AF605919

CONSTITUTIONAL POLITICS IN CANADA AND THE UNITED STATES

SUNY series in American Constitutionalism

Robert J. Spitzer, editor

CONSTITUTIONAL POLITICS IN CANADA AND THE UNITED STATES

EDITED BY

Stephen L. Newman

State University of New York Press

Published by
State University of New York Press, Albany

Printed in the United States of America

For information, address State University of New York Press,
90 State Street, Suite 700, Albany, NY 12207

Production by Diane Ganeles
Marketing by Jennifer Giovani

Library of Congress Cataloging-in-Publication Data

Constitutional politics in Canada and the United States / Stephen L. Newman, editor.
p. cm. — (SUNY series in American constitutionalism)
Includes bibliographical references and index.
ISBN 0-7914-5937-3 (alk. paper)
1. Constitutional law—Canada. 2. Civil rights—Canada. 3. Judicial review—Canada. 4. Constitutional law—United States. 5. Civil rights—United States. 6. Judicial review—United States. I. Newman, Stephen L. II. Series.

KDZ548.C665 2004
342.71—dc21

2002045250

10 9 8 7 6 5 4 3 2 1

Contents

Acknowledgments

I owe a special debt of thanks to my friend Robert Spitzer, the editor of the series in which this volume appears, for encouraging me to undertake the project. My thanks also to each of my contributors, without whom a volume of this quality would not have been possible. I received informed guidance throughout the early stages of preparing the manuscript from my editor at SUNY Press, Michael Rinella. Diane Ganeles, Senior Production Editor at the press, provided expert assistance in readying the manuscript for publication. I am grateful to York University for its generous sabbatical leave policy and the award of a Research Development Fellowship that enabled me to complete the project sooner than might otherwise have been the case.

Introduction

Stephen L. Newman

Relatively little attention has been paid by political scientists to comparative study of the American and Canadian constitutions. This may be due to the fact that for a very long time they were fundamentally unalike. For one thing, Canada, which remained loyal to the British Empire after the United States declared its independence in 1776, retained the British parliamentary system; the United States, meanwhile, adopted an innovative system of checks and balances separating the executive from the legislature and creating the judiciary as a third and coequal branch of government. As part of its system of checks and balances the eighteenth-century U.S. Constitution featured a bill of rights guaranteeing fundamental freedoms, like freedom of speech and of the press and freedom of religion, as well as various due process rights intended to protect the individual from arbitrary arrest and imprisonment and other abuses of political power. The early Canadian constitution contained no equivalent guarantees. Similar protections existed in law and custom, but unlike in the United States these did not have the status of supreme law. A further difference between American and Canadian constitutionalism had to do with the role of the courts. American courts, armed with the power of judicial review, soon emerged as powerful political actors in the new republic. In recent times, the American judiciary's willingness to apply the protections of the Bill of Rights aggressively and to expand rights claims beyond the plain language of the Constitution has had an enormous impact on public policy. In contrast, throughout the nineteenth century and into the modern era, Canadian courts were inclined to show deference to the federal and provincial legislatures, largely eschewing judicial activism in favor of judicial restraint.

For most of their history Americans and Canadians did not even share the same understanding of what a constitution is. The U.S. Constitution was conceived as a written charter of government describing the nation's basic political institutions, detailing their powers, and setting limits on the exercise of those powers. In essence, it codified the nation's fundamental constitutional rules. The nineteenth-century Canadian constitution, on the other hand, was nowhere written down in one place. As in the British political tradition, it did not consist of a single document but rather formed a compendium of acts and statutes along with common law decisions and customary practices that together organized the political life of the nation and prescribed the way in which government was to do business. The closest thing Canada had to an American-style constitution was the British North America Act of 1867, which created the Dominion of Canada out of what were then three separate provinces.[1] The U.S. Constitution had been drafted by political elites but was submitted to the people for ratification, making it a symbol of the revolutionary doctrine of popular sovereignty. In contrast, although drafted by the Canadian "Fathers of Confederation," the B.N.A. Act was formally enacted as an ordinary piece of legislation by the United Kingdom Parliament. Thus, unlike the American constitution, the act was in no way symbolic of a people's aspiration to self-government. In keeping with Canada's subordinate political status the act did not provide for a domestic amending procedure, requiring Canadians to go back to the U.K. Parliament to effect constitutional change. And even after the creation of a Canadian Supreme Court in 1875, the Judicial Committee of the Privy Council in London remained Canada's highest court of appeal on constitutional questions until the mid-twentieth century.

In a formal sense, the most the American and Canadian constitutions shared up until 1982 was federalism; and even here there were significant differences, with the Canadian provinces enjoying substantially more autonomy in the modern era than the American states. The situation changed dramatically, however, with passage of the Canada Act of 1982, which terminated the authority of the U.K. Parliament and patriated the Canadian constitution. Schedule B of the Canada Act was the Constitution Act, 1982. Like the B.N.A. Act before it, the Constitution Act was a product of long and arduous negotiations among Canadian elites, who had been trying since 1927 to reach agreement on a domestic amending formula. The act adopted a compromise that had at last obtained the near unanimous consent of the provinces and the federal government (only Quebec demurred). In addition to specifying procedures for amending the constitution, it declared a list of thirty acts and statutes, including the Constitution Act itself along with the B.N.A. Act (renamed the Constitution Act, 1867), to be the supreme law of Canada. Included in this list of fundamental laws is a new Charter of Rights and Freedoms, constitutionally entrenching fundamental personal freedoms and due process rights for the first time in Canadian history. The Canadian constitution is still more capacious and more loosely defined than its American counterpart, but the principle of constitutional supremacy and the protections contained in the Charter, along with the new role these assign to the courts, give them much more in common.

Since enactment of the Charter there has been significant convergence in the constitutional politics of Canada and the United States along two fronts:

rights jurisprudence and judicial activism. The Canadian Supreme Court's constitutional caseload almost quadrupled in the first ten years under the Charter, with Charter cases accounting for fully 80 percent of the Court's constitutional judgements in that period. Between 1982 and 2000, 20 percent of the Court's total caseload involved Charter issues; and since 1987 the proportion of Charter cases has never fallen below 21 percent and represents an average of 26 percent of all decisions. Comparatively, one-third of the caseload of the United States Supreme Court since 1954 (the year *Brown v. Board of Education* was decided) has been made up by Bill of Rights cases. The Canadian Supreme Court used the Charter to strike down a total of thirty-four federal and thirty-one provincial statutes in whole or in part during the Charter's first eighteen years, giving it a 16 percent "nullification rate" (64 of 401 Charter cases).[2] The nullification rate is actually much higher—over 30 percent—if we follow F. L. Morton and Rainer Knopff in looking only at Charter cases actually involving a direct challenge to legislation.[3] In sum, these data show that Canada and the United States now have similar levels of rights-based litigation and judicial activism.[4] Judicial intervention in the policy process has long been a hot-button issue in American politics, and it has proven to be no less politically controversial for Canadian courts.[5]

Seven of the eleven essays collected in the present volume touch on the rights revolution. The remainder deal with other aspects of American and Canadian constitutionalism, including competing notions of constitutional identity in the two nations, shared strategies of constitutional interpretation, the history of judicial review in both contexts, and amendment procedures. The collection is by no means exhaustive of the topics it covers, nor does it exhaust all that could be said about constitutional politics in Canada and the United States. Rather, it represents a modest contribution to a surprisingly neglected area of scholarship. The contributors are political scientists, political theorists, and legal scholars. As might be expected, their essays come at the subject from different angles of vision. Some focus on the politics of constitutional litigation, others on the substance of judicial decisions, still others on the theoretical implications of judicial doctrine. The essays also differ methodologically. Some employ quantitative analysis, others qualitative analysis. The only constraint placed on contributors by the editor was that their pieces be comparative; but even here we find variations on a theme. Some tilt in the direction of politics, others lean toward the law. Some make straightforward comparisons of constitutional cases, others test insights gleaned from the study of judicial politics in the United States in the Canadian context. On the whole, Canada receives more attention than the United States in these essays; but this seems only fair, given how little attention Americans usually pay to their northern neighbor.

Taken together, the following chapters chart areas of similarity and difference in the constitutional politics of Canada and the United States and suggest reasons why this is so. Under the heading of constitutional convergence we can point to the emerging consensus on first generation "negative" rights discussed by Ran Hirschl in chapter 3. Charter jurisprudence, like its American counterpart under the Bill of Rights, has shown extraordinary sensitivity to the importance of fundamental freedoms (freedom of conscience and religion; freedom of expression and of the press; freedom of assembly and association) and demonstrated heightened concern for the due process rights of the criminally accused. There has also been significant convergence on the right of privacy, including abortion rights. Moreover, as Hirschl reports, the American and Canadian high courts for the most part share a reluctance to embrace second-generation "positive" rights claims that would impose affirmative obligations on government. These doctrinal affinities are at least partially explained by structural features of the American and Canadian constitutions, both of which entrench a series of negative rights intended to protect the individual from political tyranny but neither of which explicitly guarantees positive or social rights.

Other of the contributors also point to a degree of structurally induced convergence. Sheldon Pollack in chapter 2, for example, discusses how the doctrine of constitutional supremacy, which compels the judiciary to rule on the validity of legislation, inevitably causes judges to stumble over the ambiguous constitutional language they must interpret, creating a similar hermeneutical problem for the courts of both nations. This problem haunts the exercise of judicial review, pitting the interpretive judgment of an unelected judiciary against the will of democratically elected legislators and fueling no end of controversy over the legitimacy of judicial activism. In chapter 10, Ray Bazowski points out that the politics of judicial review has its own structural dynamic governed by the complex institutional relationship that exists between courts and legislatures in Canada and the United States. To account for periodic alternations in the courts' posture, from judicial deference to judicial activism, Bazowski suggests that this relationship must be viewed historically against the background provided in each country by competing social and economic forces as they struggle for political dominance. Thus, we find that the hermeneutical problem arising from certain formal features of American and Canadian constitutionalism comes to be nested in the institutional design of government and the agonistic character of American and Canadian politics. Although they proceed from a different starting point, Ian Brodie and F. L. Morton arrive at a similar conclusion in chapter 9, where they examine the striking success of a number of "have not" groups in Canadian society in getting the courts to validate their Charter claims.

There are, of course, formal differences between the American and Canadian constitutions, even in regard to rights. The Canadian constitution is perhaps most notably distinguished by the Charter's "reasonable limits" provision and "notwithstanding clause." Section 1 of the Charter provides that the rights and freedoms guaranteed by the Charter are "subject only to such reasonable limits prescribed by law as can be demonstrably justified in a free and democratic society." Section 33 allows the federal parliament or a provincial legislature to declare a piece of legislation effective "notwithstanding a provision" included in section 2 (fundamental freedoms) or sections 7 to 15 (due process and equality rights) of the Charter. A "notwithstanding declaration" effectively insulates the legislation from judicial review, but only for a period of up to five years. It may, however, be renewed indefinitely by the issuing legislature at the end of each five-year period.

Although sections 1 and 33 might at first glance appear to make the guarantees contained in the Canadian Charter of Rights less robust than the protections afforded by the American Bill of Rights, this is in fact not the case. As a practical matter, even fundamental rights cannot be absolute (despite the stirring language of the U.S. First Amendment); individual rights must sometimes yield where the security of the state or other, equally important objectives are at stake. Faced with the necessity of balancing rights against other important societal interests, courts must develop rules to guide their application of constitutional guarantees. In effect, section 1 of the Charter inscribes within the Canadian constitution something akin to the "compelling state interest test" devised by the U.S. Supreme Court in applying "strict scrutiny" to legislation affecting fundamental rights. Like their American counterparts, Canadian courts will uphold legislation found to abridge a fundamental right only if it serves a sufficiently important objective and is carefully drawn to impair the right as little as possible.[6] Meanwhile, section 33 of the Charter, though potentially more detrimental to rights than section 1, has turned out to be more or less an empty threat. Rarely invoked, the override provision is widely considered a political dead letter.[7]

As Hirschl points out, a more significant constitutional difference emerges in connection with the Charter's protection of group rights, a category of rights unknown to the U.S. Constitution. Three such rights—minority language education rights, aboriginal rights, and a constitutional shield for affirmative action programs—are found in the Charter.[8] (For a comparison of the Canadian and American approaches to affirmative action, see chapter 8 below by Sandra Clancy.) The inclusion of group rights in the Canadian constitution signals an important feature of the Canadian political reality that distinguishes Canada from the United States. Minority-language education rights, which serve to insure that French speakers outside of Quebec will have access to French language instruction in the public schools, reflect the sharp cleavages in Canadian society. The French and the English form two distinct societies cohabiting within a single nation. The aboriginal peoples, whose treaty rights are expressly recognized by the Charter, form a third society. And it is conceivable that other social groups in the Canadian mosaic may think about themselves in the same way. For the most part, American politics is not troubled by strong group identities of these sorts. Unlike Canadian multiculturalism, which embraces linguistic and cultural diversity, American pluralism tends to soften the differences between social and cultural groups through assimilation to a common national identity. To the extent the American and Canadian societies are unalike, the two nations confront dissimilar political challenges. Bridging the distances that separate social groups is a priority in Canada but not in the United States, and this colors the distinctive constitutional vision of the two nations.

The degree to which Canadian constitutionalism values accommodation is clearly visible in Ian Greene's account (chapter 11) of the struggle to arrive at a domestic amending formula agreeable to all of the provinces, and afterward, to satisfy Quebec's demand for recognition as a "distinct society." The failure of the Meech Lake and Charlottetown constitutional accords, which were intended to conclude Canada's 1982 constitutional settlement, testifies to the fractious nature of identity-based political claims and the difficulties they create for the Canadian nation. Small wonder the Charter includes provisions affirming official bilingualism (sections 16 through 22), minority-language education rights (section 23), aboriginal rights (section 25), Canada's multicultural heritage (section 27), and women's equality (section 28). The goal is social harmony through recognition, accommodation, and inclusion. Robert Vipond argues in chapter 4 that this is how Canadians understood the purpose of rights even before the Charter. According to Vipond, the lesson reform-minded Canadian students and feminists of the 1960s learned from the American civil rights movement was that rights expand democracy by making the political process more inclusive. In chapter 5 Ronalda Murphy builds on this insight to argue that comparative constitutional law scholars interested in the relationship between abstract right and justice ought to assess rights claims contextually, looking to discover whether they in fact expand the range of political opportunities available to socially marginal and previously excluded individuals and groups.

The constitutional imperative to preserve the harmony of Canada's multicultural mosaic has affected the Canadian Supreme Court's disposition of cases bearing on the freedom of expression, opening a rift between Canadian and American rights jurisprudence. The right of freedom of expression has the status of a preferred freedom in American constitutional law, and the U.S. Supreme Court has shown it self reluctant to uphold any impairment of the right not intended to prevent some grave and imminent danger to life or property. Speech that is merely offensive or derisory, including so-called hate speech that demonizes the members of the target group and pornography that treats women as sexual objects, is not deemed sufficiently harmful to deprive it of First Amendment protection. The Supreme Court of Canada, however, has upheld the criminal suppression of both hate speech and pornography, finding the laws in question to constitute reasonable limits on the right of freedom of expression. Samuel LaSelva argues in chapter 6 that this does not indicate that the Canadian court is any less zealous in defense of constitutional rights, only that it responsibly adapts the freedom of expression to fit the circumstances of Canadian society, where offensive speech is believed to pose more of a threat to individual well-being and social harmony. In effect, the Canadian high court has imposed a minimal civility requirement on free speech that rules out incitement to hatred and violent or degrading pornography. While this requirement is inconsistent with America's liberal First Amendment jurisprudence, Stephen Newman argues in chapter 7 that it is in keeping with the republican perspective adopted by a number of the American court's domestic critics. To the extent the Canadian court has adopted their point of view, its rulings in these cases may be said to represent an alternative reading of a shared tradition of constitutional liberty.

For Peter Russell, the major difference between American and Canadian constitutionalism is not so much theoretical as experiential. In chapter 1 he argues that while the American political experience has forged a single nationality in a unified nation, Canada is more aptly described as a nation consisting of multiple nationalities that do not and cannot form a single, sovereign people in the American sense. Canadians are not one people, but several—English and French, settler and aboriginal, old immigrant and new immigrant. The multicultural Canadian experience, which defies the assimilationist tendencies of American pluralism, leads to a more profound appreciation of social difference. Politically, this recommends an open-minded approach to negotiating constitutional arrangements that provide linguistic and cultural groups with a reasonable degree of autonomy, including in some cases a limited measure of self-government. Russell thinks this makes Canada a model for the postnationalist age of the twenty-first century in which uninational nation-states will increasingly give way to multinational civic nations. If he is right, a more culturally diverse and less well unified United States may one day be looking to Canada and the Canadian constitution for inspiration.

Notes

1. The B.N.A. Act united Nova Scotia, New Brunswick, and the United Province of Canada, which comprised present-day Ontario and Quebec.

2. I am obliged to Ran Hirschl for these data on the Court's caseload. His extensive data set on the court's Charter-era decisions is discussed in chapter 5 of his forthcoming book, *Towards Juristocracy: A Comparative Inquiry into the Origins and Conse-*

quences of the New Constitutionalism, to be published by Harvard University Press. See also his "Negative Rights vs. Positive Entitlements: A Comparative Study of Judicial Interpretations of Rights in an Emerging Neo-Liberal Economic Order," *Human Rights Quarterly* 22 (2000): 1060–98.

3. F. L. Morton and Rainer Knopff, *The Charter Revolution and the Court Party,* 2d ed. (Peterborough, Ont.: Broadview Press, 2000), chap. 1.

4. Cf. Christopher P. Manfredi, "Rights and the Judicialization of Politics in Canada and the United States," in *Canada and the United States: Differences that Count,* ed. David M. Thomas (Peterborough, Ont.: Broadview Press, 2000); and Charles R. Epp, *The Rights Revolution: Lawyers, Activists, and Supreme Courts in Comparative Perspective* (Chicago: University of Chicago Press, 1998).

5. See, for example, Michael Mandel, *The Charter of Rights and the Legalization of Politics in Canada,* rev. ed. (Toronto: Thompson, 1994); and Christopher P. Manfredi, *Judicial Power and the Charter: Canada and the Paradox of Liberal Constitutionalism,* 2d ed. (Oxford: Oxford University Press, 2001).

6. As interpreted by the Supreme Court of Canada, section 1 imposes a four-pronged test on legislation found to impair a fundamental right: it must serve a sufficiently important objective; it must be rationally related to that objective; it must impair the right in question no more than is necessary to accomplish the objective; and it must not have a disproportionately severe effect on the persons to whom it applies. See *R. v. Oakes* [1986] 1 S.C.R. 103.

7. The very first use of sec. 33 was by Quebec, which almost immediately after the enactment of the charter proceeded to immunize all of its existing statutes and all new statutes against charter review; however, this practice was not continued by the subsequent government. Outside Quebec, the override clause has been used only once. See Ian Greene, *The Charter of Rights* (Toronto: James Lorimer & Co., 1989), 56–57; also Peter Hogg, *Constitutional Law,* 1997 Student Edition (Toronto: Carswell, 1997), 738–41; 732–34.

8. Minority-language education rights, which guarantee to French and English speakers the right to receive primary and secondary school instruction in their own language even when they constitute a minority in the province in which they reside, are described in section 23. Aboriginal treaty and other rights are acknowledged in section 25. The constitutional shield for affirmative action programs is found in section 15(2). It qualifies the guarantee of equality before and under the law provided by section 15(1).

CHAPTER 1

Can the Canadians Be a Sovereign People? The Question Revisited

Peter H. Russell

In 1991 I published an article entitled "Can the Canadians Be a Sovereign People?"[1] The article was my presidential address to the Canadian Political Science Association. Subsequently this question (with the verb "be" changed to "become") became the subtitle of *Constitutional Odyssey,* a book-length account of Canada's constitutional politics.[2] Though my question angered some and puzzled others, and after another decade of constitutional politics I still do not have a firm answer to it, I continue to think that asking it is a good way to explore the most profound difference between Canadian and American constitutionalism. The question also illuminates the tension in Canadian constitutional politics between the way a generation of Canadians wished to resolve their constitutional differences and the kind of resolution that suits their present circumstances.

What Does the Question Mean?

In raising this question, I did not mean to impugn Canada's claim to being a sovereign state. The claim of the governments of Canada to having a monopoly of legitimate force over Canadian territory is as good as that of other members of the United Nations. And as a country that is either one of the world's strongest middle powers or one of its lesser great powers, this claim is more than legal bravado. Still, as Stephen Clarkson and other Canadian political economists continue to show us,[3] given Canada's tight fastening to the American economic orbit, this formal sovereignty should not be equated with policy independence—especially in the economic realm. But my question is not aimed at this (and other constraints) on what our governments can do with their constitutional powers. The target of my question is concern about the legitimacy of the constitutional order through which Canadians aspire to govern themselves.

Nor in asking my question do I mean to deny that Canadians are already *in some sense* a people. The Canadian people are certainly defined juridically by

Canada's citizenship laws, and can be—and often are—discussed in terms of their defining characteristics, as diverse as they may be. I would go further than this and claim that with respect to outside interference in Canada's constitutional affairs, the Canadians are a "people" with the right to self-determination. Canadians may be deeply divided on certain constitutional issues, the most fundamental of which is recognition of the Québécois and the aboriginal peoples as "peoples" within Canada who have the right to self-determination (including the right to secede). Nonetheless, I believe that Canadians—Québécois, the aboriginal peoples, and all the rest—would and should assert their collective right to self-determination against any outside power that might try to intervene and sort us out.

What I have in mind in questioning whether Canadians can become a sovereign people is a constitutional ideal. It is the ideal of Canadians with all of their diversity agreeing formally and democratically to their constitutional order. It is the ideal of the social contract in classical European political thought. It is the ideal of Canadians constituting themselves "a people" in John Locke's terms by agreeing to form a political community with a common system of government. It is the ideal of Canadians being a "We the people," as in the opening words of the U.S. Constitution. It is the ideal of a constitution expressing the will of a sovereign people. That is the ideal that came to enthrall so many Canadians in the last three decades of the last century but that proved to be so illusive. It is the possibility of realizing that ideal through some grand final resolution of their constitutional differences that I call into question.

Now, of course, the actual "We the people" who participated in the making and adoption of the U.S. Constitution were a very exclusive "we." The majority of the people, including women, Afro-Americans, and Indians, were excluded. But over time, as the American political community became more inclusive, the idea that the U.S. Constitution expresses the will of the American people became a popular, legitimating myth at the very center of its people's sense of national identity. In this sense the Constitution constituted the American nation.

In Canada, by way of contrast, there was no founding myth of the people as a constituent power. The point is not that the actual process that produced the Canadian federation's founding constitution in 1867 was remarkably less democratic than the founding of the United States. Elite accommodation among elected politicians was the crucial process in the founding of both federations. True, the Canadian politicians did not submit the product of their constitutional bargaining to popular conventions, nor (with one exception)[4] did they submit themselves to the approval of the electorate before the constitution they had designed came into force. But the debate of the Confederation proposals in the legislative assemblies, newspapers, and public meetings of the British North American colonies was about as robust and participatory as that which preceded the American founding.[5] The real difference was that unlike the American founding fathers, Canada's did not believe that the people were, in principle, sovereign. They made this very clear in leaving the sovereign power to amend Canada's constitution in the hands of the British Parliament.

The Fathers of Confederation's willingness to leaving custody of Canada's constitution in British hands was not the result of any absence of mind nor failure to deal with some difficult unfinished constitutional business. No, these British North Americans believed that that is where constitutional sovereignty over Canada belonged—in the imperial parliament. As three of them wrote in a letter to the British colonial secretary, explaining how "the basis of the Confederation now proposed" differs from the United States: "It does not profess to be derived from the people but would be the constitution provided by the imperial parliament, thus remedying any defect."[6] Canada's founders were divided on many weighty constitutional matters, including the merits of federalism and the nature of the new nationality they were fashioning. But they were not divided on where the locus of constitutional sovereignty should be. They did not subscribe to the doctrine of popular sovereignty. Nor did they think of the constitution as a great charter setting out, comprehensively, how the country was to be governed. The most important principles and practices of parliamentary government they were happy to leave to unwritten political conventions. Thus, at Canada's founding there was no basis in fact or in thought for an American-style Lockean constitutionalism in which the constitution is understood as expressing the will of a sovereign people.

The constitutionalism of Canada's founders I have characterized as Burkean rather than Lockean. I don't mean by this that they were greatly influenced by the writings of Edmund Burke. They were, generally, much less philosophically inclined than the American founders, and those who did read political philosophy probably knew Locke better than Burke. But their practice and working assumptions conformed with Burke's skepticism about the Enlightenment's unbridled optimism in the capacity of the rational individual to discern absolute political truths. In their constitutional rhetoric one will find no talk about natural rights. The rights and responsibilities they (and Burke) believed in were quite concrete and man-made, growing out of the understandings and conventions that over time hold a society together. If they believed in any social contract, it was one unfolding along Burkean lines as each generation passes on to the next the product of its collective wisdom. In Daniel Elazar's terms, the constitutionalism they practiced was organic, not convenantal.[7] For them the constitution was not a single document drawn up at a foundational moment inscribing a people's agreement on the governance of their political community, but a collection of laws, institutions, and political practices that survive the test of time and are found to serve well the needs of a society.

For most of the Canadian federation's first century its constitutional system evolved in an organic manner along Burkean lines. Canadians settled into being a thoroughly federal country, much more so that the United States, whose founders had been so philosophically lucid about federalism. Around the edges adjustments were made, and the federation was completed territorially and institutionally through political practice, intergovernmental accords, judicial decisions, and statutes creating new institutions (like the Supreme Court of Canada). These "informal" constitutional changes were augmented by a handful of constitutional amendments, formally made in Britain but always at Canadian governments' behest. From 1867 right up to the early 1960s, constitutional politics were of little interest to the Canadian people. All this changed in the mid-1960s, when Canadian governments, and increasingly the people who elected them, became intensely engaged in constitutional debate. This period of constitutional turbulence went on almost nonstop for a quarter of a century, coming to an end with the defeat of the Charlottetown Accord in the 1992 Referendum. What plunged Canadians into this constitutional maelstrom is a complex story.[8] Suffice it to say, the proximate cause was the Canadian governments' getting serious about what was now seen—universally—as a serious piece of unfinished constitutional business, namely, a "constitutional patriation," the project of transferring the power to amend the constitution from Britain to Canada. That project involved much more than technical, legal issues. Deciding who can amend the formal constitution, the country's highest law, raises nothing less than the question of who or what is constitutionally sovereign. And that question leads pretty quickly to a debate over what kind of a political community Canada is—a community of equal individual citizens? a community of equal provinces? a community formed by two founding peoples? or a multinational federal partnership of English-speaking Canadians with the Québécois and the aboriginal peoples?

As Canada swirled through five rounds of exhausting efforts to resolve not just the patriation issue but also all the other constitutional matters it inevitably opened up, the Canadian people became ever more insistent that their constitutional sovereignty be recognized. When Clyde Wells, then premier of Newfoundland, stated in 1990 that "The constitution belongs to the *people* of Canada—the ultimate source of sovereignty in the nation,"[9] no one disputed his view. The people of Burke had become—at least for a season—the people of Locke. The problem was that this "people" was so deeply divided over what kind of a people it was that it could not act in democratic concert as a single sovereign people expressing its will in a grand constitutional charter.

It was at that time, and in that context, that I asked my question.

The Legacy of Our "Mega" Efforts

I dubbed the five intense rounds of constitutional politics Canada went through between 1967 and 1992 as exercises in "megaconstitutional politics." They were "mega" in the sense of aiming at a grand-slam solution to our constitutional difference, and precisely because they were so ambitious they were also "mega" in the sense of monopolizing the political attention of Canadians. When one of these rounds was on and reaching a climax, nothing else seemed to matter to the country. The constitutional issue was all-absorbing at these moments—like a squabbling family trying finally to sort out its differences. As they recall the Victoria Charter, the attempt at a whole new constitution in the Trudeau government's Bill C-60, patriation and the peoples' package, Meach Lake and Charlottetown, Canadians are apt to blush. So much was attempted, so little achieved.

These "mega" efforts, though far from providing a final constitutional solution, did have enduring effects. To begin with, the patriation project, which had initiated the country's gargantuan constitutional efforts, was—at least in a formal legal sense—completed. In 1982, the Canadian constitution was patriated. Britain terminated its formal legal authority over Canada's constitution, and a new and complex all-Canadian process of amending the constitution came into force. Along with patriation, and taking star billing in what Trudeau called his "people's package" of constitutional reform, came the Canadian Charter of Rights and Freedoms, a full-blown constitutional bill of rights with many distinctively Canadian bells and whistles. In that package, too, but only after some strenuous lobbying by indigenous-support groups, was a constitutional declaration recognizing and affirming the "existing" aboriginal and treaty rights of Canada's Aboriginal peoples.

The Constitution Act, 1982, containing the only formal constitutional changes resulting from the five "mega" rounds, does look like quite an achievement. Certainly, for Pierre Trudeau, the patriation package's political architect, it was enough—enough to ensure "the federation was set to last a thousand years."[10] For many Canadians, probably a majority, who like Trudeau think of their country primarily as a community of equal rights-bearing individuals, the 1982 changes were enough to settle the country's biggest constitutional issues. But Trudeau and his supporters had not converted sections of the Canadian population who have a different sense of national identity from the Trudeauian vision of Canada. Quebec nationalists and aboriginal peoples did not accept the patriation package as an adequate response to their aspiration to be recognized as nations within Canada. Quebec's National Assembly, the only provincial legislature that voted on the patriation package, and the legislature of the only province whose government did not agree to the package, passed a decree, on 25 November 1981, rejecting it. The Canada-wide organizations that represented the Indian and Inuit peoples were united in their opposition to the package.[11]

For Quebec nationalists, the patriation package fell well short of their conditions for supporting the patriation project. First, it failed to give Quebec the additional autonomy that its governments, both federalist and *independeniste,* had been insisting were necessary if Quebec were to be truly *maître chez nous.* More fundamentally, the new rules for amending the constitution denied Quebec a veto over constitutional changes that affect its vital interests in the structure of the federation.[12] If Quebec is viewed as just one of ten equal provinces forming the Canadian federation, then denying it a veto is unobjectionable. But for a majority of Quebeckers—then, now, and in the past—the Province of Quebec is not viewed as a province like all the rest but as the homeland of a founding people. Denying Quebec constitutional security for its existing status as well as its demands for additional autonomy by a deal pushed through by an antinationalist federal prime minister, Pierre Trudeau, and the premiers of the nine provinces with English-speaking majorities was widely viewed in Quebec as an act of betrayal. Rather than settling the so-called national unity issue, patriation in this manner meant that the constitution was brought back from Britain to a home more bitterly divided than ever.

The constitutional turbulence created by the struggle to accommodate Quebec nationalism enabled aboriginal leaders to get a hearing for their peoples' claims for national recognition. Though recognition of "existing" aboriginal and treaty rights in the Constitution Act, 1982 was an important breakthrough, the word "existing," inserted at the insistence of some recalcitrant provincial premiers, suggested that the rights being recognized were only a small residue that had survived over a century and a half of colonial domination by the settler majority. Aboriginal peoples who had never consciously surrendered their right to self-government would now insist on explicit recognition of that right as a condition of their consent to the Canadian constitution. The 1982 patriation package acknowledged the need to clarify "existing aboriginal rights" by scheduling a constitutional conference for this purpose with representatives of the aboriginal peoples.

The unsettled "nationalist" claims of the Québécois and the aboriginal peoples, while the most unsettling blemishes of patriation, were by no means its only shortfalls. The people and governments of "regional Canada"—i.e., the four Atlantic and four western provinces—had developed a battery of proposals to better secure their interests in the Canadian federation. Of central importance was reform of the Senate, the upper house of the federal parliament. With all of its members appointed by the federal prime minister, the Senate was a total failure in providing a counterweight to central Canada's (i.e., Ontario's and Quebec's) domination of the elected House of Commons. Testimony to the inadequacies of patriation and the fissures it deepened were the sweaty but abortive efforts at constitutional reform that followed in its wake: four constitutional conferences on aboriginal rights, the attempt to appease Quebec with the Meech Lake Accord, and then the Charlottetown Accord with its potpourri of sixty proposals—a little something for everyone but hardly enough for anyone.

Though these rounds of "megaconstitutional" politics did not produce a new Canadian social contract, they had a decisive effect on the country's constitutional culture: they democratized it. Making changes to the written constitution the most important political issue in the country for an entire generation, constant talk about the constitution as ideally incorporating a "vision" of the country, a mirror in which all Canadians should be able to see themselves, a document inscribing "what we are all about"—all of this convinced the Canadian public that the constitution was far too important to leave to the politicians and that they must have a crucial say in making any important changes in it.

In Canada, political elites will still play the leading role in negotiating and drafting proposals for constitutional change—as they do in all democracies—but to be legitimate, proposals that are seen as of primary importance must be ratified by the people voting in referenda. This is essentially a political rather than a legal imperative. At the time of the Charlottetown Accord, although only two provinces, Alberta and British Columbia, had legislation requiring a referendum before their legislatures could consider proposals to amend the constitution, and Quebec was legislatively bound to have a referendum by 26 October 1992, the federal leaders and premiers of provinces not committed to referenda knew that it would be political suicide not to seek the direct approval of all Canadians for the accord they had fashioned. In effect, the country's political leadership accepted Clyde Wells's verdict that the constitution belongs to the people of Canada. The trouble was that in rejecting—by a 54 percent majority—an accord agreed to by the federal government, the governments of all ten provinces, the leaders of what at that time were Canada's three main political parties, and the leaders of four Canada-wide indigenous organizations, Canada's sovereign people were too divided to be able to act as a constituent power.

The sovereign people were not only divided, they were now absolutely exhausted by all that had been tried to bridge their differences. Constitutional exhaustion is the other major consequence of the "mega" rounds. This exhaustion was not short term—it continues. The one post-Charlottetown attempt to initiate a round of megaconstitutional change was prompted entirely by Quebec. On 30 October 1995, Quebec had its second "sovereignty" referendum. The first took place in May 1980 when René Levesque's Parti Québécois government asked the people of Quebec for a mandate to negotiate an arrangement that would give Quebec political sovereignty but an economic association with Canada, on condition that whatever was negotiated would be submitted to a second referendum. On that occasion Quebeckers refused—by a 60 percent majority—to give such a mandate. The referendum question in 1995 was equally fuzzy. Voters were asked to approve an effort by Quebec to negotiate sovereignty/association with Canada, but this time a win for the "yes" side would mean that Quebec's independence would automatically come about if the negotiations failed. The vote was much closer than in 1980: a paper-thin majority of 50.58 percent said "no" to the proposal. After this, few on either side in Quebec had any stomach for rushing into a third referendum. The near majority of Quebeckers voting for the breakup of Canada may have shown how deeply divided Canada was, but the closeness of the vote and the passions the referendum campaign aroused showed equally how deeply divided Quebec was.

A Return to Organic Constitutional Change

Since 1992, contrary to rumor, Canada has not been in a constitutional "deep freeze." To Canadians who became addicted to the grand-slam efforts of the "mega" rounds, it may seem that nothing has been happening on the constitutional front. But they are wrong. Constitutional development has been taking place not through a great new social contract, but, in Elazar's terms, organically "in bits and pieces."

Among the "bits and pieces" were four formal constitutional amendments. All four were done bilaterally, with the federal government cooperating with a province to use the part of the amending formula that provides for changes that apply to some but not all of the provinces.[13] In 1993, the New Brunswick Act was amended, giving "equality of status and equal rights and privileges" to that province's English and French communities.[14] This amendment made New Brunswick Canada's only province that is officially bicultural as well as bilingual, a development very much in keeping with the historic position of New Brunswick's Acadian people (34 percent of the population). Such an amendment had been requested by New Brunswick's government in both the Meech Lake and Charlottetown rounds. In that same year, Prince Edward Island's Terms of Union with Canada were altered to permit a ferryboat service to the mainland to be replaced by a bridge. This change, involving as it did a wrenching challenge to Islander identity, came after a warmly contested island referendum. In 1997, in response to a unanimous resolution of Quebec's National Assembly, the federal parliament supported an amendment making the guarantee of denominational school rights inapplicable in Quebec.[15] In effect this amendment responded to the secularization of Quebec society and the desire of English and French Quebeckers to organize schools around language communities rather than around religious communities. Secularization was also evident in the important change made in 1998 to Term 17 of the Terms of Union Newfoundland agreed to in 1949. Term 17 had granted six religious dominations the right to publicly supported school systems. The 1998 amendment finally removed the constitutional guarantee of a costly and divisive educational system and replaced it with a provision requiring the provincial legislature to provide for courses in religion that are not specific to any denomination and permitting religious observances in schools where requested by parents. The 1998 amendment (which replaced a 1997 amendment providing for interdenominational schools in Newfoundland) was approved by a 73 percent majority in a province-wide referendum.

While none of these amendments involved any changes to the structure of the federation, each was important to the people of a particular province. In Canada, provincial constitutions, unlike state constitutions in the United States, are very underplayed; in Nelson Wiseman's words, they "barely dwell in the world of the subconscious."[16] Many of their most important terms involve the conditions on which a province became part of Canada, and on these matters the federal parliament continues to play a role. The spate of amendments in the 1990s adjusting individual provinces' constitutional arrangements shows how this dimension of patriation has introduced an element of flexibility into Canada's constitutional system, and displays yet another facet of Canadian diversity. Quebec, which had rejected the patriation package, did not spurn this part of the new all-Canadian amending process.

During the 1990s the structure and functioning of the Canadian federation was changing, but through informal political agreements rather than formal constitutional amendments. Changes in the federal system were now quite self-consciously not promoted as attempts to accommodate Quebec. Instead they were advertised, especially by the federal government, as designed to make the federation more efficient. In reality, they were motivated in large measure by the federal government's effort to reduce its staggering fiscal deficit, and also in part they were a response to the pressures of the global economy. The most important example of the latter was the intergovernmental Agreement on Internal Trade (AIT), which was signed in July 1994 and came into effect a year later.

The AIT was a classic effort to achieve by informal political agreement what had proved to impossible to accomplish through the legal instruments of the constitution. Canada's original constitution contains a free trade clause (section 121) that requires "Articles of the Growth, Produce or Manufacture of any one province to be admitted free into each of the other provinces." This section has been virtually a dead letter of the constitution. The courts (and Canadian business) have largely ignored it. In the modern period the Supreme Court of Canada has made federal jurisdiction over international and interprovincial trade virtually a plenary power, but federal governments have been too timid to use this power to dismantle the many ways in which the provinces have restricted internal free trade. During the patriation round, the Trudeau government failed to get the provinces to agree to a strengthening of section 121. A much watered-down constitutional commitment to "Canadian economic union" was a casualty of the Charlottetown Accord debacle. Eventually it was the embarrassing possibility that Canada's internal market might become more restrictive of trade than the external markets that NAFTA and GATT were opening up for Canada that induced federal and provincial leaders to enter into an internal agreement on trade.

The AIT is a big disappointment to economic liberals. It leaves ample scope for provincial governments to restrict access to provincial markets by pursuing "legitimate policy objectives," and it lacks effective monitoring and enforcement provisions. Still, AIT has contributed to Canada's economic integration in a number areas, including government procurement, labor mobility, and the harmonization of professional and occupational standards. It represents about as much as can be achieved through the consensual ways in which Canadians have come to operate their federation.[17]

After the defeat of the Charlottetown Accord in 1992 and the election of the Chrétien Liberal government the following year, a quiet process of adjusting federal relationships through intergovernmental agreements got under way. In effect this was a return to the method of managing the federal relationship that was dominant in the years immediately following World War II before Canada plunged into megaconstitutional politics. The instruments of this process, political agreements between governments, are not in the formal sense constitutional amendments. However, if the constitutional system is understood in the larger Burkean sense as the understandings and conventions that hold a society together, this emergent system of accords should be seen as having constitutional significance. This intergovernmental process has had three general characteristics: first, it has been broadly decentralizing; second, it has been religiously symmetrical—not offering deals to one province that are denied to others; and third, it has been thoroughly elitist, government-driven, and largely out of sight politically.[18]

A program of federal "rebalancing" with at least the first two of these characteristics fitted well the changing political climate of Canada in the 1990s. By the mid 1990s, the most dynamic challenges to the political status quo were coming from the right-of-center Reform Party, the only party in English Canada that opposed the Charlottetown Accord, and from similarly oriented Conservative governments led by Mike Harris in Ontario and Ralph Klein in Alberta, committed to shrinking government in general and federal government in particular. In the run-up to the Quebec referendum, the federal government also saw advantage in promising decentralizing changes that, while available to all provinces, might demonstrate to Quebeckers how Canadian federalism could give them room to be *maîtres chez nous*. This strategy seems to have had negligible effects in increasing support for the "no" side in the referendum. But after the referendum, when Prime Minister Chrétien brought Stephane Dion, a brilliant Quebec political scientist, into his cabinet to manage intergovernmental affairs, it gained momentum and a higher political profile. Rebalancing the federation to make it more efficient and consensual became Plan A for responding to being at the brink of breakup in the October 1995 referendum. Plan B, by way of contrast with the cozy, quiet style of Plan A, would involve risking the dangerous politics of clarifying what should happen, constitutionally, were the Quebec sovereignists to win a referendum.

Much of the federal rebalancing was achieved by the federal government agreeing to stop spending money on activities that are mainly, if not entirely, under provincial jurisdiction.[19] Thus, Ottawa largely withdrew from the sectors of mining and forestry, recreation and tourism—all of which it had been prepared to do as part of the Charlottetown Accord. The federal government also agreed to permit provinces and territories to take over full responsibility for job training with money from the unemployment insurance fund. Though federal "interference" in this dimension of education had been the reason given by the Quebec government for backing out of the Victoria Charter in 1971, by 1995 Quebec nationalists had raised the ante way past the point where federal withdrawal from this field could pacify their objections to the constitutional status quo. In other areas, where a strong federal presence was still recognized as necessary, progress was made to better define and coordinate the functions of the two levels of government. A 1998 agreement on environmental harmonization is a prime example.

The biggest move in this intergovernmental process, the agreement that cut across a number of program areas and dealt with issues of process as well as of substance, was the Social Union Agreement of 1999, signed with a great deal of fanfare on 4 February 1999.[20] The "social union" terminology was a bit of constitutional hype borrowed from the Charlottetown Accord. Only its elite inventors and a few academics had a clue what it meant. The "Framework to Improve the Social Union for Canadians" targeted areas of social policy largely under provincial jurisdiction—education, health, and social welfare—in which the federal government, using its superior taxing capacity and a spending power subject to few constitutional constraints, had come to play a leadership role in building the Canadian welfare state. Over the years the principal opposition to Ottawa's interventions in these areas came from Quebec. The idea behind the Social Union was not to curtail federal involvement in social policy but to manage it in a more cooperative and consensual manner through its Council of Ministers.

The Social Union agreement accepts the legitimacy of federal spending in areas of provincial responsibility, but requires the approval of a majority of provinces for any new social policy initiatives that are to be funded through intergovernmental transfers. Governments that opt out can still receive their share of federal funding so long as their own programs meet Canada-wide objectives and satisfy accountability standards. The provinces must be consulted three months before introducing any new federal social programs that transfer funds directly to individual citizens or organizations (for instance, the Millennium Scholarship Fund). Though these restrictions on federal spending went further than those agreed to by the Quebec Liberal government that negotiated the Meech Lake Accord, they did not go far enough for Lucien Bouchard's Parti Québécois government. The Social Union agreement was signed by the federal government and all of the provincial and territorial governments—except Quebec. Confronted with a strategy designed to treat it as simply a province like all the rest, Quebec was insisting on its special status.

The difficulty in achieving more than a de facto recognition of Quebec's distinctiveness was demonstrated by Prime Minister Chrétien's attempt after the Quebec referendum to make yet another effort to appease Quebec nationalism through constitutional reform. In opposition, Chrétien had taken his constitutional cues from his mentor, Pierre Trudeau, and bitterly opposed both the Meech Lake and Charlottetown Accords. But in the final days of the referendum campaign, as prime minister and a desperate captain of the federalist team, he promised Quebeckers that under his leadership Canada would recognize Quebec as a distinct society and restore its full veto over constitutional change. Chrétien's promise probably had little effect on the outcome of the referendum, but his effort to fulfill it surely dampened Canadians' interest in renewing the old megaconstitutional game.

On 28 November 1995, less than a month after the referendum, Chrétien announced that he would keep his promise to Quebeckers by three unilateral federal initiatives. The House of Commons would pass a resolution recognizing Quebec as a distinct society, and the federal government would introduce legislation under which constitutional amendments would have to be consented to by Quebec as well as by Ontario, provinces representing 50 percent of western Canada's population and two provinces representing 50 percent of Atlantic Canada's population, respectively—before the federal government would support them. The third item was the promise to devolve labor-market training to the provinces.[21] The Chrétien package of "semiconstitutional" changes went over like the proverbial lead balloon. It was immediately repudiated as too little too late by Quebec sovereignists and failed to win endorsement by Quebec federalists as a satisfactory basis for reengaging in a process of constitutional renewal. As for the English-speaking provinces, a number of premiers were quick to condemn Chrétien's distinct society resolution (which was already watered down from the version in the Meech Lake Accord) as endangering the principle of provincial equality.[22] Eventually, in September 1997, the premiers of the English-speaking provinces and the heads of the two northern territories came up with their own version, the so-called Calgary Declaration, according to which "All provinces, while diverse in their characteristics, have equality of status," but at the same time, "the unique character of Quebec society, including its French-speaking majority, its culture and its tradition of civil law" is recognized as "fundamental to the well-being of Canada."[23] To which Lucien Bouchard growled, "Quebec will accept nothing less than to be recognized as a people, as a nation capable of deciding its political future."[24] Mercifully, this put an end to the foolish attempt to solve Canada's national unity problem by playing definition games.

The second part of Chrétien's semiconstitutional package, committing the House of Commons not to play its necessary role in the constitution-amending process without the approval of Canada's regions, was equally a fiasco. The very idea of Ottawa "lending" its constitutional veto to the four regions was bizarre. It seems to have come right off the top of the prime minister's head, catching even his justice minister, Alan Rock, by surprise. Roger Gibbins, an Alberta-based political scientist, said it was "little short of a constitutional *coup d'état* by the Prime Minister."[25] Chrétien's proposal went down particularly badly in Alberta and British Columbia, the most rapidly growing Canadian provinces, whose chattering class could not abide the idea that they were just two provinces of western Canada and not on a par with Ontario or Quebec. British Columbia seemed to bleat the loudest. So within a few days Justice Minister Rock persuaded his cabinet colleagues to lend Ottawa's veto to British Columbia, too.[26] Thus, the final version that came into force in February 1996 superimposes five regional vetoes on the operation of the "7/50" amendment rule in the constitution.[27] So long as this legislation stands, amendments to most parts of the constitution must have the support of the federal parliament, British Columbia, Ontario, Quebec, at least two of the prairie provinces comprising 50 percent of their combined population (at current population levels, this means Alberta plus either Manitoba or Saskatchewan), and at least two of the Atlantic provinces with 50 percent of that region's population. As a result, the consent of provinces representing at least 92 percent of Canada's population is now required for any important constitutional amendment. The Chrétien legislation is worded so that the regional approvals can be given by referenda—which indeed is how the politics of the day dictates they must be given. And so the "little guy from Shawinigan" has succeeded in putting Canada's sovereign people into one very tight constitutional straightjacket.

Prime Minister Chrétien's personal contributions to this period of organic constitutional adaptation are surely the "bits and pieces" that are least deserving of respect by future generations. A Burkean constitutional culture does not thrive on prime ministerial fiat.

Since the 1995 Quebec referendum, Canada's only heavy duty bout of constitutional politics has concerned Plan B—establishing the constitutional ground rules for Quebec secession. This saga was played out in two episodes—one judicial and the other legislative. The judicial part was initiated by Guy Bertrand, a former Pequiste politician, who had undergone a total conversion to federalism and challenged the assumption of his former party that if a majority of Quebeckers voted for independence, Quebec legally—under international law, if not under Canadian law—could secede from Canada unilaterally. Bertrand began his challenge before the 1995 referendum, as the legitimacy of unilateral secession was implicit in the referendum question.[28] A Quebec trial judge ruled that Bertrand's challenge had merit but refused to give him the remedy of stopping the referendum. After the referendum Bertrand returned to court to challenge the PQ's declared intent to continue to pursue sovereignty on its terms. While Premier Bouchard was in no hurry to have another referendum—he said he would wait for "winning conditions"—he and his government were anxious to establish that Quebec's constitutional future was to be determined solely by a majority of Quebeckers. At this point the federal government decided it could no longer avoid the dynamite question of the legality of a unilateral Quebec secession and referred Bertrand's challenge to the Supreme Court of Canada.

On 20 August 1998, the Supreme Court rendered its historic decision. To the question of whether Quebec, following a referendum win by the sovereignists, could unilaterally separate from Canada, the court's nine judges gave a firm "no" answer. While the democratic principle requires that the will of a provincial majority expressed in a referendum be given real weight, the court recognized that other principles at the foundation of Canada's constitutional system are equally important—namely, the rule of law, federalism, and minority rights. The rule of law requires that any constitutional change, including removing a province from the federation, must be carried out according to the legal rules governing constitutional amendment.[29] As citizens of a federation, all Canadian citizens, including Quebeckers, exercise their democratic rights by participating in the building of two majorities, one national and one provincial. Both majorities must participate in fundamental constitutional change. Majoritarian democracy in Canada at both the federal and provincial levels must be balanced by a respect for minorities—in particular, the English in Quebec, the French in the other provinces, and aboriginal peoples, all of whose rights are enshrined in the constitution. The combination of these principles means that for Quebec to declare its independence of Canada solely on the basis of a majority vote of the province's electorate would be to violate both the letter and the spirit of Canada's constitution.

The Supreme Court also gave a firm "no" to the question of whether under international law the principle of the self-determination of peoples gives Quebec a right to secede unilaterally.[30] The court sidestepped the delicate question of whether a Quebec people exists or whether such a people encompasses the entirety of the Quebec population by finding that under international law as it has evolved, the right to self-determination gives rise to a right to secede only for a people suffering oppressive colonial subjugation, conditions that, it concluded, "are manifestly inapplicable in Quebec under existing circumstances."[31]

The Supreme Court's decision was not entirely negative for the Quebec sovereignists. In what is undoubtedly the most creative part of their judgment, the justices held that if in Quebec "a clear majority on a clear question" vote for secession, the rest of Canada is constitutionally bound to negotiate with Quebec. The aim of such negotiations is not necessarily to effect Quebec's secession but to see whether through good-faith bargaining Quebec's status can be changed in a manner that is fair to the rights and interests of all Canadians affected by such a change. The court acknowledges that these negotiations would be extremely difficult, involving all of the players in Canada's constitutional process—the ten provinces, representatives of the aboriginal peoples, and the federal parliament and government—and raising questions possibly as volatile as the borders of an independent Quebec. The court did not speculate on what happens if the negotiations fail—except to say that the legitimacy of actions taken by Quebec or Canada would depend on the extent to which "the legitimate interests of others" were respected.[32]

The Supreme Court's decision on Quebec secession was one of those very rare occasions when the governments of Canada and of Quebec, federalists and sovereignists, shared positive feelings about anything constitutional. The denial of a unilateral right to secede coupled with the affirmation of a duty to negotiate if a secession referendum succeeds gave both sides something to cheer about. The same cannot be said for the federal legislative initiative that followed—the so-called Clarity Bill. On 10 December 1999, the federal government introduced legislation designed "to give effect" to the Supreme Court's decision by identifying the circumstances under which it would be obliged to negotiate the terms of secession with Quebec (or any other province). The Supreme Court said that questions concerning what constitutes a "clear question" and a "clear majority" must be settled by the "political actors," not by the courts. Now one of the political actors, the federal government and parliament, was legislating its treatment of these questions.

According to the Clarity Bill, when the government of a province indicates the question it intends to submit to a provincial referendum on secession, the House of Commons will decide whether the question could result "in a clear expression of the will of the population of a province on whether the province should cease to be part of Canada and become an independent state."[33] The legislation rules out a referendum question like that used in the 1980 referendum asking only for a mandate to negotiate, and a question like that used in 1995, which envisages softer alternatives to secession such as continuing economic or political arrangements with Canada. In the event that a secession referendum takes place on a question that passes the clarity test, again the House of Commons will decide whether a win for the "yes" side can be treated as expressing a clear majority of the population of a province. The legislation does not stipulate any numerical requirement but implies that a bare majority of 50 percent plus one of those voting might not be enough.

The Clarity Bill was opposed in the House by the Bloc Québécois and the Progressive Conservatives, and after a rough ride in the Senate was enacted at the end of June 2000. It was bitterly opposed by the Bouchard government in Quebec, which answered back with its own "Self-determination Bill" asserting "the right of the Quebec people to self-determination" and of the Quebec people alone "to decide the nature, scope and mode of exercise" of that right.[34] The Quebec bill became law on 5 December 2000. The Quebec legislation does not assert an intention to change Quebec's constitutional status unilaterally and Premier Bouchard's acceptance of the Supreme Court's ruling (and indeed his entire leadership of the Quebec sovereignist movement) suggests that after a referendum win (on his question) he would prefer to negotiate a change in Quebec's status with the rest of Canada rather than undertake a radical and unilateral break with Canada. What the exchange of legislative missiles over the secession process shows is that Burkean organic change can shape the terms on which a society is held together, not the terms on which it can be torn asunder.

In this period of organic constitutional change, the most substantial progress has been made in relations with aboriginal peoples. After the Charlottetown Accord, aboriginal leaders had no interest in resuming efforts to achieve a restructuring of their relationship with Canada through some grand amendment of the Canadian constitution. Instead they preferred to return to the process through which relations between indigenous peoples and the settler society had originally been ordered and have individual native communities make treatylike agreements with the Crown, a Crown represented now by federal and provincial governments.

The groundwork for proceeding in this way was laid by the Supreme Court and a royal commission. In 1990, in the *Sparrow* case,[35] the court rendered its first decision on the "existing Aboriginal and treaty rights" recognized and affirmed in the Constitution Act, 1982. It said that these rights must be given "a generous, liberal interpretation" and that, among other things, they protected aboriginal peoples' right to carry on activities that are an integral part of their distinctive culture. The court's decision in the 1997

Delgamuukw case made it clear that included in the constitutionally protected aboriginal rights is "native title" to land occupied at the time British sovereignty was asserted and not surrendered or clearly extinguished by Britain or Canada.[36] The court urged that unsettled native title claims be dealt with through negotiation, not litigation. Only in that way, it argued, can "a genuine reconciliation" be achieved. Two years later, in the *Marshall* case,[37] the Supreme Court found that the Nova Scotia Mi'kmaq, under a 1760 treaty securing their alliance with Britain, had a right to harvest and trade fish and other wildlife to provide the "necessaries" of life. This capped a long series of decisions in which there was an effort to interpret historic treaties in a way that "best reconciles the interests of both parties at the time the treaty was signed." Treaty rights, like all aboriginal rights, could be infringed by government, but only by meeting a strict justification test of public interest and in as consensual a manner as possible.

The Royal Commission on Aboriginal Peoples (RCAP) was appointed by the Mulroney Conservative government in 1991 in the wake of the Oka crisis in which the Mohawks of Kanesatake and Kahnawake, resisting the building of a golf course on traditional burial grounds, through the summer of 1990 confronted the Canadian army over barricades outside Montreal. RCAP was the first time in the history of settler-native relations—anywhere on earth—that leading representatives of native and non-native societies reviewed together their past and present relations, and agreed on a plan for improving their relationship in the future.[38] The plan set out in RCAP's 1996 voluminous final report has two branches: one aimed at pulling up living conditions from the third-world standards experienced by most aboriginal Canadians and the other at restructuring political relationships through treatylike, nation-to-nation agreements.[39] The plan's two dimensions are interrelated. The commissioners recognize that enabling native Canadians to rebuild self-governing and economically self-reliant societies requires a massive commitment to overcoming the poverty, poor health, family violence, and educational failure that beset so many indigenous communities.

While the Royal Commission was sitting, the federal and provincial governments agreed to implement the aboriginal right of self-government *within Canada,*[40] which they had agreed to recognize in the abortive Charlottetown Accord. The method of implementation would be negotiated agreements with individual aboriginal communities—some of these would be historic Indian nations, others more contemporary groupings. In the Northern Territories the federal government alone represents the Crown, but south of the 60th parallel provincial governments are also parties to agreements. In many cases the negotiations deal with unsettled land claims as well as self-government, and aim at agreements that, like land-claim agreements, have the constitutional status of treaties.[41] By the end of the

1990s self-government negotiations were underway at some eighty "tables" involving aboriginal peoples in all parts of the country.

This project of reconciliation with indigenous peoples is unprecedented in world history. As I have written elsewhere, "In no other political jurisdiction, ancient or modern, has there been such an effort to reverse the subjugation of one set of peoples by another and to establish new relationships based on mutual respect and consent"[42]—and, I would add, a relationship involving shared citizenship.[43] This effort at ordering relations with indigenous peoples through agreements that are truly consensual is in its earliest stages. So far, its major achievements have been in Canada's far north. In 1999 an agreement between Canada and the Inuit people of the eastern Arctic that took over twenty years to negotiate and that was ratified by the Inuit in 1993 came into force. The agreement carved Nunavut (which means "our land'), a new self-governing territory, out of Canada's Northwest Territories. Nunavut encompasses over 2 million square kilometers, 23 percent of Canada's land mass.[44] Under the land settlement part of the agreement, the Inuit have collective ownership of 350,000 square kilometers of land. The self-government part, which takes the form of an Act of Parliament, gives its 27,000 people, 85 percent of whom are Inuit, self-government powers analogous to those which Greenlanders have as part of Denmark. Progress was also made in Yukon, the westernmost of Canada's northern territories, in implementing a 1993 umbrella agreement on land and self-government with individual first nations in the territory.[45] Earlier, in 1984, the Inuvaluit people in Canada's western Arctic had made a land settlement treaty with Canada, and in the 1990s similar agreements were negotiated with the Sahtu Dene, Metis, and Gwichin peoples further down the Mackenzie River Valley in the western part of the Northwest Territories.[46]

Progress has been much slower in the provinces where negotiations raise land and governance issues of vital concern to provincial governments and non-native majorities. A major breakthrough came with the 5,500 Nisga'a people of the Nass Valley in northwest British Columbia.[47] For over a century the Nisga'a had been endeavoring to make a treaty with Canada.[48] It was their persistence that led to the inauguration of comprehensive land-claim agreements in Canada in the 1970s. The Nisga'a were unwilling to settle land issues until it was possible to include self-government rights in a modern treaty. While the 1998 Nisga'a Agreement they signed with Canada and British Columbia, and ratified through a referendum, gives them ownership of only 10 percent of the lands and waters they claimed as traditional lands, it recognizes that the Lisims (central) and village governments of the Nisga'a nation may exercise extensive powers. In areas such as health, social services, transportation, environmental protection, and public order, Nisga'a laws have to give way if they conflict with federal or provincial legislation.[49] But in matters that are essential to their enduring as a distinct self-governing people—their constitution, membership, language, culture, and collectively owned land—Nisga'a laws prevail over conflicting federal or provincial laws.[50] Thus, through the agreement the Nisga'a are recognized as having a share of sovereign law-making power in Canada. It is this implication of the agreement, more than any other, that has provoked a great deal of concern among the non-native majority—particularly in British Columbia. British Columbia's NDP government pushed ratification of the agreement through the legislature by curtailing debate. The Nisga'a Agreement again encountered considerable opposition in the Canadian Senate, some of it from Liberals, but was finally fully ratified and became law on 13 April 2000. In July 2000, Justice Paul Williamson of the British Columbia Supreme Court rejected a court challenge to the constitutionality of the Nisga'a Agreement brought by the opposition B.C. Liberal Party.[51]

Opposition to the Nisga'a Agreement was not confined to the non-native side. Some Nisga'a and many other aboriginal people, including representatives of First Nations involved in the British Columbia Treaty Commission,[52] criticized the agreement for giving up too much land and too much self-government. Canada has made as much, if not more, progress than any other settler country in reaching a postcolonial relationship with its native peoples. Still, the struggle over ratification of the Nisga'a Agreement shows that native and non-native Canadians are still far from a genuinely consensual and popular resolution of their constitutional differences.

Can the Sovereign People Learn to be Multi-National?

Nearly a decade has gone by since the last attempt in the Charlottetown Accord to have the Canadian people act in a deliberate Lockean way as a constituent sovereign power. During these years—except for the 1995 Quebec referendum—Canadians have enjoyed constitutional peace, and a little bit of constitutional progress. The federation has been tidied up and made to work more efficiently. Provinces have updated their constitutions. The groundwork has been laid for restructuring relations with aboriginal peoples. But, it must be conceded, big unresolved constitutional issues remain unresolved. The question is not whether matters that deeply divide Canadians constitutionally can be left as they are. In history the status quo is always an illusion. The real question is whether the resolution of these issues is to be worked out quietly and gradually in a Burkean manner or through yet another heroic effort at a popular Lockean social contract.

The most fundamental issue dividing Canadians has to do with identity—about who "we" are. There are two groups of Canadians who identify primarily with a "we" who form a "nation" or "people" within Canada. These are the nationalist-inclined French-speaking Quebeckers and most aboriginal people. Many—I would think a majority—in both groups identify also with Canada, but that identity is of a weaker kind, too weak for them to feel comfortable thinking of their participation in Canada, their Canadian citizenship, as the core of their national identity. Quebec nationalists and aboriginal peoples want their societies recognized as "nations" or "peoples" within Canada. The only Canada to which they can give their allegiance is a multination Canada, one that has room for nations within. A handful of English Canadian intellectuals can identify with a multinational Canada (including the author),[53] but most English-speaking Canadians do not. They believe in a Canada, albeit a federal Canada, with a single, undivided sense of national identity—truly a nation-state. Tom Flanagan is surely empirically right when he tells us that a multinational Canada is not the vision of Canada he had when he immigrated in 1968, nor is it "what most Canadians want for themselves and their children."[54]

The situation is complicated by multiculturalism. Canada has pioneered in building a multicultural society that respects the cultural diversity that immigrants from all parts of the world bring to the country. Canada was the first country to inscribe a commitment to multiculturalism in its constitution. As Will Kymlicka has so convincingly shown, Canada's multicultural policies have not been barriers to the integration of immigrants into Canadian society.[55] Retaining the language and culture of their former homelands has not prevented "new Canadians" from learning English or French and participating fully in Canadian institutions. Though both multiculturalism and multinationalism respect cultural diversity, they entail very different constitutional aspirations. The Québécois and aboriginal peoples formed political communities on Canadian soil before the founding of the Canadian state. Their sense of distinct identity survived efforts by the British to conquer and assimilate them. These peoples' only homeland is within the boundaries of Canada, and their consent to be participants in the Canadian state is conditional on having governmental powers sufficient to ensure their survival as distinct societies. By way of contrast, the ethnic groups who support and benefit from multiculturalism have ties to former homelands elsewhere. They do not seek the same level of constitutional recognition or the governmental powers sought by the Québécois and aboriginal peoples. However, many members of these ethnic group resent these "national minorities" receiving any special treatment beyond multiculturalism. Like most Canadians of British background, the nation with which they identify is Canada.

The conflict between these two views of Canada, these two different senses of who "we" are—the uninational and the multinational—begins to surface now whenever Canadians touch the hot buttons of constitutional change. This was evident in the passions aroused by the 1995 Quebec referendum. It was evident in Prime Minister Chrétien's and the English-speaking premiers' efforts after the referendum to conciliate Quebec without recognizing its special status and the repudiation of those gestures by Premier Bouchard and other Quebec nationalists. It was abundantly clear in the showdown between the federal Clarity Bill and Quebec's Self-determination Bill. And it was evident again in the rough ride the Nisga'a Agreement had in being ratified in the British Columbia and federal legislatures and the equally rough ride aboriginal critics gave it from the opposite perspective.

Recent experience with constitutional politics has not whetted Canadian appetites for a return to the great megaconstitutional game. This is as much the case for Francophone Quebec as for the rest of the country. Premier Bouchard is having a devil of a time finding those "winning conditions" for another referendum. Perhaps he and those who support his moderation are learning that the people of Quebec, like the people of Canada, do not share a common sense of national identity, are not a single "we." The Quebec population contains members of nine Indian nations and the Inuit people of Nunavik, whose primary national identity is with their aboriginal community, as well as several million non-native federalists—French and English-speaking—whose attachment to Canada is as great or greater than their Quebec identity. Forcing a reopening of the big constitutional question of Quebec's relationship with Canada is bound to open up the equally troublesome question of restructuring Quebec—no matter what a majority of Quebeckers vote for in a referendum.

In English Canada, the main temptation to return to the big constitutional game is likely to come from Senate reformers. Even if the intent was to make Senate reform a single issue project, an attempt to restructure the Senate by formal constitutional amendment would lead inexorably to a heavy round of constitutional warfare. Canadians may be united on two *E*'s of Senate reform—on making it elected and effective—but they are surely deeply divided on the third *E* of equality. English Canada has the constitutional power to force through a reform of the Senate that treats Quebec as simply a province equal to all the rest, but not without serious risk of restoring the constitutional energy of Quebec nationalism. There are ways of attacking the democratic deficit in the functioning of our federal government that are more consensual and do not involve a difficult process of formal constitutional amendment. These include parliamentary reform and reform of the electoral system.[56]

Whether Canadians like it or not, the possibility of their country with its present borders being based on the consent of its people—and all of its peoples—depends on their learning to be citizens of a multinational state. For sure, this is a tenuous kind of unity. It means maintaining a federal country whose citizens do not share a common sense of national identity. It means conceding a right of secession to parts of the federation—something that must literally blow the minds of Americans glorying in their "perpetual union." At the same time, on the part of those whose primary identity is with a nation within, it requires a willingness to participate with some interest and enthusiasm in the political institutions of the larger Canadian community, and in that sense share a common civic identity with their fellow Canadian citizens. Operating such a political community is no easy matter, in part because it is a matter the political science of modern states knows little about. And yet, as we watch the evolution of the European Union and the efforts of its present and future member states to accommodate their "nations within," it can be argued that Canada's management of the constitutional politics of a multinational community has much more salience for the twenty-first century than the American constitutional paradigm.

In his recent book on how we Canadians might "find our way," Will Kymlicka suggests that Canadian unity could be strengthened by "moving in the direction of a more explicitly multinational federation."[57] The "explicitness" he envisages need not produce a shared identity, but it should produce a shared political conversation or discourse about the conditions of justice in a multination federation. The bonds of social union in such a political community are surely nurtured best through the "bits and pieces" of Burkean organic constitutional growth rather than through a grand populist effort at reconciling differences. To adapt some language from the Supreme Court's decision in the Quebec secession case, a multination political community "is built when the communities that comprise it make compromises, when they offer each other guarantees. The threads of a thousand acts of accommodation are the fabric" of such a state.[58]

Notes

1. Peter H. Russell, "Can the Canadians Be a Sovereign People?" *Canadian Journal of Political Science* 24 (1991): 691–709.

2. Peter H. Russell, *Constitutional Odyssey: Can Canadians Become a Sovereign People?* (Toronto: University of Toronto Press, 1992). A second edition was published in 1993 after the defeat of the Charlottetown Accord.

3. See, for instance, Stephen Clarkson, "Do Deficits Imply Surpluses? Toward a Democratic Audit of North America," in *Democracy Beyond the State?*, ed. Michael Th. Greven and Louis W. Pauly (Toronto: University of Toronto Press, 2000).

4. The exception is New Brunswick, which had two elections just before Confederation. The pro-Confederation politicians lost the first badly, but, helped by the threat of a Fenian invasion from the United States, won the second.

5. For two excellent accounts, see Donald Creighton, *The Road to Confederation: The Emergence of Canada, 1863–1867* (Toronto: Macmillan, 1964); and P. B. Waite, *The Life and Times of Confederation, 1864–1867* (Toronto: University of Toronto Press, 1962.)

6. Quoted in Russell, *Constitutional Odyssey,* 3.

7. See Daniel J. Elazar, "Constitution-making: The Pre-eminently Political Act," in *Redesigning the State: The Politics of Constitutional Change in Industrial Nations,* ed. Keith G. Banting and Richard Simeon (Toronto: University of Toronto Press, 1985).

8. My own account is chapter 6 of Russell, *Constitutional Odyssey.*

9. Quoted in ibid., 3.

10. Quoted in ibid., 126.

11. The only major native organization that approved the package was the Metis Association of Alberta. See ibid., 122.

12. While changes to a few provisions, such as the amending rules themselves, would require the unanimous approval of all the provinces and the federal parliament, most provisions, including changes in provincial powers, require approval of two-thirds of the provincial legislatures representing 50 percent of the population plus the federal parliament. A dissenting province can opt out of an amendment transferring jurisdiction to Ottawa (and receive fiscal compensation if the amendment relates to education or other cultural matters). Quebec's main vulnerability would be to amendments reducing its role in the federal government and parliament.

13. This is section 43 of the Constitution Act, 1982. An amendment under this section requires approval by the federal parliament and the legislative assembly of the province(s) to which it applies.

14. For details on all of these amendments, see Peter W. Hogg, *Constitutional Law of Canada,* 4th ed. (Toronto: Carswell, 1999), 1–7.

15. For accounts of this amendment and the Newfoundland schools amendment, see Stephane Dion, *Straight Talk: Speeches and Writings on Canadian Unity* (Montreal and Kingston: McGill-Queen's University Press, 1999), 80–92.

16. Nelson Wiseman, "Clarifying Provincial Constitutions," *National Journal of Constitutional Law* 6 (1994–95): 269–94.

17. For two appraisals, see Robert H. Knox, "Economic Integration in Canada through the Agreement on Internal Trade," and Daniel Schwanen, "Canadian Regardless of Origin: Negative Integration and the Agreement on Internal Trade," in *Canada: The State of the Federation 1997, Non-Constitutional Renewal,* ed. Harvey Lazar (Kingston, Ont.: Institute of Intergovernmental Relations, Queen's University, 1998).

18. For a critical appraisal of this intergovernmental process, see Roger Gibbins, "Time Out: Assessing Incremental Strategies for Enhancing the Canadian Political Union," in *The Referendum Papers: Essays on Secession and National Unity,* ed. David Cameron (Toronto: University of Toronto Press, 1999).

19. For an account of these reforms of the federation, see Dion, *Straight Talk,* 93–102.

20. Anne McIlroy and Brian Laghi, "PM Gets Social-Union Deal but Quebec Won't Sign," *Globe & Mail,* 5 February 1999, A1.

21. Susan Delacourt, "PM Offers Quebec Distinct Status," *Globe & Mail,* 28 November 1995, A1.

22. According to Chrétien's distinct society resolution, the House of Commons (not the courts) would "undertake to be guided" by the reality that "Quebec is a distinct society within Canada."

23. Brian Laghi and Graham Fraser, "Premiers Develop Unity Plan," *Globe & Mail,* 15 September 1997, A1.

24. Rheal Seguin, "Bouchard Reviles Unity Proposal," *Globe & Mail,* 17 September 1997, A1.

25. Miro Cernetig, "Chrétien's Veto Proposal Backfires in West," *Globe & Mail,* 29 November 1995, A7.

26. Susan Delacourt and Miro Cernetig, "BC Wins Constitutional Veto," *Globe & Mail,* 8 December 1995, A1.

27. *Constitutional Amendments Act,* Statutes of Canada, 1996, chap. 1. (For more on the amendment process in Canada, see chapter 11 of the present volume, "Constitutional Amendment in Canada and the United States," by Ian Greene.)

28. For an account of the background to the Quebec secession case, the Supreme Court's decision, and comments on it, see David Schneiderman, ed., *The Quebec Decision* (Toronto: James Lorimer, 1999).

29. On how the constitutional amendment rules apply to an agreement on Quebec secession, see Peter Russell and Bruce Ryder, "Ratifying a Postreferendum Agreement on Quebec Sovereignty," in Cameron, *Referendum Papers.*

30. The court's negative answer to this question meant that it did not have to answer the third question in the reference, namely, if international law conflicts with Canadian constitutional law, which should prevail?

31. *Reference re the Secession of Quebec* (1998) 2 S.C.R. 217, #138.

32. Ibid., #100.

33. Bill C-20, section 1(3).

34. For the text of the Quebec bill, see *Globe & Mail,* 16 December 1999, A11.

35. *R. v. Sparrow* (1990) 1 S.C.R. 1075.

36. *Delgamuukw v. British Columbia* (1997) 3 S.C.R. 1010.

37. *R. v. Marshall* (1999) 3 S.C.R. 456.

38. Four members of the seven-person commission were aboriginal, and three were nonaboriginal. They were selected by the recently retired chief justice of the

Supreme Court after a countrywide consultation. The commission's administrative and research staff was similarly bicultural in its composition.

39. The report had five volumes. It was published by Canada Communication Group and can be obtained through the Internet at www.libraxus.com/RCAP.

40. The Royal Commission's 1992 commentary, *The Right of Aboriginal Self-Government and the Constitution,* set out the rationale for this recognition.

41. The first amendment to the patriated constitution stated "for greater certainty" that constitutionally recognized treaty rights include rights obtained through land-claims agreements. *Constitution Amendment Proclamation, 1983.*

42. Peter H. Russell, "Aboriginal Peoples Do Have Inherent Rights," *Cité Libre* 27 (fall 1999): 56.

43. On the importance of shared citizenship, see Alan C. Cairns, *Citizens Plus: Aboriginal Peoples and the Canadian State* (Vancouver: University of British Columbia Press, 2000).

44. For a detailed account of Nunavut and the events leading to its establishment, see Jens Dahl, Jack Hicks, and Peter Jull, eds., *Nunavut: Inuit Regain Control of Their Lands and Their Lives* (Copenhagen: International Working Group for Indigenous Affairs, 2000).

45. Council of Yukon First Nations, *Understanding the Yukon Umbrella Agreement,* 4th ed. (Whitehorse, 1997).

46. For details, see Royal Commission on Aboriginal Peoples, *Report,* vol. 2, chap. 4.

47. This is not the first "modern treaty" within a province. The first comprehensive land claim was the James Bay and Northern Quebec Agreement of 1975, but it had very little in it by way of self-government rights.

48. For an account of the background to the Nisga'a Agreement and a range of opinions about it, see *The Nisga'a Treaty* (special issue of *BC Studies,* winter 1998/99).

49. The text of the Nisga'a Final Agreement can be obtained on the Internet at www.inac.gc.ca.

50. Section 9 of the agreement states that it "does not alter the Constitution of Canada," and section 9 states that the Canadian Charter of Rights and Freedoms applies to Nisga'a government.

51. Rod Mickleburgh, "B.C. Court Rejects Liberal Challenge of Aboriginal Self-Government," *Globe & Mail,* 25 July 2000.

52. For information on the B.C. Treaty Commission, go to www.bctreaty.net

53. I would include Samuel LaSelva, Philip Resnick, Charles Taylor, and James Tully in this group. For a discussion of this school of Canadian political thought, see Michael Ignatieff, *The Rights Revolution* (Toronto: Anansi, 2000), chap. 1.

54. Tom Flanagan, *First Nations, Second Thoughts* (Montreal and Kingston: McGill-Queen's University Press, 2000), 5.

55. Will Kymlicka, *Finding Our Way: Rethinking Ethnocultural Relations in Canada* (Toronto: Oxford University Press, 1998), see esp. chap. 1.

56. Many alternatives to first-past-the-post method of representation could be introduced without formal constitutional amendment.

57. Kymlicka, *Finding Our Way,* 177.

58. The quoted words are from the oral submission of the attorney general of Saskatchewan. I have substituted "multination political community" for "nation" in the original. *Reference re the Secession of Quebec, #96.*

CHAPTER 2

Constitutional Interpretation from Two Perspectives: Canada and the United States

Sheldon D. Pollack

Introduction

Canada and the United States both have written constitutions and independent judiciaries that possess the exclusive legal authority to interpret those constitutions. The origins and nature of this important political power to interpret the constitutional text is the subject of this chapter.

Prior to achieving independence from Britain, the American colonists already had experienced a long history of written constitutions (or "charters"). However, the Canadian experience with constitutions and English colonialism was quite different. Canada never experienced a radical break from Britain, only a long evolutionary movement toward independence. The British North America Act of 1867 (renamed the "Constitution Act, 1867" in 1982) is the closest thing Canada has to a written constitution in the nature of that ratified by the American states. The drafters of the Constitution Act, 1867 had a very limited concern—creating a governmental superstructure (the "Dominion of Canada") for the three English colonies in North America. Accordingly, the Constitution Act, 1867 did not include a bill of rights. Under the federal system adopted, the provincial governments retained considerable autonomy, and the Dominion as a whole remained under the authority of the English Crown until independence in 1982.

Because the United States and Canada took such divergent historical routes to independence, it is not surprising that two different constitutional regimes should have evolved. Nonetheless, there are striking similarities. Most notably, both have federal structures and have long struggled with the problems that arise when local constituent governments remain semiautonomous. Indeed, strife between the federal and local governments has been a hallmark of the histories of Canada and the United States. It has fallen to the judiciaries of both countries to delineate the boundaries between the two levels of government, as well as to define the rights of national citizenship. To this end, the Supreme Courts of Canada and the United States have performed the important role of interpreting and enforcing their respective constitutions.

Interpreting a constitution would seem to involve the same basic activity wherever there is a written constitution. Where the text is indeterminate, the courts are called upon to fashion a meaning. How the highest courts in these two liberal democracies came to assume this role in interpreting the constitutional text was greatly influenced by the seminal decisions of John Marshall, chief justice of the U.S. Supreme Court from 1801 to 1835. Marshall's approach to textual interpretation and the political implications that follow from a high court's exercise of the power of judicial review are explored below. Thereafter, the contemporary academic debate over theories of textual interpretation is examined.

Constitutional Interpretation as Political Choice

In the United States, with its written constitution that delineates the institutional boundaries within the federal structure and defines the rights and privileges of U.S. citizenship, interpreting the constitutional text has been the preeminent activity of the Supreme Court for nearly two hundred years. Indeed, the Supreme Court interpreting the written constitutional text *is* the essence of constitutional law in the United States. In Canada, which did not have a constitutional bill of rights until the entrenchment of the Charter of Rights and Freedoms in 1982, the Supreme Court traditionally was concerned with cases involving the federal structure: "Historically, federalism cases have been the heart and soul of Canadian constitutional law."[1] However, significant changes were made to the Canadian constitution in 1982. Since then, the Supreme Court of Canada has undergone a radical transformation, actively developing a jurisprudence of rights under the authority of the Charter. Changing the constitutional text had important repercussions for the judiciary, as well as for the entire political system. Accordingly, the starting point of this inquiry is to ask, What does it mean to organize a political regime around a written constitution? This in turn leads to the question of how a court should read or interpret the constitutional text.

Very early in its history, the American judiciary adopted and advanced a very peculiar understanding of "constitutionalism" founded upon the singular premise that the political regime shall be organized and governed by a written constitution—the meaning of which, when called into question, shall be determined by the judiciary. This view has its roots in Chief Justice John Marshall's seminal decisions. Notwithstanding widespread acceptance of this unique understanding of the relationship between the constitution and the judiciary, there always remains deep disagreement over *how* courts should interpret the text. The depth of this disagreement can be seen in the clash of opinions in recent years among constitutional jurists and political elites regarding the tenability of a jurisprudence of "original intentions." Much the same issues are raised in the recurring debate over judicial restraint versus judicial activism. There has been comparable disagreement in Canada over how active a role, and to what purpose, the Supreme Court should play in divining and articulating rights under the authority of the Charter. The divergence of opinion is reflected in the ongoing and lively debate within the academic community concerning the nature of constitutional interpretation. These disagreements share an underlying misperception of the problem as one of method and interpretation, rather than as a conflict of political choices.

Within the American constitutional tradition, which has as one of its fundamental goals limiting governmental power (and hence "tyranny") by way of a written text, this conflict of political visions is often cast deceptively as a dispute over interpretative methodology. The mainstream constitutional tradition regards the text as the source of all legitimate political authority, and hence as establishing the organizational principles of the regime. The predominance of this perspective on the bench and in the law schools provides the basis for a judicial ideology that seldom questions the theoretical justification of its own enterprise. As one political scientist has observed with a critical eye: "American constitutional interpretation takes for granted the elemental preposterousness of its subject, namely the presumption that a political world can be constructed and controlled with words."[2] This skepticism is justified in terms of the capacity of a written text to contain raw political power. However, such a judicial ideology can and does have a strong impact on politics. To the extent that judges believe they are bound by the text of a constitution, they behave differently than where they feel no such constraint. The judiciary's tenuous position as a political institution within the political system necessitates that the Supreme Court cling to the constitutional text as the source of legitimacy of its own authority. Consequently, the text and how it is interpreted are crucial in determining how the judiciary functions as a political institution.

One of the main objectives of liberal constitutionalism is to restrain political elites by imposing a structure of imperatives on them through law. Regardless of the theoretical possibility of controlling the judiciary and politics by way of a written text, the impact of this widespread view as a vital ideological tenet has been significant in shaping political practice. Conversely, if justices no longer feel impelled to adhere to the written text of a constitution and embrace an interpretive approach that facilitates the creation of new meanings by the judiciary, then the power of that constitution as a body of fundamental organizational principles will be greatly diminished. Of course, this is precisely the intention of those who promulgate new theories of interpretation in pursuit of their own political agenda. They would recast the constitutional regime through a rereading of the constitutional text. This is possible because constitutional interpretation involves political choices with serious consequences for the regime. The constitutional text establishes the rules and principles that govern the legitimate uses and goals for the exercise of political power—the "metalaw," as Lawrence Tribe has called it.[3] Pursuit of an alternative method of textual interpretation will necessarily reshape this metalaw, thereby reconstituting the extant constitutional regime. Inevitably within the context of a functioning political regime, the words of the constitutional text will give rise to specific practices and procedures that are shaped by the meanings attached to the text by the legal system. Adopting a new method of textual interpretation will transform those established practices, and hence will have important political consequences.[4]

Of course, it is not possible to permanently freeze political practice through adherence to a written text. One of the most mystifying self-delusions of the American constitutional tradition is the notion that it is possible to pronounce as final and permanent certain values and principles simply by codifying them in a constitutional text, which elevates them beyond the political realm. This position is untenable. Constitutional decision-making always involves an active and present choice among various meanings for the text. Likewise, different approaches to textual interpretation inevitably enhance or diminish the role of the judiciary in the political process. For this reason, the more extreme political attacks on the judiciary (from both the Left and the Right) take as their goal the reconstitution of the constitutional text itself. Such a reconstitution may be achieved through textual (re)interpretation, avoiding the much more difficult task of building a broad political consensus in favor of an outright change of the text. Although a constitutional amendment is always possible, a subtle rereading of the text is considerably easier and achieves much the same result. This approach was followed by mainstream liberals in the United States in the 1960s and 1970s in pursuit of an agenda of civil rights. For their part, political conservatives have been anxious to limit the jurisdiction of the courts in certain areas of constitutional law despite strong textual and historical foundation for a more active judicial role in those areas. An example of this can be found in attacks by conservatives in the 1960s on the liberal Warren Court's expansion of the rights of accused persons. Likewise, conservatives in Canada have been highly critical of the lack of judicial restraint of the Supreme Court of Canada since entrenchment of the Charter in 1982.[5]

Both sides of the political spectrum recognize the attractiveness of using textual interpretation to work subtle political changes that otherwise cannot be achieved through the political process. In this way, a battle that is essentially political in nature is recast in the language of methodology and textual interpretation.

Judicial Review as Political Power

Textual interpretation from the bench is very different from literary or academic interpretation. The difference lies in the position of the *interpreter*—namely, the role of the judiciary as a political institution. To the extent that a court's meanings are accepted as legitimate and authoritative by other political actors, any exercise of the power of interpretation enhances the role of the judiciary.

The Origins of Judicial Review

Whatever the intentions of the drafters and adopters of the U.S. Constitution, the Supreme Court's first successful exertion of the power of judicial review had a significant influence upon the development of the federal system as a whole. Of course, this was precisely Alexander Hamilton's argument in *The Federalist Papers.* Hamilton justified a judicial power derived from the capacity to pronounce an authoritative textual meaning on the grounds that this would strengthen the Supreme Court vis-à-vis the legislative branch and its presumed self-aggrandizing tendencies.[6] Hamilton's argument for a power to interpret the text was actually an instrumental tactic intended to limit *legislative* power, as he assumed an aristocratic judiciary endangered by an unchecked democratic legislature.

It was not until Chief Justice John Marshall supplied his justifications of the power of judicial review that the potential was fully revealed for utilizing the authority to interpret the text as a powerful political tool.[7] In the course of claiming this power of judicial review for the Court in *Marbury v. Madison,*[8] Marshall established the foundation for the American constitutional tradition in which the written constitutional text is regarded as the source of a "supreme law," and it is the Supreme Court's exclusive responsibility to interpret the text. Marshall's claim was that the necessity for judicial interpretation is inherent within the very notion of constitutionalism as adherence to a written text. According to Marshall, for the Supreme Court to exercise its delegated authority under Article 3, the power to review and interpret the Constitution was necessarily a judicial function. Marshall asked, more rhetorically than not, "Could it be the intention of those who gave this power, to say that in using it the Constitution should not be looked into? That a case arising under the Constitution should be decided without examining the instrument under which it arises?"[9] On the weak logic of this argument, Marshall rested a broad structural theory of the judiciary and its role vis-à-vis the other branches of government.

In *Marbury,* Chief Justice Marshall relied on a peculiarly limited conception of textual interpretation in defining the judicial role. Obviously, Marshall recognized the tenuousness of claims for judicial power in relation to Congress and the president, and he treaded carefully. Marshall implied that the art of interpretation involves a literal application of standards clearly evident in the Constitution. The examples he uses in *Marbury* to illustrate the act of interpretation are the kind of "easy cases" that give rise to the view that a text can be determinate. These examples entail such a literal application of standards that virtually no interpretation is even required. For instance, Marshall notes that conviction for treason demands the testimony of "two witnesses" in open court. Presumably, it is a relatively straightforward affair to "look into" the text here and apply the prescribed constitutional standard. To apply the rule, just count the number of witnesses. Marshall implies that applying the prohibition against bills of attainder and ex post facto laws similarly involves a literal invoking of the text—although subsequent cases suggest that these terms are a good deal more elusive than that.

In *Marbury,* Marshall portrayed textual interpretation as involving a nearly literal application of an express constitutional standard. However, he later showed that he was quite capable of employing a far more expansive reading of the text. In *McCulloch v. Maryland,*[10] Marshall demonstrated how a theory of interpretation could support a different political vision as he read the words "necessary and proper" from Article 1, Section 8, in a much broader fashion to sustain a significant extension of federal power over state government. Marshall's change in his approach to reading the Constitution was not unprincipled; rather, he knew that reading the text cannot be divorced from broader political questions. Marshall's political vision distinguished between exercising the judicial power *within* the federal government vis-à-vis the other two branches and the use of judicial power on behalf of the federal government *against* the state governments. Marshall's description of the art of textual interpretation in *McCulloch* supports an expansion of the federal government, even without stating that as an explicit goal. Obviously, such a method of textual interpretation supports and reflects an underlying political vision and is simply the same view of politics articulated in a different language—the language of constitutional law.

In Canada, the judiciary had the opportunity to emulate Marshall's broad reading of the "necessary and proper clause." The preamble to section 91 of the Constitution Act, 1867 grants the federal government the authority to enact all laws for the "peace, order and good government" of the country. This broad language would seem to grant the federal government a good deal of discretion over the provincial governments. Arguably, the preamble creates a catchall power justifying federal intrusion into any policy area not expressly reserved to the provincial governments. This reading of the text follows Marshall's interpretation of the "necessary and proper" clause as bestowing on the federal government broad and expansive powers to carry out its plenary powers. There was one problem with this interpretation of the "peace, order and good government" clause. Nothing in the Constitution Act, 1867 expressly states the supremacy of federal law over provincial law, or even of the constitution itself over statutory law. This flaw in the structure of the federal system was not rectified until the entrenchment of the Constitution Act, 1982, which provides that: "The Constitution of Canada is the supreme law of Canada, and any law that is inconsistent with the provision of the Constitution is, to the extent of the inconsistency, null and void."[11] To deal with the uncertainty prior to 1982, the federal courts developed the judicial doctrine of "paramountcy."[12] Echoing Marshall in *McCulloch,* the federal courts took the position that in cases of conflict between federal and provincial law, "the federal law is paramount and the provincial law is inoperative to the extent of the conflict."[13] The text itself does not expressly state this, but the courts discerned this result in the overall structure of the Canadian constitution.

Textual indeterminacy such as this can also be resolved by reference to an implicit political perspective, such as the nationalist vision that supports Marshall's decision in *McCulloch.* An interesting example of such an approach is found in the U.S. case of *Missouri v. Holland.*[14] In litigation, the state of Missouri challenged the enforcement of the Migratory Bird Treaty Act of 1918, a statute implementing a treaty negotiated by the president and Great Britain. The treaty and statute were challenged as unconstitutional infringements upon the powers reserved to the states under the Tenth Amendment of the U.S. Constitution. The Supreme Court was forced to consider how two specific clauses of the text interact—or, in this case, decide which clause would dominate in providing a coherent meaning for the document as a whole. Article 6 provides that treaties made under the "Authority of the United States" are to be regarded as the "supreme Law of the Land," along with the Constitution itself. However, Missouri argued that the traditional state power to regulate wildlife within its domain had been guaranteed by the Tenth Amendment. The question was, Can a treaty (which is part of the "supreme law of the land") and the statute enacting it cut back the powers seemingly reserved to the states by the Tenth Amendment?

The majority opinion of Justice Oliver Wendell Holmes Jr. in *Holland* illustrates how interpretation requires much more than merely defining terms and often slides into broader constitutional "construction." Construction is the "drawing of conclusions respecting subjects that lie beyond the direct expression of the text, from elements known from and given in the text—conclusions which are in the spirit though not the letter of the text."[15] The Constitution itself provides no method of determining how two clauses at issue should be integrated, and no historical investigation into the framers' intentions or legislative history could reveal the unforeseen contradiction. Holmes could have read the conflict out of the text by simply locating the power to regulate migratory birds under an established federal power (such as the Commerce Clause), thus preempting state regulation and rendering moot the Tenth Amendment claim. Instead, he constructed a broader meaning of the Constitution that would resolve this textual contradiction or ambiguity. Holmes invoked the now familiar metaphor of the Constitution as a flexible, "living" document (which inevitably precedes an expansion of the traditional meanings of the text). He described the text as a "constituent act" that "called into life a being the development of which could not have been foreseen completely by the most gifted of its begetters."[16] The text is incomplete and indeterminate on this question, and the issue could only be resolved by reference to some external political principle. This Holmes willingly supplied.

Echoing the nationalist sentiments of Marshall, Holmes saw the U.S. Constitution as a document that "created a nation," and thus must be understood in "the light of our whole experience and not merely in that of what was said a hundred years ago." The national experience as well as Holmes's personal experience included the Civil War, which had cost "much sweat and blood" resolving the balance of power between nation and state. Holmes refused to read the Tenth Amendment as preserving forever whatever powers the states exercised in 1787. Since the treaty did not "contravene any prohibitory words to be found in the Constitution," Holmes answered the easier question of ambiguity by resolving it in favor of the federal government. "Here a national interest of very nearly the first magnitude is involved. It can be protected only by national action in concert with that of another power. . . . It is not sufficient to rely upon the States."[17]

The *Holland* case neatly illustrates how a court confronts a multiplicity of political choices in resolving constitutional conflicts. The text often does not provide a clear standard or any derivative result. In light of ambiguity, contradiction, a conceptual gap, or simply "open-ended" language, the interpreter is free to actively construct any number of solutions by appeal to sources external to the text. Sources such as the framers' "intent" or historical practice offer the interpreter the opportunity to fashion a result almost without restraint (other than the negative check of other justices who may pursue an alternative vision). The absence of any textual guidance as to specific procedures and patterns of interbranch relations may invite a so-called structuralist approach to constitutional interpretation, but this is really a political decision.

Under a structuralist approach, a court supposedly interprets the indeterminate constitutional text in light of the justice's understanding of the nature of the constitutional regime as a whole. "Structural arguments are inferences from the existence of constitutional structures and the relationships which the Constitution ordains among these structures. They are to be distinguished from textual and historical arguments, which construe a particular constitutional passage and then use that construction in the reasoning of an opinion. . . ."[18] As such, structural arguments are largely devoid of fact and depend on deceptively simple logical inferences derived from the interpreter's understanding of the entire constitutional regime. Of course, those possessing very different political philosophies will likely arrive at very different conclusions employing a structuralist approach in interpreting any individual clause in the constitutional text.

This is not to say that the individual justice is free to impose his or her own subjective political preferences on the text. Rather, there is more than enough room and occasion to make choices regarding how to construe the constitutional text through the expression of a logically consistent political worldview. Within the inevitable ambiguities of the text, sufficient space is provided for the construction of an "unwritten constitution" reflecting the judicial ideology that can currently muster a majority on the Supreme Court. Of course, this power would be extended far beyond anything that Marshall and Holmes would have tolerated, to the extent that justices on the bench no longer feel *any* restraints in exercising their political power to interpret the constitutional text.

Judicial Review and Canadian Federalism

In 1867, the drafters of the new Canadian constitution had before them the prime example of the United States—especially with respect to its federal system of government. The drafters were familiar with John Marshall's conscious effort to read the constitutional text to justify the supremacy of federal law over that of the states. It appears that the drafters were consciously attempting to locate greater powers with the federal government, although it is difficult to discern the "original intent" of the drafters, as very little is known of their motives and there is no record of most of the discussions at the conferences held in Charlottetown, Quebec, and London that led up to the British North America Act of 1867.[19] With such scant historical evidence of the original intent of the drafters, the constitutional text provides the only real guidance for courts attempting to delineate the boundaries between the federal and provincial governments.

Unlike the U.S. Constitution, the Constitution Act, 1867 provides quite specific lists of apparently limitless and "exclusive" powers for *both* levels of government. Unless otherwise stated, these powers are mutually exclusive, rather than concurrent or shared.[20] Section 91 grants the federal government exclusive authority over issues of national importance.[21] At least on paper, the drafters of the Canadian constitution created a stronger federal government than had their counterparts in the United States. For instance, the Canadian federal government has jurisdiction over all "trade and commerce," not just interstate commerce—the more limited power granted to the U.S. Congress.

Likewise, criminal law and family law was federalized in Canada, rather than retained as a power of the local governments, as in the United States.

Section 92 in turn grants the provincial governments "exclusive" authority in a number of broadly defined legislative areas. These include management of natural resources, land, conservation, education, the family and social institutions, "property and civil rights," and all other matters of a "merely local or private nature." The provincial governments were granted shared jurisdiction over agriculture, and they too were authorized to borrow and incorporate companies "for provincial objects" (e.g., roads, bridges, public works, etc.). Whatever the drafters may have had in mind when they allocated these "exclusive" powers to the respective legislatures, many areas of public policy inevitably fall within the domain of *both* the federal and provincial governments. For this reason, Canadian courts were forced to wrestle with the inevitable conflict between jurisdictions, as if nothing had been learned from John Marshall and the American experience. While the constitutional text would suggest that the new Canadian federal structure was considerably more centralized than in the United States, the provincial governments actually retained a good deal more autonomy in practice. This left the Canadian federal courts and the Law Lords of the Privy Council with the task of drawing boundaries between the federal government in Ottawa and the provincial governments. Prior to 1982, the basic question to ask with respect to particular legislation was whether the policy addressed by the statute actually fell within the jurisdiction of the legislative body that enacted it. If not, it would be pronounced unconstitutional.

Understandably, the federal courts were reluctant to interpret the Canadian constitution to mean that federal powers *always* trump those of the provincial governments. This certainly was not the line taken in the early federalism cases, in which the courts struggled to discern where and when the federal power trumps the powers of the provincial governments. For example, in the 1896 case of *AG Ontario v. AG Canada*[22] (also known as the "Local Prohibition Reference" case), the Privy Council wrestled with competing claims of jurisdiction—specifically, as to whether a provincial legislature had the power to impose prohibition. To complicate matters, also at issue was the power of the government in Ottawa to legislate on liquor control. In considering the limits to the power of the federal government, Lord Watson emphasized that "the Dominion Parliament has no authority to encroach upon any class of subjects which is exclusively assigned to provincial legislatures by s. 92." Nevertheless, Lord Watson acknowledged that there are instances when the national interest requires that federal power take priority over the powers reserved to provincial governments: "Their Lordships do not doubt that some matters, in their origin local and provincial, might attain such dimensions as to affect the body politic of the Dominion, and to justify the Canadian Parliament in passing laws for their regulation or abolition in the interest of the Dominion." The difficulty lies in developing clear legal standards and rules for identifying such instances.

Not until after the entrenchment of the constitution of 1982 did the Supreme Court of Canada expressly articulate the implications of the "peace, order, and good government" clause for the balance of power within the federal structure. In 1988 case of *Crown Zellerbach,*[23] the Supreme Court developed a test of "rationality" and "proportionality" to be followed in delineating the boundaries between federal and provincial powers. At issue was a challenge by a private logging company to a federal statute regulating marine pollution. The Supreme Court took the position that in deciding whether Ottawa's power to provide "peace, order, and good government" trumps an express power of a provincial government (namely, environmental management) depends upon whether there is a rational reason for giving the national power priority and whether it can be demonstrated that the exercise of such power does not unnecessarily invade provincial powers.

In *Crown Zellerbach,* the Court balanced the competing claims of sovereignty of the two levels of government. This political decision becomes a *judicial* function in the absence of any ordering rules provided in the constitution itself. Just as Justice Holmes could find no such ordering rules in the U.S. Constitution, but nevertheless discerned them in the overall "structure" of the regime, so too has the Supreme Court of Canada discerned within the structure of the Canadian federal system when national priorities take precedence over provincial powers. The Court enunciated purportedly neutral rules for determining when such national priorities trump local sovereignty. In fact, what the Court did was supply its own interpretation of an indeterminate aspect of the text, thereby influencing the development of the Canadian constitutional regime—a political role for the judiciary, if ever there was one.

Theories of Constitutional Interpretation

Any constitutional theory entails a normative understanding of how the polity should be organized in accordance with those principles deemed to be "fundamental." Chief Justice Marshall laid the foundation for a peculiarly American formulation of constitutionalism based on the premise that fundamental principles of politics can be given lasting expression in a written text. The idea that a constitution is vital to organizing a political regime became the dominant view within the liberal political tradition. However, the American constitutional tradition adopted several other tenets as well—in particular, the notion that the written constitution is the supreme text and the belief that it is the unique responsibility of the judiciary to give meaning to that text.

The notion that the judiciary is the sole legitimate body to interpret the constitutional text necessarily expresses a normative political philosophy. Likewise, any theory of textual interpretation necessarily reflects an underlying political vision. For this reason, contrasting theories of textual interpretation invoke differences of political theory. There is a rich literature that has developed in the last two decades among constitutional jurists, both Canadian and American, to describe these competing theories of textual interpretation.

Originalism, Intentionalism, and Interpretivism

The underlying political implications of the various conceptions of textual interpretation can be best understood by focusing on the most extreme and diametrically opposed views. These theories of textual interpretation, along with the broader theories of politics with which they are associated, reflect the limits and boundaries of a liberal politics committed to a notion of constitutionalism in which a written text is the source of legitimacy for the exercise of political power.

At one extreme is an understanding of constitutionalism rigidly committed to a judicial doctrine embracing an "originalist" theory of textual interpretation.[24] From this perspective, the constitutional text must be read *only* in light of its "original meaning." The commitment to originalism is manifested in several forms and variations, although they are underscored by related political objectives. Sometimes the objective is the search for the original meaning of the text. Sometimes the goal is to find the original intentions of the drafters or "Founding Fathers." For this reason, the theory is occasionally referred to as intentionalism, rather than originalism.[25] In cases where the text itself betrays no discernible original meaning, historical research may be required to discern the authentic meaning of the text.[26] As in cases of statutory ambiguity, "intent" may be found in the legislative history accompanying the enactment of the text.

Most proponents of originalism share a common political concern: limiting the impact of the judiciary by imposing a restrictive method of textual interpretation upon the federal courts, thereby limiting the discretion afforded the courts within the arena of constitutional politics. The most sophisticated advocates of originalism recognize that the discretion of judges in interpreting the text can never be wholly eliminated. They understand that originalist interpretation is not easy and requires that judges make reasonable and persuasive arguments in favor of their interpretations of the text. Originalism also may require an active judiciary striking down acts of the legislature and executive as contrary to the original meaning of the text, showing "deference only to the Constitution and to the limits of human knowledge, not to contemporary politicians."[27]

One thing is certain: Imposing an "original" meaning upon the text will curtail the Supreme Court's role in discovering new constitutional rights. Indeed, this is the intention of advocates of originalism. Specific political issues will be expelled from the arena of constitutional law, and either will be left by default to other political institutions or excluded from consideration altogether. In some cases, it is difficult to distinguish between originalist rhetoric aimed at an overly active judiciary and a politically motivated attack on the federal courts for actively pursuing the "wrong" (i.e., liberal) agenda. Clearly, some conservative partisans would employ originalism selectively. Thoughtful critics recognize that there are serious problems in expanding judicial power to embrace an overly optimistic and utopian effort to read our "highest" contemporary moral sensibilities into the constitutional text—the utopian quest for perfection and progress in constitutional law. The best objections to such a judicial moral crusade should reflect a cautious view of the possibilities of politics, as well as a fear of law (both judicial and legislative) intruding too far into our private lives.

Originalism can be a potent weapon as a judicial doctrine from the bench. To the extent that it is followed by the relevant political actors themselves, its impact on the direction of the federal judiciary will be important. Several conservatives currently on the U.S. Supreme Court have expressed adherence to an originalist position.[28] The impact on the judiciary as a political institution of an emergent majority supporting some version of originalism would be comparable to stacking the Court with "strict constructionists."[29] The level of activity of the judiciary and the kind of issues brought into the arena of the federal courts would be greatly affected by a shift on the Court toward a jurisprudence of originalism.

Accepting that originalism is a viable judicial doctrine, the question remains whether it is a coherent theoretical position. Its basic premises have been significantly challenged at a number of levels.[30] As a guiding principle of textual interpretation, originalism suggests that the courts should apply only those "plain" meanings explicitly evident in the text. This position resembles the politically instrumental portrait of textual interpretation that Chief Justice Marshall laid out in *Marbury*. In the academic debate, such a theory of textual interpretation is known as "clause-bound interpretation" or strict interpretation, following the terminology of John Hart Ely in his influential book *Democracy and Distrust*.[31] According to Ely, strict interpretivism is an unworkable approach to textual interpretation in all but the most literal cases, such as a court applying a clear constitutional standard like the thirty-five-year age requirement for U.S. presidents. Ely thus rejects the simplistic premise that the text possesses an "objective" or "plain" meaning that the court has merely to uncover in interpreting a constitution. He tries to salvage an originalist position by turning to a revised version in which the meaning of the text is derived by reference to "an inference whose starting point, whose underlying premise, is fairly discoverable" in the constitution.[32]

Ely searches for a middle ground between the impracticality of originalism and the dangerous conclusions implied by a judicial realism that declares that the text means only what the Supreme Court says it means.[33] Unfortunately, it is difficult to sustain the middle ground. On the one hand, Ely concedes the theoretical impossibility of strict interpretivism; on the other, he concludes that the open-ended nature of portions of the text invites and justifies the exercise of judicial discretion in applying constitutional standards. While highly critical of the U.S. Supreme Court for the kind of judicial review exercised in the so-called privacy cases, Ely's own reading of the open-ended language in the text tends to support the Court's most blatant "noninterpretivist" approach. In the end, Ely must acknowledge that the problem is really one of adequately defining the role of the Supreme Court as a *political* institution.

Noninterpretivism

Ultimately, Ely's constitutional jurisprudence must be judged at odds with the method and political motives of originalism and interpretivism. Peculiarly, it also offers little comfort or support for the noninterpretivist school. Noninterpretivist judicial doctrine is entirely opposed to the methods and intentions of originalism and its related theory of constitutionalism. For example, Michael Perry's pursuit of noninterpretivist review in his well-known treatise *The Constitution, the Courts, and Human Rights*[34] serves up a constitutionalism hell-bent on institutionalizing the U.S. Supreme Court as the infamous "bevy of Platonic Guardians"—Justice Learned Hand's euphemism for unbridled discretionary rule by judges.[35] Perry's defense of this constitutional theory, which is the logical result of noninterpretivist judicial review, might be too readily dismissed because of this criticism, especially given the lack of any theoretical support for his vision of the Supreme Court as an oracle of human rights. However, other sophisticated theories of textual interpretation point to essentially the same political outcome as recasting the judicial function. This position is very much evidenced in the writings of Ronald Dworkin, who suggests that justices find the content of their jurisprudence in moral philosophy and the shared values of contemporary society.[36] Certain Canadian jurists have portrayed constitutional jurisprudence as the enterprise of expressing the ideal goals or "visions" of Canadian society through the constitution.[37] Of course, those who would apply such a method to constitutional interpretation conceive of their goal precisely in terms of expressing contemporary conceptions (usually moral in content) through constitutional adjudication, rather than as an effort to preserve any original constitutional position.[38]

To noninterpretivists, legal interpretation, no less than any other kind of textual interpretation, has a responsibility to translate archaic concepts into socially meaningful structures. From this perspective, there can be no permanent or fixed text any more than there can be a recovery of an "original" understanding, precisely because such an approach denies the possibility of transhistorical meaning. The text is a forum for pronouncing contemporary values as constitutional values, to be born anew with each successive progression of human experiences. Of course, this is the ultimate expression of the "living" or "unwritten" constitution, bound by nothing other than the contemporary conceptual and moral framework of "living" justices.

Such a theory of constitutional interpretation is yet another judicial doctrine—an ideological position inherently political in nature, expressed in the language of legal discourse revolving around constitutional interpretation. The nature of such a judicial function can be located at the opposite end of the political spectrum from originalism. It is no coincidence that this vision of constitutionalism focuses on constitutional adjudication involving the rights of citizenship.[39] The text itself is most open-ended in this area, allowing the courts greater discretion. Also, in pursuing a jurisprudence of rights, the judiciary is least restrained by competing political pressures from the other political institutions (i.e., Congress or Parliament). When defining rights under the cover of documents such as the Bill of Rights and the Charter, a court's action is more often perceived as a legitimate judicial function than as an intrusion into other substantive areas that may be deemed off-limits as "political" matters to be confined within the legislative branch,[40] or as simply "nonjusticiable."[41] In rights adjudication, there often is no original meaning that can be discovered in the text or history, and thus a court is relatively free to engage in noninterpretivist review.

Noninterpretivists champion a vision of the Supreme Court as the primary enunciator of rights and moral values. The justices are seen as mediators between the constitutional text, its attendant historical meaning, and contemporary society. While the words of the document remain constant, its meaning must be continually re-created for successive generations. The Court is supposed to interpret the text for and by reference to the present needs and values of the citizenry. The late Justice William J. Brennan most forcefully expressed this vision from the bench. Brennan recognized the power attached to the capacity to pronounce the authoritative interpretation of the text, but he cast the debate in the language of methodology and textual interpretation, thereby obscuring the political nature of such judicial power. As Brennan put it: "Because judicial power resides in the authority to give meaning to the Constitution, the debate is really a debate about how to read the text, about what is legitimate interpretation."[42] Unfortunately, Brennan misses the point that the authority to interpret the text, the source of judicial power, is inherently a political power, and thus the debate is really a debate about politics, not interpretation.

The Mixed Nature of the Constitutional Text

The judicial doctrine of originalism and the rhetoric of the "living constitution" represent the polar opposites located within the narrow confines of the moderate Lockean liberalism that maintains hegemony over American political thought. It can be said that constitutionalism is driven by a dialectic of opposing impulses expressed within the narrower confines of moderate liberal jurisprudence. The judicial doctrines of originalism and noninterpretivism are manifestations of these dual impulses. Historically, one strain expresses an "institutionalist" concern, stressing the principles of the rule of law, limited government, and a generally conservative ("Whig") vision of the limits of politics, while the other essentially expresses an antinomian, egalitarian, democratic, and populist strain through the radical language of natural rights theory.

Insofar as natural rights theory is most suited to providing an external vantage point for challenging the legitimacy of an extant regime, it is a historical anomaly that it should find expression in the inherently conservative vehicle of a constitution. Ironically, the triumph of natural rights theory and its entrenched position in American political thought create an uneasy tension between rhetoric and reality. The institutionalization of natural rights theory within the constitutional text in the United States, and more recently in Canada, creates an implicit tension between democratic values and government by the judiciary. This accounts for the constant need of intellectual defenders of judicial review to "reconcile" democracy with the pursuit of a rights-based jurisprudence from the admittedly undemocratic institution of the federal judiciary.[43]

These two opposing expressions of constitutionalism were present during the 1780s as dissatisfaction with the Articles of Confederation mounted and informed the subsequent debates at the Constitutional Convention, as well as the processes of constitutional amendment and adjudication by the Supreme Court over the next two centuries. The dominant strain of constitutionalism looks to institutional solutions to the problem of the undue concentration of political power by establishing a limited federal government within fixed boundaries. This position ironically views the federal government as both a prerequisite to the preservation of liberty *and* as a danger, requiring a system of institutional checks and constraints. The other strain of constitutionalism, natural rights theory, is equally ambiguous regarding political power. Here the ambiguity lies in expressing a theory that is inherently antinomian and anti-institutionalist through the constitutional decision-making of an entrenched legal system. Grafted onto the institutionalist (Madisonian) text of the U.S. Constitution, the (Jeffersonian) natural rights theory of the Bill of Rights creates a source of uneasy tension in American constitutional law. Canada has more recently experienced this kind of constitutional schizophrenia with the entrenchment of the Charter.

Because neither the institutionalist nor natural rights position triumphed in American history, neither intellectually nor politically, elements of both have remained within the mainstream tradition of liberal constitutionalism. Indeed, both positions found expression within the U.S. Constitution as amendments were subsequently added. The resulting text is sufficiently "mixed" in nature as to facilitate either constitutionalist tradition in reading its position into the document. This mixed nature of the text explains the "ironic" argument of John Hart Ely when he observes that by a strict interpretivist reading of the text, noninterpretivism is suggested by virtue of the open-ended language in sections of the Bill of Rights.[44] The inability to settle on a particular method of reading the text reflects the historical absence of consensus regarding the nature of constitutionalism.

Sources of the Mixed Text

Grafting a natural rights document onto an institutionalist blueprint for limited government renders a constitution a mixed document that is all things to all judicial ideologies. The open-ended language of constitutional documents such as the Charter of Rights and Freedoms and the Bill of Rights of 1791 invites a broad exercise of judicial review. Even if the invitation does not extend to creating entirely new rights, there is certainly a wide range of possibilities for the extension of old rights under the headings of equal protection and due process.

Whatever the merits of the originalist or interpretivist positions as to the political reasons for restraining the capacity of the judiciary to subsume the entire arena of politics under the guise of judicial review, the actual language used by the drafters of these sections of the text justifies a much broader review than the originalists will concede. For instance, nothing in the text of the Eighth Amendment of the U.S. Constitution suggests that a phrase such as "cruel and unusual" must be restricted to its "original" late-eighteenth-century meaning—although there is also no reason why a court may not so narrowly construe its meaning. While the absence of textual specificity does not sanction the legitimacy of any single interpretation of such a phrase, it does justify a good deal of leeway in giving specific content and meaning to particular judicial interpretations. Theoretically, it is possible to imagine a constitutional text that would fully express a single theory of constitutionalism and an attendant method of textual interpretation. The particular constitutions adopted in the United States and Canada, however, do not resolve the matter in favor of any particular approach. Several features of the constitutional texts contribute to the uncertainty.

First, the absence within both constitutional texts of any procedure or method (or even authorization) for a particular method of textual interpretation denies an absolute victory for either originalism or noninterpretivism. Even if the exercise of the power of judicial review is now taken as a given, a court cannot exercise this power too strongly in favor of either form of interpretation without triggering immediate protests of illegitimacy. Neither an unrestrained noninterpretivism nor a clause-bound interpretivism is politically feasible on the bench, although academics are unfettered by such constraints. Because the text authorizes neither option, the resulting jurisprudence exercised from the bench is inevitably a mixture. No court could survive politically if it pursued in unrestrained fashion either a pure noninterpretivist articulation of natural rights rhetoric or the straightjacketed jurisprudence of originalism. The limits of noninterpretivist review were most clearly revealed by the U.S. Supreme Court's decision in *Roe v. Wade*.[45] Similarly, conservative challenges to the doctrine of "incorporation" may be historically correct, but fall on deaf ears in the legal and political community, as the question was essentially rendered moot decades ago.[46] The constitutional text dictates neither originalism nor noninterpretivism.

A second source of ambiguity in the constitutional texts stems from the lack of organizing principles. In order to resolve inconsistencies, ambiguities, and unanticipated situations, the interpreter must turn to *some* guiding principles. Where the text itself provides no specific, determinate answer, some broader principle such as federal supremacy or the preservation of state autonomy may offer substantial guidance. However, neither constitution clearly explicates such principles. On the contrary, both texts provide support for a multitude of positions. This lack of general guiding principles should be distinguished from the use of general terms (or "concepts," in Ronald Dworkin's terminology)[47] in a constitution without specifying their particular applications. For example, there is clearly some general theory of federalism inherent within the U.S. Constitution and the institutions it establishes. The problem lies in discerning *what* theory of federalism is implied. Without such a statement of principle, a proponent of states' rights on the bench could justifiably have taken a position contrary to those of Marshall and Holmes.

This absence of internal principles has given the judiciary much discretion in generating its own guiding principles. Undoubtedly, the clearest such example is the creation by the judiciary through case law of a theory of "separation of powers." Given the wide range of separation theories in contemporary eighteenth-century political thought (including mixed-government theory and corporatist theories of functional representation), the organizational principles of the U.S. Constitution are not easily discovered. Sources such as *The Federalist Papers* offer some extratextual statements of principle, but to a large extent the Supreme Court has fashioned its own theory of "checks and balances" that it has applied in significant constitutional decisions.[48]

Canada's New Jurisprudence of Rights

Obviously, a different constitutional text will necessarily generate different constitutional law. For example, a constitution that includes a very narrow bill of rights will necessarily limit the capacity of the courts to pursue an expansive jurisprudence of human rights. Likewise, where a constitution establishes a federal structure and provides a very specific and clearly enunciated allocation of power between the national and local governments, a body of constitutional law will likely develop along entirely different lines than where there is only a vague and loose allocation of powers. This is to say that constitutions matter.

Where a constitutional text is amended or augmented, the opportunity arises for a change in the role of the judiciary—for example, in pursuing a jurisprudence of rights. This has been the case in Canada. The Canadian constitution changed dramatically in 1982 when a formal constitutional bill of rights was adopted. With the entrenchment of the Charter of Rights and Freedoms, the Supreme Court began to address entirely new issues involving the balance between governmental power (that of Ottawa as well as the provincial governments) and the rights of individuals or groups of citizens.[49] This is distinct from the traditional federalism cases in which the Court has drawn boundary lines strictly between governmental entities.

As in the U.S. Bill of Rights, constitutional rights are stated in the Charter in broad and sweeping language (e.g., freedom of "conscience," "religion," "thought," "association," etc.). Not surprisingly, the Canadian federal courts have been called upon to flesh out the meaning and extent of these rights in practical terms. The Charter itself includes one very substantial limit on the breadth of constitutional rights. Such rights as are granted under the Charter are "subject only to such reasonable limits prescribed by law as can be demonstrably justified in a free and democratic society."[50] Of course, this provision inevitably meant that the courts would be required to hear cases in which laws of Parliament or provincial legislatures are challenged for excessively limiting some right provided for in the Charter. The Supreme Court is the ultimate authority in deciding when a law effects an unreasonable intrusion into the protected sphere of an individual or group.

The first Charter case reached the Supreme Court within two years of entrenchment. At the time, scholars and constitutional lawyers generally assumed that the scant pre-1982 constitutional scheme with respect to human rights had been preempted by the Charter.[51] The Supreme Court agreed. The Court realized that its own prior jurisprudence on human rights under the statutory bill of rights, as well as the long history of civil rights litigation under the U.S. Bill of Rights, was not directly applicable in construing the meaning of the newly granted rights under the Charter.[52] This left the Court relatively free to develop its own case law and determine on a case-by-case basis whether a particular statute or governmental regulation imposes unreasonable limitations on the rights of an individual or group.[53] The new Supremacy Clause of the Constitution Act, 1982 made clear that the judiciary would have the responsibility and power to interpret the constitutional text and to decide whether a particular law or governmental action was consistent with the Charter. Unlike in America, there never was a question as to the propriety of the Canadian Supreme Court's exercise of the power of judicial review.

In the case of *Regina v. Oakes*,[54] the Supreme Court developed a two-prong test under which an individual or group must first demonstrate that their constitutionally sanctioned right or freedom is in some way curtailed by the statute or governmental action. Upon making such a factual showing, the burden shifts to the government to "demonstrably" prove that a bona fide public interest is furthered by the statute or governmental action and there is no other less restrictive means for achieving that goal. Under this "proportionality" test, the government has a very strict burden of proof with respect to sustaining any measure that limits or restricts a protected constitutional right.[55] In subsequent cases, the Court has applied a broad interpretation of what rights are protected under the Charter—much as the Warren Court did in the 1960s with the U.S. Bill of Rights. The values of the Court (liberalism, egalitarianism, and democracy) have informed its interpretation of the text: "The expansive definitions that the Court has given to [freedom of expression and religion] and other human rights shows clearly how reading a constitution purposefully promotes the fundamental values on which it is based."[56] As in the United States, constitutional interpretation inevitably draws the Supreme Court of Canada into the political sphere.

In interpreting the Charter, the Supreme Court has been even more aggressive than the U.S. Supreme Court in promoting a jurisprudence of rights.[57] Of course, in cases raising alleged violations of freedom of speech or the press, or in cases arising under the Fourteenth Amendment involving claims of racial, religious, or sexual discrimination, the U.S. Supreme Court can be quite aggressive itself in protecting the rights of individuals. Here the U.S. Supreme Court applies a "strict scrutiny" test that requires the defendant (i.e., the government) to prove a "compelling state interest" that justifies the abridgment of the right at issue. Usually, the government will be unable to satisfy such a strict burden. However, in many other areas raising "lesser" constitutional rights, the Court applies a much weaker test, requiring only that the government prove a "legitimate state interest" that justifies the abridgement of the right. In this respect, the Court has taken a much more aggressive approach to limiting *any* governmental action that "unreasonably" infringes upon *any* right that can be plausibly read into the open-ended language of the Charter.[58] This has dramatically changed the Court's role: "[T]he Supreme

Court . . . has inverted the traditional understanding of constitutionalism and judicial review as conserving forces, and transformed them into instruments of social reform. Rather than serving as a prudent brake on political change, the judiciary has become a catalyst for change."[59]

Mind you, nothing in the constitutional text prescribes such doctrines to the courts. The Charter certainly does not mandate this. This is all court-made doctrine. The terse and scant language in both the Canadian and American constitutional texts grants the judiciary broad discretion in deciding whether to pursue a jurisprudence of rights. The Supreme Court of Canada has accepted the challenge, while the more conservative post-Reagan Supreme Court in the United States has backed off from the role it played during its more activist days in the 1960s. This reflects the different temperament and political philosophy of those justices who sit on the bench today.

Conclusion

The political debate over constitutional interpretation reflects the many contrasting positions expressed in the abstract (and often mystifying) academic discussions of textual interpretation. However the inquiry is framed, political commitments can be readily detected lurking beneath the surface. This is not unexpected. Within the boundaries imposed by mainstream liberalism and the dominant constitutional tradition, which emphasizes the importance of a written, binding text, such debate, when expressed in the judicial sphere, reflects much the same concerns as are expressed elsewhere in political discourse.

That the peculiarities of constitutionalism dictate that political issues be cast in a distinct judicial language when conducted in the arena of constitutional politics does not mean that genuine issues of interpretation or construction do not exist in constitutional law. Nor is it to impute hidden, underlying political motives to all judicial opinions and scholarship. It is only to recognize that any theory of constitutional interpretation will inevitably reflect an underlying commitment to a particular theory of politics. The belief that law, be it constitutional or otherwise, is some neutral ground situated outside the realm of ideology is one of the worst illusions of the liberal tradition. Quite the contrary, the very commitment to a written text—to *this* written text, as opposed to some other text—and to any understanding of how it should be "read" reflects a commitment of the highest order to a particular vision of politics. Viewing textual interpretation as the primary concern is to misperceive the nature of the disagreement and suppress its inherently political character.

The American constitutional tradition is premised upon a powerful commitment to the written text and a judicial tradition in which the opinions of the Supreme Court are necessarily framed in reference to the constitutional text. This is true in Canada as well, although the written constitution is comprised of documents of a different nature. On the one hand, any theory of interpretation (at least, one that is to be taken seriously) *must* yield a determined result in those cases where the text is specific (e.g., concerning the age requirement for the executive). On the other hand, all theories of interpretation must acknowledge the indeterminacy and open-ended quality of such constitutional standards as "equal protection," "due process," and "peace, order, and good government." The very fact that originalists must appeal to the framers' original intentions is a clear indication that the text is indeterminate with respect to the particular matter at hand.

Within the boundaries of a constitutional tradition committed to a written text that is manifestly indeterminate in particular instances, there is ample room for a struggle over competing theories of textual interpretation. Here, within the gaps of indeterminacy, underlying political commitments shape and inform theories of textual interpretation. The text itself offers no rules of interpretation, and thus does not legitimize any particular approach to reading the text. When the debate is conducted at such an abstract level (rather than through fairly disagreeing over the definition or usage of a particular word or phrase), it should be conducted in terms of competing visions of politics, rather than cloaked in the guise of a judicial doctrine. One important consequence of the current system of education and training, as well as the long-standing traditions of the American and Canadian legal communities, is that justices must necessarily speak in the language of *some* judicial doctrine rather than in overtly political discourse. Echoing a more general disdain for the "political," the legal tradition finds the apparently neutral, nonpolitical language of a scientific methodological debate inviting because it preserves the illusion of constitutional law as an objective realm outside of politics.

Obviously, one main motive for having a written constitution is to take certain decisions "outside of politics" by codifying them in the text and making it hard for future generations to alter or amend them. Where there is a sufficiently strong consensus behind fundamental values (e.g., a commitment to majority rule, electoral politics, equal protection under the law, etc.), it is possible to so constitutionalize them. Where there is no such consensus (as in the case of the deep divisions over the legal and moral standing of slavery in the United States in the 1850s), then politics quickly intrudes into the realm of constitutional law. Invariably, this produces unsatisfactory results. Fortunately, this is not the common constitutional case before the courts. As Morton and Knopff put it with respect to Charter cases: "[L]egal determinacy and judicial discretion emerge not with respect to core values, about which consensus exists, but with respect to second-order questions, about which dissensus prevails. . . . The Charter supplies few obvious answers to the second-order questions that actually come before the courts."[60] The same can be said of the U.S. Bill of Rights. There is no serious disagreement over whether citizens should be afforded "due process of law" and "equal protection." But there are legitimate disagreements over how these general standards should be applied in a wide range of individual cases. It is these "second-order" questions that require the courts to interpret the constitutional text. This is where courts formulate new doctrines, make new constitutional law, create new rights, and generally intrude into the political realm, deciding issues that ought more properly be left to legislatures elected by, and accountable to, the citizenry.[61]

Because there are genuine disagreements over what specifics a constitution dictates, some scholars question the very possibility of being governed by a written text expressing an objective, transhistorical meaning. Such portends ominously for the very idea of a constitutional regime. A loss of faith in the possibility of adjudication based on a stable text is the provocation to the current debate over textual interpretation. Calls for a return to a "principled" approach to constitutional law or denunciations of rampant "nihilism" in the law schools only miss the point. Ultimately, where consensus over fundamental values is lacking, a constitutional regime is not even possible. Fortunately, that is not the problem that we face. The broad liberal consensus has not yet given way. However, there is considerable dissension over second-order questions, and that is precisely where courts ought to tread most carefully. Where the politics is too divisive, it remains judicious for courts to defer to representative bodies better equipped for addressing these issues. In the end, no written constitution or method of textual interpretation can resolve such political conflict.

Notes

1. David Beatty, *Constitutional Law in Theory and Practice* (Toronto: University of Toronto Press, 1995), 2.

2. William F. Harris, "Bonding Word and Polity: The Logic of American Constitutionalism," 76 *Am. Pol. Sci. Rev.* 34 (1982).

3. Laurence Tribe, *Constitutional Choices* (Cambridge: Harvard University Press, 1985), 246.

4. As Tribe puts it: "Constitutional choices must be made . . . Judges must make them whenever choosing among alternative interpretations of the Constitution . . . [T]he constitutional choices we make are . . . constrained and channeled by a constitutional text and structure and history, by constitutional language and constitutional tradition, opening some paths and foreclosing others." Ibid., vii–viii.

5. A forceful conservative critique of the "new" activist Supreme Court of Canada in the post-Charter era is F. L. Morton and Rainer Knopff, *The Charter Revolution and the Court Party* (Peterborough, Ont.: Broadview Press, 2000). See also F. L. Morton and Rainer Knopff, "Permanence and Change in a Written Constitution: and the Living Tree Doctrine and the Charter of Rights," *Supreme Court Law Review,* 2d ser., 1 (1990): 533–46.

6. *Federalist No. 78* (Alexander Hamilton), in *The Federalist Papers,* ed. Clinton Rossiter (New York: New American Library, 1961), 464–72.

7. For a history of American judicial review from 1776 through the end of Marshall's long tenure on the Court, see Sylvia Snowliss, *Judicial Review and the Law of the Constitution* (New Haven: Yale University Press, 1990).

8. 5 U.S. (1 Cranch) 137 (1803).

9. *Marbury,* 5 U.S. at 179.

10. 17 U.S. (4 Wheat.) 415 (1819).

11. Section 52(1) of the Constitution Act, 1982.

12. For a discussion of the paramountcy doctrine, see Peter W. Hogg, *Constitutional Law of Canada,* 4th ed. (Toronto: Carswell Company, 1997), chap. 16.

13. P. Macklem, K. E. Swinton et al., *Canadian Constitutional Law,* 2d ed. (Toronto: Emond Montgomery Publications, 1997), 207.

14. 252 U.S. 416 (1920).

15. *Holland,* 252 U.S. at 433.

16. Id.

17. Id. at 435.

18. Philip Bobbit, *Constitutional Fate: Theory of the Constitution* (New York: Oxford University Press, 1982), 74. See also Charles Black, *Structure and Relationship in Constitutional Law* (Baton Rouge: Louisiana State University Press, 1969). An example of a Supreme Court case decided in some measure on the basis of an underlying structuralist interpretation is *National League of Cities v. Usery,* 426 U.S. 833 (1976).

19. Hogg, *Constitutional Law of Canada,* § 1.2. See also G. P. Browne, *Documents on the Confederation of British North America* (Toronto: McClelland & Stewart, 1969).

20. Sections 92(3) and 95 of the Constitution Act, 1867 make clear that the drafters recognized that in some cases, jurisdiction would be concurrent.

21. These national powers are enumerated in twenty-nine specific paragraphs, and include the unlimited power to tax and borrow, and provide for the national "defence," as well as the authority to regulate "trade and commerce," Indians and their lands, currency, banking, bankruptcy, marriage and divorce, criminal law, and so on.

22. *A.G. Ontario v. A.G. Canada* (Local Prohibition Reference) (1896) AC 348 (PC), 360–61.

23. *R. v. Crown Zellerbach Canada Ltd.* 49 DLR (4th) 161 (1988).

24. Associate Justice Scalia argues for an originalist approach to reading the text. See Antonin Scalia, *A Matter of Interpretation: Federal Courts and the Law* (Princeton: Princeton University Press, 1997), 44–47. For a discussion of Scalia's development of textualist principles, see Bradley C. Karkkainen, "'Plain Meaning': Justice Scalia's Jurisprudence of Strict Statutory Construction," 17 *Harv. J.L. & Pub. Pol'y* 401 (1994). See also William J. Michael, "The Original Understanding of Original Intent: A Textual Analysis," 26 *Ohio N.U.L. Rev.* 201 (2000); Frank H. Easterbrook, "The Role of Original Intent in Statutory Construction," 11 *Harv. J.L. & Pub. Pol'y* 59 (1988).

25. The leading academic proponent of intentionalism is Raoul Berger. See Raoul Berger, *Government by Judiciary* (Cambridge: Harvard University Press, 1977); idem, *Federalism: The Founders' Design* (Norman: University of Oklahoma Press, 1987).

26. See Paul Finkelman, "The Constitution and the Intentions of the Framers: The Limits of Historical Analysis," 50 *U. Pitt. L. Rev.* 349 (1989); Robert N. Clinton, "Original Understanding, Legal Realism, and the Interpretation of 'This Constitution,'" 72 *Iowa L. Rev.* 1177 (1987).

27. Keith E. Whittington, *Constitutional Interpretation: Textual Meaning, Original Intent, and Judicial Review* (Lawrence: University of Kansas Press, 1999), 4.

28. Chief Justice Rehnquist has made reference to a jurisprudence of original intent and has been critical of the rhetoric of the "living constitution." William H. Rehnquist, "The Notion of a Living Constitution," 54 *Tex. L. Rev.* 693 (1976). Justices Thomas and Scalia have also been critical of the notion of a living constitution.

29. The reference is to President Nixon's attempt to appoint "strict constructionists" to the Court. President Reagan appointed adherents of some modified expression of originalism.

30. See Sotirios A. Barber, *On What the Constitution Means* (Baltimore: Johns Hopkins University Press, 1984), chap. 2; Brest, "The Misconceived Quest for Original Understanding," 36.

31. John H. Ely, *Democracy and Distrust* (Cambridge: Harvard University Press, 1980).

32. Ibid., 2.

33. See Charles Evans Hughes, speech to the Elmira Chamber of Commerce, New York, 3 May 1907: "We are under a Constitution but the Constitution is what the judges say it is." Charles Evans Hughes, *Addresses and Papers* (New York: G. P. Putnam's Sons, 1908), 139.

34. Michael J. Perry, *The Constitution, the Courts, and Human Rights* (New Haven: Yale University Press, 1982). See also Perry, *The Constitution in the Courts* (New Haven: Yale University Press, 1994).

35. Learned Hand, *The Bill of Rights* (Cambridge: Harvard University Press, 1958).

36. Ronald Dworkin, *Taking Rights Seriously* (Cambridge: Harvard University Press, 1977); A *Matter of Principle* (Cambridge: Harvard University Press, 1985); idem, *Law's Empire* (Cambridge: Harvard University Press, 1986); idem, *Freedom's Law: The Moral Reading of the Constitution* (Cambridge: Harvard University Press, 1996).

37. The leading proponent of "visionary" jurisprudence, wherein a constitution is viewed as an "image" that is the "product of the legal community's imagination," is William E. Conklin, *Images of a Constitution* (Toronto: University of Toronto Press, 1989).

38. This is the basic theme of Sotirios Barber. See Barber, *On What the Constitution Means.*

39. For example, see Perry's discussion of the privacy cases. Perry, *The Constitution, the Courts, and Human Rights,* 73. But see Robert H. Bork, "Neutral Principles and Some First Amendment Problems," 47 *Ind. L.J. 1* (1971) (an attempt to constrain judicial decision-making in this realm).

40. See, e.g., *Powell v. McCormack,* 395 U.S. 486 (1969).

41. For a discussion of the doctrine of "justiciability" (i.e., which matters courts may decide and which are moot, hypothetical, political in nature, or not yet ripe for a decision) as it has evolved in Canada, see Lorne Sossin, *The Boundaries of Judicial Review: The Law of Justiciability in Canada* (Scarborough, Ont.: Carswell, 1999).

42. Associate Justice William J. Brennan Jr., speech delivered at Georgetown University on 12 October 1985 (reprinted in *N.Y. Times,* 13 October 1985, 36, col. 1).

43. Peter Hogg and Allison Bushell have defended the role of the Supreme Court of Canada against claims that judicial review under the Charter is undemocratic. They argue that judicial review is best understood as "part of a 'dialogue' between the judges and the legislatures." This is because when the Court holds an act unconstitutional under the Charter, the legislature is free to reenact the statute under section 33, which allows for an express legislative "override" of the Court with respect to decisions under sections 2 and 7–15 of the Charter. Peter W. Hogg and Allison A. Bushell, "The Charter Dialogue between Courts and Legislatures," 35 *Osgoode Hall L.J.* 75 (1997). Manfredi and Kelly argue that Hogg and Bushell overstated the extent of "dialogue" between the Court and legislatures. Christopher P. Manfredi and James B. Kelly, "Six Degrees of Dialogue: A Response to Hogg and Bushell," 37 *Osgoode Hall L.J.* 513 (1999).

44. Ely, *Democracy and Distrust,* 13.

45. 410 U.S. 113 (1973).

46. The applicability of the Bill of Rights to the states was first raised in *Barron v. Mayor and City Council of Baltimore,* 31 U.S. 464 (1833), in which the Marshall Court held that the Bill of Rights restricted only the national government and not the states. By the 1930s and 1940s, the majority of the court followed Justices Cardozo and Frankfurter in arguing for a "selective" incorporation. See *Palko v. Connecticut,* 302 U.S. 319 (1937) (Cardozo, J.); *Adamson v. California,* 332 U.S. 46 (1947) (Frankfurter, J., concurring). In his dissent in *Adamson,* Justice Black, joined by Justice Douglas, argued

for the "total incorporation" of the Bill of Rights, claiming that such was the "original purpose" of the Fourteenth Amendment. Id. at 89 (Black, J., dissenting).

47. Dworkin, *Taking Rights Seriously,* 134–36.

48. In recent decades, the Supreme Court has articulated a theory of separation of powers in a number of significant cases. See *Immigration and Naturalization Serv. v. Chadha,* 462 U.S. 919 (1983); *Buckley v. Valeo,* 421 U.S. 1 (1976); *United States v. Nixon,* 418 U.S. 683 (1974); *Powell v. McCormack,* 395 U.S. 486 (1969); *Youngstown Sheet & Tube Co. v. Sawyer,* 343 U.S. 579 (1952).

49. Unlike the U.S. Bill of Rights or the Canadian Bill of Rights enacted by the Canadian Parliament in 1960, the Charter explicitly recognizes human rights *and* group rights (e.g., those of the "aboriginal peoples," including the Indian, Inuit, and Métis tribes). In addition, the special status of the French-speaking minority is expressly recognized and protected under the Charter.

50. Schedule B to Canada Act 1982, Constitution Act, 1982, Part 1, sec 1.

51. Luc B. Tremblay, *The Rule of Law, Justice, and Interpretation* (Montreal: McGill-Queen's University Press, 1997), 9.

52. Beatty, *Constitutional Law in Theory and Practice,* 63. Beatty takes a particularly optimistic view of the Charter as expressing a clear set of liberal, democratic preferences that require little "interpretation" from the judges sitting on the Court.

53. This view is expressed in Paul Bender, "The Canadian Charter of Rights and Freedoms and the United States Bill of Rights: A Comparison," 28 *McGill L.J.* 811 (1983); Peter W. Hogg, "The Charter of Rights and American Theories of Interpretation," 25 *Osgoode Hall L.J.* 87 (1987).

54. 26 DLR (4th) 200 (1986).

55. "The state must establish that the objective of any law that infringes a Charter right is in conformity with the rights-protecting regime. Moreover, the state must prove that the impugned law is rationally connected to its permissible objective and minimally impairs the right as well. Finally, the state must establish that the impugned law's objective, as well as its beneficial effects, outweighs its deleterious effects on the rights guarantee." Lorraine Eisenstat Weinrib, "Canada's Constitutional Revolution: From Legislative to Constitutional State," 33 *Israel L. Rev.* 13, 33 (1999).

56. Beatty, *Constitutional Law in Theory and Practice,* 68.

57. For a historical overview of the Court's decision-making under the Charter, see James B. Kelly, "The Charter of Rights and Freedoms and the Rebalancing of Liberal Constitutionalism in Canada, 1982–1997," 37 *Osgoode Hall L.J.* 625 (1999). See also F. L. Morton, P. H. Russell, and T. Riddell, "The Canadian Charter of Rights and Freedoms: A Descriptive Analysis of the First Decade, 1982–1992," 5 *N.J.C.L.* 1 (1994).

58. For a critical analysis from the Left of the Canadian Supreme Court's "liberal" jurisprudence of rights under the Charter, see Allan C. Hutchinson, *Waiting for Coraf: A Critique of Law and Rights* (Toronto: University of Toronto Press, 1995). See also

Andrew Petter and Alan Hutchinson, "Private Rights/Public Wrongs: The Liberal Lie of the Charter," 38 U. Toronto L.J. 278 (1988); Michael Mandel, *The Charter of Rights and the Legalization of Politics in Canada,* rev. ed. (Toronto: Thompson, 1994).

59. Morton and Knopff, *Charter Revolution and the Court Party,* 41.

60. Ibid., 17.

61. With great foresight, Peter Russell warned that the sentiment behind the Charter movement was for "transferring the policymaking focus from the legislature to the judicial arena," and that this represented a "flight from politics." Peter H. Russell, "The Effect of a Charter of Rights on the Policy-Making Role of Canadian Courts," 25 *Canadian Pub. Ad.* 1, no. 32 (1982).

CHAPTER 3

Constitutional Rights Jurisprudence in Canada and the United States: Significant Convergence or Enduring Divergence?

Ran Hirschl

Introduction

Few could doubt that the introduction of the Canadian Charter of Rights and Freedoms in 1982 marked a dramatic change in the de jure status of rights and liberties in Canada, and provided the Supreme Court of Canada (SCC) with the necessary institutional framework to become more effective in its efforts to protect the basic rights of disadvantaged groups and individuals. In fact, since the enactment of the Charter, the SCC has become one of the country's most important policy-making bodies, much like its U.S. counterpart. Beyond its traditionally significant role in adjudicating disputes involving federalism and the separation of powers, it has been called upon to decide on fundamental rights and liberties, such as freedom of expression, religion, and assembly; due process rights; the right to privacy and the right to have an abortion; equality rights; the rights of indigenous peoples; language rights; and the political and cultural status of Quebec. Indeed, in 1992, ten years after the Charter had come into effect, Chief Justice Lamer of the Canadian Supreme Court declared that "the introduction of the Charter has been nothing less than a revolution on the scale of the introduction of the metric system, the great medical discoveries of Louis Pasteur, and the invention of penicillin and the laser."[1]

At first glance, the question of whether patterns of constitutional rights jurisprudence in Canada and the United States are converging appears to be clear-cut. Most observers would agree that the 1982 constitutionalization of rights and fortification of judicial review in Canada have not only ushered in a new era in Canadian constitutional law and politics, but have also elevated the level of judicial activism and the scope of constitutional rights jurisprudence in Canada to the level and scope seen in the United States throughout the post-*Brown* era (1954 to present). However, a closer look at prevalent patterns of judicial interpretation of rights in Canada and in the United States suggests that the answer to the question of convergence in the two countries' constitutional rights jurisprudence is more nuanced than it might initially seem.

A well-known distinction has been drawn by political theorists between negative (or "first generation") rights, positive (or "second generation") rights, and collective (or "third generation") rights. Negative rights consist of fundamental freedoms such as freedom of speech, religious tolerance, freedom from arbitrary arrest, and so on. Positive rights traditionally consist of social rights such as the universal right to services that meet basic human needs (e.g., health care, basic housing, education, social security and welfare, and an adequate standard of living). The term "positive rights" is often used to describe these basic social rights, as they require the state to act positively to promote the well-being of its citizens, rather than merely refraining from acting or restraining other individuals from acting. Thus, a positive right is a claim to something, whereas a negative right is a call either for the prohibition of some action or for the right not to be interfered with. Although positive rights require a more interventionist state, they remain essentially individualistic, as the material welfare guaranteed by these provisions is secured on behalf of the individual. Collective rights, or third-generation group rights, have to do with communities, entire peoples, or individuals who are members of a specific group, rather than with individual persons as such. These rights include minority language and education rights, group rights to self-determination and autonomous jurisdiction over matters pertaining to that group's traditions, or some forms of affirmative action designed to advance the status of historically disenfranchised groups through the enhancement of their members.[2]

Over the past few years, critics have questioned the validity of the theoretical distinction between negative rights and positive rights, primarily because many rights traditionally labeled as negative actually require some kind of public funding or state intervention, just as positive entitlements do.[3] However, Canadian and American courts and judges generally do not seem to accept the fundamental logic of this critique. In this chapter, I suggest that in analyzing recent Canadian and American constitutional rights jurisprudence, the traditional distinction between negative, positive, and group rights continues to provide an organizing principle for understanding prevalent patterns of convergence and divergence in the two countries' contemporary rights jurisprudence.

More specifically, I will suggest three points in this chapter. First, over the past two decades, the rights jurisprudence of the two countries has converged rapidly in matters that deal with the Lockean-style "negative liberty" aspects of constitutional rights; with a few notable caveats the SCC has adopted its U.S. counterpart's traditional conception of constitutional rights as protecting the private sphere (human and economic) from interference by the "collective" (often understood as the state and its regulatory institutions). Second, a more moderate (albeit significant) convergence has developed over the past few years in the two countries' judicial interpretation of positive entitlements—the Canadian Supreme Court (admittedly to a lesser degree than its U.S. counterpart) has excluded positive social welfare rights from the ambit of the Charter of Rights and Freedoms. Third, in spite of the powerful centripetal forces of convergence found within Canadian and American constitutional rights jurisprudence, there still remains a significant difference between the two countries' constitutional rights adjudication pertaining to group rights. Over the past two decades, certain types of group rights—primarily minority language and education rights, aboriginal peoples' rights, and affirmative action guarantees—have been awarded wider constitutional recognition and relatively more generous judicial interpretation in Canada than in the United States.

In the following pages, I examine recent trends in American and Canadian rights jurisprudence relating to criminal due process and legal rights, freedom of religion and association, privacy and formal equality rights (classic "first generation" negative liberties); subsistence social rights ("second generation" positive rights); and language rights, affirmative action and aboriginal peoples' rights ("third generation" collective rights). This comparative examination charts the vacillation in the two countries' rights jurisprudence between (1) a predominantly neoliberal conception of rights that reflects and promotes a commitment to a Lockean-style individual autonomy and minimal visible (redistributive and regulatory) state intervention, both in the economic sphere and in what judges have considered to be the protected bodily sphere; (2) an egalitarian conception of rights as encompassing individual entitlement to subsistence social welfare and imposing a complementary moral duty on the state to actively neutralize the consequences of its members' arbitrary misfortune; and (3) a conception of rights as claims for the preservation and enhancement of minority cultures and essential collectively owned public goods.

Substantive Convergence: Negative Liberties

The Macroquantitative Picture

Before discussing several examples of significant convergence and divergence in Canadian and American rights jurisprudence in detail, it is helpful to assess the two countries' recent constitutional adjudication in terms of the types of rights that tend to be given a more generous interpretation by their respective national high courts. At least three interesting comparisons can be drawn from a systematic quantitative analysis of interpretations of constitutional rights provisions by the U.S. Supreme Court (from January 1975 to June 2002) and by its Canadian counterpart (from April 1982 to June 2002).[4]

First, negative rights litigation accounted for 83 percent (342/413) and 92 percent (1038/1127) of all BOR cases heard by the SCC and by the U.S. Supreme Court, respectively, in comparison with 17 percent (71/413) and 8 percent (89/1127), respectively, of these courts' cases that dealt with positive rights and collective rights litigation.[5]

Second, the success rate of classic civil liberties and negative rights claims has been 39 percent (133/342) in Canada and 41 percent (426/1038) in the United States, whereas the success rate of positive rights and collective rights claims has been somewhat lower—27 percent (19/71) in Canada and only 16 percent (14/89) in the United States. In other words, although the success rate of positive and collective rights claims was relatively low in both countries, it was still significantly higher in Canada than in the United States. This finding may be explained by the fact that whereas some third-generation group rights are protected by Canada's constitutional catalog of rights, no such rights are directly protected by the U.S. Constitution.

Third, the difference in absolute numbers between cases involving successful negative rights claims and those involving successful positive rights and collective rights claims is substantial. Whereas negative rights claimants won 133 cases in the SCC between 1982 and 2002, and 426 cases in the U.S. Supreme Court between 1975 and 2002, claimants for positive and collective rights had only 19 victories (that is, 19/133, or a ratio of 7 to 1) in Canada, and merely 14 victories (that is, 14/426, or a ratio of 30 to 1) in the United States. In short, a systematic macroquantitative analysis of the two countries' records of constitutional rights jurisprudence reveals a clear and common tendency to adopt a narrow conception of constitutional rights, with the emphasis on their negative liberty aspects. That being said, positive and collective rights claims found greater support overall in the SCC than in its U.S. counterpart.

Due Process Rights

Due process rights are usually thought of as classic civil liberties. These rights include, inter alia, constitutional guarantees against unreasonable search and seizure, as well as against arbitrary detention or imprisonment. They also guarantee protection of the right to counsel, the right to be tried within a reasonable period of time, the right to a fair trial, and so on. This core of due process rights also entails a set of secondary procedural rights aimed at protecting detainees, suspects, and the accused against abuses of power by the police and other state authorities.

The U.S. Supreme Court's series of landmark rulings pertaining to the rights of the criminally accused has been seen by many as the pinnacle of American progressive constitutional rights jurisprudence for the past four decades. From *Mapp v. Ohio* (defining the inadmissibility of illegally obtained evidence) to *Miranda v. Arizona* (establishing the right to remain silent) to *United States v. Wade* to *Gideon v. Wainright* (establishing the right to counsel), the Warren Court (1953–69) significantly expanded the rights of the criminally accused with its broad interpretation of the various due process provisions of the Bill of Rights.[6] Most of the Warren Court's landmark due process rulings have been upheld by the fairly conservative Burger and Rehnquist Courts, including the recent rejection by the U.S. Supreme Court of a congressional statute that would have had the reactionary effect of overruling *Miranda* altogether.[7] Recently, the U.S. Supreme Court went on to revisit one of the markers of its reactionary jurisprudence—the constitutionality of capital punishment—based on due process and fundamental fairness considerations.[8] From a quantitative point of view, cases involving the rights of the criminally accused accounted for over two-thirds of the U.S. Supreme Court's rights agenda during the 1960s, and have never since fallen below 40 percent of the Court's rights cases.[9] In short, Justice Frankfurter's frequently cited statement that "the history of liberty has largely been the history of the observance of procedural safeguards" seems to capture the U.S. Supreme Court's interpretative approach towards due process rights over the past four decades.[10]

The picture has been similar in the Canada during the Charter era. The greater part of judicial activity under the Canadian Charter of Rights and Freedoms has concerned the questions of criminal procedure—questions that have also formed the bulk of U.S. constitutional litigation for years. Two-thirds of the Charter cases decided by the SCC between April 1982 and June 2002 (279 of 429 Charter cases) were criminal due process and legal rights cases. Whereas the cumulative success rate in other litigated rights categories has been approximately 20 percent to 25 percent, the overall success rate of criminal due process and legal rights claimants as of June 2002 was approximately 30 percent. These include a spate of landmark SCC rulings concerning the right to counsel and to an interpreter; the right to a fair trial and to fair administrative hearings; the right to be tried within a reasonable period of time; inadmissibility of improperly obtained evidence; and guarantees against unreasonable search and seizure, as well as against arbitrary detention, arrest, or imprisonment.

The list of important Canadian criminal due process cases is too long to reproduce here. It is clear, however, that the significance of legal rights litigation extends far beyond the mere fact of their prevalence. Perhaps the best example of the prominence of cases involving Charter-based due process provisions on the SCC agenda can be seen in the *Singh* case (1985)—one of the first Charter of Rights rulings issued by the SCC.[11] At issue here was Mr. Singh's claim that the absence of a right to a hearing in the procedures under the Immigration Act undertaken to determine whether a person was entitled to stay in Canada as a political refugee violated sec. 7 of the Charter of Rights (which protects the "right to life, liberty, and security of the person"). In a landmark ruling, the SCC held that sec. 7 of the Charter required that government procedures depriving persons of their life, liberty, or security be procedurally fair. Some justices went on to declare that the due process protections afforded by sec. 7 extended to "every human being who is physically present in Canada."

Or consider the SCC ruling in the *Askov* case (1990) that dealt with the right to be tried within a reasonable time.[12] Here, the Court found a twenty-three-month delay between committal and trial to be unreasonable, and went on to redefine a reasonable time lag between committal and trial as not exceeding six to eight months. In a few later rulings the Court softened somewhat the *Askov* guidelines to better reflect the realities of Canada's criminal justice system. Nonetheless, the expansive interpretation in *Askov* of the right to be tried within a reasonable time has had far-reaching consequences over the past decade on the granting of stay or withdrawal of unreasonably overdue criminal charges.

Over the past two decades, the SCC has persistently fortified the status of procedural rights, not only by protecting Charter-based due process rights of people such as Mr. Singh or Mr. Askov, but also by acquitting defendants whose guilt was likely to be otherwise proven, but whose cases involved a procedural error either during their investigation or trial in the lower courts. Over the past decade alone, there were acquittals of this nature for cases ranging from tax evasion, racketeering, and financial misconduct to murder, manslaughter, sexual assault on children, rape, robbery, and the importation of heroin. Moreover, the SCC has recently started to block the extradition of Canadian residents facing serious criminal charges in foreign jurisdictions when application at trial of reasonable procedural fairness standards is in doubt.[13]

The *Feeney* case illustrates the generous interpretation of procedural due process rights guaranteed by the Charter in the SCC.[14] A police officer investigating a murder knocked on the door of Mr. Feeney's place of residence (an equipment trailer), and then entered. Finding Mr. Feeney asleep, the officer woke him up and found bloodstains on his shirt. The police officer seized the shirt and took Mr. Feeney to a local police detachment for further questioning. The officer had no warrant, and Mr. Feeney had no lawyer. Based upon the interrogation, a warrant to search the trailer was obtained, and additional incriminating evidence was found there the following day. At the trial, the evidence against Mr. Feeney was admitted, and he was declared guilty of second-degree murder. But Mr. Feeney appealed, citing the Charter; he claimed both unreasonable search and seizure and that he had not been adequately advised of his right to counsel. In a split decision, the Court ruled that "arrests made in private dwellings must be carried out with respect for individual rights and especially the right to be secure against unreasonable search and seizures." Moreover, the Court ruled that when the officer touched Mr. Feeney's leg and ordered him to get out of bed, Mr. Feeney's Charter rights to retain and instruct counsel without delay were engaged. The Court then applied the standard remedy prescribed by the Charter for such violations, and excluded the improperly attained evidence—thereby overturning Mr. Feeney's conviction.[15]

Such potentially problematic decisions attributable to the prioritization of procedural rights in constitutional rights jurisprudence are further illustrated in the SCC's decision in the *CIP* case (1992).[16] Here a company was charged under occupational health and safety legislation with causing the death of an employee, and chose to invoke in its defense section 11(b) of the Charter (the right to trial within a reasonable time). As a result, the trial was adjourned several times for administrative reasons, and the case reached the SCC almost two years after the charge was initially laid. The Court eventually decided that section 11(b) protected corporations as well as human beings, and that the delay in trial constituted a violation of the corporation's section 11(b) right. According to Justice Stevenson, the purpose of that law was to ensure that the accused (whether human or corporate) had access to a fair trial. Human rights provisions are, therefore, not limited to human beings, but include corporate entities as well.

The trend towards a generous interpretation of procedural rights in recent Canadian constitutional jurisprudence has led to other problematic outcomes. Consider, for example, the SCC's decision in the *Seaboyer* case (1991). Section 276(1) of the Canadian Criminal Code prohibited the introduction of evidence in sexual assault trials that "concern[ed] the sexual activity of the complainant with any person other than the accused." It had been enacted in response to strong lobbying by women's organizations, which criticized common law rules permitting evidence of past sexual history on the grounds that such evidence had little probative value, led to biased and irrelevant moral judgment of the victim, and discouraged women from reporting sexual assault because of the ordeal of being cross-examined on their past sexual histories. Nonetheless, in *Seaboyer* the SCC struck down section 276(1) on the basis that it violated the accused's right, protected by section 7 of the Charter, to present a full answer and defense to a charge.[17]

Using the same rationale, in the *O'Connor* case (1995), the Court struck down restrictions on the accused's access to the complainant's private and confidential counseling records in rape and sexual assault cases.[18] The government reacted by enacting Bill C-46, which responds to the minority opinion in *O'Connor* to reintroduce legislative restrictions on judicial and defense access to a complainant's private counseling records in sexual violence cases. In its recent decision in the *Mills* case (1999), the Court upheld the constitutionality of Bill C-46, giving precedence to the complainant's constitutional right to privacy over the accused's constitutional right to present a full answer and defense to a charge.[19] In other words, the right of the accused to a fair trial (procedural equality) was limited only in the interests of protecting the right to privacy of other right bearers. Moreover, it was only under immense political pressure from the federal government and feminist activists that the Court overruled its highly controversial decision in the *O'Connor* case.

In short, we can safely say that over the past two decades, Canadian constitutional jurisprudence pertaining to procedural due process rights has rapidly converged with, and in some areas has even exceeded, the fairly progressive due process standards set by the U.S. Supreme Court over the past few decades.

Demarcating the Private Sphere

In a similar spirit, the SCC followed the steps of its U.S. counterpart in issuing a series of landmark Charter-based rulings that fortify and expand the boundaries of the private sphere in the context of assembly and association rights, freedom of expression and religion, freedom of movement, the right to privacy (including abortion rights), and formal equality. Consider, for example, the following illustrations of converging Canadian and American constitutional jurisprudence concerning the "negative liberty" aspect of several fundamental rights: freedom of religion, freedom of expression, and freedom from discrimination on the basis of sexual preference.

From *Sherbert v. Verner* to *Wisconsin v. Yoder* to *Church of the Lukumi Babalu Aye v. City of Hialeah* (and with the notable exception of *Oregon v. Smith,* which led to the subsequent Religious Freedom Restoration Act saga), support of a religious practice over state regulation (that is, strict adherence to the free exercise principle), has been the U.S. Supreme Court's long-standing principle in freedom of religion cases over the past four decades.[20] Over the past two decades, the SCC appears to have adopted a similar approach to freedom of religion. In marked contrast with its pre-Charter approach to mandatory Sunday closing laws, in *Big M Drug Mart* (1985), the SCC struck down the federal Lord's Day Act (a mandatory Sunday closing legislation enacted to promote Christian religious belief and practice), on the grounds that it was enacted to establish a specific religious faith (Christianity) while ignoring the status of non-Christian religious faiths, and was therefore in breach of sec. 2(a) the Charter—the major constitutional provision protecting freedom of religion in Canada. The Lord's Day Act violated the principle of a clear separation of church and state, and therefore non-Christian customers' and business owners' freedom of religion.[21]

Or we might consider the gradual convergence of Canadian and American rights jurisprudence regarding freedom of expression, primarily in the realms of hate propaganda, child pornography, and commercial speech. The U.S. Supreme Court has long tended to view restrictions on racist speech as a violation of the First Amendment. In its landmark decision in *R.A.V. v. City of St. Paul* (1992), for example, the U.S. Supreme Court unanimously invalidated St. Paul's hate-speech ordinance that banned cross burning, swastika displays, and other expressions of racial supremacy, and held that even within the category of fighting words, governments might not bar or penalize the expression of some but not other words, based on their content.[22]

The SCC's adoption of the "content neutrality" doctrine in freedom of expression cases has not been as firm as the U.S. Supreme Court's stance (due, inter alia, to the above-mentioned sec. 1 "limitation clause"). However, it would be fair to say that disseminators of hate propaganda have done quite well in "Charterland." Mr. Keegstra, for example, taught his Alberta high school students that "Jewish people [were] evil, sadistic, money-loving child killers who caused the world's ills, sought to destroy Christianity, and fabricated the Holocaust." He was charged under the Criminal Code for "promoting hatred against a section of the public distinguished by religion and ethnic origin." The SCC found that Keegstra's speech was indeed "invidious and obnoxious," but that this was not a reason for denying it protection under sec. 2(b) of the Charter.[23] "The content of a statement cannot deprive it of the protection accorded by s. 2(b), no matter how offensive it may be." It further held that this section protected all messages "however unpopular, distasteful or contrary to the mainstream." The Court thus found that the Criminal Code's restrictions on hate speech under which Keegstra had been charged limited his freedom of expression. However, in a 4:3 decision, the Court ruled that the specific section in the Criminal Code under which Keegstra had been charged satisfied the criteria set by sec. 1 and by the *Oakes* test, and should therefore stand.

But even sec. 1 could not block Ernst Zundel, one of the world's leading producers of Holocaust denial literature, from disseminating his neo-Nazi hate propaganda. Mr. Zundel was charged under another section of the Canadian Criminal Code for publishing a booklet entitled *Did Six Million Really Die?*, the central thesis of which was that the Nazis did not kill six million Jewish people, and that dissemination of this "fact" was part of a worldwide Jewish conspiracy. False news, such as hate literature, might be undesirable or even harmful in some cases, the SCC held in 1992, but that was not sufficient reason to deny it prima facie protection as a form of expression.[24] Unlike in its decision in *Keegstra,* however, the Court ruled that the law restricting false news was too broad in its scope; it did not specify any particular type of statement or harm to the public interest, and therefore did not meet the standards set by the *Oakes* test. In *R. v. Lucas* (1998), the SCC confirmed its Zundel holding that s. 2(b) of the Charter protects the dissemination of deliberate falsehoods.[25]

The SCC employed a similar balancing approach in another controversial freedom of expression case—*Sharpe* (2001).[26] Mr. Sharpe was charged under the Criminal Code with two counts of possession of child pornography and two counts of possession of child pornography for the purposes of distribution and sale. Sharpe argued that the provisions upon which the charges against him were based infringed upon his constitutionally entrenched right to freedom of expression. The Crown conceded that the relevant provisions infringed sec. 2(b) of the Charter but argued that the infringement was justifiable under sec. 1 of the Charter. The Court ruled that, taken as a whole, the said provisions reflected an appropriate balance between the potential harm to children child pornography may cause and the (pedophiles') right to free expression, and should therefore be upheld. However, the Court added that when child pornography material is created, depicted, and held by the accused alone and intended exclusively for personal usage, it might be allowed, as it poses relatively little harm to children. To this extent, held the Court, the law banning the creation and possession of child pornography was disproportionate in its effects, and the infringement of freedom of expression could not be justified by sec. 1.

In the same spirit, the SCC has expanded the ambit of the Charter's freedom of expression provision to protect commercial speech. A clear illustration of this trend can be seen in the landmark decision of the Supreme Court of Canada in the *RJR MacDonald* case.[27] At issue in this case was a governmental act that prohibited the advertising and promotion of tobacco products offered for sale in Canada, and which required manufacturers to add to their packaging an unattributed warning about the dangers of smoking. Two tobacco companies successfully challenged the act in the Supreme Court, arguing that the act was inconsistent with their right to freedom of expression under sec. 2(b) of the Charter. The Court accepted the tobacco companies' claim that the Charter's freedom of expression provisions protected commercial speech and defied, in principle, unreasonable regulatory consumer-protection measures. In balancing the government's duty to protect the public health against the tobacco companies' right to freedom of expression, the Court held that the act was not "the least drastic means" for accomplishing the objective of reducing the consumption of tobacco products. The Court also noted that when it came to regulation of commercial speech, freedom of expression should be understood as entailing not just the right to express one's own ideas, but also the right not to speak and not to be required to communicate someone else's message (even when this "someone else" is a government whose concern is for the health of the public).

We might also consider a less obvious example of convergence in the realm of negative liberties: the recent wave of Canadian constitutional jurisprudence regarding discrimination on the grounds of sexual preference. In three landmark rulings in the 1990s, the SCC significantly expanded the recognition accorded to sexual preference as a legitimate basis for right to privacy and antidiscrimination/formal equality of opportunity claims. In *Egan* (1995), the Court held that a law defining "spouse" so as to exclude homosexual couples unfairly discriminated against homosexuals and therefore violated the Charter's equality rights provisions (sec. 15).[28] It then went on to hold in *Vriend* (1998) that Alberta's Individual Rights Protection Act contravened the Charter, because it failed to include sexual orientation as a prohibited ground of discrimination, and ordered that the words "sexual orientation" be read into the act, effectively expanding its scope to cover lesbians and gay men.[29] It also held that sec. 15(1) of the Charter entitled same-sex couples to sue for spousal support on the same basis as common-law heterosexual couples *(M v. H)*.[30] Similarly, the U.S. Supreme Court struck down in *Romer v. Evans* (1996) an amendment to the Colorado state constitution (known as Amendment 2) repealing progressive local laws passed by a number of Colorado's major cities that made sexual orientation an impermissible ground upon which to discriminate.[31] In spite of the fact that the amendment had been adopted by a statewide referendum, the U.S. Supreme Court held that "Amendment 2 classifies homosexuals not to further a proper legislative end but to make them unequal to everyone else. This Colorado cannot do. A State cannot so deem a class of persons a stranger to its laws."

An apparent deviation from this trend is the U.S. Supreme Court's recent ruling in *Boy Scouts of America v. Dale* (2000).[32] In a 5:4 decision, the Court held that requiring Boy Scouts of America to uphold the membership and scoutmaster status of an outspoken homosexual violated the organization's First Amendment right of expressive association. The Court accepted the argument of Boy Scouts that the very presence of gays as scoutmasters would send a message contradicting the organization's fundamental belief that homosexuality is immoral. Despite its outcome, however, Boy Scouts is a textbook example of how deeply embedded is the notion of the demarcated private sphere in the U.S. Supreme Court's constitutional jurisprudence. The Court's decision was based on the classification of Boy Scouts of America as a private entity, and on the Court's determination that as a private entity, the organization had the right to impose a certain moral code on its members (who joined voluntarily), however contested that code might be.

The SCC's decisions in the *Vriend* and *M. v. H* cases, as well as that of the U.S. Supreme Court in *Romer*, represent historic landmarks in the Canadian and American gay and lesbian communities' continuing fight for recognition and equal treatment by state laws. However, a closer look at these progressive rulings suggests that these decisions fit a preexisting pattern of protecting negative liberties simply by redefining an individual's sexual preference as an extension of his or her private sphere. The conduct in question should therefore enjoy the same protection from the public, the state, or an employer as any other personal character trait. As crucial as these landmark judgments are in enhancing the everyday life of millions of historically discriminated-against people, the establishment of the "sameness" principle in the realm of sexual orientation simply expands the scope of personal characteristics that ought to be recognized as belonging to one's protected private sphere. The outcome is that sexual orientation, along with other personal characteristics, cannot serve as the basis for differential treatment by the state and its organs. However, neither Court was concerned in these specific decisions with expanding (or even preserving) the circle of positive responsibilities of the state or employers. Thus, even progressive adjudications with regard to sexual preference—the hallmark of progressive constitutional rights jurisprudence in Canada and in the United States—have been decided drawing upon the same logic that conceptualizes constitutional rights as primarily negative rights of nonintervention.

In sum, we can safely say that a clear pattern of convergence emphasizing the "negative liberty" aspects of constitutional rights has established itself over the past two decades in Canadian and American constitutional rights jurisprudence. An analysis of the two countries' records of constitutional rights jurisprudence reveals a common tendency to emphasize the dyadic and antistatist aspects of constitutional rights. In spite of the open-ended wording of the constitutional catalogs of rights in Canada and the United States, the national high courts of these two countries tend to understand the purpose of rights as protecting the private sphere (human and economic) from interference by the "collective" (often understood as the state and its regulatory institutions). With a few notable exceptions that I discuss below, both the U.S. Supreme Court and the SCC tend to regard state regulation as a greater threat to human liberty and equality than the potentially oppressive and exploitative social relations and institutions of the so-called private sphere, whether human or economic.

Between Convergence and Divergence: Positive Entitlements

Neither the U.S. Constitution nor the Canadian Charter of Rights and Freedoms explicitly protect positive social welfare rights. However, several provisions of the constitutional catalogs of rights in Canada and the United States can be interpreted by the national high courts of these countries as protecting fundamental subsistence social welfare rights (such as the right to basic education, health care, basic housing, access to safe water, and so forth). However, such positive rights have been effectively deprived of their binding force by the U.S. Supreme Court as well as by the SCC, and are regarded by neither Court as essential components of full citizenship.

Perhaps the clearest example of the exclusion of positive entitlements and substantive equality claims from the ambit of the U.S. Bill of Rights is the U.S. Supreme Court's landmark judgment in *San Antonio Independent School District v. Rodriguez* (1973).[33] In this case, Mexican-American parents whose children attended public schools in a severely underfunded school district in a poor section of San Antonio, Texas, challenged the constitutionality of the state's formula for distributing education funds (which resulted in low levels of financial support for economically depressed districts) under the Equal Protection Clause. The parents' general argument made two claims: first, that the right to education was a necessary precondition for the pursuit of happiness and a fundamental element of any meaningful "equal protection" constitutional scheme, and therefore ought to be provided indiscriminately by the state; second, that in order to eradicate economic discrimination and inequality, poverty should be elevated to a suspect category status (alongside categories such as race or gender). In rejecting these two claims, the U.S. Supreme Court ruled that although "the grave significance of education both to the individual and to our society cannot to be doubted . . . education is not among the rights afforded explicit protection under the Federal Constitution. Nor do we find any basis for saying it is implicitly so protected."[34] The Court expressly held that the poor were not a suspect class. Unlike other groups that were granted such status, the Court found that the poor were neither an easily identified nor a politically powerless group; moreover, as a group, they did not have a history of overt discrimination.

While in the United States attempts to entrench social welfare rights have never gained political momentum, several attempts have been made by Canadian legislators and social rights activists over the past two decades to initiate the enactment of a complementary social charter explicitly requiring the state to commit to basic health, education, and housing provisions. In spite of these efforts, none of the attempts to grant elevated constitutional status to positive entitlements have been successful. The most important of these failed attempts was a "social union" provision included in the Charlottetown Accord, which was defeated by a national referendum in 1992.[35]

From the perspective of constitutional jurisprudence, the SCC has rejected positive claims that would have required the state to provide benefits to rights-holders, either directly by means of social programs (such as health care and unemployment benefits), or indirectly, through social legislation that would have imposed obligations on private actors (for example, minimum wage, pay equity, and rent control legislation). According to Chief Justice Lamer, "It would be a very big step for this court to interpret the Charter in a manner which imposes a positive constitutional obligation on governments."[36] Social rights claimants have repeatedly failed in their efforts to challenge the concept of the state-as-Leviathan embedded in the Court's jurisprudence. Most of these attempts have been based on the Charter's equality rights (sec. 15). But in its interpretation of this hotly contested section, the Court ruled that "[i]t does not provide for equality between individuals or groups within society in a general or abstract sense, nor does it impose on individuals or groups an obligation to accord equal treatment to others. It is concerned with the application of the law."[37]

Sec. 15 is thus confined to state action—"the application of law"—and does not govern state *inaction,* in other words, its unwillingness to act to promote "equality between individuals or groups." Another example of the exclusion of social rights from the Charter is *Finlay,* in which the SCC held that the Canadian provinces "are not obliged by the Charter or by any other constitutional document to provide a minimum standard of welfare benefits equivalent to the basic requirements of a person in need."[38]

A somewhat different illustration of how positive duties are excluded from the reach of the Charter's equality rights provision can be seen in the *Adler* affair.[39] According to sec. 93(1) of the Constitution Act, 1867, the provinces' exclusive power to legislate with regard to education is subject to a historical pact between Ontario and Quebec (reached prior to Canada's unification in 1867), whereby minority denominational schools at the time of union were entitled to get funding from the provincial governments. The practical implications of this provision have been that only Roman Catholic schools in Ontario and Protestant schools in Quebec have been entitled to public funding, as they were the only recognized minority denominational schools in 1867. In 1996, the parents of children attending private Jewish schools and independent Christian schools challenged Ontario's education funding scheme, which (in addition to funding the entire secular public school system) awarded full funding to private Catholic schools only, while withholding equivalent support from other independent denominational schools. The parents argued that such a selective funding scheme violated their religious and equality rights, and asked the Court to order the government of Ontario to provide equal funding to non-Catholic denominational schools. In rejecting the petitioners' request, the SCC held that the failure to fund denominational schools did not breach the Charter's freedom of religion or equality rights, as the original intent of sec. 93(1) was to preserve the unique culture of Roman Catholics in Ontario and Protestants in Quebec at the time of union. This provision, the Court stated, was the product of "[a]n historical compromise which was a crucial step along the road leading to Confederation. Without this 'solemn pact', there would have been no Confederation. . . . Given that the appellants cannot bring themselves within the terms of s. 93's guarantees, they have no claim to public funding for their schools."[40]

Two interesting exceptions to the SCC's narrow interpretation of the "positive" aspect of equality rights (at least at first glance) are *Schachter* (1992) and *Eldridge* (1997). In *Schachter,* the Court held that the right in sec. 15(1) to equal benefit of the law was a positive right, requiring "special considerations in the remedial context."[41] In *Eldridge,* the Court interpreted sec. 15(1) as requiring the state to ensure that disadvantaged members of society had the resources necessary to take full advantage of benefits provided by the government to the general population.[42] However, a closer look reveals that in the specific circumstances of these two cases, the Court was concerned only with imposing limits on how the state could act *if* it decided to act. In practice, these decisions do not require the state to act in the first place. In other words, the negative character of the Charter's equality rights has remained largely unaltered in the wake of *Schachter* and *Eldridge.*

That said, legislative attempts to constitutionalize various social and economic subsistence rights, as well as Charter-based litigation concerning claims for positive entitlements, are still among the most contentious issues on Canada's constitutional politics agenda. And as we have already seen, there is still a difference both in terms of absolute numbers and relative success rates of positive rights claims between Canada and the United States in this respect. Positive social welfare rights claims have at least been given serious consideration by the SCC, whereas such rights have long been conclusively excluded from the scope of any meaningful protection by the U.S. Supreme Court's rights jurisprudence.

Divergence: Group Rights

In spite of the powerful forces of convergence in American and Canadian constitutional rights jurisprudence, there remains a major difference between the two countries' constitutional recognition of *group rights.* Whereas no collective rights are directly protected by the U.S. Constitution, or have been unequivocally protected by the U.S. Supreme Court, at least three categories of such rights—minority language and education rights, rights of aboriginal peoples, and a constitutional shield for affirmative action programs—are recognized and affirmed by the Canadian Constitution Act, 1982, and have been further established by the SCC's Charter-based constitutional rights adjudication.

Indeed, the appropriate recognition of Canada's two major linguistic communities has long been a matter of the greatest importance at every stage of Canadian constitutional development and rights discourse. Language rights in Canada are protected by sec. 133 of the Constitution Act, 1867, and by secs. 16–23 of the Charter. The introduction of the latter provisions marked a fairly expansive conceptualization of Canadian citizenship entitlements for members of French and English minority language communities on the part of the Charter framers. This pattern is reflected in the amendment provisions of the Constitution Act, 1982, which require unanimous provincial support for changes to the constitution in respect to language. Over the past two decades, the SCC has become one of the crucial arenas for translating these constitutional provisions into a set of practical guidelines for protecting minority language and education rights in Canada. Some would even argue that the very enactment of the above-mentioned language rights provisions was part of the Canadian federal government's constitutional battle against the separatist movement in Quebec in general, and against the contentious Bill 101 in particular.[43]

In its most important pre-Charter ruling (*Blaikie,* 1979), the SCC upheld the federal bilingualism policy by determining that the Quebec National Assembly's production of only unofficial English translations of its enactments did not meet the requirements of sec. 133 of the Constitution Act, 1867.[44] In a similar spirit, the SCC went on to rule in 1984 that the education provisions of Quebec's Bill 101 (requiring that teaching in Quebec be in French only) contradicted sec. 23 of the Charter and should, therefore, be struck down;[45] and four years later, that the provisions of Quebec's Bill 101 requiring that public signs and advertisements might only be written in French violated the Charter's freedom of expression guarantee.[46]

The Court's generous interpretation of minority language and education rights has not been confined to the struggles generated by Quebec's separatist aspirations. In the 1985 *Manitoba Language Rights Reference,* for example, the SCC declared unconstitutional an 1890 Manitoba Act that set down that only English could be the language of the legislature and the courts in that province, further stipulating that Manitoba be granted five years "to translate, reenact, and publish" all its legislation in French as well as in English.[47] In a similar vein, in its landmark decision in *Mahe v. Alberta,* the Court held that in accordance with sec. 23 of the Charter, the Alberta provincial government was responsible for actively providing and funding educational facilities and intensive instruction in French for the francophone minority in that province, as well as for ensuring proportional representation of French-speaking parents in the management of their children's French-language education.[48] In a recent ruling the Court reaffirmed its decision in *Mahe,* holding that sec. 23 mandates that provincial governments do whatever is practically possible to preserve and promote minority language education.[49] In this case, the imposition upon francophone children in a PEI town of a daily two-hour ride to and from a French school in another town, instead of funding schooling in French on-site constituted an unreasonable constraint upon the children's parents' sec. 23 rights.

In stark contrast to the gradually expanded recognition of group rights by the SCC, there has been significant erosion of the U.S. Supreme Court's willingness to recognize and affirm such rights over the past two decades. For example, we might consider the Court's hostility towards bilingualism and affirmative action, let alone more comprehensive attempts to promote multiculturalism at the expense of the traditional U.S. assimilationist approach. From a legal perspective, a strong argument can be made for treating language minorities as a "suspect" or "quasi-suspect" class in claims for equal protection. Such classifications would be especially timely given the widespread backlash over the past few years against the so-called coloring of America and the accompanying rise of Official English movements driven by antipathy towards non-English speakers and aimed at imposing monolingualism upon America's major language minorities (primarily groups of Hispanic or Asian descent). In spite of these trends, American courts have so far been unwilling to deem language minorities a quasi-suspect class for equal protection analysis when such parties claim an affirmative right to governmental accommodation of their minority language rights. In a series of important "nondecisions" over the past few years, the U.S. Supreme Court has decided to remain silent on the issue of minority language rights by denying numerous applications for leave to appeal against rulings that reject claims to a constitutional and statutory right to bilingual education and against various English-only public services. In a similar fashion, the Court recently drew upon a narrow conception of standing rights granted by Title VI of the 1964 Civil Rights Act, thereby refraining from dealing with the questionable constitutionality of English-only policies implemented by state and publicly funded enterprises.[50]

Another clear illustration of this trend is the U.S. Supreme Court's gradual disqualification of group-targeted affirmative action schemes in the name of not violating the Fourteenth Amendment's Equal Protection Clause. In its landmark (yet somewhat ambiguous) ruling in *Bakke*—an Equal Protection Clause challenge to a public university's policy admitting a specific number of minority applicants, even at the expense of rejecting white applicants who had better qualifications—the U.S. Supreme Court held that affirmative action programs that set quotas for particular racial or ethnic groups violated the Equal Protection Clause. While the Court held that specific racial and ethnic backgrounds might permissibly be deemed advantageous by universities seeking to assemble a diverse student body, it added that minority status could not be the only factor determining admissions outcomes.[51] Nevertheless, however ambiguous the Court's ruling in *Bakke* (both in its reasoning and implications), it has come to be viewed by proponents of affirmative action as a form of constitutional approval, however implicit and tentative, for implementing such programs. But even the dubious Bakke-based gesture towards affirmative action and the challenges posed by the concrete reality of vast social disparity have not been able to withstand the U.S. Supreme Court's embedded hostility towards generous interpretation of group rights.

Indeed, in a series of landmark rulings over the past two decades, the U.S. Supreme Court has practically eliminated the use of affirmative action programs as an effective means of remedying the consequences of systematic racial discrimination in education, economic well-being, and political representation. In *Wygant* (1986), for example, the Court struck down on equal protection grounds a Michigan school board collective bargaining agreement that permitted necessary layoffs of teachers, provided that at no time would there be a greater percentage of minority personnel laid off than the percentage of minority personnel employed at the time of the layoff.[52] The Court rejected the school board's claim that correcting the effects of past discrimination and providing black faculty "role models" with whom black students might identify justified the elevated protection for minority teachers. Outlining the reasoning behind the Court's ruling in *Wygant,* Justice Powell pointed out that "[N]o one doubts that there has been serious racial discrimination in this country. But as the basis for imposing discriminatory legal remedies that work against innocent people, societal discrimination is insufficient and overexpansive."

In *City of Richmond v. J.A. Croson* (1989), the Court struck down a city plan that required that at least 30 percent of the dollar amount of construction contracts issued by the Richmond City Council be awarded to minority business enterprises. This was done in spite of the fact that 50 percent of Richmond's population was black, while historically, less than 1 percent of the city's construction business had been awarded to minority contractors.[53] In *Adarand* (1995)—another hard-line antiaffirmative action ruling—the Court struck down a similar federal program requiring that no less than 10 percent of federal funds designated for highway construction "be expended with small business concerns owned and controlled by socially and economically disadvantaged individuals."[54] In striking down this program, the Court applied the same strict scrutiny standards to the federal government as to state and local governments, thus placing almost all meaningful affirmative action and "set-aside" schemes beyond the bounds of constitutional protection.

In a similar spirit, the U.S. Supreme Court went on to rule in *Shaw v. Reno* (1993) that congressional districts created to maximize minority representation might be unconstitutional on equal protection grounds.[55] Applying this principle, the Court went on in 1995 to strike down a redrawing of Georgia's eleventh congressional district designed to maximize black representation, therefore calling into question the validity of hundreds of majority-minority congressional, state, and local districts created during that decade.[56] In *Bush v. Vera* (1996) the Court went on to hold unconstitutional on equal protection grounds a Texas redistricting plan that had created two majority-black districts and a majority-Latino district.[57] One of the high points as of yet of the U.S. Supreme Court's battle against affirmative action and political representation came in 1999 in the *Department of Commerce* case, when the Court invalidated a plan by the Clinton administration to use statistical sampling techniques in conducting the year 2000 decennial census in order to correct for the chronic and growing problem of undercounting (and therefore underrepresentation) of racial minorities in past decennial censuses.[58]

The divergence of recent Canadian and American constitutional rights jurisprudence pertaining to group rights is further illustrated by the emerging role of the Canadian constitution and Supreme Court in recognizing and affirming the rights of aboriginal peoples. While it is true that up until 1982, the constitutional status of American Indians was better protected than the status of aboriginal Canadians, this trend has changed significantly over the past two decades. Although judicial protection of American Indians' recognized right to self-government has waxed and waned over time, the U.S. Supreme Court's recent adjudication has been markedly unpredictable, if not downright reactionary, on the question of aboriginal self-government. In fact, in the process of a spate of decisions by the conservative Burger Court (1969–85), the U.S. Supreme Court has struck crushing blows to American Indian sovereignty.

The role of the Canadian constitution and courts has been relatively more positive. Sec. 35 of the Constitution Act, 1982 formally recognizes and affirms "existing" aboriginal and treaty rights, defines the "Aboriginal Peoples" as including Indians, Inuit, and Metis, and provides that modern land-claim agreements are "treaties" within the meaning of this section. Sec. 35 is therefore the main constitutional source for protecting the rights of the aboriginal peoples of Canada. While several post-1982 rounds of constitutional talks to define these rights have failed, they have inspired political and legal action by proponents of aboriginal peoples' rights, and have influenced Canadian courts to construct a new legal foundation for aboriginal rights.

Consider the following examples, which are only a representative few of the spate of recent sec. 35-based landmark rulings by the SCC. In the *Sparrow* case (1990), the SCC was asked to determine the meaning of the word "existing" in sec. 35, to set concrete legal tests to establish when an infringement of an existing right had occurred, and to establish when such an infringement might be justified.[59] In what has become the most important judgment pertaining to the status of Canadian First Nations' rights, the SCC ruled that the word "existing" in sec. 35 meant "unextinguished"—i.e., that if a right had not been validly extinguished before 1982, it was protected by sec. 35. A federal regulatory statute would have the effect of extinguishing aboriginal rights only if its intention to do so was "clear and plain." To receive constitutional protection, an aboriginal right must have existed in 1982, and must relate to aboriginal practices that were in use at the time of contact between First Nations and Europeans.[60]

The Court's crucial role in translating the various constitutional provisions dealing with aboriginal peoples' rights into a set of practical guidelines for public life has not been limited to its interpretation of aboriginal peoples' economic rights. In *Delgamuukw* (1997) it ruled that when aboriginal rights to specific land are infringed (a situation that, through implementing the tests set by the Court, should rarely come about), fair compensation by the government would be the appropriate remedy.[61] Nonetheless, the practical implications of *Delgamuukw* remain unclear.

In the late 1990s, the Court was called upon to interpret the constitutional status of aboriginal treaty rights to fish and hunt vis-à-vis regulatory federal laws (*Badger* 1996, *Marshall I* & *II* 1999).[62] In *Marshall I,* for example, the SCC found that there was an unjustified infringement by the Crown of an unextinguished Mi'kmaq (an Indian tribe that resides primarily in Nova Scotia and New Brunswick) treaty right to fish eel for food and to obtain moderate livelihood through trading their catch. In *Marshall II,* however, the Court reopened the case by drawing upon a rarely used procedure, and declared that the outcome of its first judgment could not be generalized to a declaration that licensing restrictions or closed seasons could never be imposed as part of the government's regulation of aboriginal peoples' limited commercial right to fish. The Court concluded that "[t]he federal and provincial governments have the authority to regulate the exercise of a treaty right where justified on conservation or other grounds."

In short, from a constitutional jurisprudence standpoint, it would be fair to say that the SCC has been quite generous in its interpretation of aboriginal peoples' rights at the declarative level, but far more hesitant to translate its abstract recognition of Aboriginal rights into redistribution of land or the establishment of aboriginal self-governed territories. That said, there is little doubt that over the past two decades, American and Canadian constitutional recognition and interpretation of aboriginal peoples' rights, as well as of other groups' collective rights, have taken different directions.

Conclusion

Whereas the U.S. legacy of active judicial review and constitutional rights jurisprudence is nearing its bicentennial anniversary, the Canadian constitutional rights revolution is still in its formative stages. Although it is still too early to identify prevalent patterns of judicial interpretation of constitutional rights in Canada, I believe some general, provisional conclusions can be drawn from the comparative analysis presented in this chapter.

First, given the rapid "Americanization" of Canadian politics, society, and mass culture, the introduction of NAFTA and the removal of trade barriers between the United States and its northern neighbor, the adoption of neoliberal economic policies in the two countries, and (most importantly) the 1982 constitutionalization of rights and fortification of judicial review in Canada, the gradual convergence of the two countries' rights discourses appears to be inevitable. As we have seen, a conception of rights patterned on that of the United States has indeed established itself in Canada over the past two decades. Moreover, although Canada inherited the doctrine of parliamentary supremacy and judicial restraint from Britain, there is little question that during the Charter era, Canada has converged with the United States with respect to judicial activism, the judicialization of politics, and, most notably, with the scope of its constitutional rights jurisprudence.

Second, my brief analysis of the two countries' records of constitutional rights jurisprudence reveals a common tendency to adopt a narrow conception of rights, one that emphasizes Lockean individualism and the dyadic and antistatist aspects of constitutional rights. In spite of the open-ended wording of the constitutional catalogs of rights in Canada and in the United States, the two countries' Supreme Courts tend, as has been said before, to conceptualize the purpose of rights as protecting the private sphere (human and economic) from interference by the "collective" (often understood as the state and its regulatory institutions). Constitutional rights jurisprudence in the two countries has thus tended to regard state regulation as a threat to human liberty and equality, more so than the potentially oppressive and exploitative social relations and institutions of the so-called private sector. Moreover, it often occurs that the same constitutional rights provisions are given a generous interpretation by these courts in the context of negative rights claims, but a much narrower interpretation in the context of positive rights.

In other words, as far as negative liberties are concerned (especially those rights associated with the protection of privacy and personal autonomy, due process, and formal equality—all of which require that the state refrain from interfering in private human and economic spheres), the judicial interpretation of rights is inclined to be much more generous, and thus has the potential to plant the seeds of social change. By contrast, judicial interpretations of constitutional rights in both countries seem to hold only a very limited capacity for advancing progressive notions of social justice in arenas (such as employment, health, housing, and education) that require greater state intervention and more public expenditure. Unlike in the United States, however, the uphill battle against the complete exclusion of positive entitlements to subsistence social welfare from the scope of Canadian constitutional rights provisions has not yet sunk into constitutional oblivion.

Third, in spite of the broad and rapid convergence of U.S. and Canadian rights discourses, deeply entrenched differences between the two countries' social, cultural, and political legacies continue to promote divergence in the two countries' constitutional recognition and judicial interpretation of group rights. Whereas the relatively greater emphasis on collective values in Canada has failed, by and large, to block the "Americanization" of Canadian rights discourse concerning first-generation negative liberties and second-generation positive entitlements, there is little doubt that over the past two decades, certain types of group rights—primarily minority language and education rights, aboriginal peoples' rights, and affirmative action guarantees—have been awarded much wider constitutional recognition and relatively more generous judicial interpretation in Canada than in the United States.

Finally, the prevalent patterns of constitutional rights jurisprudence I have discussed in this chapter highlight an important difference in the challenges Canadian and American jurists will have to face in the years to come. The SCC is bound to find itself at the center of a clash between the increasingly hegemonic views of a neoliberal society, with its emphasis on the individualistic aspects of constitutional rights, and counterpressure to preserve the Canadian legacy of relative collectivism and meaningful multicultural accommodation. The U.S. Supreme Court, on the other hand, will have to reconsider its strict adherence to a Lockean-style antistatist conception of constitutional rights in view of the vast racial, regional, linguistic, and economic disparities in U.S. society, as well as the large-scale demographic changes it is undergoing. It might well have to develop a more accommodating approach towards differentiated citizenship rights and progressive notions of distributive justice. If such a change does occur, then the United States and Canada will indeed see a convergence of their rights discourses, and the transformation of their respective national high courts' rights jurisprudence in the process.

Notes

1. "How the Charter Changes Justice" (an interview with Chief Justice Lamer), *Globe and Mail,* 17 April 1992, A11.

2. For thorough discussions of the classic distinction between these three types of rights, and of the major normative justifications for protecting positive and collective rights, see Charles Fried, *Right and Wrong* (Cambridge: Harvard University Press, 1978); Cecile Fabre, *Social Rights Under the Constitution* (Oxford: Clarendon Press,

2000); Henry Shue, *Basic Rights: Subsistence, Affluence, and U.S. Foreign Policy* (Princeton: Princeton University Press, 1980).

3. See, for example, Stephen Holmes and Cass Sunstein, *The Cost of Rights* (New York: W. W. Norton, 1999).

4. This systematic analysis is based on a complete survey conducted by the author of this chapter of all reported Charter cases decided by the SCC from 1982 to 2002, and of all reported Bill of Rights cases decided by the U.S. Supreme Court from 1975 to 2002. The complete databases are on file with the author.

5. These figures do not include cases that dealt exclusively with technical aspects of the BOR (e.g., application and jurisdiction). For further elaboration on data gathering, collation, and coding issues related to this analysis, see Ran Hirschl, *Towards Juristocracy: A Comparative Inquiry into the Origins and Consequences of the New Constitutionalism* (Cambridge: Harvard University Press, 2003), chap. 5.

6. *Mapp v. Ohio,* 367 U.S. 643 (1961): no evidence of guilt could be used if it was obtained in the course of an illegal search and seizure; *Miranda v. Arizona,* 384 U.S. 436 (1966): once a suspect has been taken into police custody, that person must be warned of certain rights, including the right to remain silent, and be granted an attorney during questioning; in *Gideon v. Wainright,* 372 U.S. 335 (1963), the Warren Court established the Sixth Amendment-based right to counsel, as well as the right to government-provided attorneys to indigent defendants in state trials.

7. *Dickerson v. United States,* 530 U.S. 428 (2000).

8. *Walton v. Arizona* (decision released 20 June 2002): the execution of a mentally retarded criminal constitutes cruel and unusual punishment that is prohibited by the Eighth Amendment; *Ring v. Arizona* (decision released 24 June 2002): holding unconstitutional a practice of having a judge, rather than a jury, decide the critical sentencing issues in a death penalty case.

9. Charles Epp, *The Rights Revolution: Lawyers, Activists, and Supreme Courts in Comparative Perspective* (Chicago: University of Chicago Press, 1998), 28.

10. *McNabb v. United States* 318 U.S. 322, 347 (1942).

11. *Singh v. Minister of Employment and Immigration,* [1985] 1 S.C.R. 177.

12. *Askov v. The Queen,* [1990] 2 S.C.R. 1199.

13. *United States of America v. Cobb,* [2001] 1 S.C.R. 587; *United States of America v. Shulman,* [2001] 1 S.C.R. 616.

14. *R. v. Feeney,* [1997] 2 S.C.R. 117.

15. In a similar spirit, the SCC held recently (*R. v. Golden,* 2001) that strip search in public space of suspects in drug trafficking and selling contravened the Charter's privacy provisions. The downright incriminating evidence gathered through such searches was held inadmissible.

16. *R. v. CIP Inc.,* [1992] 1 S.C.R. 843. See Joel Bakan, *Just Words* (Toronto: University of Toronto Press, 1997), 91–92.

17. *R. v. Seaboyer,* [1991] 2 S.C.R. 577.

18. *R. v. O'Connor,* [1995] 4 S.C.R. 411. See also *R. v. Daviault,* [1994] 3 S.C.R 63.

19. *R. v. Mills,* [1999] 3 S.C.R. 668.

20. *Sherbert v. Verner,* 374 U.S. 398 (1963) (denial of unemployment benefits because a person refuses to work on her Sabbath day violates the "free exercise" clause; the state must show a "compelling interest" in limiting freedom of religion); *Wisconsin v. Yoder,* 406 U.S. 205 (1972) (Amish children could leave school earlier than otherwise allowed under Wisconsin's compulsory education laws; the latter may not infringe upon minority groups' right to preserve their collective identity through extended autonomy over their children's education); *Church of the Lukumi Babalu Aye v. City of Hialeah,* 508 U.S. 520 (1993) (a city ordinance prohibiting animal sacrifice for religious purposes by adherents of the Santeria religion violated the "free exercise" clause); *Oregon v. Smith,* 494 U.S. 872 (1990) (smoking peyote for sacramental purposes in religious ceremonies by state employees on duty is not protected by the free exercise clause and may constitute a criminal offense).

21. *R. v. Big M Drug Mart Ltd.* [1985] 1 S.C.R. 295.

22. *R.A.V. v. City of St. Paul, Minnesota,* 505 U.S. 377 (1992). In an equally contested decision, the U.S. Supreme Court relied primarily on the "content neutrality" doctrine to strike down Texas's flag-burning law. See *Texas v. Johnson,* 491 U.S. 397 (1989).

23. *R. v. Keegstra,* [1990] 3 S.C.R. 697.

24. *R. v. Zundel,* [1992] 2 S.C.R. 731. See also *Ross v. New Brunswick School District No. 15,* [1996] 1 S.C.R. 825.

25. *R. v. Lucas,* [1998] 1 S.C.R. 439.

26. *R. v. Sharpe,* [2001] 1 S.C.R. 45.

27. *RJR MacDonald Inc. v. Canada,* [1995] 3 S.C.R. 199.

28. *Egan v. Canada,* [1995] 2 S.C.R. 513. However, the specific discriminatory provision in question was reinstated by the "reasonableness" test of sec. 1.

29. *Vriend v. Alberta,* [1998] 1 S.C.R 493. The de facto meaning of this decision is that the state has an obligation to enact human rights legislation that is broad enough to allow human rights claims to be made concerning discrimination based on sexual orientation.

30. *M v. H,* [1999] 2 S.C.R. 3.

31. *Romer v. Evans,* 517 U.S. 620 (1996).

32. *Boy Scouts of America v. Dale,* 530 U.S. 640 (2000).

33. *San Antonio Independent School District v. Rodriguez,* 411 U.S. 1 (1973).

34. Id., at 35.

35. It is worth noting that the proposed provision stated clearly that its intention was not to afford social rights the same status as rights protected by the Charter, and

it would not have the effect of modifying the interpretation of the rights and freedoms protected by the Charter.

36. *R. v. Prosper,* [1994] 3 S.C.R. 236.

37. *Andrews v. Law Society of British Columbia,* [1989] 1 S.C.R. 143, 163–64.

38. *Finlay v. Canada (Minister of Finance),* [1993] 1 S.C.R. 1080.

39. *Adler et al. v. The Queen in Right of Ontario et al.,* [1996] 3 S.C.R. 609.

40. Id., at 613. Following the Court's decision, the parents presented the case before the U.N. Human Rights Committee (UNHRC). In 1999, the committee released a recommendation stating that Ontario's refusal to fund non-Roman Catholic denominational schools amounted to a violation of fundamental freedom of religion and equality rights. See *Waldman v. Canada* (1999), CCPR/C/C7/694/1999.

41. *Schachter v. Canada,* [1992] 2 S.C.R. 679. The Court held that unemployment insurance child-care benefits had to be provided equally to both natural and adoptive parents, and that the Unemployment Insurance Act's provision of such benefits to the latter but not to the former was therefore unconstitutional.

42. *Eldridge v. British Columbia,* [1997] 3 S.C.R. 624. The Court held that the failure of hospitals and doctors to provide publicly funded sign-language interpretation as part of the provision of medical services discriminated against deaf patients of the B.C. Medicare system.

43. Without going into detail, the Quebec Bill 101 *(Charte de la langue française),* enacted by the newly elected Parti Quebecois government in 1977, was intended to promote the use of French in Quebec by restricting the use of English in businesses and in schools in the province.

44. *Attorney-General of Quebec v. Blaikie,* [1979] 2 S.C.R. 1016.

45. *Attorney-General of Quebec v. Quebec Protestant School Board,* [1984] 2 S.C.R. 66.

46. *Ford v. Attorney-General of Quebec,* [1988] 2 S.C.R. 712. The SCC also held that the blanket use of an override declaration by the Quebec government (Bill 178) was an improper and invalid application of the Charter's override clause.

47. *Reference re Manitoba Language Rights,* [1985] 1 S.C.R. 721.

48. *Mahe v. Alberta,* [1990] 1 S.C.R. 342.

49. *Aresenault-Cameron v. Prince Edward Island,* [2000] 1 S.C.R. 3.

50. *Alexander v. Sandoval,* 121 S.Ct. 1511 (2001).

51. *Regents of the University of California v. Bakke,* 438 U.S. 265 (1978).

52. *Wygant v. Jackson Board of Education,* 476 U.S. 267 (1986).

53. *City of Richmond v. J. A. Croson,* 488 U.S. 469 (1989).

54. *Adarand Constructions, Inc. v. Pena,* 515 U.S. 200 (1995).

55. *Shaw v. Reno,* 509 U.S. 630 (1993). See also *Shaw v. Hunt,* 517 U.S. 899 (1996).

56. *Miller v. Johnson,* 515 U.S. 900 (1995). In a follow-up ruling in *Abrams v. Johnson,* 521 U.S. 74 (1997), the Court held that Georgia was not required to make any increase in the number of majority-minority voting districts in the state.

57. *Bush v. Vera,* 517 U.S. 952 (1996).

58. *Department of Commerce v. United States House of Representatives,* 525 U.S. 316 (1999).

59. *R. v. Sparrow,* [1990] 1 S.C.R. 1075.

60. The Court added, however, that even if an aboriginal right met these criteria, a court could still find that government restrictions on it were justified. See, for example, *R. v. Van der Peet,* [1996] 2 S.C.R. 507; *R. v. Gladstone,* [1996] 2 S.C.R. 672; *R. v. N.T.C. Smokehouse,* [1996] 2 S.C.R. 572.

61. *Delgamuukw v. British Colombia,* [1997] 3 S.C.R. 1010. See also *R. v. Pamajewon,* [1996] 2 S.C.R. 821, in which the Court narrowly defined the right of First Nations to self-government under sec. 35 of the Charter.

62. *R. v. Badger,* [1996] 1 S.C.R. 771; *R. v. Marshall I,* [1999] 3 S.C.R. 456; *R. v. Marshall II,* [1999] 3 S.C.R. 533.

CHAPTER 4

The Civil Rights Movement Comes to Winnipeg: American Influence on "Rights Talk" in Canada, 1968–71

Robert Vipond

I

One weekend in September 1970, a group of high school student council leaders in Winnipeg traveled to a nearby conference center to discuss their plans, individual and collective, for the new school year. Organized by the student union at the University of Manitoba, the retreat was a bit of a gamble. There was only the loosest of organizing structures that connected the various student councils in Winnipeg, and no one really knew if these student leaders would find common cause. They did. As discussion proceeded, it became clear that many of the students shared a common and deep frustration that their local principal and school board did not take them seriously, and that, as students, they had "no say in the decisions that affect them" and their education. From this basic insight followed a series of other complaints: that student-run newspapers were routinely censored; that dress codes suppressed individual expression; that students were subject to arbitrary and unjust disciplinary measures. From these various concerns emerged a clear consensus. What they needed, the students agreed, was a bill of rights for students that would "protect the individual rights of students and student governments" and "give students a greater voice in the decisions that affect them."[1]

For the smaller group of students who accepted the challenge of drafting the Winnipeg student bill of rights over the course of the school year, the practical problem was how to translate the fine sentiments articulated at the retreat into language that would both stir students and engage principals and school boards. A couple of sympathetic law students at the University of Manitoba provided some tips on the niceties of legal writing, and Jerry Farber's famous essay, "The Student as Nigger," provided a broader and richer context for their intuitions. But it was not until the student committee turned up a student bill of rights from New York City, complete with commentary by the ACLU, that the Winnipeg students began to hit their stride. To be sure, some of the advice provided by the ACLU did not resonate strongly with the Winnipeg students; curbing the presence of police in the schools was simply not what most of them worried about. Still, the New York example turned out to be crucial for providing the Winnipeg students with a model for their own bill. Indeed, in a broadsheet distributed to several thousand Winnipeg high school students in March 1971, the drafting committee quoted extensively from the New York bill, the ACLU gloss, and even from a couple of U.S. federal court decisions that gave constitutional weight to student rights. As the Winnipeg drafting committee proudly confessed, the New York bill "provided inspiration"[2] for their own efforts. In the end, the efforts of the Winnipeg students came to nought. The student bill of rights attracted a brief flurry of media attention, but the organizers simply lacked the ability to mobilize their fellow students, much less overcome the entrenched opposition of most principals and school boards.

I should confess at the outset that I have a personal interest in the Winnipeg student bill of rights story, as I was one of the students who helped draft and defend it. My purpose here, however, is not personal. What I want to suggest is that the Winnipeg student bill of rights provides a helpful snapshot of, and an introduction to, English-Canadian "rights talk" in the late 1960s and early 1970s. Appropriately enlarged with other documentary materials, what emerges from an analysis of this period is a public discussion that is different both from the conventional story of how Canadians came to embrace a Charter of Rights and how rights questions are typically framed in this, the post-Charter period. Less centered on the question of national unity, more concerned with establishing the conditions for a vibrant democratic polity, and largely silent about the power of courts—this is a discussion not simply worth remembering, but worth recapturing.

II

In the many retellings of the story of how Canadians came to the Charter of Rights, there are two elements that are fixed. The first is that Pierre Trudeau is the central character of the story, for whom establishing a Charter of Rights became "a magnificent obsession."[3] He rose to national prominence in 1967 when, newly installed as minister of justice, he introduced the Charter as a national priority. He made it the centrepiece of his successful campaign for the leadership of the Liberal Party and touted the Charter and other features of a "just society" in the 1968 general election. Moreover, no name is more closely associated with the political strategy and negotiations that led to the enactment of the Charter of Rights in 1982 than Pierre Trudeau. In short, no one is more central to the creation of the Charter than Trudeau, and no account of its creation can ignore him.

The second element of commonality informs the first. The Charter of Rights was so important to Trudeau because, in his view, it provided a powerful counterpoise to the divisive potential of Quebec nationalism. The Charter would articulate a set of fundamental, shared values that would "define the common thread that binds us together" so as to combat the "forces of self-interest [that would] tear us apart."[4] The Charter was, in this sense, central to Trudeau's national unity strategy. There are, to be sure, deep and important interpretive differences among the many scholars and journalists who have told and retold the Charter story. Whether Trudeau was too liberal or not liberal enough and whether his obsession with the Charter blunted Quebec nationalism or actually fueled it remain topics of considerable debate. Still, the consensus about what Trudeau was attempting to accomplish and his central role in the Charter drama is so monolithic it can almost be reduced to a formula: no Trudeau, no Charter. And for Trudeau, there was this corollary: no Charter, no Canada.[5]

Trudeau was a larger-than-life figure, and it is easy enough to understand why friend and foe alike would identify the Charter project so closely and so fully with him. There is a problem, however, with this preoccupation with Trudeau's contribution to the Charter. For in concentrating on Trudeau, both admirers and critics have tended to marginalize the equally important story of how other Canadians, especially English Canadians, came to speak the language of rights and welcome the creation of something like a Charter. Given Trudeau's intellectual and political presence and leadership, most accounts of the pre-Charter era seem to assume that the broader public essentially followed his cues. Take the Winnipeg students, for example. The Winnipeg students, after all, took up the cause of creating a student bill of rights just as Trudeau began to build serious political momentum for the Charter, and it would be easy enough to infer from the timing of both initiatives that the students followed in Trudeau's intellectual slipstream. And, true enough, a few of them had cut their political teeth by working for Trudeau in the 1968 election. In fact, however, these were the exception, not the rule, and there is precious little other evidence to suggest that the students who busied themselves writing a student bill of rights were inspired by Trudeau in any direct way, much less that they were deeply concerned about national unity or any of the other questions that preoccupied the prime minister.

What I want to suggest here is simply that it is dangerous to assume that in understanding Trudeau, we understand how Canadians came to the Charter. The evidence suggests, on the contrary, that even in the years of Trudeau's first Charter offensive—that is, from roughly 1968 to 1971—"rights talk" in

Canada was far more diffuse, far more varied, and far more "American" than the Trudeaucentric account of the Charter's development would suggest. Rights talk was so widespread in public discussion, indeed, that any attempt to catalog all of its variants is well beyond the scope of this chapter. So let me begin by focusing on one of the most important forums for Canadian rights talk of the day, the popular newsmagazine *Maclean's,* as a way of illustrating just how diffuse, varied, and subtly different from Trudeau's apparently authoritative understanding of rights this public discussion was.

Maclean's is a useful guide to the broader discussion of rights in Canada for several reasons. In the first place, it was one of English Canada's most widely read newsmagazines. Published monthly, *Maclean's* had an average monthly circulation of over 700,000 copies during the period 1968–71, higher than the Canadian edition of *Time* magazine, which averaged slightly under 500,000, and far higher than other "highbrow" magazines, such as *Saturday Night* (90,000), *Canadian Forum* (1,500), and *This Magazine* (3,500). Only *Chatelaine,* with a circulation of close to 1 million a month, and *The Canadian Magazine* (which was included as a Saturday supplement to Southam newspapers) reached as many Canadians.[6] Moreover, *Maclean's* was the only high-circulation magazine that combined extended commentary and analysis of current events broadly political in nature. *Time* magazine concentrated then (as now) on shorter "news" stories. And while both *Chatelaine* and the *Canadian Magazine* included some longer articles on political subjects, in neither case was political analysis and commentary their raison d'être. For *Maclean's* it was.

If one thing is clear from even a cursory reading of *Maclean's* in the years 1968–71, it is that rights talk—giving political priority to protecting individual liberty, promoting equality, and strengthening democracy—flourished. *Maclean's* served as a forum for discussing student rights and student power in the universities. (Following a feature-length debate between student leader Steven Langdon and Claude Bissell, the president of the University of Toronto, *Maclean's* endorsed the publication of student evaluations as a form of "consumer protection" that would give "undergraduates more freedom to choose" their courses.)[7] Not surprisingly, the legalization of abortion was vigorously debated in its pages.[8] The arbitrary powers of the police and the absence of protection for individual liberty against the state were commonly deplored.[9] In the wake of the Royal Commission on the Status of Women, there was considerable discussion of gender equality, equality of opportunity, and individual dignity.[10] The glaring gap between the liberal myth of America and the conduct of its affairs abroad was both searchingly exposed and cleverly satirized.[11] And, of course, there were thematic articles on Quebec, including an acute analysis of René Levesque's political moderation, which showed considerable familiarity with the subtle differences embedded in rights language. Whereas more strident nationalists argued that the use of English in Quebec was a "privilege," wrote Blair Fraser, Levesque defended the more generous notion that choice of language is one of "the rights of the English minority in a sovereign Quebec."[12] Stated quantitatively, in the years 1968–71 *Maclean's* published slightly over twenty articles per year that dealt thematically with such rights questions. Nor did this interest only suddenly appear. In fact, in the three previous years (1964–67) before those summarized here, the extent of rights talk in *Maclean's* was actually more widespread.

III

The simple point here is that the public discussion of rights in the early Trudeau years (1968–71) was widespread and varied. By now one might have thought this was an observation so self-evident that it hardly needed making. Yet, oddly enough, in the historical reconstruction of how the Charter of Rights came to be, the period 1968–71 has largely been passed over by Canadian historians, political scientists, and journalists.[13] It is therefore important, in the first instance, to establish some sort of baseline. A survey of *Maclean's*, though not representative in every way, does just that by providing an enlarged snapshot of mainstream, liberal-leaning, widely read journalism. The larger and more important background question is this: What was the tone and content of this public "rights talk" and how, if at all, did it relate to Trudeau's defense of the Charter?

Michael Ignatieff has recently written that "the entire spirit" of Trudeau's Charter "was to protect individuals from the tyranny of the state and the tyranny of majorities."[14] As we will shortly see, Ignatieff's statement is almost certainly too categorical, but it does illuminate an essential element of Trudeau's thought and action: namely, his solicitude for what is conventionally called "negative liberty." Trudeau's famous quip that the state has no business in the bedrooms of the nation remains to this day a versatile liberal emblem. He defended language rights as the rights of individuals to speak the language of their choice, even or especially when in the minority.[15] As prime minister, he lectured the premiers on the importance of protecting "fundamental, natural and unalterable" individual rights, among them "the right to life and property, and the freedoms of opinion, speech and religion."[16] Even Trudeau's critics tacitly acknowledged his civil libertarian core. After all, when the prime minister was criticized for imposing the War Measures Act in 1970 in response to the actions of the FLQ (Fédération pour la libération du Québec), the sharpest rebuke came from those who said he had betrayed his own civil libertarian principles, which give priority to individual freedom over the open-ended and arbitrary powers of government.

The value of protecting individual freedom and choice resonated publicly. The idea that individual freedom and freedom of choice are good things and in need of more robust protection was clearly central to the Winnipeg students' campaign for a bill of rights. Indeed, freedom of expression, freedom of the press, and freedom of dress all featured prominently in the draft bill, and their justification for the inclusion of these rights was classically liberal. Without these protections, the students argued, their colleagues did not speak out for fear of intimidation, censorship had a chilling effect on what they wrote in their student newspapers, and dress codes stifled self-expression. Nor were these the only ways in which talk of individual rights figured. The students were concerned, in a somewhat different vein, to ensure that students could appeal unjust disciplinary actions. This, too, was put in the language of individual rights—in this case, the right of individual students to be protected against the arbitrary power of principals and school boards. In making their case for including procedural rights in the draft student bill of rights, the Winnipeg students cited a U.S. appeals court decision that nicely summed up their claim: "When a school board undertakes to expel a public school student, it is undertaking to apply the terrible organized force of the state, just as surely as it is applied by the police, the courts, the prison, or the militia. . . . It is time to broaden the constitutional community by including within its protection young people, whose claim to dignity matches that of their elders."[17]

Nor were the Winnipeg students alone in worrying about the fragility of individual freedom. The debate over abortion, so much a fixture of rights debate in Canada over the past two decades, was already by the late 1960s framed in terms of reproductive autonomy, on the one hand, and the rights of the unborn, on the other. *Maclean's* took special interest in chronicling and debating the place of the "hippie movement" in Canadian society. Here, too, the issues were not infrequently framed in terms of freedom of expression, police harassment, and trumped-up charges of loitering as a means of removing an unwanted minority from the streets—"a clear-cut case of a civil liberty," according to one *Maclean's* staff writer.[18] Indeed, it seems fair to say that one of the goals of *Maclean's* in this period was to expose the misuse of police power, the inequalities built in to the administration of justice, and the "cavalier attitude" displayed by many judges to the sanctity of "individual freedom." At stake in exposing the deficiencies of the justice system, one staff writer argued, was "the value of individual liberty."[19]

Yet as central as individual liberty was for Trudeau, the Winnipeg students, and the informed public alike, it is clear, pace Ignatieff, that the rights debate in Canada was about more than protecting individuals from "the tyranny of the state and the tyranny of majorities."[20] The journalist Margaret Daly, writing for *Maclean's* in 1970, neatly captured the complexity of the debate in a striking article entitled "How Women in Power Keep Other

Women Powerless." "Respectable though freedom for women may have become," she argued, "the idea of a mass movement to achieve it—like the labor movement, civil-rights movement, or mass movement of the poor which is beginning to show stirrings—that's something else." An individual woman's freedom and success was nothing more than "a phony illusion" unless she recognized and supported "one of the most important movements of our day: the trend toward real equality of the sexes."[21] Women, especially professionally successful women, must not repeat the errors of African Americans before the civil rights movement who "tried to beat the system by making it as outstanding individuals—the UN's Ralphe Bunche for example." Rather, the only way to achieve "real liberation" was to do as the "next black generation" had done and stand together in "a mass movement."[22]

I quote at some length from Daly's article because it illustrates or represents an important turn in the Canadian rights debate. What Daly (and others) wanted to do was turn the conventional debate away from understanding rights simply in terms of individual, negative rights protected from state intrusion and to embrace, instead, a notion of rights that focused on the state's obligation to ensure equality. Daly's real target here was the Royal Commission on the Status of Women, but her egalitarian sentiments, once generalized, rippled through Canadian rights discourse in an extremely powerful way in the late 1960s and early 1970s. Indeed, an equality-seeking strategy went to the heart of the entire rights debate of the era. And in describing and defending the fundamental importance of equality, no example or metaphor was as powerful, as widely used, or as resonant as that of the civil rights movement in the United States.

The late Judith Shklar used to argue that the institution of slavery framed American political discourse by defining an evil against which political and social reformers could measure their own position and aspirations.[23] To be free meant, above all, to be able to vote and to earn one's living. It is thus not at all coincidental that voting and working for a wage have loomed so large in the history of American political thought and social reform. Curiously enough, in the Canada of the late 1960s and early 1970s, the American civil rights movement had a similarly architectonic effect on Canadian constitutional discourse. As Americans historically have measured their own situation in light of slavery, so, in the 1960s and early 1970s, Canadians began to situate their own efforts at political and constitutional reform in light of American attempts to overcome the legacy of racism.

Not surprisingly, the struggles of the civil rights movement served several different purposes when imported to Canada and adapted for Canadian use. Probably the most famous invocation of the American racial analogy in Canada was by Pierre Vallières, whose book *White Niggers of America*[24] became a leading text of radical Quebec nationalism. A journalist and a supporter of the FLQ, Vallières wrote the book largely while being held in the Manhattan House of Detention for Men while awaiting extradition to Canada to stand trial in a murder case. Published in French in 1968, it was translated into English and published with considerable fanfare following the October Crisis of 1970. For Vallières, the metaphor of African American slavery helped to describe the situation of Québécois in Canada. The reviewer for the *New York Times,* Laurier Lapierre, agreed that this central metaphor resonated powerfully: "Vallières is quite right when he writes that 'The liberation struggle launched by the American blacks . . . arouses growing interest among the French-Canadian population, for the workers of Quebec are aware of their condition as niggers, exploited men, second-class citizens.'"[25] Most of the reviewers seem to have found the slavery analogy illuminating or even compelling. Christopher Lehmann-Haupt, for instance, predicted that Vallière's autobiography "will take its place alongside the writings of Malcolm X, Eldridge Cleaver, Frantz Fanon, Che Guevera, and Regis Debray."[26]

Somewhat unwittingly, I think, Lehmann-Haupt put his finger on the central limitation of Vallière's rhetorical strategy. For the fact is that Vallières's intellectual commitments grew out of, and were inspired by, the anti- and postcolonial movements represented by thinkers like Fanon, not the American liberal tradition. So while the metaphor of "white niggers" was initially arresting, it quickly became clear that Vallière's prescription of world revolution went far beyond anything in the American (or Canadian) tradition. Mainstream Canadian constitutional discourse in the late 1960s, like that of the civil rights movement, was essentially liberal: egalitarian, to be sure, but egalitarian in a way that was defined and constrained by the liberal framework in which it worked and the liberal tradition to which it appealed. Ultimately, Canadians were far more likely to be moved by Martin Luther King than by Malcolm X.

Alan Borovoy has written that the "civil rights movement around Martin Luther King" was "the most inspiring embodiment of liberal values this continent has probably ever experienced."[27] Borovoy is in a position to know. Before becoming executive director of the Canadian Civil Liberties Association, he was on staff at the Labour Committee for Human Rights, a civil rights organization that had grown out of the Jewish Labour Committee. Throughout the 1950s and 1960s, the Jewish Labour Committee (JLC) and the Labour Committee for Human Rights (LCHR) organized actively to combat discrimination and to promote civil rights in Canada. They had close relations with like-minded organizations in the United States (including the NAACP), sponsored educational workshops with American civil rights leaders, and were generally happy to borrow ideas and strategy from their American counterparts. Though the legislative and judicial landscape was different in the two countries, the problems—especially, in this case, discrimination in employment on the basis of race and religion—were similar enough to permit the LCHR leadership to look to the civil rights movement as a model. Nor were they alone. Much of the debate engendered by the Royal Commission on the Status of Women was about gender equality, and in this debate the civil rights movement and Dr. King became lightning rods for opinion on both sides of the issue. Pauline Jewett, noted academic and activist, described the importance of the Royal Commission in terms that were entirely reminiscent of the civil rights struggle. The hearings before the Royal Commission, she argued, "have given women a new determination to ensure that they may yet be treated, in dignity and worth, as the equals of men."[28] Indeed, the message of social justice and nonviolence had become sufficiently powerful and attractive in Canada that Dr. King himself was asked to deliver the prestigious Massey Lectures in the fall of 1967. Broadcast to a national radio audience on the CBC, the lectures, taped in New York and Atlanta, were interrupted while Dr. King served his now famous jail sentence for contempt of court in Birmingham, Alabama.

For Pierre Trudeau, on the other hand, the struggle for civil rights provided a helpful way of explaining his strategy of combating Quebec nationalism. In his signature collection of essays, *Federalism and the French Canadians,* published in English in 1968,[29] Trudeau used the constitutional vocabulary created by *Brown v. Board* to explain to English Canadians that Quebeckers needed to feel as if they belonged in Canada. What Quebeckers wanted and needed, he argued, was real linguistic equality throughout Canada. But this would require something more than good will, something like constitutional guarantees. "Like the United States," he said, "we must move beyond separate but equal to complete integration."[30] In the United States, the courts had ruled that separate but equal educational facilities engendered a sense of inferiority that was inconsistent with the idea of equality of opportunity. In subsequent decisions, federal courts held that simple nondiscrimination or neutrality may be insufficient to eliminate racial inequality "root and branch." The Constitution not only prohibited governments from doing certain things they wanted to do (e.g., running racially segregated schools), but also forced governments to do certain things they didn't want to do (e.g., busing students to integrated schools). What Mr. Trudeau meant to say, by analogy, was that it no longer sufficed simply to prohibit discrimination against French Canadians. Positive government action, of the sort that was embedded in the Official Languages Act, for instance, was needed to integrate them more fully into Canadian life.

As numerous commentators have noted, Trudeau's vision, like that of the U.S. Supreme Court, was a fundamentally individualist one. His goal was to guarantee the equality of individual French Canadians, much as the Supreme Court in the United States has said that the equal protection clause is directed at the equality of individual African Americans. Whatever the merits of the constitutional argument in the United States, Trudeau's use of it in the Canadian case arguably created as many problems as it solved. As Michael Ignatieff has pointed out, the equality of individual rights is "simply not enough" in the Canadian case, because it "fails to recognize and protect the rights of constituent nations and peoples to maintain their distinctive identities."[31] In this view, aboriginal peoples and Quebeckers are "nations, not collections of individuals with similar characteristics."[32] That is, they are not minorities in the sense that the *Brown* court understood the term, in which the question is not usually whether African Americans belong to the moral community that has been created by a sovereign people but whether they enjoy the "equal protection of the law" that is due all members of the American constitutional order. The prior question about membership in the moral community—about whether African Americans belong—was answered definitively at the time of the Civil War. In other words, the Canadian constitutional debate has been stuck at an earlier stage than the American. Thus, as Peter Russell has put it so well,[33] the fundamental question in Canada is less about the rules that should guide and govern a sovereign people than it is about whether a single, sovereign people really exists in the first place. In choosing to formulate his constitutional argument in American terms, Trudeau chose to expound an alternative to group identity, not to accommodate it. He chose to assume an answer to the sovereignty question rather than to open it. Whether this was ultimately the best strategy remains, to this day, an open question and central to assessing his legacy. What is not open to question is Trudeau's debt to American constitutional paradigms and precedents.

For the Winnipeg students, the influence of the civil rights movement played out in a different way altogether. If there was one text that became essential reading for the students involved in drafting the student bill of rights, it was Jerry Farber's famous essay "The Student As Nigger," which I mentioned above. Farber's essay had originally been published in a low-circulation, alternative newspaper in California, but it quickly achieved underground fame and was circulated far and wide—including to the Winnipeg students—in various informal ways. Farber's rhetorical style was direct and unsubtle. "Students are niggers," the article began. "When you get that straight, our schools begin to make sense." What caught the attention of the Winnipeg students was Farber's thematic account of the undemocratic nature of the school system: "Students at Cal State are politically disenfranchised. They are in an academic Lowndes County. Most of them can vote in national elections—their average age is about 26—but they have no voice in the decisions which affect their academic lives. The students, it is true, [are] allowed to have a toy government of their own. It is government run, for the most part, by Uncle Toms, concerned principally with trivia. The faculty and administrators decide what courses will be offered: the students get to choose their own Homecoming Queen." He concluded: "Students, like black people, have immense unused power. They could, theoretically, insist on participating in their own education. They could make academic freedom bilateral. . . . They could. They have the power. But only in a few places, like Berkeley, have they even begun to think about using it."[34]

This emphasis on power and participation helps to clarify just what the Winnipeg students believed they could, and needed to, achieve by constructing a student bill of rights. Part of their motivation, as I have noted above, had to do with protecting individual rights—to speak out, to dress as one wants, and so on—without fear of reprisal. And one could probably interpret their draft bill of rights as a statement about the importance of equality and individual dignity—although it is interesting that the words "equality" and "discrimination" never appear in their draft. Yet what clearly stands out as the single most important purpose of the draft bill of rights is the need to defend "the right to participate in the decision-making process in all areas of policy which affect the student body directly." The bill was designed, as the students themselves formulated it, "to give students greater voice in the decisions that affect them," and it is no coincidence, therefore, that the first two articles of the draft bill aim to entrench the rights of student government. Only later do they introduce provisions to guarantee freedom of expression, freedom of the press, and what they called freedom of dress.

Besides, the Winnipeg students seem to have understood, long before John Hart Ely had developed the notion theoretically,[35] that freedom of expression and freedom of the press serve a democratic purpose. And this is the point. The Winnipeg student bill of rights was, centrally and essentially, a democratic instrument. "The Bill of Rights," they explained, "is a basis for education reform, not on a piecemeal scale, but on a scale that will truly replace authoritarianism with democracy. The Bill of Rights is for every student and will not succeed if there is not mass student support." The Winnipeg students believed that, in their own way, they had responded to Jerry Farber's rhetorical question: "What have black people done? They have, first of all, faced the fact of their slavery. . . . They've organized. They've decided to get freedom now, they've started taking it."

In point of fact, the actual text of the Winnipeg bill of rights did not really match the rhetorical claims in which it was bundled. In retrospect, indeed, the striking thing about the Winnipeg bill is just how timid the suggested reforms were. The draft bill did not actually challenge the statutory authority of principals or school boards, the repeated emphasis was on representation rather than on direct action and activism, and even in matters of representation the students shied away from a standard like parity in favor of the malleable standard of "reasonable representation." Still, what is noteworthy is that, for the Winnipeg students, to have rights meant, first and foremost, to participate in making decisions about their education. For them, the basic purpose of a bill of rights was to enshrine this fundamental, procedural principle.

I linger on the example of the student bill of rights because in many ways the Winnipeg students seem to have captured the spirit of their age. The students were struck by the disproportion between the importance of education, on the one hand, and their lack of control over it, on the other, and they viewed a bill of rights as one way to reduce the distance between them. The same worry about "disproportionality"[36] was widely shared. Claude Bissell, president of the University of Toronto, clearly worried about student "discontent" and believed that "the university must more insistently respond to democratic pressures" to ensure "wide involvement" of students and faculty in governance in ways that would produce "loyalty and a sense of cohesion."[37] The editors at *Maclean's* found Bissell's arguments persuasive. In the same issue in which the magazine published a long discussion between Bissell and the student Steven Langdon, the editors praised Bissell and his moderate democratic reforms. The university needed to remind itself that it was a "place of learning," not a "political cockpit," and should not engender "a false equality" between student and professor. Still, undergraduates "are at least the consumers of education, and a customer has a right to say where the shoe pinches him." Why not offer students "a representative voice—not a veto—on the curriculum, on faculty appointments and promotions, and even on the administration of the university?"[38]

In a special editorial for the January 1969 issue of the magazine, the *Maclean's* editors broadened both their analysis of, and their prescription for, the problem of disproportionality. "The feeling is growing among millions of ordinary people," they opined, "that, in some new and unexplained way, *things are coming apart.* Was there ever another time like this, so fearful, so violent, so uncertain? Has there ever been personal loneliness and mass insanity on so vast and frightening a scale?" The problem, they argued, was that "the world is getting worse because technology is crushing people. Institutions and power structures (the bad guys) are subjugating human beings (the good guys)." The common link between the invasion of Czechoslovakia and the Democratic convention in Chicago was that in both cases "power" triumphed over "people." The only solution to the problem was for people "to demand more involvement in the governing process," to embrace what they called "People Power." This was the significance of the phenomenon dubbed Trudeaumania, the retirement of Lyndon Johnson, and incipient reforms in the Catholic Church. The editorial concluded: "People, in other words, are beginning to run their own show at last. And this is the real meaning of what's happening in the chaotic, uncertain world of the 1960s. They're less willing than ever before to accept structures that limit their potential for self-development."[39] It all sounded, as Larry Zolf put it, like what many called the American Dream, where individuals were not only "human" but "an involved participant, an equal."[40] Here, in a nutshell, was the spirit that generated support for the Charter in those early years.

IV

I have wanted to argue that the debate that led to the Canadian Charter of Rights was both broad and diffuse, that it dwelled especially on notions of equality and democratic participation, and that it used American experience consistently as a reference point. Now, one might object that, in interpreting rights debates, silences can be as important as the debate itself, and that inattention to these silences may distort the analysis. Just because property rights, for instance, were not widely discussed in the constitutional debate I have canvassed, for instance, does not mean that they were unimportant. In fact, it arguably means precisely the opposite. Property rights have been so successfully entrenched in the liberal mind that they have been effectively "organized out" of ordinary political discourse. It is as if questioning the sanctity of certain sorts of individual rights is essentially out of bounds in ordinary political discourse. In liberal politics, fundamental rights are meant to be protected from the "vicissitudes of politics," and constitutional courts understand their function first and foremost as patrolling the boundary between majoritarian politics and individual autonomy. As Ran Hirschl has demonstrated in detail in this volume and elsewhere,[41] a fundamental commitment to maintaining the boundary between individual rights and democratic politics remains essential to the courts' self-understanding in Canada and elsewhere.

Still, something did change in the way Canadians came to think about rights in the late 1960s and early 1970s that forged a connection between a growing sense of the importance of equality and democratic participation, on the one hand, and constitutional change, on the other. To give one final example: In his campaign for greater, and ultimately constitutional, protection for language rights, Pierre Trudeau developed two related lines of argument. In one version, Trudeau identified language rights as a species of individual rights that needed to be protected from majoritarian pressures. In this sense, linguistic minorities in Canada are like individuals who are silenced because they hold unpopular views. Both need protection from overbearing majorities that seek to enforce conformity. In the other version of the argument, however, Trudeau developed an egalitarian argument for language rights, claiming that French Canadians should be considered a marginalized minority within Canada to whom equality of respect and treatment are due. We now know that Trudeau's campaign for language rights largely succeeded in English

Canada. Moreover, we know that it succeeded because the egalitarian argument resonated (and continues to resonate) in the public mind. That is, most supporters of language rights think of language rights in the context of a larger concern for equality, and it is this fundamental commitment to equality that informs their support of minority linguistic rights. By the same token, however, English Canadians simply do not think of language rights as a species of individual rights. The notion, pressed vigorously by Trudeau, that an individual's right to speak the language of one's choice is like the right to read what one wants or speak one's mind freely simply did not take. In this sense, the 1968–71 debate I have described here was an important harbinger.[42]

There is one other silence in the early debate, however, that merits greater attention. Gerald Rosenberg has argued that, in the United States, the public discussion of civil rights in the 1950s and 1960s proceeded largely apart from, and in ignorance of, Supreme Court decisions.[43] The conventional wisdom among many court-watchers that pivotal cases like *Brown v. Board* defined and inspired public debate of civil rights is, according to Rosenberg, simply untrue. Public debate was attentive to the civil rights movement, not, by and large, to court decisions.[44] The same seems to have been true in Canada. What is most striking about the rights debate in Canada between 1968 and 1971 is the almost complete absence of references to courts and to judicial review. Thus, while the Winnipeg students quoted freely from U.S. court decisions in the material that accompanied their bill of rights, the bill itself said virtually nothing about how these rights were to be enforced—and what enforcement they did anticipate was purely internal to the school itself. The pages of *Maclean's* were full of discussions of rights, but here too the connection to judicial review was notably absent. (The one major exception to this rule was in the area of criminal rights, where, not unexpectedly, discussions of reform did indeed center on the role of courts.) Even Pierre Trudeau himself rarely spoke thematically about the judicial protection of rights. In fact, he almost never mentioned the place of courts in a fully constitutionalized—or as Canadians would say, "entrenched"—Charter of Rights in those early years, even when speaking to lawyers. And while it goes beyond the scope of this chapter, it is worthwhile noting that even law schools at the time were slow to recognize the growing importance of legal rights protection. Indeed, in the late 1960s there were only two law schools in Canada that offered a regular course devoted to the study of civil liberties, and both of these were taught by professors who actually opposed entrenchment. In this sense, the vocal Canadian critics of "judicial activism" may have a point when they refer to the introduction of constitutionalized judicial review and "activist" courts in Canada as a sort of "revolution."[45] In the pre-Charter years the public discussion of rights not only outpaced the discussion of judicial review, it was largely disconnected from it. It is small wonder, then, that in some eyes the new role for courts must indeed have seemed revolutionary.

But the disconnect between the pre-Charter discussion of rights and judicial review has had another, potentially more insidious, effect on Canadians' understanding of the Charter. For the critics of judicial activism, the fundamental problem with judicial review is that, in the words of the late Alexander Bickel, courts are "counter-majoritarian" and so lack democratic legitimacy.[46] When courts begin to "make policy" rather than "declare law," they cross the boundary into terrain where unelected bodies ought not to stray.[47] One of the problems with this view is that it depends on an extremely formal definition of what constitutes democracy. Democracy is, pure and simple, about being elected. What is ignored or abandoned by the definition is the possibility that a robust definition of democracy may also entail consideration of participation beyond voting, the treatment of citizens as equals, and the creation of what I earlier referred to as "proportionality" in politics. Yet these were precisely the sorts of questions and considerations that motivated the Canadians I have canvassed in this chapter to think in terms of rights and, ultimately, a Charter.

The rights debate in the period 1968–71 was all about democracy, but democracy understood in a way that included, but was not limited to, the process of elections. It is perhaps an artifact of this commitment to democratic principles writ large that to this day most Canadians remain relatively untroubled by the institution of judicial review, for they perhaps understand better than some of the Court's critics that judicial review is not necessarily and in every way incompatible with democratic principles.[48] And there is a delicious irony here as well. The critics of robust judicial review in Canada, as in the United States, like to argue that courts ought to be guided by the "original intentions" of the constitutional framers, for this is one of the few ways to ensure that present-day judges do not freelance by "reading in" their own views of what constitutes such potentially open-ended constitutional terms as freedom, equality, and security of the person. But if I am right that the debate about the meaning of the Charter began at the moment Pierre Trudeau introduced it to public debate in the late 1960s, then this period should be part of the historical record that informs our understanding of what was "originally" intended. And if I am right that the debate that led to the Charter borrowed liberally from the American civil rights movement in order to create an extended definition of democracy, cast in terms of equality and participation, then it would seem to follow that the "original" meaning of the Charter was broader, more capacious, and more hospitable to a "democratic" vision of the Charter than the critics of "judicial activism" would have us believe. Which is why history matters, and why a complete account of American influence on Canadian rights talk in the 1960s and 1970s would be a story worth telling.

Notes

1. Interim Report of the Greater Winnipeg Student Bill of Rights Committee," 17 March 1971. Available from Human Rights Documentation Centre, University of Ottawa.

2. Ibid.

3. The phrase is taken from the subtitle of Stephen Clarkson and Christina McCall, *Trudeau and Our Times,* vol. 1 (Toronto: McClelland and Steward, 1990).

4. Cited in Paul Sniderman, Joseph Fletcher, Peter Russell and Philip Tetlock, *The Clash of Rights: Liberty, Equality, and Legitimacy in Pluralist Democracy* (New Haven: Yale University Press, 1996), 3.

5. Some of the best accounts of Trudeau's Charter strategy include Kent R. Weaver, ed., *The Collapse of Canada?* (Washington, D.C.: Brookings Institution, 1992); Kenneth McRoberts, *English Canada and Quebec: Avoiding the Issue* (Toronto: York University, Robarts Centre for Canadian Studies, 1991); Andrew Cohen and J. L. Granatstein, eds., *Trudeau's Shadow: The Life and Legacy of Pierre Elliott Trudeau* (Toronto: Random House, 1998); Alan C. Cairns, *Charter versus Federalism: The Dilemmas of Constitutional Reform* (Montreal: McGill-Queen's University Press, 1992); and Michael Mandel, *The Charter of Rights and the Legalization of Politics in Canada* (Toronto: Wall and Thompson, 1989).

6. All circulation data are taken from *Canadian Advertising Rates and Data* (Toronto), various years.

7. See "Student Power," *Maclean's,* November 1968; "Give Students a Voice but Let's Not Let Student Power Spell Destruction," *Maclean's,* November 1968; and "How to Steer Clear of Professor Fossilhead," *Maclean's,* March 1969.

8. See, for instance, "Cheer Up, Girls, Help Is on the Way," *Maclean's,* January 1968; "Your Local Friendly Abortionist," *Maclean's,* May 1968; "Childbirth: 'Birthright'—for Girls in Trouble," *Maclean's,* May 1970; "I'm Married, Happy, and Went through Hell for a Legal Abortion," *Maclean's,* October 1970.

9. "The Hippie and the Cop," *Maclean's,* July 1968; "Arms and the Man: 1 and 2," *Maclean's,* July 1968; "Special Report: The Law on Trial in Canada," *Maclean's,* October 1968; "Ten Days Inside the Don Jail," *Maclean's,* November 1970.

10. "Cheer Up, Girls, Help Is on the Way," *Maclean's,* January 1968; "Where Were the Men?" *Maclean's,* December 1968; "Who Downgrades Women? Women," *Maclean's,* August 1968; "Jobs for Women: Put Up or Shut Up," *Maclean's,* February 1970.

11. "Our War," *Maclean's,* February 1968; Larry Zolf, "Boil Me No Melting Pots, Dream Me No Dreams," *Maclean's,* October 1968.

12. "Blair Fraser: Rene Levesque and the Separatists," *Maclean's,* July 1968.

13. Although there has been new interest shown in the history of "rights talk" in Canada, most of the new scholarship focuses on earlier periods. See, for instance, James W. St. G. Walker, *"Race," Rights, and the Law in the Supreme Court of Canada* (Waterloo, Ont.: Wilfrid Laurier University Press, 1997). A notable exception to my generalization is Cynthia Williams, "The Changing Nature of Citizen Rights," in *Constitutionalism, Citizenship, and Society in Canada,* ed. Alan Cairns and Cynthia Williams (Toronto: University of Toronto Press, 1985).

14. Michael Ignatieff, *The Rights Revolution* (Toronto: Anansi, 2000), 65.

15. See Robert C. Vipond, "Citizenship and the Charter of Rights: The Two Sides of Pierre Trudeau," *International Journal of Canadian Studies,* fall 1996, 179–92.

16. Federal-Provincial Constitutional Conference, *Proceedings* (Ottawa: Canadian Intergovernmental Conference Secretariat, February 1969).

17. Winnipeg Student Bill of Rights, citing a 1969 appeals court decision, *Breen v. Kahl.*

18. See "We Just Want to Do Our Thing," *Maclean's,* July 1968. See also "Some of the Best People Smoke Pot," *Maclean's,* January 1969; "The Happy Emergence of People Power," *Maclean's,* January 1969; and "My First Real Big-Time Campus Sit-In: We Win!" *Maclean's,* June 1970.

19. "The People of Canada vs. the Crown," *Maclean's,* October 1968.

20. Ignatieff, *Rights Revolution.*

21. "How Women in Power Keep Other Women Powerless," *Maclean's,* March 1970.

22. Ibid.

23. Judith N. Shklar, *American Citizenship: The Search for Inclusion* (Cambridge: Harvard University Press, 1991).

24. The book was subtitled "The Precocious Autobiography of a Quebec 'Terrorist.'" Translated by Joan Pinkham (New York: Monthly Review Press, 1970).

25. *New York Times Book Review,* 11 April 1971, 1.

26. *New York Times,* 6 April 1971, 37.

27. A. Alan Borovoy, *The New Anti-Liberals* (Toronto: Canadian Scholars' Press: 1999), xviii.

28. "Where Were the MEN When Canada Set Out to Find What Makes Life Tough for Its Women?" *Maclean's,* December 1968.

29. Pierre Trudeau, *Federalism and the French Canadians* (Toronto: Macmillan, 1968).

30. Ibid., 48.

31. Ignatieff, *Rights Revolution,* 65–66.

32. Ibid., 66.

33. Peter H. Russell, *Constitutional Odyssey: Can Canadians Be a Sovereign People?* (Toronto: University of Toronto Press, 1992).

34. Jerry Farber, "The Student as Nigger," typescript dated 4 March 1970.

35. John Hart Ely, *Democracy and Distrust* (Cambridge: Harvard University Press, 1980).

36. I am grateful to John Whyte for this notion.

37. *Maclean's,* November 1968.

38. Ibid.

39. *Maclean's,* January 1969. Italics in original.

40. Larry Zolf, "Boil Me No Melting Pots, Dream Me No Dreams," *Maclean's,* November 1968.

41. See chapter 3 of the present volume by Ran Hirschl, "Constitutional Rights Jurisprudence in Canada and the United States: Significant Convergence or Enduring Divergence?" See also, by the same author, "Negative Rights versus Positive Entitlements: A Comparative Study of Judicial Interpretations of Rights in an Emerging Neo-Liberal Economic Order," *Human Rights Quarterly* 22 (2000): 1060–98.

42. I have developed this argument in "Citizenship and the Charter of Rights: The Two Sides of Pierre Trudeau," *International Journal of Canadian Studies* 14 (1996): 179–92.

43. Gerald N. Rosenberg, *The Hollow Hope: Can Courts Bring About Social Change?* (Chicago: University of Chicago Press, 1991).

44. For a vigorous defense of the way in which courts did indeed shape the American agenda, see Morton J. Horwitz, *The Warren Court and the Pursuit of Justice* (New York: Hill and Wang, 1998).

45. F. L. Morton and Rainer Knopff, *The Charter Revolution and the Court Party* (Peterborough, Ont.: Broadview, 2000). Note, though, that by the 1970s, Canadians were already building a legal infrastructure that the Charter would build on and extend. On this point, see Charles Epp, *The Rights Revolution: Lawyers, Activists, and Supreme Courts in Comparative Perspective* (Chicago: University of Chicago Press, 1998), chaps. 9 and 10. Still, the point is that, in what I consider to be the formative period of Charter discussion, the role of courts was almost invisible.

46. Alexander Bickel, *The Least Dangerous Branch: The Supreme Court at the Bar of Politics* (Indianapolis: Bobbs-Merrill, 1962).

47. See, for instance, Morton and Knopff, *Charter Revolution,* 40–53. This theme—the countermajoritarian nature of judicial review—has received more than its share of journalistic treatment as well. See, for instance, Jeffrey Simpson *The Anxious Years: Politics in the Age of Mulroney and Chrétien* (Toronto: Lester, 1996), 87–93; idem, "After Fifteen Years, the Charter Has Sunk Deep Roots in Canada's Psyche," *Globe and*

Mail, 18 April 1997; and Kirk Makin, "Manu Judges Uneasy with Charter Powers," *Globe and Mail,* 22 December 1998. Generally, see Kent Roach, *The Supreme Court on Trial: Judicial Activism and Democracy* (Toronto: 2001), the first chapter of which contains several other examples of journalistic critiques of judicial activism.

48. Joseph F. Fletcher and Paul Howe, "Canadian Attitudes toward the Charter and the Courts in Comparative Perspective," *Choices* 6, no. 3 (May 2000).

CHAPTER 5

The Politics of Comparative Constitutional Law: Implications for Theories of Justice

Ronalda Murphy

Introduction

There are several traditional justifications for comparative law scholarship.[1] The main one is simply that any knowledge is good and potentially helpful. But then a question arises: helpful to whom? This raises the issue of focus in comparative scholarship. An inward focus involves exploring a jurisdiction to see whether what has been done elsewhere generates an argument for application or nonapplication of an approach to a legal issue in the examiner's jurisdiction. Or the focus can be outward; the examiner may be arguing for the application or nonapplication of his or her jurisdiction's approach to a legal issue in another jurisdiction. Either way, the effect is to deepen understanding about the place of law in society. Often a comparative analysis will yield the insight that the same laws do radically different things in different jurisdictions, while very different laws can end up doing similar things in different jurisdictions. The grid of sameness/difference seems implicit in the act of comparison, and this generates immediate and complex issues of methodology and politics. While issues of methodology and politics are present in all forms of legal scholarship, they are especially apparent and unavoidable in comparative law. Methodology involves deciding how to "do" comparative research. What is the legal issue being considered? How is that initial act of description of the issue decided upon, given that it will determine the scope of research? What are the units of comparison (e.g., legal topic, nation-state, legal family, etc.)? What are the sources of law being examined? These are standard—if unresolved—issues in comparative law.[2] Politics is directly implicated in the purpose and effect of comparative scholarship, and also indirectly in the choices made about methodology. The political aspect can be appreciated by the following questions: What motivates the research? What is the standard by which the ascriptions of "same" and "different" are reached? Is a common standard possible? What is the effect of a conclusion that something is the same or that it is different? What is the sameness or difference being measured in relation to? These are large and undertheorized issues in comparative law, but the dominant approach is one that understands the objective of the scholarship as value-neutral and descriptive:

> The basic methodological principle of all comparative law is that of *functionality*. From this basic principle stem all the other rules which determine the choice of laws to compare, the scope of the undertaking, the creation of a system of comparative law, and so on. Incomparables cannot usefully be compared, and in law the only things which are comparable are those which fulfill the same function. . . . The proposition rests on what every comparativist learns, namely that the legal system of every society faces essentially the same problems, and solves these problems by quite different means though often with very similar results. The question to which any comparativist study is devoted must be posed in purely functional terms; the problem must be stated without any reference to the concepts of one's own legal system.[3]

I reject the dominant conception of comparative law as driven by the value in exposing functional equivalencies among legal phenomena. Claims to a politics-free functional approach reveal rather than escape the politics implicit in methodological choices. First, the "functional" approach hides or denies the reality that comparative scholarship cannot escape using some "standard" of comparison. Second, functionalism asserts a false objective stance from which law is observed and described in different jurisdictions. Third, it diverts attention away from identifying *and* critically assessing the role of political forces in the purposes and effects of comparative law,[4] and, more significantly, the role of political forces *within* legal phenomena itself. Comparative constitutional scholarship should accommodate explicit recognition of constitutional law as a very important form of *political* expression and action within communities.

Comparative constitutional law is especially prone to this problem of avoidance of political context, because often the point of contrast is with respect to a particular constitutional right. Mainstream defenders of human rights justify them by reference to the fact that the rights are accorded to people because they are people, and not because they are the participants in any particular constitutional order. No one should be tortured regardless of what jurisdiction they live in. The arguments in support of the standard set of civil and political rights usually found in constitutions are also not tied to any given community's need or history regarding those rights. Everyone, everywhere, should have freedom of speech and association. In other words, constitutional rights are typically universalist claims. Yet constitutions are not universalist in this way; rather, they are the expressions of specific political decisions by a community that can be altered by legal (amendments) or nonlegal (revolutions) means. Increasingly, however, there is a burgeoning business in constitutional borrowings or transplantations of rights between jurisdictions, and comparative constitutional analysis can have a powerful impact. In this complicated interplay, it is especially important for theorists of rights and constitutional lawyers to address the way in which claims for recognition of specific constitutional rights may be consistent or inconsistent with claims to justice, of which rights are a key component.

Comparative constitutionalists should confront the manner in which history and politics are reflected in the choice of rights within a constitutional regime. I acknowledge this is problematic, as it reveals law and politics to have similar, and similarly unstable, foundations from which to offer communities the type of certainties that constitutions appear to promise. Yet I suggest that it can be liberating—rather than threatening—to accommodate the political contingency of specific legal concepts and events, including principles of constitutional law. Help from rights theorists is not always forthcoming, however, as they often fail to accommodate historical and political context, or they simply theorize it away. I argue that recognition of the political in the analysis of comparative information teaches a great deal about the role of law itself. A study in comparative constitutional law can suggest that legal theorists of rights need to address the way in which rights claims used at particular moments of legal time may *or may not* actually be progressive when considered from a standpoint of justice for all members of a community. To illustrate this point, in the last section I describe gender rights claims that arose during the period of constitutional negotiation over the transition in South Africa from apartheid to democracy, and I contrast these with similar developments in Canada and the United States at the same historical time period. I deploy the case study to support the claim that the most significant value of comparative law scholarship lies in its ability to force those trained in law to engage directly with political contingency in formulating theories of constitutionalism.

Comparative Law as Relational

Comparative law is always about relationships between jurisdictions. Engaging with comparative law is difficult in the same way that any personal relationship is difficult, and for similar reasons. First, you have to know your own self, and for a comparative lawyer that means the law of the jurisdiction in which one is trained, and this alone involves command of a demanding and constantly changing mass of information, even in specialized topics areas. Second, you have to know enough about the other jurisdiction to comprehend its legal system. That may involve learning another language, and certainly another legal vocabulary and procedural structure. Third, formal law-on-the-books may be only a superficial or even a misleading statement about the law of a community, so it is essential to figure out how the legal principles being studied operate in practice in the jurisdictions being examined. Fourth—and this is the most disquieting aspect of the endeavor—it turns out that learning the law is not likely to be adequate as a basis for making statements about the law in another jurisdiction. In my experience, it is necessary to turn to a variety of additional disciplines—economics, sociology, literature, politics, and so on—to accurately account for the law that you are comparing. At a minimum, historical context will be required.

A metaphor that captures the array of comparative projects while also revealing underappreciated political overtones is travel. There is a difference between going to live in a new part of the world for a period of time and spending a week at a Club Med resort; moreover, it is possible to live elsewhere and never be truly engaged with the place or its inhabitants. Gunter Frankenberg warns that: "As long as we understand foreign places as like or unlike home, we cannot fully begin to appreciate them, or ourselves. . . . Only close attention to detail—variety and heterogeneity—can prevent our leveling others in images taken from our vision of the order of the world."[5] He argues that it is possible to achieve genuine intellectual openness in comparative law, but only if there is tolerance of ambiguity and self-reflection:

> A comparative perspective can be *one* of the methods for questioning and distancing oneself from dominant legal consciousness. . . . Distance requires taking nothing for granted. . . . A liberating distance begins with investigating what the law does to us, to our world views, and to human relations. . . . I believe that the comparativist is in a privileged position by the very fact that she is confronted with different legal forms and categories, with alternative legal and non-legal strategies all of which may be more or less realistic, adequate, mystifying, reifying, alienating, and so forth.[6]

The ability to tolerate difference, to bother to understand it, to live with complexity, and to be open to the new and unexpected is certainly an ideal in travel and, in my view, in comparative law scholarship. Observance of the ideal can do more, however, than offer a antinecessitarian basis from which to critique "dominant legal consciousness" as asserted by Frankenberg. It can also generate insights concerning the significance of comparative law for legal theory generally and especially for theories of justice. I have noted that comparative constitutional scholarship is important in that it can accommodate explicit recognition of the significance of political, social, cultural, and historical factors in understanding legal phenomena. Good constitutional comparison projects acknowledge, rather than minimize, the impact of social and political factors on the choice of constitutional laws made in one jurisdiction. In the face of this jurisdictional contingency, however, analysts invariably confront the issue of how to account for similarity and difference between jurisdictions.

There are standard analytical responses to this dilemma. At one extreme, there is the celebration of difference, which involves the claim that comparative analysis will demonstrate that each jurisdiction is unique and inherently valid because it is simply the self-expression of that political community. This version of "legal culture" relativism asserts that we cannot properly evaluate any jurisdiction by reference to a common standard of "law," because there is no universal agreement on what "law" ought to be, and there is no common uncontested source of knowledge that would provide the basis of assessment between different jurisdictions. At the opposite extreme is the claim that a comparative approach is valid and important precisely because it allows us to discover that there is a common system of law that can be described and defended. This latter view is expressed in the standard texts of comparative law. For example, in what is seen as the "bible"[7] of comparative law, the authors Zweigert and Kötz state that legal comparativists are motivated by the "ultimate goal of discovering the truth," and the value of the enterprise is to "deepen our belief in the existence of a unitary sense of justice."[8]

Although the topic is law, we can readily appreciate this as a version of the familiar philosophical debate between the particular and the universal.[9] It can be a central preoccupation of comparative law, or really any comparative study. While it is easy enough to criticize extreme positions,[10] my point is that both extremes preclude cognizance of the relational character of comparative law and limit what can actually be learned from engaging in this scholarship. Those who highlight differences between jurisdictions do so in part to ensure each society is given due recognition for its legal development, which seems to be jeopardized by an emphasis on similarity, and even the traditional defenders of universalism in comparative law steer well clear of claiming for it what they see as explicitly morally loaded areas of law, such as law regulating the family or the succession of property.[11] This can be an acute problem for comparative constitutional law, with its paradoxical embrace of universally grounded rights in an moment of explicit political choice for any given jurisdiction. So it is interesting to consider how to deal with the "new" law of human rights in light of the tension between universalism and particularism, and to consider what impact comparative analysis of rights may have on legal theory generally.

The Implicit Universalism of Human Rights Claims

Fundamental rights or human rights theories are not conceptually tied to any one jurisdiction, and they are defended on the basis of their philosophical correctness. As a result, comparative law on rights is especially prone to universalism. In contrast, I argue that notwithstanding its intellectual heritage, constitutional law is largely subservient to outcomes of contests of political power, even when that lineage is adamantly denied by the articulators of the law in a society. I suspect that this may well be itself a universal phenomena, but in this chapter I support the claim by a case study of rights discourse based on my experience in the legal communities of the United States, Canada, and South Africa. As a preliminary matter, however, I need to explain the significance of my qualification "largely subservient" to political demands and constraints. I use this phrase to warn of several critical limits in my argument. I do not claim that law is the same as politics, or that law's legitimacy is utterly dependent upon the politics from which it springs forth. Law provides a different set of resources for social actors to deploy than does conventional political discourse, even if there is a very great overlap between the two discourses. Law—as a technique—also provides for constraints that may not exist in politics. If, for example, there is an explicit constitutional guarantee of property rights, it is impossible to argue that there is no legal protection for property rights. Until such a provision is changed or rendered useless by judicial interpretation, that argument is "not on." By contrast, nothing is off-limits in the political arena, at least in theory, and actual power—military or electoral—will determine most of the outcomes. But this is less true of legal claims. Law as a discourse operates to both widen and delimit what can be asserted.

What is peculiar about law is that the discourse of constitutional rights makes it very difficult to openly identify legal claims as politically motivated and their resolution as politically charged. It is particularly difficult to address the political aspects of legal claims within a specific jurisdiction. There is a obvious reason for this difficulty: while it is common enough for a specific jurisdiction to explain its choice of basic laws (a constitution or whatever is seen as the fundamental law) as reflecting the community's values, history, and cultural context, equally common is the tendency thereafter to eliminate the political context and treat those laws as universal, inherent, rational, or the product of objectively valid agreement.

Innumerable theories attempt to account for the power of law apart from its validity as a form of expression of a state (however that state is constituted). If law is the same as the state's expression of its will, there is no legitimacy crisis: one follows from or falls with the other. But much of the intellectual history of law is about finding another source of legitimation to account for instances when law is interpreted in a manner that is not necessarily consistent with the desire of a particular ruling body. Traditionally the sources were religious or naturalist, and today the preferred source of justification is a conception of human rights. Now there are many competing theories of rights, so there remains much to justify, and even if law is about rights, it is not obvious why unelected judges are the institutional form of rights protection. But leaving aside the institutionalization issue, the interesting question now becomes one of figuring out why "rights" are seen as capable of legitimating law.

To address this issue more directly, it is important to acknowledge the deepening relationship between democracy and law, and in particular, to consider the form of constitutionalized democracy. Constitutional law norms are defended as legitimate because they ensure the preconditions for democratic will-formation. After that, it becomes a debate about what those conditions are and what rights are needed to reflect commitment to them. Obviously, the right to participate in the conditions by which democratic will is formed and expressed are key, and even a skeletal claim like a right to vote requires some combined recognition of the norms of equality and autonomy. But what else? How thick or thin of an account of rights is justifiable and by what standard? In my view, this is where things get troubled. It is a mistake to believe that rights discourse or theory is capable of answering this question. But the mistake is not one of offending some notion of respect for different legal cultures. My point is rather that it is a mistake to assume we can tell in advance, simply by reference to rights theories, what version of rights is appropriate for any given jurisdiction. And comparative law reveals this error readily.

To illustrate this argument I contrast the emergence and impact of the race and class critique of women's claims for rights in Canada and the United States with the emergence of an independent women's movement in South Africa. The successful invocation of the political category of "women" in South Africa is fascinating, given that it occurs at a moment when the political and philosophical integrity of the category was thoroughly deconstructed in Canada and the United States at the same period of time. I argue that there were important objectives achieved by the deployment of the race and class critique within the Canadian and American women's movement, and the chief one is that it allowed for the necessary democratization of the movement and its practices. I dispute, however, that the race and class critiques represent a discourse of feminism that is inherently just or appropriate for any women's movement. I explain the emergence of the political category of "women" in South Africa at precisely the same period in an effort to illustrate the need to assess all discourses as sites of power and contestation, and to reserve assessment of them until they are understood in relation to the political context in which they emerge.

Case Study: Gender, Race, and Class

Law—including constitutional law—is one of many sites of power and emancipation, and as such is the target of many forms of political intervention.

Feminism engages in legal rights discourse on a variety of levels but draws upon the existence of a movement of women in support of specific claims. When dealing with constitutional rights, such as claims over whether free speech includes restrictions on sexual speech such as pornography, feminists are often divided. Some argue such expression is harmful to women, others say it is liberating. But either way, there is a political category "women." However, this category was destabilized by fundamental critiques of feminism as racist and classist in Canada and the United States in the 1980s. By the early 1990s, the critiques were pervasive, and this had significant implications for women's organizations and feminist theory in general, and rights theories in particular. Angela Davis's famous statement reported in 1989 in a Canadian grassroots publication is symbolic of the overall direction of the critique: "At the risk of being controversial, in the 1990's all 'white' women's organizations should strive to make themselves obsolete."[12] In this section I summarize my examination of the history of the emergence of the race and class critiques of the women's movement in Canada.[13] I argue that the significance of the discourse lies in its political effects: it successfully contested exclusionary practices and accounts of feminism. In both Canada and the United States, it was and remains a progressive intervention that aims to secure democratization in the political movements of women and in the theories of feminism they employ in responding to the conditions of their lives. In this chapter I use mostly Canadian sources to illustrate my point, since these are less well known and merit attention. In both Canada and the United States, however, the race and class critique of gender as a category of thought and organization followed a common trajectory.

I then turn to South Africa. My intent here is to document the early 1990s phenomena of the emergence of an independent "women's" movement. Such a development is surprising in light of the opposite trend in Canada and the United States. But there is an explanation of this development that once again points to the need to assess theories and practices about rights—in this instance, gender rights—as part of a larger social context. In South Africa, there were very good reasons to support the political category of "women," and these relate to the near-hegemonic status of race and class narratives in both apartheid and its opposition movements. The decision to create a distinct women's movement in the early 1990s to press for constitutional rights and other forms of response to deprivation of needs cannot be judged by reference to whether it would make sense to do that in Canada or the United States at the same period of time. It is thus my view that insistence in Canada and the United States on the theoretical and strategic coherence of "women's" rights in the early 1990s had very different effects (overwhelmingly negative) than the same insistence in South Africa at the same period of time (overwhelmingly positive). My point is that you cannot understand women's rights discourses without situating them historically, and certainly it would be unwise to judge them without assessing their political purpose and effect.

The Canadian Context

The National Action Committee on the Status of Women (NAC) is the major institutional site of feminism in Canada. A quick review of NAC's history provides a context within which to situate the basic features of the Canadian women's movement.[14] NAC reflected and produced a feminist discourse in which gender was identified as *the* determinative category of social thought and action pertaining to the status of women. This discourse was extremely effective during NAC's first decade and, given NAC's orientation to the state, it successfully opposed the discourses of progressive conservatism and liberalism in the male-dominated Canadian political milieu. Race and class had no real existence as discourses within the movement in that first decade. There were sporadic references to "visible minority women."[15] For many years the institutional women's movement simply did not recognize racism as an important issue, while class also took a backseat to dominant concerns such as violence, pension reform, constitutional reform, sexuality, and reproductive issues. By the time the race and class critique of feminism gained momentum in NAC, it had already succeeded in the grass-roots women's movement. There are many illustrations of the noninstitutional deployment of the race and class debate, and in other work I trace this as well.[16] It is sufficient here, however, to explain the logic of the critique.

The race and class discourses were launched in a cultural context: an emerging, affirmative, culturewide embrace of the discourse of "identity" based on sexual orientation, national origin, language, and so on. Identity politics is an extremely powerful challenge to the liberal state's denial of difference, and while feminism in the United States and Canada was never simply or wholly liberal, it was extremely resistant to differences between women in the context of the feminist project. We can appreciate this by recalling feminist claims made in the late 1970s and early 1980s. In the nascent days of the development of feminist theory, a central thesis was that feminism differed from socialism in its rejection of class as the dominant narrative, and differed from liberalism in its rejection of individualism as the dominant principle. In other words, feminism began with an embrace of the idea of the group in opposition to the individual, and with a declaration of the inadequacy of forms of difference other than gender for the purposes of explaining disadvantage among women. When women of color began to press their claims, there was an unarticulated resentment of them by white women, because their critique and arguments necessitated a return to a form of analytical reference in which "gender" is not exclusive. For a lengthy period of time, the battle to protect and maintain the movement's gender focus was the most important battle waged in the women's movement. To the movement's white, middle-class leaders it seemed harsh to have to give up the focus that had finally won the movement credibility in its contest with their oppressors—namely, white men and the state.

But the struggles waged by white women feminists was never the struggle of aboriginal women or women of color. When these latter women found themselves being constituted by a discourse of gender exclusivity, it was, from their perspective, yet another form of oppressive treatment—one that they would be powerless to contest until they created and deployed a counternarrative challenging the legitimacy of the basic claims of the women's movement. One required action was to simply point out how white feminists either ignored women of color and aboriginal women altogether or, even worse, claimed to speak on their behalf without ever having consulted with them. This criticism triggered panic and guilt within the movement and was met with the rhetoric of inclusion and a concession that major women's groups—such as NAC—had failed to accurately "represent" the interests of nonwhite women. On this level were the many attempts to manage the race and class critique by ensuring that more (any) women of color and aboriginal women were invited to join the movement. There was as of yet almost no sense that the content of the movement's agenda for the improvement of the status of women would also have to change. This need would be no more than dimly perceived for several years. For a lengthy period of time these challenges to the movement were managed in a therapeutic fashion with workshops on "unlearning racism" and through the personal confessions of limited knowledge and perspective of individual white women.

Eventually there were two main responses in the Canadian women's movement to the race and class critique. First and foremost, the criticism was conceptualized as a form of moral condemnation to which feminists responded defensively by recitation of various initiatives undertaken by the women's movement that "demonstrated" an absence of racism or classism. Accordingly, the first response to the race and class critique was to create and disseminate a historical résumé of the movement's inclusionary endeavors. To make this plausible it was essential to devote more attention to more groups. I will call this the "inclusionary response" to the race and class critique, where the goal is to ensure that everyone's story of struggle is told. A subsequent response, however, proved more powerful. Now dominant, this response interpreted the race and class critique as primarily directed at theory itself. The challenge is to the philosophical integrity of the concept of "women" for its inability to represent women who are not white or financially secure, for example. Feminist theory was recast in terms that avoided "essentializing" the "nature" of the "woman." The object was to eliminate the practice of positing as the "universal woman" a woman in fact representative of only a particular community of women: the white, educated middle class. Perhaps the most brilliant exposition of this critique was Elizabeth Spelman's *Inessential Woman: Problems of Exclusion in Feminist Thought.*[17] Although reconceiving feminism in antiessentialist terms is laudable, it can have the perverse effect of camouflaging the "political" element of the race and class critique as it emerged, and can redirect political contests into debates over how to ensure the correct articulation of philosophy. The point is not that the philosophical responses to the race and class critiques have subverted the political power of these critiques; they have not. The point is that if we understand the matter as political, and not simply philosophical or personal, we can begin to understand why there are times when race and class are not deployed by women in a position to advance them.

I interpret the race and class critique as one primarily effective in securing participation in a movement that was more than merely frequently racist and classist, but one that, through the rhetoric of representation, claimed to speak on the behalf of *all* women. The feminist movement's response categorizes racism and classism as problems to be solved; and that the solution is a matter of finding a way to continue telling the truth about women, but all women. It remains, then, a question of subjectivity, a belief in the political power of telling the truth about women and now also about "black women" and "aboriginal women" and "disabled women" and "women of color." While I do not disparage this analysis, I do believe that it overlooks the most powerful implication of these events. I believe that race and class challenges have been "managed" in this way partly because feminists have failed to fully conceptualize the discourses themselves as locations of power and thus subject to democratic critique. It is critical that we understand the discourses of race and class as politically strategic sites of democratic contestation *against* the forms of power wielded by the discourse of feminism that had become hegemonic and institutionalized. While feminism is certainly not the most powerful source of the oppression facing those contesting racism and classism, it is one such source nonetheless.

The discourse of identity of race and class deployed against the feminist movement successfully undermined both the feminist movement's foundation of authenticity and forced it to understand that legitimacy is not a given, but rather something to be achieved. I think these developments in feminist politics are extremely positive: necessary advances in feminism and democracy alike. But can we conclude from this history that the emerging discourse of a Canadian or American feminism that incorporates a simultaneous opposition to all forms of oppression is inherently progressive? Have we solved the analytical and personal problems to such an extent that we can now articulate this new feminism as *the* universal feminism of the future? I argue that this feminism is not inherently progressive in the way that activists and theorists desire. It is contextually progressive: in Canada and the United States, at this moment. However, it may not operate progressively everywhere—a fact that disrupts feminism's continuing tendency towards "truth" and "subjectivity" as a basis for legitimacy.

I consider events in South African feminism in order to study the way in which discourses of race, class, and gender operated in opposition to apartheid and in the subsequent creation of a democratic state. I conclude that the discourses of race and class were poised to smother the emerging oppositional narratives of South African women, whose gender analysis did not suffer from the endemic exclusionary practices found in North American feminist work. The progressive struggle for justice for women in South Africa presents a marked counternarrative to the account of feminism in the United States and Canada, especially in the legal arena. From the period of time beginning immediately before the successful challenge of apartheid to the period of the creation of an interim constitutional democracy for the transition to a fully legitimate state, the most effective oppositional discourse deployed by South African women to subvert the existing relations of power was one that deliberately invoked the category of "women." South African women did not opt for this gender discourse because they were white; indeed, they were overwhelmingly not. Nor were they were merely trailing a few years behind the North American women's movement, as was often assumed during this period. Rather, South African women used the category of "women" because it was effective against the very precise and historically conditioned discourses of those who defended apartheid and those who opposed it. A narrative in which race, class, and gender were equivalent would have simply failed to disrupt the power relationships that were impairing the ability of women in South Africa to be actors in a participatory democracy. In the next section I support my argument by briefly reviewing the following: women's distinctive struggles in South African history, the incendiary race-class debate in popular political movements and in academic discourse in South Africa, and the emergence of the Women's National Coalition (WNC) in the period of transition from apartheid to democracy.[18]

The South African Context

Historical Struggles. The history of women's movements in South Africa during apartheid is detailed and complex, but there is no debate over the absence of a feminist consciousness in the various struggles in which women in South Africa were engaged.[19] Race mattered more than anything else and competed only with class as the major conceptual basis upon which all women of South

Africa understood their realities. Perhaps in no place on earth is the utter paucity of the claim of female "sisterhood" more readily revealed. This is not, however, to say that black women did not successfully organize with sympathetic white women, as indeed they have done at significant moments in South African history. It is to claim that when they did, it was *not* in the name of sisterhood. The three main episodes of women's historical movements involve resistance to the apartheid legal system, specifically against laws that regulated the vote, the sale of beer, and passes (documents used to restrict movement of people).

The voting struggle was resolved in racist terms: white women eventually obtained it, but they did so because granting it to them served to dilute the still-existing black male vote in one region of the country (subsequently taken away). But even the struggle for voting rights by white women was not feminist. The "Beer Protests" are an infamous period in South African history, and this was a struggle of black women. While women's activities in the early 1900s were controlled by the decision-making authority vested in men in traditional societies,[20] making money from the sale of beer represented an autonomous source of income for women. The white South African government made the production or consumption of beer illegal, unless done in the newly constructed beer halls—called canteens—that were owned by white municipalities. Beer protests were well-known in South Africa, and they drew the attention of political and social historians. However, until the late 1980s, the gendered nature of the protests was not appreciated. Helen Bradford, writing from a feminist perspective, introduced her nuanced analysis of the history of a specific set of protests with the following statement: "Patriarchal relations have frequently been collapsed into those of class exploitation and national opposition—and in the process, the resistance of black women against brewing restrictions has been at best distorted and at worst hidden from history."[21]

The most clearly transformative political action undertaken by women under apartheid involved resistance to "pass laws."[22] "Passes" in South Africa were documents that determined whether and on what terms black people could either live or work in areas designated exclusively for whites. It was African women who were most associated with the protests of the pass laws in South Africa. The resistance of these women is historically significant, because their concerted protests marked the first mass action against apartheid since the ANC (originally called the South African Native National Conference) was formed in 1912. Neither the ANC nor the African People's Organization allowed women to be admitted to full membership.[23] Since women were not permitted to join the organizations as members, they formed autonomous groups. The early enforcement of pass laws against women produced arrests (when women did not produce their passes or burned them), and this provided the occasion for "open defiance" of the laws by women. In her analysis of this period of challenge by women, Cheryl Walker concludes that these protests had little if anything to do with any modern notion of women's rights:

> The anti-pass campaign of 1913/14 had nothing to do with the women's right's movement then rocking the western world and to which white South African suffragists looked. It can in fact be argued that in defying the law as vociferously as they had, African women were looking back to a cultural tradition that allowed women a great deal more independence and authority than western society considered either "natural" or "respectable" at the time.[24]

The most important lesson, Walker argues, that women drew from the antipass campaign was one that is best understood within notions of black nationalist thinking.[25]

With victory of the National Party in 1948, apartheid took a new, more draconian form, and restricting the movement of black people became a priority. The antipass campaigns of the later period were unique in that they developed within a national movement to challenge the entire apartheid system (at this time the resistance movement was generally well-organized as the Congress Alliance but was restricted to passive and nonviolent methods), but they were eventually spearheaded by women's organizations. The ANC Women's League was formed, a Women's Charter was formulated, and the Federation of South African Women (ANCWL) was launched in the 1950s. While the women's antipass campaigns were incredible, they were not conceptualized as protests for women; they were clearly part of the larger struggle by many organizations against apartheid.[26] In conclusion, South African history involves extraordinary periods of protest by women but not as part of a women's movement.

Race and Class Narratives in South Africa. The dominance of the race- and class-based accounts of apartheid can hardly be overstated. Gender was not ignored as much as theorized to be either subsumed within the liberation struggle or understood to simply be unimportant as a political issue until after the liberation struggle was won. The liberation heroines could advocate gender issues ultimately because they had spent their lives sacrificing for the nationalist and liberationist struggles. The gradual emergence of a discourse on gender was not primarily a function of the interventions of a few prominent women; rather, women on the ground were beginning to question the wisdom of a strategy that places gender-specific demands at the bottom of the hierarchy. In this section I explore the fact that "[p]olitical organization of women in South Africa has always been (and still is) overshadowed by what are considered to be the central, most important issues—race and economics."[27]

The ANC took tentative steps while in exile to acknowledge the growing pressure to talk about women's issues, and these included the passage of resolutions committing the organization to paying attention to women. Previously, it had been "almost taboo to talk about women's emancipation."[28] In debates among ANC members, "[i]t was felt that two aspects affecting women, race and class oppression, were being dealt with while the other one of patriarchy was being overlooked."[29] In 1987, one commentator observed that over a seventy-five-year period, "the women's question has moved through distinct phases where the issue was not being considered at all, to the contemporary period where women are beginning to articulate women's demands as part of the national political struggle."[30] Others also noted that "[g]ender oppression has been, and continues to be, an issue of secondary or little importance in the political life of South Africa."[31]

Within the various working-class movements and union activities in the late 1980s, the gender issue was finally being addressed.[32] The Congress of South African Trade Union (COSATU) held its first conference in 1988, and a Women's Forum was formed. However, it is critical to note that the women's issue was formulated entirely within a class struggle paradigm. In the Mass Democratic Movement (an alliance of powerful antiapartheid organizations) a serious attempt was made in 1987 to develop a national women's group, but the state of emergency imposed extreme and disabling restrictions on political organizations, and none were able to function adequately.

In 1990 the ANC held the now famous Malibongwe Conference in Amsterdam, on gender issues.[33] The Malibongwe meeting is described as a "watershed"[34] in the history of women in South Africa, and in the ANC in particular, because at it women's concerns were "legitimated as political issues to be addressed within the process of national liberation."[35] While this is accurate, the analysis offered to delegates at the Malibongwe Conference nonetheless remained firmly caught within the hegemonic narratives of race and class.[36]

In May 1990 the ANC leadership issued a document entitled "Statement on the Emancipation of Women in South Africa."[37] In this important document the ANC states that it realizes that in its commitment to eradicate racism, oppression, and exploitation in South Africa, it "cannot fail to address also the question of the emancipation of women."[38] After articulating its understanding of the oppression that women endure in South Africa and committing to rid itself of sexist patterns and practices, the ANC called on its Women's League to initiate a campaign for a "Charter of Women's Rights" that would be designed to "elaborate and reinforce our new constitution."[39] The mobilizing effects of such a campaign were touted as one way to redress the lack of full participation of women in the liberation movement's operations. Although careful to state that men must not be excluded from the process, and after noting the acute exploitation of African women, the statement asserts that the Charter for Women's Rights should "draw in and represent the wishes of women from all sections of South African society, and as such be an important step in preparing over half the population for full citizenship and equality."[40]

The idea of a Women's Charter was workshopped within the ANCWL when the league officially relaunched in South Africa on 9 August 1990. Some women began to assert that the role of the women's organization simply had to change from being primarily absorbed with the liberation movement if gender were to successfully be on the negotiating table in the processes governing the transition to democracy. Equally important was the necessity of challenging the use of conceptual frameworks that on the one level seem progressive (because they acknowledge the codetermination of factors such as race, class, and gender), but in the context of South Africa serve to once again ignore the gender aspect of women's worlds. The value of developing a more gender-oriented approach was conceptualized as politically useful, because it would widen the support base for liberation movements. Shireen Hassim argued, for example, that

> [w]ithin women's organizations, analysis of patriarchy has not extended beyond the notion of triple oppression with its concomitant focus on the needs of black working class women. . . . Broadening the scope of politics to include these issues [control over women's bodies, women's labor, sexuality, and the social legitimation of violence against women] would mean that the ANCWL can begin to appeal to a much wider constituency, not merely those that suffer "triple oppression."[41]

The ANCWL committed itself to organizing a "Charter for Women," and at the foundation meeting on 30 September 1991, the ANCWL hosted delegates from thirty organizations to launch a campaign in support of it. There was express acknowledgment that "the process of developing the Women's Charter is as important as the product itself."[42] In addition to the launch of the Women's Charter, efforts began to ensure that women would be involved in the process of negotiation for the transition to democracy.[43] While this merits its own analysis, in this next section I discuss only briefly the Women's National Coalition (WNC).

The Women's National Coalition

On 25 April 1992 the WNC was formally established by national women's organizations and eight regional and local coalitions of women.[44] Frene Ginwala, the ANC activist who went on to become the convener of the WNC, addressed the organizations directly on the issue of divisions among women in South Africa and articulated a vision of the movement as able to acknowledge differences but still work together to create unity among women. Ginwala explained:

> Our common past, over these last four decades especially, is of separation; divided by race, ethnicity, language, by poverty and privilege; divisions entrenched in law and sanctified by practice. These we have shared as South Africans, men, women and children alike. But we have also been divided as women, isolating ourselves in separate struggles and because the over-arching divisions in our society have placed women in unequal power relations with each other. . . . ALL this is part of our history, but though we cannot forget, we do not have to be overcome by the past. We are all the products of history, but each of us can choose whether or not to become its victims. Our past can become the reason for retaining our divisions, or can be something we move beyond as we go forward together. That is our choice. Our presence here today indicates, that despite the many things past and present that divide us, women are anxious to work together for a common future.[45]

This discourse of unity is not valid because "unity" is the best philosophical position; quite the contrary, it is valid because it reflects a strategic understanding that the dominant justice narratives of race and class oppression served to silence women. The challenge of the WNC was to break that silence in a politically effective manner. Although the regions in South Africa vary widely in almost every conceivable dimension, the attitude of unity was sustained throughout the life of the WNC.[46]

The Final Report of the WNC offers the following assessment of the positive features of their campaign:

> The Coalition's Charter Campaign stimulated public awareness about and promoted considerable debate on women's issues. It gave women the opportunity to act together to begin to change their lives. The Campaign unified women, both within and outside established organizational structures, on issues that affected their lives. It constituted a unified women's movement where none had existed before. The Charter which was the product of this unity is more than an important political document. It is a symbol that speaks about women's empowerment and their desire to take an active role in transforming their lives.[47]

The WNC, then, can be seen as a success. It was a fully representative body that managed to reach out to a wide cross-section of South African society. It sustained its commitment to democratic, grass-roots determination of what women's needs and rights are, and it functioned as a political mechanism for women to ensure some of those issues were dealt with in accordance with women's articulated demands.[48] By the end of the campaign, there were over ninety-two national groups and thirteen regional coalitions supporting the WNC. It was the most representative women's group ever formed in South Africa, and the single strand that connected the women was a belief in the importance of their united pressure on the incredibly fast-paced political process that was spinning wildly away from all women in South Africa.[49]

Conclusion to the Case Study: Gender, Race, and Class

Apartheid destroyed the lives of people, and it did so overwhelmingly on the basis of their race and their class. Apartheid deployed narratives of difference based on race, and it was opposed primarily by a narrative of justice that argued against the recourse to racial categories at all. Apartheid constantly denied its economic dimension, while the opposition movements constantly stressed the exploitation of the poor and working classes. Gender and "women" were chosen concepts; they were not forced on the women's movement by advocates of Western feminism. Moreover, the use of "women" as both a mobilizing and a conceptual framework was completely intelligible from the perspective of politics in South Africa. It was never the case that the women involved in politics in South Africa did not appreciate the intersection of race, class, and sex. But the dominance of race and class narratives exhausted all the space for justice, and the invocation of the concept of "triple oppression" was of little value unless gender first achieved some political content. The emergence of the WNC reflects both a decision to develop a concept of gender specificity and the political unity of organizing around the notion of "women." But most significantly, it reflects the need to locate these developments squarely within their precise historical context before any judgment about their philosophical value is made. Organizing around gender, with a unifying call to women, was not merely strategically correct for women in South Africa, it was the only course of action that would ensure representativity in the women's movement.

I hope to have demonstrated that the South Africa women's movement articulated a gender politics independent of the dominant theories of race and class politics. When faced with this contradiction, the temptation is to figure out which approach is correct, or to try and synthesize the two approaches to come up with a new and better truth. But justice claims may not be about developing a "true" or universally valid discourse of rights; I believe they are primarily about contesting unequal distributions of power. The temptation to choose between these diverse models of feminism and find the one that tells more "truth" about women's subjectivity is an understandable desire, but it has often come at the expense of a more concrete examination of why women develop the rights discourses that they do, and how they secure participation through the deployment of different ones in different locations.

Conclusion

In our world it is quite simple to ascertain what "rights" exist in different parts of the world. Comparative constitutional analysis can help disseminate that information. But it is important to locate the embrace of comparative analysis within wider debates about the role of law generally. I do not offer an argument in this chapter that would "legitimate" law per se. I understand the desire for "law" to carry the burden of legitimating power. My point is that one cannot assume that "rights" are inherently capable of justice. It depends. It is necessary to assess whether rights claims are being deployed to advance or diminish democratic possibilities within a political community. My concern is that contemporary preoccupation with justification and legitimacy of all law tends toward the construction of rights as being "inherently" good and thus hard to criticize. The immunity of rights from politics (which is not understood as delivering inherent goodness as a product) can actually make those additional factors appear to be "outside" the rights discourse, and thus unavailable. This happens because of the dominance of universalist or abstract justification for rights generally. It also occurs because political communities tend to produce narratives about their moment of self-constitution that hide the political compromises that reflect the impact of history, power, and indeed nonreason in discourse about constitutional rights.

The case study I have discussed is but one illustration of a larger phenomena. I believe that analysis of the origin of recognized rights in particular constitutions reveals that it is impossible to conclude rights are chosen out of a recognition of their "inherent" quality or their universalism. Rather, they appear in an already charged political context. I am interested in this slippage from the contextual to the universal, and a comparative law analysis helps to identify the phenomena while suggesting more radically that little in law is universal, objective, or the product of reasoned agreement. While I do not address these points in this paper, comparative law also suggests the significance of political and disturbingly contingent factors such as mistakes and individual personalities in understanding why specific rights claims achieve recognition in a particular community.[50] Finally, it suggests that if law continues to be a major site of the contestation of power in different societies, rights claims must also be forms of struggle, and ought not to be idealized as the antithesis of power itself.

Notes

The author would like to thank Stephen Newman for his excellent editorial comments, and the participants at the Legal Theory Workshop at McGill Law School for their encouraging feedback on an earlier version of this essay. The student assistance of Elaine Craig in preparing the text for publication is gratefully acknowledged.

1. See, for example, Basil Markesinis, *Foreign Law and Comparative Methodology: A Subject and a Thesis* (Oxford: Hart Publishing, 1997), 45. He identifies the aims of comparativists as "to increase mutual understanding; to destroy artificial barriers; to promote reconsideration of sacred doctrines; to encourage the bringing together of lawyers with common interests."

2. Methodology of comparative law occupies the third chapter of Konrad Zweigert and Hein Kötz, *An Introduction to Comparative Law,* trans. Tony Weir, 3d ed. (Oxford: Clarendon Press, 1998). The chapter begins with a warning that these questions of methodology may not be capable of resolution at all.

3. Ibid., 34.

4. See ibid., 25, where the authors point to improvements in economic efficiency as one of the purposes and effects of comparative law.

5.Gunter Frankenberg, "Critical Comparisons: Re-thinking Comparative Law," *Harv. Int'l. L. J.* 26 (1985): 411, reprinted in *Comparative Constitutional Law,* ed. Vicki C. Jackson and Mark Tushnet (New York: Foundation Press, 1999), 150–52.

6. Ibid.

7. The reference is made by Basil Markesinis in *Always on the Same Path: Essays on Foreign Law and Comparative Methodology* (Oxford and Portland, Ore.: Hart Publishing, 2001), 37.

8. Zweigert and Kötz, *Introduction to Comparative Law,* 3.

9. Ernesto LaClau, "Universalism, Particularism and the Question of Identity," in his *Emancipations* (London: Verso, 1996).

10. Frankenberg, "Critical Comparisons," offers a provocative but thoughtful analysis of scholars who adopt one extreme or the other:

> The dilemma of understanding foreign (legal) cultures and of transcending the domestic (legal) culture can neither be resolved by "going rational" nor by "going native." The rigorous rationalist who relies on conceptual or evolutionary functional universals is prone to give her world-view and norms, her language and biases only a different label. In the end, she may bring home from her comparative enterprise nothing but dead facts and living errors, the progeny of ethnocentrism. The rigorous relativist who naively deludes herself into believing that cultural baggage and identities can be dropped at will, is prone to oscillate between ventriloquism and mystification. As a cultural ventriloquist she would reproduce ethnocentrism under the guise of a pseudo-authentic understanding. As a cultural immigrant she might over-identify with the mystified new way and thereby be unable or unwilling to relate anything her sympathetic eye happens upon in travel to what she learns at home. (151)

11. Cf. Zweigert and Kötz, *Introduction to Comparative Law,* 40.

12. Angela Davis, "International: Consciously Interrupting Oppression," *Kinesis* (British Columbia), May 1989, 18–19 (on file with the author).

13. I fully document the history of the discourse of race and class in the Canadian women's movement as reflected in a variety of locations between 1970 and 1990 in my doctoral thesis, "Theories of Justice: A Contextual Approach" (J.S.D. thesis, Harvard University, 1998). For an account of the South African case more detailed than was possible within the confines of the present essay, see my contribution to *Women, Politics, and Constitutional Change,* ed. Alexander Dobrowolsky and Vivien Hart (Palgrave Press, forthcoming).

14. I draw on Jill Vickers, *Politics As If Women Mattered: A Political Analysis of the National Action Committee on the Status of Women* (Toronto: University of Toronto Press, 1993) and my own review of available NAC resolutions and documents over a twenty-year period, 1970–90.

15. On the virtual invisibility of women of color, immigrant women, women with disabilities, poor women, and lesbians in NAC's first decade, see Anne Molgat, *An Action That Will Not be Allowed to Subside: NAC's First Twenty Years* (National Action Committee on the Status of Women, 1982), 2.

16. Ronalda Murphy, review of available NAC resolutions and documents from 1970 to 1990.

17. Elizabeth V. Spelman, *Inessential Woman: Problems of Exclusion in Feminist Thought* (Boston: Beacon Press, 1988).

18. Excellent treatments on the history of women's political activity in South Africa include the following: Belinda Bozolli, *Women of Phokeng: Consciousness, Life Strategy, and Migrancy in South Africa, 1900–1983* (written with the assistance of Mmanantho Nkotsoe) (Johannesburg: Raven Press, 1991); Cheryl Walker, "The Women's Suffrage Movement," in *Women and Gender in South Africa to 1945,* ed. Cheryl Walker (Cape Town: David Philip Publishers, 1990), 313; Walker, *Women and Resistance in South Africa,* 2d ed. (Capetown: David Philip Publishers, 1991); Shireen Hassim, "Family, Motherhood, and Zulu Nationalism: The Politics of the Inkatha Women's Brigade," *Feminist Review* 1, no. 43 (spring 1993); Jo Beall et al., "'A Bit on the Side'?: Gender Struggles in the Politics of Transformation in South Africa," *Feminist Review* 33 (summer 1989); Christina Murray and Catherine O'Regan, "Putting Women into the Constitution," in *Putting Women on the Agenda,* ed. Susan Bazilli (Cape Town: Raven Press, 1991), 33–55; Jacklyn Cock, *Women and War in South Africa* (Cleveland, Ohio: Pilgrim Press, 1993).

19. Walker, *Women and Gender in South Africa,* 343.

20. See Helen Bradford, "'We are now men': Women's Beer Protests in the Natal Countryside, 1929," in Belinda Bozolli, ed., *Class, Community and Conflict: South African Perspectives* (Johannesburg: Raven, 1987), 295–296.

21. Ibid., 292–293.

22. Julia Wells and Cheryl Walker both examine the pass law issue and provide excellent summaries of the history on which I draw in this section. They come to dif-

ferent accounts of the implications for feminism, however. See Wells, *We Now Demand! The History of Women's Resistance to Pass Laws in South Africa* (Johannesburg: Witwatersrand University, 1993) and Walker, *Women and Resistance in South Africa.*

23. Walker, *Women and Resistance in South Africa,* 34.

24. Ibid., 32.

25.Ibid.

26. Lillian Ngoyi, a highly regarded South African activist, stated in 1959: "It is important to understand that the struggle against passes is controlled by the African National Congress. The struggle of women is merely part of the general struggle for the African people." Quoted in Walker, *Women and Resistance in South Africa,* 220.

27. Murray and O'Regan, "Putting Women into the Constitution."

28. Pethu Serote, "National Liberation Equals Women's Emancipation: A Myth Totally Exploded," *Agenda: A Journal about Women and Gender* 10 (1991): 5.

29. Mavivi Manzini, "Women's Liberation and the Struggle for National Liberation" (LL.M. thesis, ISS, The Hague, 1998), 100.

30. Leila Patel, "South African Women's Struggles in the 1980s," *Agenda: A Journal about Women and Gender* 2 (1988): 34, 28–35.

31. Julia Segar and Caroline White, "Constructing Gender: Discrimination and the Law in South Africa," *Agenda: A Journal about Women and Gender* 1 (1987): 95, 95–112.

32. Gay Seidman, "No Freedom Without the Women: Mobilization and Gender in South Africa, 1970–1992," *Signs: Journal of Women in Culture and Society* 18, no. 2 (winter 1993): 291–309.

33. See the discussion of this event in Bridget Mabandla, "Protecting Women's Rights and Promoting Gender Equality in a Democratic Non-Racial and Non-Sexist South Africa," paper presented at the Lawyers for Human Rights International Conference, Amsterdam, 23–25 November 1990.

34. Andrew Charman et al., "The Politics of Gender: Negotiating Liberation," *Transformations* 15 (1991): 40–64, 41.

35. Memo dated 20 January 1990 summarizing the conference and the resolutions that were passed. (On file with the author.)

36. Charman, "The Politics of Gender," 40–64.

37. National Executive Committee of the African National Congress, *Statement of the National Executive Committee of the African National Congress on the Emancipation of Women in South Africa* (May 1990). (On file with the author.)

38. Ibid., 1

39. Ibid., 4.

40. Ibid.

41. Shireen Hassim, "From Handmaiden to Comrade: The ANCWL and the Question of Political Power," paper presented at the Lawyers for Human Rights Conference: Putting Women on the Agenda, Johannesburg, 22–23 November 1990), 5. (On file with the author.)

42. Women's Charter Campaign, "Motivation" (Johannesburg, 1991), 1. (On file with the author.)

43. A Gender Advisory Committee was set up to advise on the "gender implications" of CODESA's structures and decisions after much public and political pressure by women. CODESA was the Conference of a Democratic South Africa and existed in two incarnations during the early 1990s. For history and assessment of the effects of the Gender Advisory Committee, see Cathi Albertyn, "Women and the Transition to Democracy," in *Gender and the New South African Legal Order*, ed. Christina Murray (Capetown: Rustica Press, 1994), 39–63.

44. See the discussion in Bridgette Mabandla, "Changes in South Africa—Advances for Women?" in *Ours By Right: Women's Rights as Human Rights,* ed. Joanna Kerr (London: Zed Books, 1993), 19–26.

45. Frene Ginwala, "Non-Racial Democracy—Soon Non-Sexism—How?," speech given at the Women's National Coalition-National Worship, Johannesburg, 25–26 April 1992, 1.

46. In the constitution of the Women's National Coalition, section 2 states that the role of the WNC is "to coordinate a national campaign for the development and education of women which will (1) acquire and disseminate information about women's needs and aspirations and (2) unify women in formulating and adopting a Charter to entrench equality for women in the new Constitution." (On file with the author.) The campaign itself was pursued from November 1992 until February 1994.

47. Women's National Coalition, "The Origins, History, and Process of the Women's National Coalition: Research Report of the Women's National Coalition" (Johannesburg, 1994), 29. (On file with the author.)

48. The debate over customary law was a vivid illustration of this effect. See Albertyn, "Women and the Transition to Democracy."

49. Women's National Coalition, "The Origins, History and Process of the Women's National Coalition," 19: "The initiative to launch a representative umbrella organization was chiefly motivated by the fear that women would again be excluded from key political processes that were taking place and which were determining the future of South Africa. The WNC was animated by women's exclusion from the negotiation process. . . . This exclusion was an important source of organizational coherence for an extremely heterogenous grouping."

50. An illustration of this in the South African context can be found in Richard Spitz, with Mathew Chaskalason, *Transition: A Hidden History of South Africa's Negotiated Settlement* (Oxford: Hart Publishing, 2000).

CHAPTER 6

"I Know It When I See It": Pornography and Constitutional Vision in Canada and the United States

Samuel V. LaSelva

Few statements about pornography are more intriguing than U.S. Supreme Court Justice Stewart's remark "I know it when I see it." On its face, the statement seems incredible. The phenomenological truth about the perception of pornography appears to be much closer to Justice Douglas' candid admission, "What shocks me may be sustenance for my neighbor." Obscenity, Douglas continued, "is a hodge-podge. To send men to jail for violating standards they cannot understand, construe and apply is a monstrous thing to do in a Nation dedicated to fair trials and due process."[1] But Justice Stewart's remark is not primarily an exercise in phenomenological analysis, nor a denial of the need for reasonably precise standards in obscenity cases. His now famous remark does not stand on its own. On the contrary, it is embedded in an opinion that articulates a complex constitutional doctrine. "I have reached the conclusion, . . . confirmed at least by negative implication in . . . *Roth* and *Alberts*," he wrote, "that under the First and Fourteenth Amendments criminal laws in this area are constitutionally limited to hard-core pornography." He admitted that even hard-core pornography is difficult to define. "But I know it when it see it, and the motion picture involved in this case is not that."[2] Justice Stewart's famous remark is as much about constitutional vision as it is about the phenomenology of pornography.

My objective is to use Justice Stewart's remark as a stepping-stone, in an attempt to clarify competing constitutional visions and their implications for the problem of pornography. What I shall suggest is that key obscenity decisions by the U.S. Supreme Court presuppose a distinctive constitutional vision, one that stands in sharp contrast to the constitutional vision that underpins the Canadian Supreme Court's landmark decision in *R. v. Butler*. *Butler* has become the best-known Canadian Supreme Court case within the United States; it has also met with the approval of well-known American feminists. Catharine MacKinnon, for example, welcomed it as "a stunning legal victory for women" and "of world historic importance."[3] She also criticized American judges for failing to embrace its reasoning. Implicit in MacKinnon's praise of *Butler* is an assumption of universalism and a belief that the question of pornography must have one right answer. Assumptions of this kind are present in many other discussions of pornography, including Ronald Dworkin's influential defense of *American Booksellers v. Hudnut,* a decision that emphatically rejected the feminist understanding of pornography. But the assumption of universalism and the belief in a single answer are highly questionable positions, especially in the human sciences. They can be questioned without embracing relativism, skepticism, or historicism. All that is required is to acknowledge there is more than one way of life. If ways of life are plural, then there is no reason to suppose that there must be a single, best constitutional vision or a single solution to the problem of pornography. Moreover, since criticism presupposes self-understanding, even those who criticize decisions like *Butler* or *American Booksellers* need to take seriously the existence of diverse ways of life.

A Worthy Tradition: Free Speech in the United States

In both Canada and the United States, courts have upheld the constitutionality of laws that restrict and regulate pornography. But they have not offered the same reasons for their decisions, with the result that different kinds of pornographic materials are regarded as obscene and as unworthy of constitutional protection. The Canadian decisions are more restrictive of individual liberty, the American decisions less so. This fact is significant, because both countries have a bill or charter of rights that guarantees the freedom of speech or expression. What makes it even more significant is that the U.S. Bill of Rights not only has historical precedence, but is widely regarded as the leading exemplar of liberal constitutionalism, and departures from it are often viewed with skepticism. The judges of both countries are acutely aware that their decisions are final rather than infallible, yet the free speech decisions of the U.S. Supreme Court are accorded considerable respect, and some of them are justly celebrated as signal contributions to the theory of constitutional government. The Court's pornography decisions are an integral part of American free speech theory and derivative of it. Consequently, the divergences from American freedom speech theory in the Canadian Supreme Court's *Butler* decision are matters of interest and importance to both Canadians and Americans, and in need of explanation.

But the explanation cannot begin with the *Butler* decision. It must begin with American free speech theory. Moreover, no account of free speech in the United States can ignore *Schneck* or its progeny *Abrams,* or the crucial contribution of Justice Holmes. Decided in 1919, *Schenck* raised the question of free speech in wartime. Writing for the Court, Justice Holmes announced the clear and present danger test and proclaimed that "[t]he most stringent protection of free speech would not protect a man in falsely shouting fire in a theatre." Speech can be suppressed, in other words, if there is "a clear and present danger" that it will bring about "the substantive evils that Congress has a right to prevent."[4] *Abrams* was decided only eight months after *Schenck,* but Holmes had second thoughts and expressed them in a famous dissent. One difference is that *Schenck* countenanced restriction based on the bad tendencies of an utterance, while the *Abrams* dissent insisted that its apprehended dangers had to be imminent. Even more significant was Holmes's articulation of a philosophy of free speech, which transformed the clear and present danger test into a speech-protective formula. The test of truth, he said, is not the power of persecution to "sweep away all opposition," but the ability of thought "to get itself accepted in the competition of the market." In the *Abrams* dissent, Holmes not only noted that "time has upset many fighting faiths," but he also advocated a "free trade in ideas," and warned Americans to be "eternally vigilant against attempts to check the expression of opinions that we loathe."[5]

Roscoe Pound described the *Abrams* dissent as a document of human liberty worthy of a Socrates, a Milton, or a Mill.[6] The dissent also had its critics, and the clear and present danger test was of little help in protecting the free speech of Communists in the early years of the Cold War. Still, Holmes transformed the discussion of free speech in the United States. In his hands, free speech became part of a philosophy of life and the key component of the American constitutional system. Holmes found the foundations of free speech in human fallibility and the quest for truth. That is why he spoke of the Constitution as "an experiment," and described human beings as wagering their "salvation upon some prophecy based upon imperfect knowledge."[7] Holmes wrote other opinions after *Abrams,* and supported Justice Brandeis's concurring opinion in *Whitney.* Brandeis not only restated the clear and present danger test, but also expanded the philosophical exploration that Holmes had begun. Brandeis said that free speech was essential if people were to "develop their faculties." He insisted that "public discussion was a political duty." He underlined the importance of free speech for the discussion of "supposed grievances and proposed remedies." Suppression was justified, he said, if "the incidence of the evil apprehended is so imminent that it may befall before there is opportunity for full discussion." But if there was time to expose the falsehood through discussion, or to avert the evil by education, then "the remedy to be applied is more speech, not enforced silence."[8]

Schneck, Abrams, and *Whitney* are not obscenity cases. Still, they contain a test for the suppression of speech and explore the philosophical and constitutional foundations of free speech in the United States. After Holmes's dissent and Brandeis's concurring opinion, it was no longer possible to think of free speech in quite the same way. Speech questions now required an analysis of free speech values. It became imperative to ask: Is the First Amendment's guarantee of free speech based on the role of free speech in the search for truth? Or on the importance of free speech for political democracy? Or on its contribution to the development of the individual? Is there a justification for suppressing speech that embodies free speech values? And what happens to "speech" that has little or no connection to the values of the First Amendment? Like speech in wartime, obscenity raises these questions. The difference is that by the time the Supreme Court came to address the obscenity issue, its earlier decisions revealed glimpses of a philosophy of free speech.

In 1957 the Supreme Court decided *Roth,* the first case in which the dispositive question was whether "obscenity is utterance within the area of protected speech and press." Writing for the majority, Justice Brennan said that the Court had always assumed that it was not, and the assumption was justified. After reviewing both constitutional history and the history of libel laws, he said that "the unconditional phrasing of the First Amendment was not intended to protect every utterance." He also quoted the *Chaplinsky* decision in which the Court explicitly recognized the existence of classes of speech, such as fighting words and the obscene, "the prevention and punishment of which have never been thought to raise any Constitutional problem." And he noted that the First Amendment was fashioned "to assure unfettered exchange of ideas" and that "all ideas having even the slightest redeeming social importance" came within its ambit, but that obscenity was "utterly without redeeming social importance" and should be restrained. Crucial for his argument is the distinction between sex and obscenity. Sex, he said, is not the same as obscenity. On the contrary, sex is "one of the vital problems of human interest and public concern." Unlike sex, obscenity was not protected by the First Amendment, and part of the test for it was "whether to the average person, applying contemporary community standards, the dominant theme of the material taken as a whole appeals to prurient interest."[9]

After *Roth* comes *Miller,* and then *American Booksellers*. In *Miller,* Chief Justice Burger said that although obscenity is "utterly without redeeming social importance," what the prosecution has to show is that "the work, taken as a whole, lacks serious literary, artistic, political or scientific value."[10] *Miller* not only restates *Roth,* but also softens the test for obscenity by bringing more materials within its ambit. In *American Booksellers,* Judge Easterbrook declared the Indianapolis ordinance unconstitutional. One of the main purposes of the ordinance was to define pornography as a practice that discriminates against women, and to protect them from it. But the ordinance, said Judge Easterbrook, departed from the Supreme Court's test for obscenity. It did not refer to "the prurient interest" or to "community standards," nor did it exempt works based on their "serious value." He acknowledged that sexist pornography often creates harmful stereotypes and produces other negative effects; "[y]et this simply demonstrates the power of pornography as speech." Moreover, the ordinance discriminated based on the content of speech and was not neutral with respect to viewpoint. Quoting Justice Jackson, Judge Easterbrook said that "no official . . . can prescribe what shall be orthodox." He also insisted that a key difference between "our society" and totalitarian government is "our absolute right to propagate opinions that the government finds wrong or even hateful."[11]

American Booksellers is not without its critics; *Roth* and *Miller* also have their critics. In fact, *Roth* and *Miller* were the decisions of a sharply divided Court. In both cases one of the chief concerns of the dissenting judges was the dangers of censorship. Justice Douglas complained that, by the standards of *Roth,* "punishment is inflicted for thoughts provoked, not for overt acts or antisocial conduct."[12] Part of Justice Harlan's concern was that the censorship of pornography should be left to the States, because "the dangers of federal censorship in this field are far greater than anything the States may do."[13] Even Chief Justice Warren's concurring opinion in *Roth* cautioned that obscenity legislation often suppressed great books and stifled social controversy. In *Miller,* Justice Brennan joined the dissenters. Although he had authored the *Roth* opinion, he had since come to believe that a new direction should be embraced. His proposed new direction would let consenting adults make their own decisions about sexually oriented material without interference from the state. Judicial experience had demonstrated, he said, the inability of the Court to separate obscenity from constitutionally protected speech. The Court's obscenity decisions were, in their effect, too restrictive of free speech and should be abandoned.[14]

Brennan's proposed new course was strikingly similar to that recommended by the Commission on Obscenity and Pornography in its 1970 *Report.* The commissioners acknowledged the need to regulate the sale of sexual materials to young persons and to protect all persons from having such materials thrust upon them; but once these safeguards were in place, government should not "interfere with the right of adults . . . to read, obtain, or view explicit sexual materials."[15] However, the Supreme Court implicitly rejected this recommendation in *Paris Adult Theatre.* "We categorically disapprove the theory," wrote Chief Justice Burger, ". . . that obscene, pornographic films acquire constitutional immunity . . . simply because they are exhibited for consenting adults only." Writing for a majority, the chief justice reiterated that obscenity is not protected speech and that the states have a legitimate interest in regulating its use "in local commerce and in all places of public accommodation." The states can regulate obscenity, if they choose, based on its perceived harm to the quality of social life, to family values, and to the development of human personality. A state can "quite reasonably determine" that exposure to obscene materials increases antisocial behavior. Modern societies, the chief justice said, do not leave "disposal of garbage and sewage up to the individual 'free will,' but impose regulation to protect both public health and the appearance of public places."[16] American society can deal with obscenity in the same way.

If American society can treat obscenity as a form of harmful trash, why should sexist pornography be treated any differently? Radical feminists like Catharine MacKinnon deny that it should. As a key supporter of the Indianapolis Ordinance, she is also one of the most forceful critics of Judge Easterbrook's ruling in *American Booksellers*. Part of her argument is that American society neglects the harms of sexist pornography. Exposure to it, she argues, increases violence against women, legitimates their relegation to low-paying jobs by perpetuating degrading stereotypes, and politically disenfranchises women by silencing them. If equality for women is to be achieved, then sexist pornography cannot circulate freely.[17] Such an assessment is compelling by the standards of *Paris Adult Theatre*. But *Paris Adult Theatre* was an obscenity case that did not bring the First Amendment into play. Under the First Amendment, free speech enjoys a preferred status that extends even to the kind of sexist pornography that radical feminists condemn. Judge Easterbrook said as much, in language that was decidedly Holmesian. He talked about "a market place of ideas," and noted that even "[s]editious libel is protected speech unless the danger is not only grave but also imminent."[18] He implied that sexist pornography and seditious libel should be judged by the same test, and when so judged, the harms of sexist pornography were insufficient to justify the restriction of protected speech. What he seemed to say was that the Indianapolis Ordinance put too little faith in the American tradition of free speech, a tradition immortalized by Holmes and Brandeis.[19]

Pornography and Hate: From Keegstra to Butler

R. v. Butler highlights an important difference between Canada and the United States. In the United States, obscenity and sexist pornography raise, each in their own way, fundamental questions about the First Amendment. The starting point, in other words, is provided by free speech values and their preferred position in the American constitutional system. In Canada, there is a different starting point and a different focus. The core of *R. v. Butler* is a discussion of the concept of harm and the ways in which the harms of pornography justify restrictions on free expression. The contrast is aptly illustrated by striking differences in constitutional language. The U.S. Bill of Rights enacts that "Congress shall make no law . . . abridging freedom of speech." Section 1 of the Canadian Charter of Rights and Freedoms stipulates that free expression is subject to "reasonable limits." "No law" versus "reasonable limits" is a distinction that has made a difference. Equally important are the divergences between Canadian and American case law. When Judge Easterbrook declared the Indianapolis ordinance unconstitutional in *American Booksellers,* he could not ignore the looming presence of Oliver Wendell Holmes and the American tradition of free speech. In *Butler,* there is also a looming presence, but it appears in the figure of James Keegstra and Canada's antihate law.

Decided only two years before *Butler, Keegstra* deals with a recurring and long-standing problem in Canadian society. James Keegstra was a high school teacher in Eckville, Alberta; he taught anti-Semitic views and expected his students to reproduce his teaching. Occasionally, his hate messages also included Blacks, Catholics and other groups. For the Supreme Court, the question was whether or not hate speech was protected by the Charter. The Court held that it was not, because the restriction of hate propaganda was justified under the Charter's reasonable limits clause, and was consistent with Canada's commitment to a free and democratic society. Three judges dissented, but even they conceded that the objectives of antihate legislation were "of a most worthy nature."[20] The majority went a step further. "[T]he special role given equality and multiculturalism in the Canadian constitution," wrote Chief Justice Dickson, necessitated a departure from the position "that the suppression of hate propaganda is incompatible with the guarantee of free expression." Not only were there real and substantial harms associated with hate propaganda, but Canadian democracy was itself endangered by its presence. Hate propaganda, said the chief justice, conveys ideas that are anathema to democratic values and "inimical to the democratic aspirations of the expression guarantee."[21]

Although Chief Justice Dickson offered a variety of authorities to support his *Keegstra* opinion, he accorded pride of place to the *Report of the Special Committee on Hate Propaganda in Canada,* published in 1966. He described the *Report* as the product of "a particularly strong committee," and emphasized that its unanimous recommendations were "most influential in changing the criminal law." He also quoted its first paragraph, which begins by insisting on "the power of words to maim," and concludes with the admonition that a free society should not permit injury to "identifiable groups innocently caught in verbal cross-fire that goes beyond legitimate debate."[22] What the authors of the *Report* discovered was that a small number of people were actively involved in the dissemination of hate propaganda in Canada. Nevertheless, hate propaganda constituted "a clear and present danger," because "in times of social stress [it] could mushroom into a real and monstrous threat to our way of life." Moreover, the corrosive effects of hate propaganda were capable of undermining "the confidence that various groups in a multicultural society must have in each other." Although a multiethnic society, Canada also had two dominant language groups that were searching for a new and lasting accommodation. Consequently, "the idea of a healthy acceptance and accommodation" implicit in antihate legislation was relevant to all groups, and "indispensable to the future well-being of Canadian Society."[23]

Butler is inconceivable without *Keegstra,* which in turn relied heavily on the *Report on Hate Propaganda.* In *Butler,* Justice Sopinka cited *Keegstra* repeatedly, affirmed its prohibition of hate propaganda, and concluded that "obscenity which degrades and dehumanizes is analogous to . . . hate propaganda." This kind of obscenity, he said, "wields the power to wreak social damage in that a significant portion of the population is humiliated by its gross misrepresentation."[24] In *Butler,* the influence of Chief Justice Dickson's *Keegstra* opinion is unmistakable. But *Keegstra* is not the only decision by Chief Justice Dickson that is essential for an understanding of *Butler.* Almost as important is *Towne Cinema,* a pre-Charter obscenity case in which Dickson analyzed the *Criminal Code's* "undue exploitation of sex" prohibition, held that "community standards" is not an exclusive test for it, and anticipated key aspects of both the *Keegstra* and *Butler* decisions. There was, he said, "no *necessary* coincidence between the undueness of publications which degrade people . . . and the community standard of tolerance." Certain sex-related materials might be within the community's standard of tolerance, yet they might still constitute "undue exploitation of sex" if "they portray persons in a degrading manner as objects of violence, cruelty or other forms of dehumanizing treatment."[25]

In *Towne Cinema,* Dickson hinted at, but did not actually say, that some forms of pornography are akin to hate propaganda. What he left unsaid the Fraser Committee, the Special Committee on Pornography and Prostitution, had no hesitation in saying. Among its recommendations were "changes to the hate literature section of the *Criminal Code* to recognize that pornography may be hate literature directed toward women." The committee also articulated a sophisticated three-tier analysis of pornography that allows some material (child pornography and violent pornography) to be forbidden, some material (erotica) to circulate freely, and still other material (simulated sexual violence that affronts equality and human rights) to be prohibited if it fails tests for artistic merit and educational or scientific purpose. The classification accepts key feminist principles, in that it distinguishes erotica and pornography, and suppresses pornography that does violence to women's aspiration of equality. But it also acknowledges the force of liberal principles by retaining the defense of artistic merit and educational or scientific purpose, and by refusing to suppress all unflattering images of women. Balancing liberty and equality, confided the committee, "has been for us . . . a difficult yet essential task."[26]

In *Butler,* the Supreme Court not only approved many of the findings of the Fraser Committee, but also took up the task of balancing liberty and equality. In doing so, it addressed the question of harm and sought to avoid the impasse that often results. It took the position that pornography is a complex phenomenon and requires an equally complex analysis of harm. A corollary of this view is that pornography becomes a less daunting constitutional problem if crude simplifications are avoided. Writing for the Court, and benefiting from the Fraser Report, Justice Sopinka said that pornography is not all of a kind but is composed of three main types: explicit sex with violence, explicit sex without violence that degrades or dehumanizes people, and explicit sex without violence that is neither degrading nor dehumanizing. This is the first step of his argument, but it is not a step that all Canadians would accept. As he noted, "Some segments of society would consider that all three categories of pornography cause harm to society because they tend to undermine its moral fibre. Others would contend that none of these categories cause harm."[27] Both sides would contend that the Court's three-tier classification of pornography is irrelevant. Far from accepting this view, Justice Sopinka believed that those who espoused it had too simple a view of pornography, failed to explore the connections between pornography and hate, and misunderstood the implications of the Charter.

Canadian judges had themselves once embraced views of pornography that the Court now rejected. Historically, the most common position has been to regard all pornography as immoral "dirt" and to insist that society should refuse to tolerate it. For many years the Supreme Court endorsed a view of this kind; it did so by accepting the *Hicklin* rule, which regards as obscene material that tends "to deprave and corrupt those whose minds are open to such immoral influences."[28] *Hicklin* had the effect of reducing adults to the status of children by limiting their interest in sex "to the standard of a child's library."[29] But *Hicklin* ceased to be sound law in 1959. In that year, Parliament amended the *Criminal Code* and defined obscenity as "the undue exploitation of sex." Interpreting this definition in *R. v. Brodie,* the Supreme Court said that sex was a legitimate subject of interest; obscenity was still forbidden, but the standard for determining it was no longer grounded in the paternalistic and moralistic assumptions of *Hicklin.*[30] In *Butler,* the Supreme Court went one step further. *Hicklin* made the courts the guardian of public morality. The Charter rendered such a role untenable, not only for the courts but for Parliament as well. "The prevention of 'dirt for dirt's sake'," said Justice Sopinka, "is not a legitimate objective which would justify the violation of one of the most important freedoms enshrined in the Charter."[31]

If all pornography were erotica or even "dirt," the case for prohibiting it would be no stronger than the flawed assumptions of *Hicklin.* However, some pornography resembles hate propaganda, and the harms associated with it are antithetical to the kind of society envisaged by the Charter. There is growing recognition, wrote Justice Sopinka, that material that exploits sex in a degrading and dehumanizing manner "will necessarily fail the community standards test . . . because it is perceived by public opinion to be harmful to society, particularly women." A direct link between obscenity and harm is difficult to establish; but the evidence is strong enough for Parliament to have "a reasoned apprehension of harm resulting from the desensitization of individuals exposed to materials which depict violence, cruelty, and dehumanization in sexual relations." Even this kind of pornography comes within the Charter's guarantee of free expression. But it does not stand "on equal footing" with the search for truth, participation in the political process, and other kinds of expression that "directly engage the 'core' of the freedom of expression values." When this kind of pornography is prohibited, the objective of avoiding harm and protecting equality normally outweighs the resulting impairment of free expression within the framework established by the Charter's reasonable limits clause. Not only does Parliament have the right "to legislate on the basis of some fundamental conception of morality for the purpose of safeguarding . . . a free and democratic society," but its "moral disapprobation" of certain forms of pornography is an appropriate response when based on Charter values.[32]

The logic of the *Butler* decision is that sexist pornography is virtually indistinguishable from hate propaganda, and just as intolerable. Moreover, to the extent that they can be distinguished, the case against violent and degrading pornography is even stronger than that against hate speech. In *Keegstra,* all the judges agreed that "the evil of hate propaganda is beyond doubt."[33] But a minority voted against sustaining Canada's antihate law because, in their view, suppression would increase media coverage of hate messages, turn hatemongers into martyrs, and defeat the purpose of antihate legislation.[34] With respect to violent and degrading pornography, reasoned Justice Sopinka, such a criticism does not apply, because "pornography is not dignified by its suppression."[35] Judging by the votes cast, Sopinka's clarification had considerable effect. For although three judges dissented in *Keegstra,* none dissented in *Butler*. If some pornography is like hate propaganda, then the argument for its suppression seems to be not merely persuasive but overwhelming, at least in the Supreme Court of Canada.

Constitutional Visions: Canadian and American

In itself, pornography is hardly the kind of issue from which to construct a constitutional vision. But when pornography is discussed in terms of free speech values or compared to hate propaganda, questions about constitutional fundamentals are difficult to avoid. To read Judge Easterbrook's opinion in *American Booksellers* or Justice Sopinka's in *Butler* is to encounter nothing less than a constitutional *Weltanschauung*. To read them together is to glimpse some of the important differences between the Canadian and American constitutional systems. Moreover, within each system, there is a constitutional faith that sustains it. "[I]f there is any principle of the [U.S.] Constitution that more imperatively calls for attachment than any other," wrote Justice Holmes, "it is the principle of free thought—not free thought for those who agree with us but freedom for the thought that we hate."[36] Holmes may not have expressed the whole of the American constitutional faith, but he did capture one of its most important elements. The Canadian constitutional faith is different, as *Keegstra* and *Butler* make plain. Canadians do not ascribe the same priority to free speech, in part because they live in a different kind of society, one in which the corrosive effects of hatred raise distinctive questions about the Canadian identity and about the ability of Canadians to live under a common constitution.[37] With differences in constitutional faith come different constitutional visions and, in turn, different understandings of the problem of pornography.

However, the best-known discussions of pornography do not always give the issue of diverging constitutional faiths the attention it deserves. Instead, they often proceed as if there are right answers independent of national differences in constitutional faith and unconnected to fundamental divergences in constitutional vision. What they take for granted is the availability of a single, universal solution. But the assumption of universalism is difficult to justify in view of the kinds of disagreements that exist. In a seminal essay, W. B. Gallie suggested that some disagreements cannot be settled by appealing to a single, correct answer. The reason is that some disagreements turn on what he called an essentially contested concept, that is, a concept capable of generating multiple conceptions, all of which can be supported "by perfectly respectable arguments and evidence." However, Gallie did not believe that contested concepts rendered argument futile. Each of the parties to a dispute, he said, can attempt to improve its own position, and work for the day when all sides are "converted" to its point of view.[38] The pornography debate often mirrors the kind of contest identified by Gallie: fundamental disagreements coupled with philosophically sophisticated attempts at conversion. One such example is the famous debate between Ronald Dworkin and Catharine MacKinnon, in which a liberal confronts a radical feminist, and the differences between Canada and the United States come into question.

What troubles Dworkin about the pornography debate is that the kind of censorship embodied in the Indianapolis ordinance has come to seem justified and even benign "to many people whose convictions are otherwise traditionally liberal." They support censorship because they increasingly regard as intolerable speech that expresses "a degrading attitude toward women." But such a position, Dworkin warns, confuses negative and positive liberty. Pornography, he admits, is "grotesquely offensive"; it is "insulting not only to women but to men as well." However, there is no evidence linking sexist pornography to an increase in rape or sexual assault; and in the absence of such evidence "the speech we hate is as much entitled to protection as any other." Are there not other kinds of harms and other kinds of liberty that buttress the case for censorship? Feminists like Catharine MacKinnon argue that sexist pornography corrupts society's image of women; it condemns women to an inauthentic existence, and it silences women by rendering them inaudible. This kind of argument, Dworkin replies, is both deceptive and dangerous. It depends on a conception of positive liberty that allows people to be governed "ruthlessly" by rulers who claim to know their "true, metaphysical will."[39] Feminist censorship, Dworkin concludes, is neither benign nor a substitute for the kind of freedom defended by Judge Easterbrook. Implicit in Dworkin's analysis is a subtle universalism, in which the classic doctrines of American free speech theory are both defended against the radical feminist onslaught and rearticulated as the surest safeguard against the lure of the "metaphysical will."

In *Only Words,* Catharine MacKinnon not only defends the Indianapolis ordinance, but also responds to Dworkin's criticism of it. The way liberal apologists such as Dworkin commonly justify freedom for pornographers is by arguing against censorship, and by identifying state control of pornography with tyranny over the mind. Some of them also attempt to portray pornographers as helpless dissidents whose freedom society should protect. But, replies MacKinnon, a world fashioned by sexist pornography is not one in which freedom flourishes. On the contrary, it is a world of oppression. In it, women are sexually abused, economically disadvantaged, and brutally displayed. Moreover, it is not enough to retort that sexist pornography is only words, and cannot possibly have these effects. For such a response, MacKinnon argues, neglects the power of words. Not only is "society . . . made up of words, whose meanings the powerful control, or try to"; but "social inequality is substantially created and enforced—that is, *done*—through words and images."[40] Ultimately, those who refuse to control sexist pornography conflate freedom with power, and such a conflation makes sense only in the kind of Orwellian universe relished by pornographers and falsely celebrated by liberal constitutionalists.

However, MacKinnon's objective is not simply to expose a pernicious conceptual confusion or to reveal the ugly truth about sexist pornography. In *Only Words,* she also contrasts Judge Easterbrook's decision in *American Booksellers* with Justice Sopinka's opinion in *Butler*. Her objective is to show that Canadian judges take seriously the harms of sexist pornography and treat with skepticism such constructs as the "slippery slope" and the litany of "political speech." "Canada's new constitution, the Charter of Rights and Freedoms," includes "an expansive equality guarantee" that the Canadian Supreme Court has interpreted "in a meaningful way—one more substantive than formal, directed toward changing unequal social relations." The Charter's equality guarantee also grounds *Keegstra,* a decision that MacKinnon applauds because "an atmosphere of group hate" destroys "equality of opportunity." For MacKinnon, the *Keegstra* and *Butler* decisions demonstrate that Canadian judges are unlike their American counterparts. They take equality seriously and refuse to reduce "the harm of hate propaganda or pornography to its 'offensiveness'." But American judges, MacKinnon insists, can achieve similar results if they accord sufficient weight to the Fourteenth Amendment's promise of equality. In the United States, sexist pornography and hate crime legislation fail judicial scrutiny, yet "they might, with constitutional equality support, survive."[41]

Catharine MacKinnon and Ronald Dworkin disagree about sexist pornography—about the harms it causes and about its implications for a free society. Behind their disagreement, however, is a common premise. Each supposes that there is a single, correct solution to the problem of pornography, one that can be applied to both Canada and the United States. That MacKinnon subscribes to this premise seems plain enough. Why else does she praise Justice Sopinka's decision in *Butler,* and criticize Judge Easterbrook for failing to arrive at a similar conclusion in *American Booksellers?* Dworkin is less explicit, but his argument also proceeds as if the solution to the problem of pornography must transcend national and jurisdictional boundaries. His key arguments in "Pornography and Hate" depend on the distinction between negative and positive liberty, a distinction that he portrays as having universal significance. At the very least, Dworkin the liberal and MacKinnon the feminist are working for the day (to quote Gallie again) when all sides are "genuinely converted" to a single point of view.

But a problem like pornography does not easily lend itself to the development of a single solution that transcends every national or jurisdictional boundary. In Canada and the United States, pornography ultimately raises constitutional issues of the first importance, yet it is far from self-evident that the resolution of these issues must be identical for both countries. "[E]very country," wrote Ivor Jennings, "must have a Constitution to suit itself, a Constitution made to measure, not one bought off the rack."[42] If, as has been frequently suggested, the Canadian and American constitutions differ, and if there are good reasons for the differences, then solutions to the problem of pornography can also differ.[43] There is no reason to suppose that there must be a single, ideal Bill of Rights or that the interpretation of the Canadian Charter must be constrained "by the textual or political constitutional imperatives of the American first amendment."[44] Moreover, the idea of a single solution depends on monistic assumptions that are less coherent than is often supposed. Monism presupposes a single scale of values and a harmonious moral universe. But, as Isaiah Berlin noted, "the notion of the perfect whole . . . seems . . . not only unattainable but conceptually incoherent." This is so because "some of the Great Goods cannot live together," and because human beings can and do pursue diverse values and even incompatible ways of life.[45] In place of monism, Berlin advocates the recognition of pluralism and the acknowledgment of different "forms of life." If different "forms of life" exist, then so do different solutions to the problem of pornography.

For Canadians, an unresolved question is how their "form of life" differs from the American, and what significance they should attach to the difference. There is no easy answer to this question, but one source of illumination is the constitutional faith of each country. Like Canadians, Americans debate the character and significance of their constitution. However, the American debate is almost always a debate about liberty, its meaning, its limits, and the best means for its realization. American constitutional history begins with the Declaration of Independence, a document that denounces tyranny and defends the inalienable rights of the individual. Freedom also animates the Constitution and the Bill of Rights, both of which are instruments for the realization of republican liberty and democratic self-government. Finally, the greatest crisis of the U.S. Constitution, the American Civil War, ends black slavery and announces "a new birth of freedom."[46] What Canadians most often debate, by contrast, is the character, the requirements, and even the possibility of national unity. The Canadian debate frequently focuses on the French-English question; but Canada also includes disparate provinces, aboriginal peoples, multicultural citizens, and a host of other groups that cannot be neglected. The great problem for Canadians is not tyranny but fragmentation, and the great challenge is to create a country that both recognizes group differences and nurtures common ties and a common identity.[47]

If a constitution is part of a "form of life," then it is significant that Canadians and Americans live under constitutions that are animated by different concerns and different principles. *American Booksellers* is not an isolated judicial decision, but a link in a chain that stretches back to *Roth* and then to *Whitney* and *Abrams*. These decisions elaborate a complex theory of free speech that is congenial to much of the American constitutional tradition and its faith in freedom. A key assumption of that theory is that Americans should be free to advocate the most diverse and extreme social and political doctrines, because "[t]he Constitution forbids the state to declare one perspective right and silence opponents."[48] If Americans are free to advocate communism or fascism, then they should be equally free to advocate worldviews that demean women or regard them as inferior to men. "It would plainly be unconstitutional," writes Ronald Dworkin, "to ban speech directly *advocating* that women occupy inferior roles. . . . So it cannot be a reason for banning pornography that it contributes to an unequal economic or social structure."[49] Dworkin's hope is that free speech will be used in the service of equality rather than against it. But it is part of the American constitutional faith that the people should also be free to choose inequality, because the alternative to freedom and democracy is political tyranny, which most Americans find even more abhorrent than sexist pornography.

The Canadian constitutional tradition is different. Not only are Canadians less concerned than Americans about political tyranny, but their identity is far more fragile. André Siegfried once said that French and English were "like brothers that hate each other . . . [and] have to dwell under one roof."[50] Others have emphasized that, in a culturally heterogeneous country like Canada, "close contacts . . . are likely to lead to strain and hostility."[51] One way of lessening strain and hostility in a society as deeply pluralistic as Canada is to control the dissemination of hate propaganda. That there is a connection between controlling hate and promoting Canadian unity seemed apparent to the committee on hate propaganda in Canada. The committee insisted that "sinister abuses of our freedom of expression . . . can tear apart a society, brutalize its dominant elements, and persecute[,] even to extermination, its minorities."[52] In *Keegstra,* the Supreme Court of Canada arrived at a similar conclusion, and upheld Canada's antihate legislation as a reasonable limit on the Charter guarantee of free expression. With *Butler,* the Court extended its ruling to cover pornographic material that resembles hate propaganda. Behind both decisions is a constitutional faith that recognizes social pluralism and diverse group identities, while promoting "a healthy acceptance and accommodation as between all groups in Canada."[53]

Not only do constitutional differences make a difference, but one of the important tasks of legal and political theory is to make sense of such differences. According to Charles Taylor, a theory of society differs from natural science precisely because it deals with institutions and practices that rest on self-understandings. "What makes our practice more clairvoyant," he suggests, "is *pro tanto* valid theory."[54] In some cases, theory will reveal that a practice or institution is vain or deeply muddled and should be abandoned. But there is a great difference between correcting a practice or an institution in a manner that takes account of a nation's constitutional experiences and abandoning a practice or institution in favor of a single or abstract model. If judges, legislators, and social theorists were more like Platonic Guardians, the problem of pornography would not only be easier to solve, but the availability of a single solution could be taken for granted. However, Platonic Guardians have privileged access to a world of immutable principles that bears no resemblance to the untidy world of pornography or to the differences in constitutional faith that distinguish Canada from the United States and ground the different responses of their highest courts to the problem of pornography. Of course, constitutional faiths are not immutable, and the day may come when Canada and the United States subscribe to the same constitutional faith and embrace the same solution to the problem of pornography.

Conclusion: "I Know It When I See It"

Pornography is commonly discussed in terms of the harm principle, or free speech values, or the idea of human dignity. It is much less often discussed in terms of contrasting constitutional visions and distinctive constitutional faiths. But the problem of pornography is part of a larger constitutional matrix that is difficult to ignore. If Canadian and American judges have decided pornography cases differently, part of the explanation is that there is no single or universally accepted solution to the problems raised by it, and none that can be completely divorced from a constitutional vision and a constitutional faith. In "Towards the Regime of Tolerance," Thomas R. Berger takes as his starting point the interaction between ideals and institutions, and asks: "What do our Canadian institutions reveal about our ideals?" Part of his answer is that "our new Canadian Constitution and Charter of Rights . . . is a valuable and uniquely Canadian undertaking and represents our own attempt to articulate the philosophical ideas undergirding the Canadian polity." He also believes that there are "strands of Canadian federalism altogether distinct from the United States variety," and that Canadians "do not share the American goal, often reiterated, . . . of integration and assimilation."[55]

If different goals and ideals, and even different conceptions of federalism and nationhood, underpin the Canadian and American polities, then Justice Stewart's "I know it when I see it" has an added significance. What his remark hints at, but does not make fully explicit, is the idea of constitutional vision. Not only is the problem of pornography commonly viewed through a constitutional lens, but the response to it depends in part on a constitutional vision. Under the U.S. Constitution, pornographic material that offends contemporary community standards can be suppressed if it lacks value as speech. At the same time, pornographic material that contains a degrading and hateful message is protected under the First Amendment, because American judges have been unable to find a state interest strong enough to justify its suppression as speech in a free and open society. The deepest rationale of these decisions is faith in the American people, and the hope that the people will use their freedom wisely. Canada is different partly because the existence of a Canadian people and a Canadian nation cannot be taken for granted. As a multinational federation that officially sanctions multiculturalism, Canada contains group identities strong enough to call into question the common sympathies required by Canadian nationhood. Strong group identities bring group hatreds, and the need to control such hatreds for the sake of common citizenship. Viewed within this framework, the *Keegstra* and *Butler* decisions are contributions to the creation of a Canadian people and the realization of a distinctively Canadian constitutional vision.[56] No less than Justice Stewart, the Supreme Court of Canada can also say in pornography cases, "I know it when I see it."

Notes

1. *Miller v. California,* 413 U.S. 40–41, 43–44 (1973) (Douglas, dissenting).

2. *Jacobellis v. Ohio,* 378 U.S. 197 (1964) (Stewart, concurring).

3. Catharine MacKinnon, as quoted in Dany Lacombe, *Blue Politics: Pornography and Law in the Age of Feminism* (Toronto: University of Toronto Press, 1994), 136; and Kent Greenawalt, *Fighting Words* (Princeton: Princeton University Press, 1996), 99.

4. *Schenck v. United States,* 249 U.S. 52 (1919) (Holmes).

5. *Abrams v. United States,* 250 U.S. 630 (1919) (Holmes dissenting).

6. Roscoe Pound as cited in Richard Pollenberg, *Fighting Faiths* (New York: Penguin Books, 1989), 241.

7. *Abrams v. United States,* 630 (Holmes dissenting).

8. *Whitney v. California,* 274 U.S. 375, 377 (1927) (Brandeis, concurring). See also Gerald Gunther, "Learned Hand and the Origins of Modern First Amendment Doctrine," *Stanford Law Review* 27 (1975): 719.

9. *Roth v. United States,* 354 U.S. 481, 483, 485, 484, 487, 489 (1957) (Brennan).

10. *Miller v. California,* 413 U.S. 431 (1973) (Burger).

11. Judge Easterbrook's opinion in *American Booksellers v. Hudnut* (1985), as reprinted in *Law and Morality,* ed. David Dyzenhaus and Arthur Ripstein (Toronto: University of Toronto Press, 1996), 617, 619, 618.

12. *Roth v. United States,* 509 (Douglas, dissenting).

13. *Roth v. United States,* 505 (Harlan, dissenting in part).

14. *Miller v. California,* 47 (Brennan dissenting). In *Miller,* Brennan called attention to his much fuller dissent in *Paris Adult Theatre 1 v. Slaton,* 413 U.S. 83–84, 103, 112–14 (1973).

15. *The Report of the Commission on Obscenity and Pornography* (New York: Bantam Books, 1970), 57.

16. *Paris Adult Theatre 1 v. Slaton,* 57, 61, 64 (Burger). See also Alexander Bickel, "On Pornography: Dissenting and Concurring Opinions," *Public Interest* 22 (winter 1971).

17. Catharine A. MacKinnon, "Pornography and the Rights of Women," in *Applied Social and Political Philosophy,* ed. Elizabeth Smith and H. Gene Blocker (Englewood Cliffs, N.J.: Prentice-Hall, 1994), 304.

18. *American Booksellers v. Hudnut,* 620.

19. See, generally, Harry Kalven Jr., *A Worthy Tradition: Freedom of Speech in America* (New York: Harper and Row, 1988), 6–19.

20. *R. v. Keegstra* (1990), 3 Canadian Rights Reporter (2d) 312 (McLachlin, dissenting).

21. *R. v. Keegstra,* 225, 240–41 (Dickson).

22. Ibid., 211–12 (Dickson).

23. *Report of the Special Committee on Hate Propaganda in Canada* (Ottawa: Queen's Printer, 1966), 24, 25, 33.

24. *R. v. Butler* (1992), 70 Canadian Criminal Cases (3d) 162 (Sopinka).

25. *Towne Cinema Theatres Ltd. v. The Queen* (1985), 18 Dominion Law Reports (4th) 11 (Dickson).

26. *Pornography and Prostitution in Canada,* vol. 1 (Ottawa: Minister of Supply and Services, 1985), 57, 264, 266, 26.

27. *R. v. Butler,* 150 (Sopinka).

28. For the Hicklin rule, see *The Queen v. Hicklin* (1868), reprinted in *Censorship Landmarks,* ed. Edward De Grazia (New York: Bowker, 1969), 9.

29. Such was Leaned Hand's opinion in *United States v. Kennerley* (1913), reprinted in De Grazia, *Censorship Landmarks,* 58.

30. *R. v. Brodie* (1962), 32 Dominion Law Reports (2d) 524 (Judson).

31. *R. v. Butler,* 156 (Sopinka).

32. *R. v. Butler,* 146–47, 164, 162, 156 (Sopinka).

33. *R. v. Keegstra,* 275.

34. Ibid., 303–5 (McLachlin).

35. *R. v. Butler,* 164; Sopkina, quoting Dickson.

36. *United States v. Schwimmer,* 279 U.S. 654–55 (Holmes, dissenting). See also Sanford Levinson, *Constitutional Faith* (Princeton: Princeton University Press, 1988), 122–54.

37. For a discussion of some of the contrasts between the constitutional faiths of Canada and the United States, see Samuel V. LaSelva, "Divided Houses: Secession and Constitutional Faith in Canada and the United States," *Vermont Law Review* 23 (1999): 771–92.

38. W. B. Gallie, "Essentially Contested Concepts," in his *Philosophy and the Historical Understanding* (New York: Schocken Books, 1968), 158, 189.

39. R. Dworkin, "Pornography and Hate," in his *Freedom's Law* (Cambridge: Harvard University Press, 1996), 215.

40. Catharine A. MacKinnon, *Only Words* (Cambridge: Harvard University Press, 1993), 30, 13. See also Andrea Dworkin, "Against the Male Flood: Censorship, Pornography, and Equality," *Harvard Women's Law Journal* 8 (1985): 1.

41. MacKinnon, *Only Words,* 102, 97–98, 99, 104, 85.

42. W. Ivor Jennings, *The Approach to Self-Government* (Boston: Beacon Press, 1963), 2.

43. See, generally, Greenawalt, *Fighting Words,* 122–23, 150–53; and Mayo Moran, "Talking about Hate Speech: A Rhetorical Analysis of American and Canadian Approaches to the Regulation of Hate Speech," in Dyzenhaus and Ripstein, *Law and Morality,* 546–55.

44. Kathleen Mahoney, "Freedom of Expression: Hate Propaganda, Pornography, and Section 1 of the Charter," in *Canadian Constitutional Dilemmas Revisited,* ed. Denis N. Magnusson and Daniel A. Soberman (Kingston, Ont.: Queen's University Institute of Intergovernmental Relations, 1997), 89.

45. Isaiah Berlin, *The Crooked Timber of Mankind* (New York: Alfred A. Knopf, 1991), 13.

46. LaSelva, "Divided Houses," 782–89.

47. Samuel V. LaSelva, *The Moral Foundations of Canadian Federalism* (Montreal: McGill-Queen's University Press, 1996), 3–16.

48. *American Booksellers v. Hudnut,* 618.

49. Dworkin, "Pornography and Hate," 219.

50. André Siegfried, *The Race Question in Canada* (1907; reprint, Toronto: McClelland and Stewart, 1966), 85.

51. Arend Lijphart, "Consociational Democracy," in *Consociational Democracy,* ed. Kenneth McRae (Toronto: McClelland and Stewart, 1974), 83. See also Arend Lijphart, "Cultural Diversity and Theories of Political Integration," *Canadian Journal of Political Science* 4 (1971): 14.

52. *Report on Hate Propaganda in Canada,* 59. Here the committee quoted Justice Jackson of the U.S. Supreme Court.

53. Ibid., 33. See also Samuel V. LaSelva, "Pluralism and Hate: Freedom, Censorship, and the Canadian Identity," in *Interpreting Censorship in Canada,* ed. Klaus Petersen and Allan Hutchinson (Toronto: University of Toronto Press, 1999), 41–55.

54. Charles Taylor, "Political Theory and Practice," in *Social Theory and Political Practice,* ed. Christopher Lloyd (Oxford: Clarendon Press, 1982), 85.

55. Thomas Berger, "Towards the Regime of Tolerance," in *Political Thought in Canada,* ed. Stephen Brooks (Toronto: Irwin Publishing, 1984), 83, 86, 84.

56. LaSelva, "Pluralism and Hate," 45–53.

CHAPTER 7

American and Canadian Perspectives on Hate Speech and the Limits of Free Expression

Stephen L. Newman

Congress shall make no law . . . abridging the freedom of expression
—First Amendment to the United States Constitution

2. Everyone has the following fundamental freedoms:
(b) freedom of thought, belief, opinion and expression
—Canadian Charter of Rights and Freedoms

In roughly parallel cases decided within two years of one another, the Supreme Court of the United States and the Supreme Court of Canada handed down diametrically opposed rulings on the constitutionality of laws proscribing hate speech. In *R.A.V. v. St. Paul* (1992),[1] the U.S. Supreme Court disallowed a municipal ordinance making it a crime to display symbols, including but not limited to a burning cross or Nazi swastika, that are known to arouse "anger, alarm or resentment" on the basis of race, color, creed, religion, or gender. In *R. v. Keegstra* (1990),[2] the Supreme Court of Canada upheld the constitutionality of sec. 319(2) of the federal *Criminal Code* penalizing the willful promotion of hatred against an "identifiable group," viz., "any section of the public distinguished by colour, race, religion or ethnic origin." The divergent rulings are puzzling, given the facial similarity of the First Amendment to the United States Constitution and sec. 2*(b)* of the Canadian Charter of Rights and Freedoms.

Some commentators have followed Chief Justice Dickson of Canada in ascribing the conflicting results to differing "constitutional visions" framed by the different historical experiences and political traditions of the two nations.[3] There are certainly significant differences to be taken into account, not least of all the newness of Canada's rights jurisprudence under the Charter and the enhanced political status of the Supreme Court as the guardian of those rights.[4] Whereas the American Supreme Court is able to draw upon two hundred years of precedent, its Canadian counterpart is literally making new law every day.[5] I, too, read Dickson's majority opinion in *Keegstra* as a self-conscious attempt to carve out a distinctive Canadian approach to defining the limits of freedom of expression. It bears keeping in mind, however, that *Keegstra* was decided by the narrowest of margins (the vote was 4 to 3) and that the dissenting opinion authored by Justice McLaughlin embraced the model presented by First Amendment jurisprudence.[6] Nor ought we overlook the fact that Dickson's groundbreaking opinion was itself deeply indebted to the American constitutional and philosophical literature on free speech. It is a fine line that distinguishes the Charter guarantee from that of the First Amendment.

Both courts agree in principle that there must be limits to free expression. The difference between them concerns where to draw the line between protected speech and constitutionally permissible censorship. I contend that this is best understood as an argument within a shared tradition of constitutional liberty between liberal and republican points of view. Are the rights of the individual normally paramount (the liberal view), or are they inherently self-limiting (the republican view)? From the liberal standpoint favored by the American court, the freedom of expression presumptively extends even to morally disreputable speakers unless it can be shown that the speaker's words will bring about some tangible injury that the state has an obligation to prevent. From the republican point of view favored by the Canadian court, however, freedom of expression must be consistent with the state's obligation to promote civic equality and thus should not extend to speech that denigrates, intimidates, or silences others.[7] In the final analysis, it is not a question of which point of view offers the correct perspective on freedom of expression—that is a political question and will always be subject to partisan dispute. But by attending closely to the reasoning of the courts in these decisions we can at least assess the usefulness of these viewpoints in marking the boundaries between constitutionally inoffensive speech and speech so vile and hateful that it deserves to be suppressed.

Racist Hate Speech and the American Tradition of Free Expression

Robert Viktora, the juvenile petitioner in *R.A.V. v. St Paul,* was charged under the city's Bias Motivated Crime Ordinance for having participated with other youths in burning a cross, crudely fashioned from pieces of broken furniture, on the lawn of a black family in his neighborhood.[8] The perpetrators were not members of an organized hate group like the Nazi party or the Ku Klux Klan; they were teenagers, bored, drunk, and high on drugs. Still, they must surely have been aware of the symbolism of the burning cross and the terror it would strike in their victims. As Justice Scalia observed in his majority opinion, the city could have charged Viktora with any number of serious crimes, such as arson or criminal damage to property. It might even have preferred charges under a state statute providing for up to five years imprisonment upon conviction for making terroristic threats.[9] That the city elected to charge Viktora under its Bias Motivated Crime Ordinance appears to have been a deliberate response to the social and political significance of his act. By charging Viktora under this ordinance, the city was attempting to counter the potent symbolism of the burning cross with an equally emphatic gesture of its own.

The trial judge dismissed the charges on First Amendment grounds. While government has every right and perhaps even a moral responsibility to communicate a message of racial tolerance, the constitutional difficulty in this instance was that St. Paul chose to express its opposition to racism by gagging the racists. Its Bias Motivated Crime Ordinance made punishable the display of a Nazi swastika, burning cross, or like symbol of hatred on account of their communicative value. There is no power to suppress speech or expressive conduct, like the act of burning a cross, solely on account of the state's disapproval of its content.

First Amendment jurisprudence is highly speech-protective. Much of that jurisprudence was fashioned in the first half of the twentieth century in response to government efforts to suppress overtly political, albeit allegedly subversive, speech. The Supreme Court was not always hostile to the government's agenda, and expression believed to jeopardize national security or threaten social order often found itself without friends among the justices. Still, the rule employed to balance First Amendment claims against the legitimate security interests of the state requires a showing of real and substantial harm flowing from the impugned expression. I refer to the clear and present danger rule formulated by Justice Holmes in *Schenck v. United States* (1919). For Holmes, "[t]he question in every case is whether the words are used in such circumstances and are of such a nature as to create a clear and present danger that they will bring about the substantive evils that Congress has a right to prevent."[10] Subsequent decisions established that the evils in question must be tangible, usually in the form of violence against persons or property, and also that the danger apprehended must be grave and imminent. Fear of what *might* result from unchecked expression is not sufficient warrant to override the First Amendment guarantee.[11]

The reasons why government ought not to be able to suppress (without ample cause) even manifestly bad ideas are eloquently expressed by Holmes's frequent collaborator, Justice Brandeis, in yet another subversive speech case, *Whitney v. California* (1927). Building on what Holmes had argued in *Schenck,* Brandeis linked the immediacy of the harm associated with speech to the loss of any opportunity for full public discussion of what the speaker has to say.[12] Given the opportunity for full discussion, he was confident that persons such as the framers of the Constitution presumed us to be are normally competent to distinguish truth from falsehood and good from evil. This is not to say he believed that individuals are always reasonable, or that truth and goodness will always prevail in public debate. The logic of Brandeis's argument in *Whitney* does not require that democratic citizens be perfectly wise and perfectly just moral agents, only that they be capable of autonomous rational deliberation and show the courage of their convictions. This was the very heart of Brandeis's liberal faith, and its conception of the citizen as a moral actor justifies allowing the freedom of expression an expansive scope. The political theorist Ronald Dworkin captures the spirit of Brandeis's liberalism when he writes, "Government insults its citizens, and denies their moral responsibility, when it decrees that they cannot be trusted to hear opinions that might persuade them to dangerous or offensive convictions."[13]

In the context of *R.A.V.* it might be objected that a burning cross is not a political manifesto and does not deserve to be treated as though it were. More generally, it might be argued that racist hate speech per se is not debatable, as are crackpot calls for revolution, because it trades on prejudice, eschewing reasoned argument and appealing instead to people's emotions. Against the liberal remedy of countering harmful speech through wide-open public debate, it might be argued that the point of hate speech is not so much to persuade others as it is to stigmatize and intimidate its targets; thus, the damage is done as soon as the words are uttered, and no amount of debate can undo it.

To the first of these objections the liberal First Amendment philosophy replies that many sorts of appeals are emotionally charged and less than fully reasonable, so hate speech cannot be distinguished on that basis alone. Assuming that individual auditors are normally competent to assess the moral implications of the ideas to which they are exposed, respect for their status as autonomous moral agents requires that they be left alone by the state to judge even highly volatile racist messages for themselves. While conceding that hate speech may have the power to intimidate, the liberal philosophy finds this insufficient reason to overlook its expressive value. Insofar as racist hate speech communicates a message, and not infrequently a message having political content, liberal doctrine insists that it deserves the same degree of protection afforded any other unpopular and potentially dangerous idea. Noxious ideas receive protection not because they might be true, nor because they are deemed inconsequential and of no real threat; their falsity may seem perfectly evident, as may the strength of their appeal to weak or prejudiced minds. But liberals believe that we have more to fear from the coercive power of the state than from malicious ideas. The former, when abused, can only be resisted by countervailing power, which an oppressed citizenry might not always be able to muster; the latter can be successfully opposed by countervailing ideas, the expression of which lies within the power of every citizen.

To claim that the racist message itself inflicts a harm that cannot be remedied through counterspeech raises a possibility not contemplated by the clear and present danger rule: an intangible injury (psychic trauma?) against which "more speech" is not an effective remedy. I understand the liberal reading of the First Amendment to reject this possibility. In keeping with the logic of Brandeis's argument, individuals targeted by hate speech must be presumed to possess the same moral and intellectual capacities as all other persons. They, too, must be trusted to have the courage of their convictions. Hate speech may indeed be unusually hurtful, as those who favor its suppression contend; but the fact is that words of hate are not the only "words that wound."[14] The liberal philosophy of free speech demands that citizens of a liberal democracy be prepared to suffer the slings and arrows of unconstrained expression. It's not that "sticks and stones may break our bones, but words will never hurt us." Rather, it's that the hurt we suffer on account of words is the price we pay for the freedom of expression.[15]

The Minnesota Supreme Court reinstated the charges against Viktora on appeal, reasoning that the impugned ordinance could be made to fit within a general exception to the First Amendment known as the "fighting words" doctrine. Fighting words constitute a narrowly drawn category of expression limited to abusive personal epithets. Contemplating the sort of "in your face" verbal provocation that leads to violence, the U.S. Supreme Court wrote in *Chaplinsky v. New Hampshire* (1942) that such words "by their very utterance inflict injury or tend to incite an immediate breach of the peace." Because fighting words are immediately connected with physical violence, and because in the eyes of the Court "such utterances are no essential part of any expression of ideas" and have only "slight social value as a step to truth," this category of speech falls outside the protection of the First Amendment.[16]

The notion of a categorical exception to the First Amendment can be squared with the liberal philosophy embodied in the clear and present danger rule only by assuming that fighting words tend to create a danger of imminent harm that justifies suppressing the free expression of ideas. Already narrowly drawn, the fighting words doctrine was further tightened in *Gooding v. Wilson* (1972) when the Supreme Court restricted its application to utterances that "have a direct tendency to cause acts of violence by the person to whom, individually, the remark is addressed."[17] Somewhat implausibly, however, this requires us to believe that St. Paul's ban on symbols of hate was intended to prevent a violent response on the part of onlookers, as though the real danger the city apprehended in Viktora's act was that his victims might strike out in anger. A more plausible assumption is that the city was attempting to ameliorate a climate of racial antagonism and in so doing to lessen the prospect of racial violence; but this assumption requires that we view the ordinance contextually and that its suppression of racist hate speech be judged contingently, in light of variable circumstances, as it would be under the clear and present danger rule. Categorically excluding the class of fighting words from the protection of the First Amendment deviates from liberal principles by insulating the ban on expression against a fact-based challenge.

Another oddity of the *Chaplinsky* decision is that it construes fighting words themselves as a source of injury, as though insults were bricks hurled at an opponent. The effect is to downplay the expressive character of such words, effectively granting them little if any communicative value. The Court then proceeds to minimize the consequences of their suppression by asserting that low-value speech of this sort forms "no essential part of the expression of ideas." The logic implicit in the Court's position is that the suppression of speech with *de minimis* expressive value poses no constitutional difficulties. The paradox is that low-value speech can only be identified by reference to its content. The ruling leaves ambiguous whether the category of fighting words is distinguished by its particularly intemperate *language* or defines a set of unduly provocative *ideas*.

The question in *R.A.V.* was not whether St. Paul's ordinance was properly understood to pertain only to fighting words; the U. S. Supreme Court showed customary deference to the reading given the scope of the law by the state supreme court. Nor was the question whether Viktora's burning cross was proscribable under the fighting words doctrine. The justices had no difficulty agreeing that this racist symbol belonged to the class of fighting words and was thus legitimately subject to proscription. To this extent, then, the consensus of opinion on the Court found the suppression of racist hate speech consistent with the First Amendment. Led by Justice White, four members of the Court argued that the ordinance should nonetheless be struck down for being "overbroad." Because the law proscribed the display of racist symbols that elicit resentment as well those that cause anger and alarm, it appeared to them to cast the net too widely, putting at risk protected speech that merely gave offense or caused hurt feelings.[18] Consistent with the liberal First Amendment philosophy, this line of reasoning linked the suppression of racist hate speech under the fighting words doctrine to the prospect of real and substantial harm. The overbreadth argument would explicitly disallow any more broadly conceived ban on disfavored expression.

Justice Scalia's majority opinion took a different tack, using this case to reconceptualize the scope and application of the fighting words doctrine. In a striking departure from tradition, Scalia insisted that fighting words are not "entirely invisible to the Constitution." Nor was it true, he argued, that they have "at most a 'de minimis' expressive content, or that their content is in all respects 'worthless and undeserving of constitutional protection'." On the contrary, he acknowledged that "sometimes they are quite expressive indeed."[19] Even so, he allowed that the class of fighting words is "proscribable" by virtue of its content. Apparently, however, he did not intend to signal that government is justified in proscribing the expression of specific *ideas*. On the contrary, "the reason why fighting words are categorically excluded from the protection of the First Amendment," he wrote, "is not that their content communicates any particular idea, but that their content embodies a particularly intolerable (and socially unnecessary) mode of expressing whatever idea the speaker wishes to convey."[20] Presumably, a message communicated through unduly provocative language could as easily be communicated in words that pose no risk of violence.

On this basis Scalia drew an analogy between the suppression of fighting words and the imposition of time, manner, and place restrictions on protected speech. The Court has long held that time, manner, and place restrictions, such as those which prevent the use of sound trucks in residential neighborhoods, are allowable so long as they do not discriminate on the basis of the content of the message the speaker wishes to communicate. (E.g., a universal ban on sound trucks in residential neighborhoods is acceptable; a ban only on sound trucks espousing the platform of the Republican Party is not.) The rationale for time, manner, and place restrictions balances the right of free expression against other societal interests, such as public convenience and privacy. So long as all speakers are subject to the same restrictions, the government has demonstrated appropriate neutrality. Neutrality matters, because under the Fourteenth Amendment government owes all persons equal protection of the laws. This means that the coercive power of the state cannot be used to advantage or disadvantage particular speakers on account of what they choose to speak about or the opinions they express. In sum, laws regulating expression must be both *content* and *viewpoint* neutral.

Scalia objected to St. Paul's ordinance because he found it tainted by content discrimination: only symbolic displays specifically targeting a person's race, color, creed, religion, or gender were proscribed.[21] Moreover, in his view the ordinance amounted in practice to actual viewpoint discrimination. It appeared to him that the city had, in effect, taken sides in a partisan dispute over racial, religious, and gender equality by granting the pro-equality side permission to use abusive personal invective while penalizing their opponents for use of the same intemperate language. The city, he complained, had no authority "to license one side of a debate to fight freestyle, while requiring the other to follow Marquis of Queensberry rules."[22] To be brought into conformity with the First Amendment and the Equal Protection Clause of the Fourteenth Amendment, the ordinance would have to impose a content- and viewpoint-neutral ban on the use of fighting words.

Scalia's revised fighting words doctrine goes further than the original in attempting to distinguish provocative ideas from the language in which they are expressed. In his account it is clearly the language—the "socially unnecessary mode of expression"—and not the ideational content of the message that defines the category. This seems to me to set the impossible task of disentangling the medium and the message. I see no way to distinguish a racial slur from the racist idea it communicates. It follows that the regulation of hate speech must necessarily be attentive to the content of what is expressed and cannot aspire to neutrality after the fashion of time, manner, and place restrictions. St. Paul's ordinance would not run afoul of the Equal Protection requirement if, as Justice Stevens argued, the city had legitimately determined that "fighting-word injuries 'based on race, colour, creed, religion or gender' are qualitatively different and more severe than fighting-word injuries based on other characteristics."[23] Scalia himself was forced to admit under pressure from Stevens's argument that content-based regulation of a subclass of fighting words poses "no significant danger of idea or viewpoint discrimination"—and is thus allowable—when "the basis for the content discrimination consists entirely of the very reason the entire class of speech at issue is proscribable."[24] This condition is surely met in regard to the suppression of hate speech as a subclass of fighting words.

Consequently, it appears that Scalia was wrong to accuse St. Paul of viewpoint discrimination. In the debate over equality, the city did not license one side to use fighting words while denying the same privilege to the other side. *Either* side was permitted to hurl fighting words at the other on the basis of their conflicting ideas; but *neither* side could resort to fighting words on the basis of the target's race, color, creed, religion, or gender. As Stevens explained, extending Scalia's pugilistic metaphor, "[T]he St. Paul ordinance simply [banned] punches 'below the belt'—by either party."[25] Still, the metaphor itself seems strained. Rhetorical punches "below the belt" are bound to occur in heated political debate, and the liberal philosophy of freedom of expression does not authorize the arbitrary imposition of a civility requirement on public discourse.

Curiously, as a result of Scalia's focus on the medium (the "mode of expression") rather than the message, his revised fighting words doctrine looks to be more useful in policing the general tone of public discourse than in staking out the limits of free speech. The logic of the majority opinion in *R.A.V.* would in effect compel St. Paul to ban *all* fighting words in order to reach the injuries specifically associated with hate speech.[26] Perversely, this means of remedying the constitutional defect in the city's ordinance would place greater, not lesser, restrictions on free expression. Commentators have suggested that Scalia's opinion was intended to strike a blow against "political correctness," but its consequences could ultimately prove more illiberal than any campus speech code or local ordinance banning the display of racist symbols.

Hate Speech and the "Reasonable Limits" to Freedom of Expression in Canada

James Keegstra, a former high school teacher in Alberta, was accused of willfully promoting hatred in violation of sec. 319(2) of the *Canadian Criminal Code* for having repeatedly made anti-Semitic remarks to his students. Keegstra described Jews to his pupils as "treacherous," "subversive," "sadistic," "money-loving," "power hungry," and "child killers," and taught them that the Jewish people seek to destroy Christianity and are responsible for depressions, anarchy, wars, and revolutions. He also denied the truth of the Holocaust, claiming that it was a Jewish hoax devised to gain the world's sympathy. His students were required to parrot these slurs or risk receiving lower grades.[27] Keegstra's abuse of his authority as an educator continued for almost ten years before his anti-Semitic diatribes became a public issue and he was dismissed from his position. Criminal charges were brought a year later. His subsequent conviction was overturned by the Court of Appeal, which ruled inter alia that the willful promotion of hatred provision of the *Criminal Code* violates sec. *2(b)* of the Charter. The case went to the Supreme Court of Canada on appeal by the Crown.

Chief Justice Dickson's majority opinion confirmed that Keegstra's anti-Semitic statements qualified as expression protected by s. *2(b)*. Earlier freedom of expression cases had established that only the communication of ideas by means of violence is excluded from the Charter guarantee. In determining Keegstra's statements to be protected speech, the Court expressly rejected a version of the American fighting words doctrine urged upon it by proponents of the law, who argued that hate speech was analogous to expressive conduct threatening violence. There was still a question, however, of whether the statute could be upheld under sec. 1 of the Charter as a reasonable limit on the freedom of expression.

Section 1 of the Canadian Charter of Rights and Freedoms states that the fundamental freedoms listed in sec. 2 are subject "to such reasonable limits prescribed by law as can be demonstrably justified in a free and democratic society." Because of the reasonable limits clause, a law plainly in violation of the sec. *2(b)* guarantee of free expression can be upheld by the courts without recourse to tenuous distinctions between high- and low-value speech. By offering a sec. 1 defense of impugned legislation, government invites the courts to balance free expression against other important societal interests.

The test for whether a limit on a right or freedom guaranteed by the Charter can be demonstrably justified in a free and democratic society derives from *R. v. Oakes* (1986).[28] Under the *Oakes* test it must first be established that the impugned state action has "an objective of pressing and substantial concern." Next, it needs to be shown that there is proportionality between this objective and the impugned measure. The balancing of individual and group interests that is the hallmark of sec. 1 analysis occurs in the assessment of proportionality, which proceeds in three stages. First, it must be demonstrated that the impugned measure is rationally related to the state's legitimate objective. Second, the impugned measure must be demonstrated to impair the right or freedom in question "as little as possible." Third, there must be a proportionality between the effects of the impugned measure and the compelling objective that justifies infringing a protected right or freedom. In applying this test, the Court announced itself in *Oakes* to be guided by "the values and principles essential to a free and democratic society," including but not limited to "respect for the inherent dignity of the human person, commitment to social justice and equality, accommodation of a wide variety of beliefs, respect for cultural and group identity, and faith in social and political institutions which enhance the participation of individuals and groups in society."[29]

The key to understanding Dickson's opinion in *Keegstra* lies in his answer to the first prong of the *Oakes* test. The objective of "pressing and substantial concern" served by the ban on hate speech was found to be the protection of members of the target groups. Chief among the harms to be prevented was the "emotional damage" inflicted by hatemongers. Hate "propaganda," as Dickson referred to this category of expression, was seen as having "a severely negative impact on the individual's sense of self-worth and acceptance." Moreover, the danger hate propaganda posed to the "self-dignity of the target group" was matched "by the *possibility* that prejudiced messages will gain some credence [within the general public], with the attendant result of discrimination, and perhaps even violence, against minority groups in Canadian society."[30]

In light of the importance the *Oakes* test assigns to the government's objective, it is significant that Dickson spoke so tentatively about the social consequences of hate speech. He did not say that it *will* bring about discrimination and violence, only that it *might* do so. Pondering the effect of hate speech on society at large, he opined that it is "*not inconceivable* that the active dissemination of hate propaganda can attract individuals to its cause, and in the process create serious discord between various cultural groups in society."[31] He had good reason to be circumspect. His primary source of empirical data on the extent of hate speech in Canada, the *Report* of the Cohen Committee (Special Committee on Hate Propaganda in Canada, 1966), contained surprisingly little evidence in support of its dire conclusions. In fact, the *Report's* two-year survey discovered relatively few pieces of hate literature to complain of.[32] The mere possibility of untoward consequences seems a rather weak foundation on which to ground a governmental objective of pressing and substantial concern. Nonetheless, Dickson was satisfied that the statute met the first and crucial part of the *Oakes* test.[33]

Perhaps Dickson's ominous view of hate speech is at least partially accounted for by his use of the term "propaganda," which deliberately calls to mind the effective use of the Big Lie by totalitarian regimes in the twentieth century. Again, his views regarding the terrible power of hate propaganda were heavily indebted to the Cohen Committee's *Report,* which argued that "individuals can be persuaded to believe 'almost anything' if information or ideas are communicated using the right technique and in the proper circumstances." In the opinion of the Committee, we are no longer justified in sharing the comfortable belief of eighteenth- and nineteenth-century philosophers that man is a rational creature, whose mind, if "trained and liberated from superstition by education, . . . would always distinguish truth from falsehood, good from evil." Dickson quoted approvingly the report's optimistic assertion that "over the long run, the human mind is repelled by blatant falsehood and seeks the good"; but he also accepted the report's caution that "it is too often true, in the short run, that emotion displaces reason and individuals perversely reject the demonstrations of truth put before them and forsake the good they know. . . . We act irresponsibly if we ignore the way in which emotion can drive reason from the field."[34]

I find in these remarks a counterpoint to the theoretical underpinnings of the U.S. Supreme Court's speech-protective First Amendment jurisprudence. It would seem that in Dickson's view the liberal faith I earlier identified with the opinions of Holmes and Brandeis is no longer relevant. We can no longer safely assume that individuals are normally competent to assess the truth value and moral implications of public discourse. We now know better than to trust in people's reasonableness or in their capacity to resist sophisticated techniques of persuasion. State censorship may be required to protect the individual and society from the ill consequences of malevolent ideas retailed as slick propaganda. Like the optimistic liberal faith it displaces, Dickson's subdued confidence in human reason and personal moral agency is a founding premise rather than an empirical fact. What he offers us is a pessimistic conception of human nature rather than a descriptive account of how human beings actually respond to hate speech.

There is a conservative, Burkean cast to Dickson's argument. Individual reason is disparaged, but we are asked to trust the collective wisdom of society, institutionally vested in the state and enforced by its agents, notably the courts. But what sort of principles are to guide the state (and its agents) in determining whose speech and which messages to suppress? I believe that Dickson's position in *Keegstra* is best characterized as a defense of republican liberty. Republicanism and liberalism share many of the same commitments, including a tradition of constitutionally entrenched rights and liberties. Republican liberty, however, is realized through citizen participation in a shared public life while liberal freedom consists in the individual's unfettered pursuit of his or her private interests. In republicanism, rights serve to empower a politically active citizenry; in liberalism, rights operate as a check on political power, which protects the individual from a tyranny of the majority.[35] Viewed through the lens of republicanism, Dickson's concern with the effects of hate speech on the self-perceptions of vulnerable groups makes perfect sense. Insofar as exposure to hate propaganda lowers the self-esteem of minority group members, it lessens the likelihood that they will participate in civic affairs. Insofar as the contagion of hate infects the majority, minority group members are less likely to meet a receptive public if they do find the courage to participate.[36] In essence, freedom for hatemongers means unfreedom—a loss of republican liberty—for their victims. If rights are thought to serve republican liberty rather than liberal freedom, there would seem to be good reason not to allow the spread of pernicious ideas intended to undermine civic equality.[37]

While Dickson's theoretical framework in *Keegstra* is republican, his social ontology is communitarian. Communitarianism is distinguished by its concern with the social context within which the members of a community acquire their personal and civic identities and shared values. Dickson considered it self-evident that the autonomy and dignity of persons targeted by hate speech were contingent on their "ability to articulate and nurture an identity derived from [group] membership."[38] It was important, then, to protect the status of vulnerable groups so that their members would have an opportunity to develop the personal resources they would need to flourish as human beings. Only by securing their group identity could they be assured entrance into the political life of the nation on a level of equality.[39] On this logic, the state was justified in limiting the free speech rights of hatemongers in order to protect the equality rights of their victims. In Dickson's view, this constitutional trade-off met the minimal impairment requirement of the second prong of the *Oakes* test while serving "the legitimate Parliamentary objective of protecting target group members and fostering harmonious social relations in a community dedicated to equality and multiculturalism."[40]

There is, however, another aspect to Dickson's solicitous concern for the targets of hate propaganda. The statute makes it a crime to willfully promote hatred of an "identifiable group," which is defined as any section of the public distinguished by color, race, religion, or ethnic origin. Since all persons may be grouped on the basis of these criteria, the law would seem on its face to ban the willful promotion of hatred against *any* person on the basis of his or her ethnic, racial, or religious identity. But Dickson chose to read the statute as prohibiting "the intentional fostering of hatred against particular members of our society, as opposed to any individual."[41] Thus, he distinguished between the public at large, which is not identified and does not self-identify in terms of color, race, religion, or ethnic origin, and the members of minority groups, who are and who do.[42] There is a whiff of prejudice to this distinction (it references racial, ethnic, and religious minorities as the cultural Other), and the odor clings to the benevolent paternalism implicit in Dickson's reading of the statute.

Dickson's proportionality analysis is troubling in a number of other respects. While he attempted to minimize the reach of the statute by construing it as a ban on the most extreme forms of hate speech—the sort of especially noxious utterances "clearly associated with vilification and detestation" that tend toward the "destruction of both the target group and of the values of our society"[43]—the logic of his argument would as easily support a much broader ban on speech that is perceived by its auditors as offensive or demeaning. The subjective nature of the offense virtually assures that culturally insecure groups will discern the willful promotion of hatred in remarks that are merely critical or unkind. It is conceivable that by politicizing group differences the law actually encourages a heightened sensitivity to disparaging comments, such that even trivial slights will be keenly felt and bitterly resented. The vagueness of the statute invites aggrieved parties to salve their wounded pride by seeking to have government suppress the hurtful expression. Worried by the absence of limiting definitions in the statute, the dissenters in *Keegstra* anxiously pointed to efforts by Muslim groups to invoke the ban on hate speech against mainstream works of literature, like Leon Uris's *The Haj* and Salmon Rushdie's *Satanic Verses,* on account of their critical portrayal of Islam. That these and other attempts were rebuffed by the government does not guarantee that all such attempts will fail. On the contrary, the decision in *Keegstra* virtually assures that more prosecutions will be sought, and undoubtedly some will be undertaken.[44]

This prospect raises troubling political implications. Because hate speech carries a negative political valence, accusing others of promoting hatred can be an effective means of discrediting not only their words but also the beliefs and values that inform what they say. Once the state steps in and invokes the legal ban on hate speech, partisan denunciation becomes official writ. The statute upheld in *Keegstra* opens the door to politically motivated claims of injury, and there is a real danger that the state's legitimate interest in promoting multiculturalism will be exploited by social groups seeking to invoke the power of the state against other groups. One scholar who has examined this issue in depth reports that state censorship in Canada, formerly employed by government chiefly as a means of policing public morals, is now more commonly wielded on behalf of politically successful groups wanting to delegitimize their rivals. He attributes this to the rise of postmodern "identity politics," which makes a fetish of difference and initiates a fierce competition for status and power among variously defined social and cultural communities.[45] It is ironic that a law intended to promote social harmony lends itself to this socially divisive cultural warfare.

Social harmony was very much on Dickson's mind in *Keegstra*. His concern for ensuring that Canada's diverse cultural communities show respect for one another was apparently born of a sense that the multicultural Canadian nation is a fragile construction. This may or may not be so. (Dickson himself presented no evidence on the question.) But contrary to the drift of his argument, a politics of mutual respect is not inconsistent with a degree of intergroup animosity and mutual dislike. A culturally diverse society is bound to be morally diverse as well, featuring multiple and incompatible beliefs about the nature of value and the elements of a good life. Consequently, a certain amount of friction seems unavoidable.[46] Disagreement over fundamental values will convince some persons that those with whom they disagree are deeply mistaken about the nature of the good. They may even conclude that the lives led by some of their fellow citizens are objectively bad. The respect that one citizen owes another does not require that persons refrain from criticizing beliefs they consider false or practices they think morally flawed, regardless of the hurt this may cause to others. What matters is that all citizens respect one another's political rights, which in a society characterized by value pluralism necessarily include the right of each to pursue the good as she and her cultural community understand it (consistent with everyone else doing the same). While some persons may in fact feel aggrieved knowing that others dispute their sacred beliefs, disdain their fundamental values, or hold them in contempt on account of their group identity, this does not appear to be the sort of injury government can or should seek to avert.[47]

The Charter allows for reasonable limits to be imposed on a fundamental freedom, but only if such limits are demonstrably justified in a free and democratic society. Dickson's republican logic treats the suppression of hate speech as a means of empowering the members of vulnerable groups. In that sense the law serves democratic ends. But the perceived necessity of such a law rests on a peculiarly weak assessment of its beneficiaries' competence to fulfill the obligations of democratic citizenship. Dickson depicted the targets of hate speech as helpless victims in need of the state's protection. There is, however, no a priori reason to assume that the members of vulnerable groups will lack a sense of their own worth strong enough to repel attacks on their self-esteem. Even if we grant that personal identity cannot be separated from group membership, it is by no means obvious why the sense of belonging to a particular cultural community would not serve individuals as a source of strength rather than as a point of vulnerability. Working from Dickson's own communitarian assumptions we would normally expect the members of a targeted group to make common cause against their tormentors, drawing upon their shared culture to defend themselves. By assuming that victims are passive in the face of hate speech, Dickson denied their ability to play a proactive role in reformulating the terms of public discourse.[48]

The preservation of republican liberty requires that citizens possess civic virtue, the disposition to protect their freedom, and the capacity to use it well. Dickson claimed in effect that victims of hate speech are prevented from acquiring the requisite form of virtue, to the detriment of participatory democracy. But it would seem from his opinion that civic virtue was in short supply more generally. A ban on hate speech was needed not only to shield vulnerable groups but to protect the majority, which was deemed no less susceptible to the hatemonger's venomous screed. It is a curious defense of democracy that shows so little faith in the moral and intellectual capacities of ordinary citizens. Dickson must not have thought Charter values very deeply rooted if they must be guarded from the contagion of hate by the criminal law and the courts.[49]

Hate Speech and the Limits of Free Expression

As boundary-setting exercises, neither the American nor the Canadian case yields entirely satisfactory results. The majority in *R.A.V.* refused to acknowledge the unique historical circumstances of racial minorities in the United States that might very well justify affording them special protection from the harms of hate speech, at least in the narrow sense provided for by the Court's traditional fighting words doctrine.[50] While all persons may feel the sting of hateful words and be discomforted by abusive epithets, it is absurd to pretend that the effects of hate speech will be uniform across the population without regard to the circumstances of particular individuals, whose personal identities have been shaped at least in part by their experience of discrimination on account of their race, color, creed, ethnicity, religion, or gender.[51] Surely, if a given society were seriously fractured along racial or ethnic lines, such as is the case in the former Yugoslavia, prudence would recommend restrictions on abusive language intended to reduce the likelihood of interracial or interethnic violence. It is not much of a stretch to argue that the United States, plagued by a long history of interracial violence and striving to deal with its social and economic consequences, might choose to restrict racially inflammatory and abusive language in order to promote the healing of a divided society. This appears to be the underlying rationale in the concurring opinions offered by Justices White and Stevens, both of whom dwell on the historical grievances of black Americans. In contrast, Justice Scalia, striving for race-neutral impartiality, failed to take seriously St. Paul's rationale for suppressing hate speech.

Meanwhile, the *Keegstra* majority can be faulted for making no attempt to establish the real effects of hate propaganda, relying instead on ungrounded assertions concerning the harm done to victims and society at large. On its own terms, Dickson's rationale for proscribing hate speech has validity only if the impugned category of expression in fact constitutes a credible threat to the victims' self-esteem and norms of civic equality. That Canadian society is a multicultural community of communities does not by itself create an irrebuttable presumption of harm attached to offensive, abusive, or hateful speech. It is always possible that group solidarities will insulate their members against the harmful effects of hurtful words. It is also possible that the majority's normative commitment to democratic values will inoculate the citizenry against hate propaganda. That government acts to suppress hate speech under color of preserving democracy in no way diminishes the risks of censorship. Social harmony in a multicultural society is purchased at a high price if harmless expression is chilled for fear of inviting prosecution.

The American and Canadian high courts agree that moral and political considerations link freedom of expression to personal autonomy and democratic self-government, creating a strong presumption against state regulation. At the same time, they both recognize a need to impose limits on free expression for compelling moral and prudential reasons, including the protection of human dignity and the maintenance of social order. I have argued that they balanced these competing considerations differently in the hate speech cases because they came at the problem from differing theoretical perspectives. Still, I would contend that the juridical task facing each Court was essentially the same. Each had an obligation to ensure that the evil apprehended by the state was genuine, that its consequences were substantial, and that impairing the right of free expression in these instances would in fact avert the danger. If, as some observers have alleged, Canadian society is more divided and more fragile than its American counterpart and its political union less resilient, Canadians may well have more to fear from hate speech.[52] This is an empirical question. The special weight constitutional and moral theory attaches to rights demands not only a compelling purpose to justify their impairment, but convincing evidence of the need to do so. If the majority in *R.A.V.* was too quick to discount the gravity of the evil represented by hate speech, the majority in *Keegstra* was surely lax in failing to assess the magnitude of the evil.

Racism, anti-Semitism, and other virulent forms of hatred constitute an evil from which neither Canada nor the United States is immune. Persons of good will in both nations hope that those who sow seeds of enmity plant in barren ground. It may be tempting to believe that by silencing the purveyors of hate we might comfort their victims and generally improve the tone of public discourse. Still, insofar as we value constitutional liberty, we need to think very carefully about the message we send by responding to bad ideas with brute force. Whether our aim is to cultivate good republican citizens or conscientious liberal individuals, surely it is better to meet lies with truth and to counter propaganda with education. We need not fear giving legitimacy to the hatemonger's illiberal and inegalitarian message by allowing it to be heard; on the contrary, our willingness to tolerate the intolerant affirms our own commitment to freedom and equality.[53] Tolerance should not be equated with indifference. Malevolent ideas antithetical to our shared democratic ideals must not be allowed to go uncontested. At the extreme, where violence threatens, their expression may legitimately be suppressed. In the normal course of affairs, however, I believe that we register our opposition to hate speech most strongly not by calling for censorship but by speaking out in defense of human dignity, civic equality, and democratic freedoms.

Notes

This chapter draws on material that appears in "Liberty, Community, and Censorship: Hate Speech and Freedom of Expression in Canada and the United States," *American Review of Canadian Studies* 23, no. 3 (autumn 2002). I want to thank Ray Bazowski, Katrin Froese, John Harles, Terry Heinrichs, and Patrick Neal for their comments and suggestions.

1. 505 U.S. 377 (1992).

2. 3 S.C.R. 697. In *R. v. Zundel,* [1992] 2 S.C.R. 731, the Court struck down a related provision of the *Criminal Code,* suggesting at the very least some degree of ambivalence in its position. Earlier, in *Canada (Human Rights Commission) v. Taylor,* [1990] 3 S.C.R. 892, the Court had upheld provisions of the Canadian Human Rights Act curtailing hate speech, and subsequently, in *Ross v. New Brunswick School District No. 15* [1996] 1 S.C.R. 825, it allowed a provincial human rights tribunal to remove a teacher from the classroom for having publicly expressed racist views. In summer 2001, a teenager in New Brunswick was charged under sec. 319(2) of the *Criminal Code* for having burned a cross on the lawn of a black family. See "N.B. Teen Pleads Guilty in Cross-Burning," *Globe and Mail* (Toronto), 25 August 2001, A9.

3. See chapter 6 of the present volume by Samuel LaSelva, "'I Know It When I See It': Pornography and Constitutional Vision in Canada and the United States." See also, by the same author, "Pluralism and Hate: Freedom, Censorship, and the Canadian Identity," in *Interpreting Censorship in Canada,* ed. K. Peterson and A. Hutchinson (Toronto: University of Toronto Press, 1999).

4. Peter McCormick, *Supreme at Last: The Evolution of the Supreme Court of Canada* (Toronto: James Lorimer & Co., 2000).

5. The Charter was adopted as part of the Constitution Act, 1982. For an overview of the Courts sec. 2*(b)* cases, see Clare Beckton, "Freedom of Expression in Canada—Thirteen Years of Charter Interpretation (Subsection 2*[b]*)," in *The Canadian Charter of Rights and Freedoms,* ed. G-A. Beaudoin and E. Mendes, 3d ed. (Toronto: Carswell, 1996), chap. 5. Also, for a thoughtful critique of the Court's approach to free speech, see Richard Moon, *The Constitutional Protection of Freedom of Expression* (Toronto: University of Toronto Press, 2000).

6. For a discussion of the extent to which the American philosophy of freedom of influenced the majority opinion and the dissent, see Lorraine Eisenstat Weinreb, "Hate Promotion in a Free Society: *R. v. Keegstra*," *McGill Law Journal* 36 (1991): 1416–49.

7. On the opposition between liberal rights and the republican tradition in the Canadian context, see Charles Taylor, "Alternative Futures: Legitimacy, Identity, and Alienation in Late-Twentieth-Century Canada," in *Constitutionalism, Citizenship, and Society in Canada*, ed. Alan Cairns and Cynthia Williams (Toronto: University of Toronto Press, 1985), 183–229.

8. For a detailed account of the incident, see Randall P. Bezanson, *Speech Stories: How Free Can Speech Be?* (New York: New York University Press, 1998), 93–113.

9. *R.A.V. v. St. Paul,* footnote 1 to the majority opinion, 381.

10. 249 U.S. 47, 52 (1919).

11. Cf. *Gitlow v. New York,* 268 U.S. 652 (1925), where the Court adopted a looser standard allowing the present suppression of subversive speech on account of it's "ill tendency" to bring about a substantive evil in the future. The *Gitlow* "bad tendency test" was effectively repudiated two years later in *Whitney v. California.*

12. "[N]o danger flowing from speech can be deemed clear and present," he wrote, "unless the incidence of the evil apprehended is so imminent that it may befall before there is opportunity for full discussion." *Whitney v. California,* 274 U.S. 357, 378 (1927).

13. Ronald Dworkin, *Freedom's Law* (Cambridge: Harvard University Press, 1996), 200.

14. For the view that racist hate speech is especially injurious, see Mari J. Matsuda, Charles R. Lawrence III, Richard Delgado, and Kimberle Williams Crenshaw, *Words That Wound: Critical Race Theory, Assaultive Speech, and the First Amendment* (Boulder, Colo.: Westview Press, 1993).

15. See Dworkin, *Freedom's Law,* 195–213.

16. 315 U.S. 568, 572 (1942).

17. 405 U.S. 518, 524 (1972).

18. Separate concurrences were filed by Justices White, Blackmun, and Stevens. White's stayed closest to the traditional fighting words doctrine with its emphasis on a narrow, categorical approach to free expression; however, all three, together with Justice O'Connor, agreed that the St. Paul ordinance was overbroad and hence, on the face of it, invalid. See *R.A.V. v. St. Paul,* 411–14.

19. *R.A.V. v. St. Paul,* 383, 385.

20. Ibid, 393.

21. Ibid., 392, 394–95.

22. Ibid., 393.

23. Ibid., 425.

24. Ibid., 388.

25. Ibid., 435.

26. Ibid., 404–5 (White, J., concurring in the judgment).

27. *R. v. Keegstra,* 714.

28. 1 S.C.R. 103.

29. *R. v. Keegstra,* 735.

30. *R. v. Keegstra,* 748 (emphasis added). In her dissent, Justice McLachlin expressed concern that persons "gullible enough" to believe hate propaganda "might be just as likely to believe that there must be some truth in the racist expression because government is trying to suppress it." Ibid., 853.

31. *R. v. Keegstra,* 747. Emphasis added.

32. Terry Heinrichs reviews the statistical evidence presented by the *Cohen Report* and finds it remarkably weak: "[T]he entire amount of hate propaganda materials distributed in Canada in [the two years covered by the report] consisted of 52 pieces!" Heinrichs, "Gitlow Redux: 'Bad Tendencies' in the Great White North" (unpublished ms.), 56.

33. On the Court's contextually deficient presumption of harm in *Keegstra,* see Jamie Cameron, "The Past, Present, and Future of Expressive Freedom under the *Charter,*" *Osgoode Hall Law Journal* 35 (1997): 18–19.

34. *R. v. Keegstra,* 747.

35. Michael P. Zuckert, *Natural Rights and the New Republicanism* (Princeton: Princeton University Press, 1994), esp. chapters 6 and 10.

36. In essence, Dickson was claiming that free speech for hatemongers silences their victims. For a critique of this line of argument, see Terry Heinrichs, "Censorship as Free Speech! Free Expression Values and the Logic of Silencing in *R. v. Keegstra,*" *Alberta Law Review* 36, no. 4 (1988): 862.

37. Cf. LaSelva, "Pluralism and Hate." An American commentator sympathetic to the Canadian approach sees its preference for equality rights as a means of bringing previously excluded groups into the political process. See Kent Greenawalt, *Fighting Words: Individuals, Communities, and Liberties of Speech* (Princeton: Princeton University Press, 1995), 122–23.

38. *R. v. Keegstra,* 763.

39. Dickson's argument assumes the primacy of group membership in the construction of personal identity; however, it is also possible that laws like sec. 319(2) of the *Criminal Code* foster this identification by educating the public to think of personal identity in these terms. See Stephen Macedo, *Diversity and Distrust: Civic Education in a Multicultural Democracy* (Cambridge: Harvard University Press, 2000), 217.

40. *R. v. Keegstra,* 763. Section 15 of the Charter, which reads much like the Equal Protection Clause of the Fourteenth Amendment, guarantees equality "before

and under the law." Section 27 states that the Charter is to be interpreted "in a manner consistent with the preservation and enhancement of the multicultural heritage of Canadians." However, neither section mandates differential treatment of minority groups.

41. Ibid., 777.

42. Heinrichs, "Censorship as Free Speech," 862.

43. *R. v. Keegstra,* 777.

44. See Stefan Braun, "Freedom of Expression and Hate Propaganda Law: Striking a Balance in Canadian Democracy" (Ph.D. diss., York University, 2001), chaps. 4 and 5.

45. Reg Whitaker, "Chameleon on a Changing Background: The Politics of Censorship in Canada," in *Interpreting Censorship in Canada,* ed. K. Peterson and A. C. Hutchinson, 19.

46. Joseph Raz points out that "[o]ne of the difficulties in making multiculturalism politically acceptable stems from the enmity between members of different cultural groups." J. Raz, *Ethics in the Public Domain* (Oxford: Clarendon Press, 1994), 163; quoted in Samuel LaSelva, "Pluralism and Hate," 51. LaSelva goes on to observe that such enmity "is not simply due to ignorance, *but is endemic to multiculturalism and other forms of value pluralism.*" (Emphasis added.)

47. Stephen L. Newman, "What Not to Do about Hate Speech: An Argument against Censorship," in *Canadian Political Philosophy: Contemporary Reflections,* ed. R. Beiner and W. Norman (Toronto: University of Toronto Press, 2001).

48. On the capacity of victims to contest the language of their oppressors, seizing on the equivocality of meaning to draw the sting of hurtful words and overcome the injury they inflict, see Judith Butler, "Sovereign Performatives in the Contemporary Scene of Utterance," *Critical Inquiry* 23 (winter 1997).

49. It is not obvious that penal laws can compensate for a lack of civic virtue. Moreover, leaving the problem to the courts may discourage citizens from standing up to the evil on their own. Joseph Magnet calls into question the effectiveness of a criminal ban on just these grounds, arguing that "hate laws are a quick fix that makes people feel better because they perceive, falsely, that something is being done about a visible, irritating problem"; however, the putative solution is in reality a "cruel illusion" that "will cripple our political capacity to take serious action against intolerance." See his "Hate Propaganda in Canada," in *Free Expression: Essays in Law and Philosophy,* ed. W. J. Waluchow (Oxford: Clarendon Press, 1994), 250.

50. This was the position taken by White and Stevens in their separate concurrences.

51. Cf. this comment from Justice John Paul Stevens's Ralph Elliot First Amendment Lecture at Yale Law School: "We should at least consider the possibility that racial, religious, and gender-based invectives can cause distinct and especially grievous injury, particularly when used by members of a powerful group against an individual

already disadvantaged by a hostile environment. Most obviously, it is in that posture that an epithet comes closest to a threat, by evoking the ever-present spectre of bias-motivated violence, and, with it, real fear in the recipient." "*The* Freedom of Speech," *Yale Law Journal* 102 (1993): 1311.

52. See Samuel LaSelva's contribution to this volume.

53. David A. J. Richards, *Toleration and the Constitution* (New York: Columbia University Press, 1992), 192.

CHAPTER 8

Affirmative Action as a Way to Overcome Disadvantage: Inspiration from Canadian Law

Sandra Clancy

In the last few years, several prominent public intellectuals in the United States have called for a reexamination of affirmative action in the face of a number of new developments, among them successful initiatives to put an end to state-sponsored programs and court cases that have forced universities to dismantle programs designed to increase minority representation in student bodies. These scholars call for an end to affirmative action as it has been previously practiced and justified and offer novel suggestions as to how to proceed with ameliorative programs in the future. While affirmative action in the United States has long been regarded either as measures to remedy discrimination against African Americans and other minorities or ways to promote diversity in academic and employment settings, these scholars propose a conceptualization of affirmative action as a way to combat disadvantages experienced by individuals. Indeed, much of their work centers on recasting the structure of the debate about affirmative action to focus on helping individuals overcome disadvantages. Further, these scholars argue convincingly that efforts to aid the disadvantaged, even those disadvantaged on the basis of race, are entirely consistent with the time-honored American value of achieving equality of opportunity for individuals. As I will explain below, it is certain that the Supreme Court will soon reexamine the underpinnings of its affirmative action jurisprudence, and the scholars whose work I discuss have attempted to structure new terms for the inevitable upcoming national discussion of affirmative action. Their efforts seem especially helpful in light of the fact that recent research demonstrates that there exists considerable consensus among white and black Americans that special programs designed to help disadvantaged individuals take advantage of educational and employment opportunities are appropriate and needed. Americans are receptive to the notion that an individual's ability and willingness to work against significant disadvantage should be recognized as an important component of that individual's merit.

In their efforts to reformulate the justification for affirmative action, Americans would benefit greatly from observing the Canadian legal formulation of affirmative action. Canadian judges and politicians have conceptualized affirmative action as "special programs" designed to better the lot of individuals who are disadvantaged. Canadians have explicitly rejected as unworkable the American understanding of affirmative action as a remedy for past discrimination. In fact, the Canadian Charter of Rights and Freedoms itself sanctions "any law, program, or activity that has as its object the amelioration of conditions of disadvantaged individuals or groups," and subsequent interpretation by the Supreme Court expresses an understanding of equality as encompassing both the protection of individuals against unfair discrimination *and* the amelioration of conditions of members of disadvantaged individuals and groups.[1] The Canadian Court has also rejected the understanding of equality implicit in the American law, one that requires identical treatment of individuals unless there is sufficient, specific evidence of past discrimination that warrants remedial action. The Canadian justices argue that the attainment of equality often requires differential treatment in the form of special programs to enable disadvantaged individuals to compete for opportunities. It may be that the American public and courts would be willing to support arguments similar to those developed in the Canadian setting.

Indeed, it is often helpful to examine arguments expressed by lawmakers in other countries, especially those that have legal traditions similar to our own. Mary Ann Glendon tells us that comparative legal analysis is particularly useful when applied to a problem our own legal system has not handled very well. It often provides "a deepened understanding of the problem and . . . a source of inspiration," as well as "help in finding our own way through the forest."[2] Canadian law provides formulations that can help Americans structure new arguments for novel types of affirmative action. Upon reflection, it is clear that a number of programs Americans support but do not consider to be affirmative action should indeed be regarded as affirmative action programs aimed at helping disadvantaged individuals. Head Start, a popular preschool program for underprivileged children, is one such program. In the midst of a reevaluation of the foundations of American affirmative action law on the part of both lawmakers and scholars, it seems worthwhile to examine and draw inspiration from the Canadian legal experience with affirmative action.

The American Supreme Court's Reevaluation of Affirmative Action

In the next few years, as I have pointed out, the Supreme Court of the United States is certain to reevaluate the very foundations of its affirmative action jurisprudence. Several lower courts have recently rendered conflicting interpretations of the important 1978 case *Regents of California v. Bakke* in which Justice Powell argued that race could be viewed as a "plus" in university admissions in the interest of creating diverse student bodies.[3] Similarly, the Court itself has so narrowed the circumstances in which affirmative action is justified that it calls into question the legitimacy of many existing programs. Given the fact that many of the Supreme Court's decisions in favor of affirmative action have been close, often supported by only five justices, it would not be surprising if the Court rejected the use of affirmative action programs both as a remedy for past discrimination and as a way to encourage diversity in employment and educational settings. An argument for affirmative action as a means to ameliorate disadvantage may fare better before a more conservative Court.

The Supreme Court's affirmative action jurisprudence has been complicated and contradictory. Remedial intent has long been at the core of the arguments put forward by the Court's supporters of affirmative action. Justice Brennan, who wrote many of the majority decisions in favor of affirmative action in the 1970s and 80s, contended that preferential treatment was necessary in order to remedy centuries of past discrimination and its lingering effects directed toward African Americans, women, and other minorities.[4] In *Bakke,* for example, in which the Court considered an affirmative action program designed to increase the number of minority students to the University of California at Davis's medical school, Brennan argued that the university's stated purpose of remedying the effects of past societal discrimination was "sufficiently important to justify the use of race-conscious admissions programs where there is a sound basis for concluding that minority underrepresentation is substantial and chronic, and that the handicap of past discrimination is impeding access to opportunities."[5]

However, affirmative action as a remedy for what has come to be known as "societal" discrimination never stood on firm foundations. In *Wygant v. Jackson Board of Education,* a majority of the Court insisted that a showing of discrimination on the part of the governmental unit that had set up an affirmative action programs was necessary to justify the use of racial classifications.[6] Over the years, the Court has reiterated this requirement. For example, in *Richmond City v. J. A. Croson Co.* the Court held that racial classifications within state and local set-aside programs were inherently suspect and were to be subject to the most searching standards of constitutional review ("strict scrutiny") under the equal protection provisions of the Fourteenth Amendment. To survive strict scrutiny, a racial classification must (1) serve a compelling state interest and (2) be narrowly tailored to achieve that interest.[7] The Court held that remedying past societal discrimination is not a compelling state interest that can justify an affirmative action program. As Justice O'Connor put it, "a governmental agency's interest in remedying 'societal' discrimination, that is[,] discrimination not traceable to its own actions, cannot be deemed sufficiently compelling to pass constitutional muster under strict scrutiny."[8] Recent majorities on the Court consider affirmative action programs to be justified only as the remedy for discrete instances of past discrimination, requiring specific evidence of identified harm in workforces as a predicate for programs.[9] Implicit in this approach is the narrow understanding of equality as identical treatment, with affirmative action as only a temporary deviation from this ideal. American justices, even those in support of affirmative action, have articulated arguments for formal equality by conceiving of affirmative action as a form of compensation for past discrimination. The impoverished nature of the American jurisprudence will become clearer when set against the Canadian.

Following Supreme Court precedent requiring specific findings of discrimination, in 1996 the Fifth Circuit Court of Appeals rendered a decision that invalidated an affirmative action program designed to increase the number of Mexican American and African American students in the University of Texas law school. *Hopwood v. State of Texas* became legally binding in states located in the Fifth Circuit (Louisiana, Mississippi, and Texas) when the Supreme Court refused to review the case.[10] The law school had devised a program in which members of these two groups were admitted with lower GPAs and LSAT scores than white applicants.[11] One goal of the program, according to the law school, was to remedy the effects of past discrimination in Texas's primary and secondary schools, discrimination that resulted in lower test scores for African American and Mexican American students. The court, however, rejected these "boundless remedies," arguing that the law school was only justified in remedying the present effects of its *own* past discrimination. The law school pointed to no evidence of its own discrimination, but insisted that the lingering reputation of the University of Texas law school as a "white" school, particularly in the minority community, the underrepresentation of minorities in the student body, and the perception that the law school was hostile to minorities justified remedial action. The court rejected these indications of past discrimination as insufficient to warrant the use of affirmative action.[12]

The law school also put forward the argument that its affirmative action program was needed to encourage diversity within its student body, an argument that had first been proposed by Justice Powell in *Bakke*. Powell had rejected the University of California at Davis's contention that remedying societal discrimination is a compelling state interest, arguing instead that universities do have a compelling interest in admitting a racially diverse class of students. He stated that "the attainment of a diverse student body . . . clearly is a constitutionally permissible goal for an institution of higher education."[13] Powell endorsed an admissions program such as the one adopted by Harvard College in which race or ethnic background could be deemed a "plus" in a particular applicant's file. Other factors universities could consider to attain "beneficial educational pluralism" included exceptional personal talents, unique work or service experience, leadership potential, maturity, demonstrated compassion, and ability to communicate with the poor.[14]

Bakke may be considered the paradigmatic American affirmative action case, since it demonstrated the Court's profound confusion about the issue. Six justices filed opinions, none of which garnered more than four votes. There were two major opinions. The one written by Justice Brennan and joined by Justices White, Blackmun, and Marshall argued that racial classifications should be subject only to "intermediate scrutiny" and upheld the ones used by the University of California as a way to serve the "substantial state interest" of remedying past societal discrimination. Justice Stevens, joined by Justices Burger, Stewart, and Rehnquist, declined to address the constitutional issue and invalidated the program based on Title VI of the Civil Rights Act of 1964, which forbids any discrimination on the basis of race.[15] Justice Powell's decision is considered a swing vote, because while he agreed with the Stevens group that the university's plan was unconstitutional because it included quotas, he argued, like the Brennan group, that under some circumstances race could be a factor in admissions decisions.

Although Justice Powell's decision provided the impetus for the creation of many affirmative action programs, there has been considerable controversy about whether it constitutes valid precedent. In *Hopwood,* the Fifth Circuit said that Powell's decision was never sound precedent because it had never received any support from other justices. "Justice Powell's argument in *Bakke* garnered only his own vote and has never represented the view of a majority of the Court in *Bakke* or any other cases."[16] Indeed, the *Hopwood* court pointed out that the Supreme Court itself had expressed doubts about the validity of Powell's decision as binding precedent.[17]

More recently, several conflicting lower court cases have set forth differing opinions about whether Powell's decision in *Bakke* is a controlling precedent. In *Gratz v. Bollinger,* Judge Patrick Duggan of the United States District Court for the Eastern District of Michigan decided that, although Powell's decision was not joined by any other justice, altogether five justices did determine that "universities may take race into account in admissions."[18] At issue in *Gratz* was the affirmative action program designed by the University of Michigan's College of Literature, Science, and Arts to increase diversity in its student body. Under the program, members of underrepresented minority groups had extra points added to their GPAs in an admissions process in which GPA and SAT scores were heavily weighed.[19] Duggan argued that while Brennan and the three justices who joined his decision defended affirmative action as a remedy for past discrimination, "Justice Brennan's silence regarding diversity could easily be interpreted as 'implicit approval'."[20] Duggan approved of the University of Michigan's affirmative action plan, concluding that Supreme Court precedent holds that the attainment of diversity is a compelling state interest and that the University of Michigan's program was narrowly enough tailored to achieve that interest.

Only three months later, another judge on the same court decided that a similar affirmative action program designed by the University of Michigan Law School was unconstitutional. In *Grutter v. Bollinger,* Judge Bernard Friedman disagreed with Duggan that Powell's discussion of diversity is a controlling precedent, stating that this part of the decision was joined by no other justice. According to Friedman,

> The clearest indication that the Brennan group did not concur with Justice Powell's conclusions regarding the diversity rationale is that, although they joined in other portions of Justice Powell's opinion, they did not join in Part IV-D, the only portion of any of the *Bakke* opinion that specifically addressed the diversity issue. Moreover, the Brennan group did not believe that the diversity rationale was before the Court, as those Justices stated that the "issue presented" in the case was "whether government may use race-conscious programs to redress the continuing effects of past discrimination." . . . The Brennan group did not so much as mention the diversity rationale in their opinion, and they specifically declined to join in the portion of Justice Powell's opinion that addressed the issue. . . . In short, while the Brennan group and Justice Powell agreed that race may be considered in admissions . . . they disagreed entirely as to the reasons why.[21]

Friedman concluded that the attainment of a racially diverse class was not a compelling state interest, because it is not recognized as such in *Bakke*. Obviously, then, he ruled that the school's affirmative action program could not be justified using the diversity rationale.

In May 2002 the Sixth Circuit Court of Appeals overturned the ruling in *Grutter* and agreed with Judge Duggan in *Gratz* that Justice Powell's opinion is binding precedent.[22] But this decision in no way settled the matter for the nation, given that a year earlier the Eleventh Circuit Court of Appeals had struck down an affirmative action program at the University of Georgia based in part on the determination that Justice Powell's opinion in *Bakke* did not establish that student body diversity is a compelling interest that can justify the use of race-based affirmative action.[23] The conflicting decisions in the courts of appeals ensure that the long-unresolved issues underlying American affirmative action law will surely garner Supreme Court attention.

Scholars Reconsider Affirmative Action Based on Race

While American courts have struggled to forge a coherent theory of affirmative action, for some time even scholars who are very much interested in overcoming the problems of racial injustice in the United States have expressed reservations about granting preferential treatment on the basis of race rather than on the basis of disadvantage. Christopher Edley, himself a member of President Clinton's task force on affirmative action, conceded that one of the basic problems Americans have with affirmative action is that many people who are not disadvantaged benefit from it.[24] Disadvantaged African Americans benefit least from affirmative action programs, because they often do not have the skills and resources to compete for the opportunities affirmative action affords.[25] William Julius Wilson, best known for his work on "the truly disadvantaged," poor, unskilled African Americans who live in hypersegregated communities, has noted that more advantaged African Americans

> reap disproportionate benefits from policies of preferential treatment based solely on race. I say this because minority individuals from the most advantaged families are likely to be disproportionately represented among the minority members most qualified for preferred positions—such as higher paying jobs, college admissions, promotions, and so forth. Accordingly, if policies of preferential treatment for such positions are conceived not in terms of actual disadvantages suffered by individuals but rather in terms of race or ethnic group membership, then these policies will further enhance the opportunities of the more advantaged without addressing the problems of the truly disadvantaged.[26]

In addition, David Hollinger, a proponent of affirmative action, has pointed out the problematic nature of conceiving of programs as a remedy for societal discrimination. The Immigration Act of 1965 brought into the United States nearly twenty million legal immigrants, three-fourths of whom automatically qualified for preferences of the kind designed to remedy historic injustices faced by African Americans.[27]

These types of concerns have encouraged calls for affirmative action based solely on economic class rather than race.[28] Such arguments in turn have been opposed by scholars who insist that the level of racial discrimination experienced in the United States by African Americans of all classes proves the continuing need for affirmative action based on race.[29] But others, like the three scholars whose work I will consider below, have tried to establish what might be regarded as a middle ground between these two positions, one that has as its focus the amelioration of disadvantage and a recognition of the many complex dimensions of disadvantage, and, importantly, one that might have a chance of convincing an increasingly conservative court. They argue that both race and class must be seen as independent sources of disadvantage in the United States. This means that even many middle-class and comparatively advantaged black individuals face disadvantages compared with similarly situated whites. These may include having attended inferior schools, living in hypersegregated communities, having parents who did not go to college, and having to work full-time while attending school. A black student who appears to be as advantaged as a white student may have faced and overcome many more disadvantages. Edley explains that "race neutral approaches don't address the fact that some African-Americans, although better off than those who are poor or living in concentrated poverty, are nevertheless disadvantaged relative to similarly situated whites, and still face various forms of discrimination and exclusion."[30] Therefore, since not all African Americans are disadvantaged or similarly disadvantaged by race, different types of programs may be appropriate in different circumstances. Edley, for example, argues that African Americans from financially privileged backgrounds should not be given the same amount of help as African Americans with far fewer privileges. In admissions to elite institutions, rather than affirmative action programs that give pluses to all minority applicants, he proposes programs that give pluses to individuals who come from poor families, are first-generation collegegoers, or who come from hypersegregated poor communities.[31]

The focus on disadvantage, while not ignoring the effects of race, calls attention to the fact that members of groups should not be reduced to a common set of attributes and encourages consideration of each individual's attributes and qualifications. No doubt, refocusing the affirmative action issue on disadvantage will not provide simple solutions to difficult questions. Edley provides an oft-cited example of the types of choices faced by admissions committees in university settings to call for renewed discussions of these very issues. If a university were faced with the option of admitting two equally qualified candidates, one the daughter of an Appalachian coal miner and the other the son of a prominent African American neurosurgeon, which one should be given preference? Edley argues that such questions deserve "a national conversation and careful consideration."[32] Recent political events and court cases have lent an air of urgency to these considerations. Three prominent scholars in particular—Carol Swain, William Julius Wilson, and Glen Loury—have focused their considerable energy toward restructuring the American debate about affirmative action to center on disadvantage, and it is to their arguments that I now turn.

Carol Swain, William Julius Wilson, and Glen Loury

Carol Swain has analyzed public opinion data, arguing that it is here that scholars will find consensus among citizens upon which to structure viable alternatives to traditional affirmative action.[33] Swain notes that there is a substantial body of literature that makes clear that the Supreme Court sooner or later falls into line with American public opinion.[34] The American public, both black and white, agree that acceptable affirmative action programs fall somewhere between color blindness and racial preferences. Therefore, if the public were provided with acceptable alternatives to current affirmative action law, this would heighten the chances that the Court would be receptive to them.

Swain found that black citizens are not, contrary to the conclusions reached by many researchers, monolithically supportive of racial preferences. A 1997 Joint Center for Political and Economic Studies survey asked a random sample of the population in the United States their attitude toward the following statement: "We should make every possible effort to improve the position of blacks even if it means giving them preferential treatment." Forty-nine percent of African Americans and 83 percent of white Americans disagreed. Similarly, a 1996 Princeton survey asked whether a company with few minority employees, confronted with hiring one of two equally qualified applicants, one minority and one nonminority, should hire the nonminority applicant or find some other way to choose between the two applicants. Eighty-two percent of whites and 71 percent of blacks said the company should find some other way to choose. Likewise, in a 1997 New York Times-CBS poll 77 percent of whites and 72 percent of blacks agreed that race should not be a factor in college admission.[35]

Swain demonstrates that there is consensus across racial lines that special programs should be designed to help *disadvantaged* individuals take advantage of opportunities. In a vignette designed to model decisions college administrators often face, respondents were presented with the following scenario: A state university is deciding between two high school seniors who have applied for admission.[36] The first student attends a public high school, has maintained a B average, is from a low-income family, and has held a job throughout high school. This student scored slightly below average on the college admissions test. The second student attends a private school, has maintained an A average, comes from a prominent family, has spent two summers studying abroad, and scored well on the college admissions test. Swain randomly assigned the race and genders of the two hypothetical students so that sixteen possible combinations of race and gender were presented to equal numbers of respondents. She found that a majority of blacks favored the "B" student, even in a mixed-race situation in which the "A" student was black. A majority of whites with a high school education or less preferred the black "B" student over a white "A" student. Only whites with a college degree favored the black "A" student over the white "B" student, indicating that they did not approve of giving the space to a somewhat less qualified student who had overcome disadvantages. Swain makes a compelling case that black and white Americans favor attempts to identify and reward efforts to overcome disadvantage.

Swain provides evidence that white Americans are willing to support special programs designed to aid individuals who are disadvantaged on account of race. For example, outreach programs to locate qualified minorities for employment opportunities are supported by an overwhelming majority of Americans. In a December 1997 New York Times-CBS poll, 59 percent of whites favored special educational programs to help minorities compete more effectively for college admissions and 64 percent favored job training programs for minorities in industries where they are underrepresented.[37]

Swain concludes that the American public holds a wider conception of merit than many researchers had previously assumed, one that takes into account more than factors such as test scores, but looks to an individual's attempts to overcome disadvantage. She explains that "many Americans are committed to principles that allow for a substantially broader definition of merit than used by the leading protagonists in the affirmative action debate. That broader definition of merit includes consideration of the obstacles and hurdles that a given person has had to overcome to achieve the scores presented to the admissions committee."[38]

Like Swain, William Julius Wilson calls for a shift away from traditional affirmative action with its focus on goals and timetables.[39] Affirmative action based solely on race does not adequately recognize that the problems faced by disadvantaged individuals are not always related to race. Low-income, poor education, crime-ridden neighborhoods, inadequate housing, and cultural and linguistic differences are disadvantages that are not only faced by minorities. But at the same time, Wilson, while favoring special efforts on the basis of class, rejects calls for affirmative action based solely on financial need, even though minorities would benefit disproportionately from it. Rather, Wilson provides a convincing analysis of how race is a significant source of disadvantage for many African Americans.

Wilson points to large racial differences in Scholastic Aptitude Test (SAT) scores even among black and white students of similar income levels.[40] He argues that standard measures of socioeconomic status understate significant differences in the family and neighborhood environments of black and white students. For example, even when black and white parents report the same average income, white parents have substantially more assets than do black parents. Whites with the same amount of schooling as blacks generally attend better colleges and universities. Children's test scores are affected not only by the socioeconomic status of their parents, but also by that of grandparents. Wilson insists that black students' life chances are restricted by race regardless of class, "because of the effects of living in segregated neighborhoods (that is, being exposed to styles of behavior, habits, and the particular skills that emerge from patterns of racial exclusion), because of the quality of de facto segregated schooling, because of nurturing by parents whose experiences have also been shaped and limited by race, which ultimately affects the resources they are able to pass on to their children."[41] For all these reasons,

Wilson argues that race-blind policies fail to acknowledge the accumulation of disadvantages faced by even middle-class black students.

Wilson makes the case for the development of a new language to describe the goal of overcoming disadvantage and achieving real equal opportunity. He suggests the use of the term "affirmative opportunity." In the academic setting, Wilson suggests moving away from university admissions procedures that heavily weigh raw tests scores and toward the use of flexible, merit-based criteria. "[U]sing flexible criteria of evaluation will ensure that we are measuring merit or potential to succeed rather than privilege. In other words, we want to use criteria that will not exclude people who have as much potential to succeed as those from more privileged backgrounds."[42] He gives examples of innovative alternatives to traditional affirmative action, among them new admissions guidelines adopted by the University of California, Irvine in the wake of the decision by the University of California's regents to eliminate affirmative action in admissions. While SAT scores and grades remain important elements in the selection process, the guidelines state that "merit is demonstrated in many forms and measured in many ways."[43] These factors include an applicant's ability to overcome personal hardship, initiative and leadership, self-awareness (that is, evidence of active commitment based on self-identified values), civic and cultural awareness, honors and awards, and specialized knowledge. No numerical guidelines are used, but a study that compared the actual makeup of the newly admitted freshman class with the hypothetical makeup of a class admitted solely on the basis of GPA and test scores showed a significant gain for African Americans, American Indians, and Chicanos under the new system.

Wilson's affirmative opportunity focuses on recognizing and overcoming disadvantage in part because affirmative action has come to be associated in the public mind with equality of results, quotas, and the lowering of standards. Wilson contends that his proposals accord with liberal individualism's time-honored commitment to equal opportunity. "Affirmative opportunity means to renew the nation's commitment to enable all Americans, regardless of income, race, or other attributes, to achieve the highest level that their abilities permit."[44]

In the same vein, Glen Loury, long known as a critic of traditional affirmative action policies, has put forward a convincing argument as to why race should still be acknowledged as an important component of disadvantage for many African Americans.[45] Like Wilson, he calls for an end to goals and timetables. Instead, he endorses what he calls "developmental affirmative action," a concept that takes seriously the fact that race still plays an important role in the development of many individuals' capacities.[46] All individuals are embedded in complex webs of associations, networks, and contacts that shape behavior and capabilities. Both the historical practice of racial oppression and the ongoing racial segmentation of American society (most prominently seen in the isolation of the ghetto underclass) are such important influences.

Loury advocates programs designed to enable blacks to enhance their performance and better take advantage of opportunities. He calls for the creation in the university setting of summer workshops to make black students more competitive in the fields of math and science, support for curriculum development at historically black colleges, and the financing of research assistantships for promising graduate students. Similarly, he supports the provisional admission of black students to state universities, conditional on their raising their academic scores to competitive levels after a year or two of study at a local community college.[47] These measures all take race into account, but they attempt to overcome disadvantage based on race and enable minority students to compete for opportunities on a par with all other students. Loury contends that developmental affirmative action, although conscious of race, is "entirely consistent with individualism as a core philosophical premise. I am simply acknowledging the additional fact that in society people are not atoms. They are, rather, situated within systems of mutual affiliation. And in our society, these systems are defined, in part, by race."[48]

The three scholars whose current work I have briefly outlined have begun a new discussion about the future of affirmative action in the United States. They suggest that policy should focus on helping worthy individuals to overcome disadvantages, including disadvantages on account of race, and their goal is to restructure the entire affirmative action debate in the United States. All three are cognizant of recent changes to case law surrounding affirmative action and expect further changes. Indeed, Swain refers to Wilson's call for affirmative opportunity to overcome disadvantage and suggests that his proposals "are part of set of unresolved issues that must be debated at greater length by those concerned with racial justice and racial harmony in America."[49] The Canadian law of employment equity has taken as its starting point the amelioration of disadvantage, and it seems worthwhile at this junction to provide some insight into how Canadians have dealt with challenges that are similar to those faced by Americans.

Canada's Special Programs

The Canadian Supreme Court has argued that the achievement of equal opportunity requires lawmakers to examine the actual economic conditions of members of minority groups to gauge the full extent of the disadvantages they face and then devise special programs to ameliorate them. Canadian judges do not consider affirmative action to be a way to remedy past discrimination or to enhance diversity, but rather as a means to address the complex and varied disadvantages that may be the product of past discrimination and that often impede certain individuals from competing equally for opportunities.

Canadian lawmakers long ago rejected the formulation of affirmative action as a remedy for past discrimination. Indeed, Canada's Charter of Rights and Freedoms not only explicitly sanctions special programs, but expresses that their purpose is to overcome disadvantage. As I have pointed out, section 15(2) allows "any law, program, or activity that has as its object the amelioration of conditions of disadvantaged individuals and groups." This wording, as well as later Supreme Court interpretation, confirms the Canadian law's understanding that the achievement of equal opportunity often requires that government and private interests make special efforts to enable individuals to overcome the disadvantages they face. A hallmark of the Court's jurisprudence surrounding affirmative action is the justices' insistence that analyses of the status of individuals and groups in the political, social, and legal contexts in which policy decisions are made must guide their judgments. The Canadian Court, unlike its American counterpart, does not hesitate to examine data and statistics in an effort to determine whether a particular group of people is disadvantaged in relation to the general population. Finally, the Court conceives of affirmative action as entirely consistent with the pursuit of equality opportunity for all individuals.

Even before the implementation of the Charter, the Canadian Supreme Court affirmed its support for affirmative action as a way to ameliorate disadvantage. As far back as 1981, the Court rejected an argument that an affirmative action program designed to enable native groups to compete for job opportunities discriminated against non-native peoples and violated their rights to equal opportunity. Alberta's Energy Resources Conservation Board had prescribed the implementation of an affirmative action program as a condition of its approval of a tar sands plant proposed by Amoco Canada Petroleum Company and other companies. Amoco argued that the program discriminated against non-natives, but the Court countered that "[t]he purpose of the plan is not to displace non-Indians from their employment, but rather to advance the lot of Indians so that they may be in a competitive position to obtain employment without regard to the handicaps which their race have inherited."[50]

In *CN v. Canada (Human Rights Commission)* the Supreme Court confirmed that affirmative action should not be conceived as a remedy for past discrimination, but rather as a way to open up opportunities in the future.[51] Action Travail des Femmes, a public-interest pressure group, had charged Canadian National Railway with discriminating against women in hiring and promotions. A tribunal set up under the Canadian Human Rights Act ordered CN to hire women in certain positions until 13 percent of the workers in "nontraditional" jobs were women. A court of appeals judge overturned the tribunal's decision, arguing that according to the Human Rights Act, an affirmative action program could not be used to remedy the effects of past discriminatory practices, but only prevent discrimination from occurring in the future.[52] In this judge's opinion, the intention of the program ordered by the tribunal was to compensate for CN's past discrimination.

The case was appealed to the Supreme Court, and the centerpiece of Justice Dickson's majority decision was the impossibility of distinguishing between remedy and prevention in affirmative action programs. The Court clearly distinguished itself from the American Court's approach, which requires that affirmative action be a remedy for discrete acts of discrimination. Dickson wrote that the goal of an employment equity program was not to "compensate past victims or even provide opportunities for specific individuals who have been unfairly refused jobs or promotions in the past . . . [but rather to] ensure that future applicants and workers from the affected groups will not face the same invidious barriers that blocked their forebears."[53] This decision put an end to any speculation that the Court would follow the American model.

After *CN v. Canada,* the affirmative action jurisprudence of lower courts began to focus squarely on disadvantage. For example, *Apsit v. Manitoba Human Rights Commission* concerned a decision by the Manitoba Department of Natural Resources to give preference to people with native backgrounds in the issuing of licenses to grow wild rice on designated Crown land.[54] Although the appeals court judge decided to invalidate the plan, the case was important, because it clearly articulated an argument for affirmative action as a way to combat disadvantage. The judge found that the object of the program, which was to help native people take a leading role in the wild rice industry, would not be furthered by giving them preferences in obtaining licenses. Rather, this group lacked the ability to take advantage of broader opportunities in the industry. The court had no trouble finding that native people are a disadvantaged group in Canada.[55] In this case, the judge argued that the native group in question needed capital and management assistance in order to take a leading role in the wild rice industry, and if a program were designed to achieve this objective, it would be acceptable.

In the Court's first equality case after the establishment of the Charter of Rights and Freedoms, it set out its preliminary interpretation of the meaning of equality under the document.[56] The case arose because Andrews, a permanent resident of Canada but a citizen of the United States, charged that British Columbia's law restricting admission to the bar to Canadian citizens infringed his equality rights under section 15(1) of the Charter of Rights and Freedoms.[57] Although the Court did not explicitly discuss affirmative action, it articulated doctrine that has since become an important foundation of its affirmative action jurisprudence. Justice McIntyre stated at the outset that equality entails the promotion of a society in which all are recognized at law as humans who deserve concern, respect, and consideration.[58] He rejected the equal-treatment approach to equality, arguing instead that in order to achieve full equality, lawmakers had to recognize differences among individuals and groups and the differential impact of laws and practices on them. "In simple terms, then, it may be said that a law which treats all identically and which provides equality of treatment between 'A' and 'B' might well cause inequality for 'C,' depending on differences in personal characteristics and situations."[59] He noted that section 15(2) is a crucial expression of the fact that identical treatment can often produce serious inequality. He further clarified that equality is a comparative concept "the condition of which may only be attained or discerned by comparison with the conditions of others in the social and political setting in which the question arises."[60]

A recently decided Supreme Court case demonstrates how the Court has applied some of these ideals to a particular dispute concerning an affirmative action program. The decision provides formulations that may be helpful to those concerned with developing a new language and practice of affirmative action in the United States. The case, *Lovelace v. Ontario,* involved a special program in the form of a partnership between the province of Ontario and Ontario's First Nations to create the province's first reserve-based commercial casino, the proceeds of which would be distributed amongst First Nations communities "to ameliorate specifically social, health, cultural, educational and economic disadvantage."[61] Between 1991 and 1993, First Nations bands approached the Ontario government for the right to control reserve-based gaming activities. The two groups discussed the terms of the partnered arrangement, and in 1996 Casino Rama opened. The province of Ontario and representatives of the aboriginal communities began negotiating the terms of distributing the casino's proceeds. At this time, representatives of nonband aboriginal groups petitioned the Ontario government in order to participate in the program and share in the proceeds. In the spring of 1996, the province informed these communities that profits would be distributed only to groups registered as bands under the Indian Act.[62] Nonband communities brought suit against the province. The case finally reached the Supreme Court, and it faced the question of whether Ontario's exclusion of nonband aboriginal groups from the program violated section 15 of the Charter of Rights and Freedoms. In the process, the Court articulated its most comprehensive justification for affirmative action as a way to overcome disadvantages and further developed its argument that affirmative action is completely consistent with the Charter's guarantee of equality for individuals.

The Court stated at the outset that the equality provisions in the Charter were created to protect against the violation of "essential human dignity." Human dignity, in turn, was concerned with the realization of personal autonomy and self-determination. These are harmed by discriminatory treatment premised on traits that do not relate to individual needs, capacities, or merit, and are enhanced by laws or programs that are sensitive to the needs and capacities of different individuals taking into consideration the context underlying these differences. "Human dignity is harmed when individuals or groups are marginalized, ignored or devalued, and is enhanced when laws recognize the full place of all individuals and groups in Canadian society."[63]

The Court argued that the attainment of equality sometimes requires that distinctions be made in order to take into account the actual circumstances of individuals as they are located in varying social, political, and economic situations. It insisted that the attainment of equality encompasses both the prevention of discrimination and the amelioration of conditions of disadvantaged persons. It further argued that affirmative action should not be construed as an exception to the attainment of equality, but rather as an integral part of it.[64]

The Court faced a fundamental question that the American Court had confronted in *Bakke* and many other cases. That is, when does an affirmative action program designed to benefit one group constitute discrimination against those not receiving the benefit? The Canadian Court has devised a novel approach to this question, one that is in important respects different from the American model. The American Court insists upon identical treatment between groups and individuals unless there is sufficient evidence of past discrimination to warrant remedial action. The Canadian Court, on the other hand, dispenses with any consideration of past discrimination and accepts that differential treatment in the form of affirmative action is required to overcome present disadvantage. However, special programs are not acceptable if the exclusion of some individuals and groups from the programs is motivated by prejudice or if it amounts to a loss of their essential human dignity.

In a previously decided case, *Law v. Canada,* the Court had articulated a three-stage formula to determine whether a breach of section 15 has occurred, and in *Lovelace* it applied this approach to affirmative action.[65] The formula required the Court to find (1) differential treatment between the parties to a dispute (2) on the basis of enumerated or analogous grounds (3) that conflict with the purpose of section 15 (1) and, thus, amount to discrimination.[66] In order to answer the third stage of the inquiry, the Court considered what it called "four contextual factors." Here, it looked at whether the group excluded from the special program suffered preexisting disadvantage, stereotyping, prejudice, or vulnerability; whether there was a correspondence between the grounds on which their claim was based and their actual needs, capacities, and circumstances; the effect of the special program on a group more disadvantaged than the beneficiaries; and the negative impact of the exclusion from the program on the nonbeneficiaries.

The Court found that there was manifest differential treatment between the band and nonband native groups but that it was not on the basis of an enumerated or analogous ground, and it did not amount to discrimination.[67] In terms of the first contextual factor, it determined that both groups faced significant disadvantages, making it fruitless to consider which was more disadvantaged. However, nonband aboriginal groups had not been excluded from the Casino Rama project because of stereotyping or prejudice. The second contextual factor proved to be the heart of the Court's resolution. It justified the exclusion of nonband aboriginal groups from participation in the program on the basis that the casino project did not correspond to their circumstances and needs. The project was designed to be located on a reserve because the Indian Act placed constraints on the use of reserve land, resulting in limited economic development opportunities. The appellant communities were of a disperse nature, holding no title to a land-base identifiable as an aboriginal community center. Similarly, there was no evidence that the *Lovelace* appellants had experience in gaming. Because the negotiations between band representatives and the province of Ontario had gone on for five years before the opening of Casino Rama and it was developed on a partnered basis, there was a high degree of correspondence between the program and the actual needs, capacities, and circumstances of the bands.

In terms of the third contextual factor, the Court reiterated that the two groups were both disadvantaged and that "the program in question was targeted at ameliorating the conditions of a specific disadvantaged group rather than a disadvantage potentially experienced by any member of society."[68] In other words, the program was designed to address one particular disadvantage and could not be held invalid because it did not address all disadvantages experienced by Canadians. Finally, when considering the effect of exclusion on the nonband groups, the Court said that it did not amount to its complete nonrecognition by the government, nor did it affect the basic aspects of full membership in Canadian society like voting or mobility. In short, the group's exclusion from the program did not have the effect of demeaning the members' essential human dignity.

Lovelace provides a viable working alternative to present American affirmative action law, one that has at its central tenet that differential treatment in the form of special programs is a necessary condition for the achievement of equal opportunity. The Canadian Supreme Court, unlike its American counterpart, has developed a coherent theory of affirmative action and a means to achieve equal opportunity. In addition, Canadian lawmakers wisely evaluate data concerning the current economic and social status of groups of citizens in order to determine disadvantage and structure programs to combat it, while the American Court has rejected as unworkable any formulation that looks beyond past instances of isolated discrimination in particular settings. Insights from the Canadian setting can help Americans shape a novel approach to affirmative action.

It may be that the types of programs that Canadians have devised would not be acceptable in the American setting. Many of the Canadian cases I have examined involve efforts to improve the conditions of native Canadians, a group that may be less economically diverse than are African Americans. Nevertheless, the arguments in support of affirmative action developed in the Canadian setting should be considered by American scholars and lawmakers. The two dominant American rationales supporting affirmative action are unworkable and seem destined to be rejected by the Supreme Court. The goal of remedying past societal discrimination seems unreasonable in the face of the fact that many African Americans now eligible to take advantage of the programs arrived or had parents who arrived in the country in the last thirty years. The goal of remedying discrete instances of discrimination in workforces and university settings ignores widespread disadvantage in society at large. Similarly, the case for the retention of racial preferences to promote diversity is confounded by the fact that many of the white applicants rejected by such schemes would bring diversity to the institutions to which they seek employment or admissions. Cheryl Hopwood, the plaintiff in *Hopwood v. Texas,* was a thirty-two-year-old white woman of modest means, married to a member of the armed forces and raising a severely handicapped child. She certainly would have brought a unique perspective to the law school class.

While there are, of course, no easy answers to the sorts of questions affirmative action raises, a focus on disadvantage rather than discrimination or diversity clarifies the fundamental objective, which is consonant with the time-honored value of equal opportunity in which peoples' fates are determined by their choices rather than by their circumstances. While Canadian law offers us a firm conceptual framework for constructing arguments for affirmative action as a way to overcome disadvantage, Swain, Wilson, and Loury offer evidence that the American public is ready for such arguments as well as examples of innovative programs that have a chance of being accepted by the American public and courts.

To return to an example with which I began, Head Start may very well be the most widely accepted affirmative action program ever created in the United States. Head Start is a tremendously popular federally funded program that helps poor preschool children prepare for school. Indeed, it may be that American in favor of affirmative action would want to emphasize the need for more of these types of special programs, and see programs at the level of employment opportunities and university admissions as secondary. If the fundamental goal of affirmative action is to combat disadvantage, the justification for it becomes weightier as one moves from entrepreneurship (minority business set-asides) to employment to education, and in turn as one moves from university-level programs to the preschool setting. The *Journal of the American Medical Association* recently published results of the Chicago Longitudinal Study, one of the most comprehensive longitudinal studies of a large-scale early intervention program, and found that it helped poor children stay in school and out of jail.[69] For fifteen years researchers observed children enrolled in the Chicago Parent-Child Center program, which was created in 1976 under the Elementary and Secondary Education Act. It is the country's second-oldest (after Head Start) federal preschool program and the oldest early intervention program. Researchers compared 989 children enrolled in the program with 550 youngsters in less-intensive early childhood programs. Most of the children, born in 1980, came from families with incomes below the poverty level. The study found that 49.7 percent of preschool participants had graduated from high school, compared with 38.5 percent of those enrolled in other programs. The former group also had a much lower rate of arrests. Participation in the program was also associated with greater cognitive skills at school entry, higher school achievement in elementary school, reduced rates of grade retention, and reduced rates of special education by early adolescence. The researchers disagreed with those they referred to as the naysayers, critics of the efficacy of antipoverty programs created in the 1960s. But at the same time, they noted that while participants in the program did better than other poor children, they had less-favorable results than children from middle-class and wealthier backgrounds, leading them to comment that "although early intervention can provide a stronger foundation for learning than would be expected, *it alone cannot ameliorate the effects of continuing disadvantages children face.*"[70] The researchers therefore recognize the need for all sorts of creative affirmative action programs designed to target disadvantage.

The American public, and in turn American courts, will be more receptive to programs justified in this manner than through the traditional rationales for affirmative action. Lawmakers should consider an array of programs that the American public has a good chance of supporting, from Head Start to special college preparation courses for inner-city youth, to employment training for minorities in industries where they are underrepresented, to aggressive outreach programs in poor neighborhoods, to conditional acceptance of promising candidates by elite schools after completion of two years at a community college, to summer workshops for college students, to innovative acceptance methods that target ability to succeed rather than raw test scores. The fundamental principle underlying all these programs is that they aspire to offer equal opportunities to all Americans by recognizing and helping them to overcome disadvantage, a goal upon which most Americans can agree.

Notes

1. Schedule B, Constitution Act 1982, (U.K.), c. 11.

2. Mary Ann Glendon, *Abortion and Divorce in Western Law* (Cambridge: Harvard University Press, 1987), 1.

3. 438 U.S. 265 (1978).

4. See *United Steelworkers v. Weber* 99 S.Ct. 2721, 2723 (1979), *Local 28 of Sheetmetal Workers v. EEOC* 106 S. Ct. 3019, 3032 (1986), and *Johnson v. Transportation Agency, Santa Clara County* 107 S.Ct. 1442, 1446 (1987).

5. 438 U.S., at 362.

6. 476 U.S. 267, 276 (1986).

7. 488 U.S. 469, 493–98 (1989).

8. Ibid., 509.

9. Kathleen Sullivan, "Sins of Discrimination: Last Year's Affirmative Action Cases," *Harvard Law Review* 100, no. 1 (1986): 92. The criticism is that this approach makes it impossible for the Court to address widespread economic and social inequalities experienced by African Americans and other minorities that can be attributed in some significant measure to past discrimination.

10. 78 F. 3d 932 (5th Cir. 1996).

11. Ibid., 935–38.

12. Ibid., 948.

13. 438 U.S., at 311–12.

14. Ibid., 317–18.

15. Title VI states, "Race cannot be the basis of excluding anyone from participation in a federally funded program." Ibid., 418.

16. F. 3D 932 (5th Circuit 1996), 944.

17. In *Adarand Constructors, Inc. v. Pena* 115 S. Ct. 2097, 2109 (1995), the Court had lamented that its own "failure in *Bakke* . . . left unresolved the proper analysis for remedial race-based government action."

18. 2000 U.S. Dist. LEXIS 18099 (December 2000), 8.

19. Ibid., 15.

20. Ibid., 9.

21. 2001 U.S. Dist. LEXIS 3256 (March 2001), 22.

22. *Grutter v. Bollinger* 2002 Fed. App. 0170P (6th Cir.).

23. *Johnson v. Board of Regents of University of Georgia* 263 F. 3d 1234 C.A. 11 (Ga.), 2001.

24. Christopher Edley, *Not All Black and White: Affirmative Action, Race and American Values* (New York: Hill and Wang 1996), 105.

25. Daniel Farber, "The Outdated Debate on Affirmative Action," *California Law Review* 82 (1994): 931.

26. William Julius Wilson, *The Truly Disadvantaged: The Inner City, the Underclass, and Public Policy* (Chicago: University of Chicago Press), 115.

27. David Hollinger, "Group Preferences, Cultural Diversity, and Social Democracy: Notes toward a Theory of Affirmative Action," in *Race and Representation: Affirmative Action,* ed. Robert Post and Michael Rogin (New York: Zone Books 1998), 106.

28. See, for example, Richard Kahlenberg, *Class, Race, and Affirmative Action* (New York: Basic Books, 1996).

29. Amy Gutmann, "Responding to Racial Injustice," in Amy Gutmann and Anthony Appiah, *Color Conscious: The Political Morality of Race* (Princeton: Princeton University Press, 1996).

30. Edley, *Not All Black and White,* 101.

31. Ibid., 138–65

32. Ibid., 157.

33. Swain is the author of *Black Faces, Black Interests: The Representation of African-Americans in Congress* (Cambridge: Harvard University Press, 1993) and the editor of *Race v. Class: The New Affirmative Action Debate* (Lanham, Md.: University Press of America, 1996).

34. Swain quotes Robert Dahl in "Decision-Making in a Democracy: The Supreme Court as a National Policy Maker," 6 *Journal of Public Law* 6 (1957): 279, 285. He argued "the policy views on the Court are never for long out of line with the policy views dominant among the law making majorities of the United States."

35. Carol Swain, "Affirmative Action, Legislative History, Judicial Interpretation, Public Consensus," in vol. 1 of *America Becoming: Racial Trends and Their Consequences,* ed. Neil Smelser, William Julius Wilson, and Faith Mitchell (Washington: National Academy Press, 2001), 337–39.

36. Swain discusses the vignette in ibid., 388–40 and in her "Life after *Bakke* Where Whites and Blacks Agree: Public Support for Fairness in Educational Opportunities," *Harvard Blackletter Law Journal* 16 (2000): 166–77.

37. Swain, "Affirmative Action, Legislative History," 340.

38. Ibid.

39. Wilson works include *The Truly Disadvantaged: The Inner City, the Underclass, and Public Policy* (Chicago: University of Chicago Press, 1987) and *When Work Disappears: The World of the New Urban Poor* (New York: Alfred Knopf, 1996). Wilson lays out his argument for a reexamination of the purpose of affirmative action in "From 'Racial Preference' to Affirmative Opportunity," in *The Bridge over the Racial Divide: Rising Inequality and Coalition Politics* (Berkeley: University of California Press, 1999) and "Affirming Opportunity," *American Prospect* 10, no. 46 (1999): 1–7.

40. Several authors point to differences in SAT scores between middle-class black and white students as evidence of race as an independent source of disadvantage in the

United States. See Amy Gutmann, *Color Conscious,* 140–41; and Andrew Hacker, *Two Nations: Black and White, Separate, Hostile, Unequal* (New York: Charles Scribner's Sons, 1992).

41. Wilson, "From 'Racial Preference' to Affirmative Opportunity," 97.

42. Ibid., 103.

43. Ibid., 105.

44. Ibid., 112.

45. Glen Loury, professor of economics at Boston University and director of its Institute on Race and Social Division, is the author of *One by One from the Inside Out: Essays and Reviews on Race and Responsibility in America* (New York: Free Press, 1996).

46. Glen Loury, "Absolute California: Can the Golden State Go Color-blind," in *New Republic,* 18 November 1996, 1–20; and idem, "Who Cares about Racial Inequality?" *Journal of Sociology and Social Welfare* 27, no. 1 (March 2000): 133–51.

47. Loury, "Who Cares about Racial Inequality," 148.

48. Ibid., 143.

49. Swain, "Affirmative Action," 337.

50. *Athabasca Tribal Council v. Amoco* [1981] 1 S. C. R. 699, p. 711.

51. [1987] 1 S. C. R. 1114.

52. The *Canadian Human Rights Act* provides that if a tribunal finds that an employer has discriminated, the tribunal can order the employer to "take measures, including adoption of a special program, plan or arrangement . . . to prevent the same or a similar practice in the future" (Ottawa: Queen's Printer [1961]), 1.

53. *CN v. Canada,* p. 1143.

54. [1988] 1 W.W.R. 629.

55. The Court looked at data presented by Statistics Canada concerning educational levels, unemployment factors, income levels, value of housing or equity in property, and general unemployment figures. *Apsit,* p. 637.

56. *Andrews v. Law Society of British Columbia* [1989] 1 S.C.R. 143.

57. Section 15(1) of the Charter guarantees that "[e]very individual is equal before and under the law and has the right to the equal protection and equal benefit of the law without discrimination and, in particular, without discrimination based on race, national or ethnic origin, color, religion, sex, age or mental or physical disability."

58. *Andrews v. Law Society of Ontario* [1989] 1 S.C.R. 143, p. 171.

59. Ibid., 165.

60. Ibid., 164.

61. *Lovelace v. Ontario* [2000] 1 S.C.R. 950, p. 968.

62. R.S.C. 1985, c 1–5. The Court said that the nonband groups could be divided into two main groups: the Lovelace nonband First Nations appellants and the Be-

Wab-Bon Metis appellants. While the Court noted that the reasons for their nonregistration under the Indian Act were "historically long-standing, community-specific, and complex," it also quoted the Lovelace appellants' counsel, who expressed the band's resistance to giving up traditional forms of self-government and the present difficulty of becoming registered under the act. Bands who are registered under the act hold reserve lands and exist under a federally based legal regime for their identification, management, and accountability (*Lovelace,* p. 965).

63. *Lovelace,* p. 984.

64. Ibid., 987–1007.

65. *Law v. Canada (Minister of Employment and Immigration)* [1999] 1 S.C.R. 497.

66. Ibid., 988. The Court has maintained that this list of enumerated grounds is not exhaustive and that there may be grounds analogous to them.

67. *Lovelace,* p. 995.

68. Ibid., 1000.

69. Arthur Reynolds, Judy Temple, Dylan Robertson, and Emily Mann, "Long-term Effects of an Early Childhood Intervention on Educational Achievement and Juvenile Arrest: A Fifteen-Year Follow-up of Low-Income Children in Public Schools," *Journal of the American Medical Association* 285, no. 18 (8 May 2001): 2339–46.

70. Ibid., 2345.

CHAPTER 9

Do the "Haves" Still Come Out Ahead in Canada?

Ian Brodie and F. L. Morton

In the past thirty years, a number of Canadian interest groups have launched American-style strategic, public interest litigation campaigns.[1] Three interests—official language minority groups, feminists, and homosexual rights groups—have been particularly successful at pursuing their objectives through the courts.[2] All three of these interests consider themselves traditionally "disadvantaged" groups in Canadian society, and so their success is puzzling. It appears to contradict the long-standing sociolegal thesis that the "haves" tend to do better than the "have nots" in litigation. We suggest a solution to this puzzle. Their success confirms the Galanter thesis that the "haves" tend to do better in court. However, the agenda that the "haves" pursue and the resources they deploy are not the agendas and resources Galanter had in mind twenty-five years ago. We suggest that these changes have come about because of two complementary trends: the process of value change in Canada and the work of the embedded state. We also suggest that, in Canada, center-periphery politics must be considered when applying the Galanter thesis. In effect, although these three successful interests consider themselves "disadvantaged," they are now part of the "have" classes.

Galanter's Sociolegal Studies Thesis

Marc Galanter's "speculations" on why the "haves" in society come out ahead in litigation are well known. His 1974 article set off a vigorous debate about how litigation can deliver social and political change. That debate continues today in the broader sociolegal studies literature.[3] Galanter suggested that the "haves" come out ahead because they are more likely to be "repeat players" in the court system. They have ample resources, and these resources let them take a long-term view of litigation and acquire legal expertise more readily. They are more likely to "play the odds" over time and more willing to fight court cases with the potential to change the rules of the game. They are more likely to have informal relations with decision-makers in the court system and the legitimacy that comes with such informal relations. They are also more likely to develop reputations for skill or perseverance in court. The "have nots" in society, by contrast, are more likely to be "one-shot" litigators. The stakes in each case are relatively more important to a one-shotter, so they are more likely to settle out of court than fight for a powerful precedent. One-shotters have less access to specialized legal expertise. Galanter was careful not to claim that all "haves" are repeat players, nor that all "have nots" are one-shotters. However, over time, he suggested, those with the resources to be repeat players will likely do better.

Galanter's article was written at a time of optimism about liberal law-reform efforts. American governments were expanding citizen entitlements, beefing up legal aid services, and creating new civil and consumer protection rights.[4] Although Galanter was wary of the prevalent spirit of optimism, he concluded his article hopefully. He suggested the kinds of reforms that would make the judicial process more useful as a tool for social change: specific rule changes, more judicial resources, and increased government legal-aid services. He also suggested aggregating one-shot players into repeat players through class action lawsuits, interest group litigation, and government offices dedicated to representing "have nots."

Needless to say, times have changed since Galanter set out his speculations. Galanter's reform agenda has been largely implemented in the United States and Canada. The creation of new law schools, the expansion of old law schools, the diversification of the law student population, and the emergence of new categories of "quasi-lawyers" have all diffused legal knowledge in both countries.[5] Access to legal expertise and legal knowledge has undoubtedly improved. Yet, some of these reforms have been cut back in recent years. Private organizations have responded to the new pressures they face as a result of the reforms. There is less optimism about liberal law-reform efforts in the United States and Canada. Public interest litigation is now well established in both countries, but the haves–have nots research agenda that Galanter set out in 1974 continues to animate sociolegal scholarship in both countries.[6]

Legal Success in Canada

Canada has also seen an active and highly charged debate about the efficacy of litigation strategies for self-proclaimed "disadvantaged groups" over the past fifteen or twenty years. On the one hand, some argue that public interest litigation has changed Canadian politics and society in important ways. Morton and Knopff, for example, see self-styled "disadvantaged" groups winning important victories in court.[7] Smith argues that the Charter's equality rights have produced meaningful improvements for disadvantaged groups in Canadian society.[8] On the other hand, scholars looking for more far-reaching and deeper "social change" have criticized litigation as a political strategy. Mandel has repeatedly warned that Charter litigation offers only the illusion of gains for disadvantaged groups. The judiciary is dominated by the "have" classes, and its decisions reflect their class interests.[9] Razack's sympathetic account of the early years of the Women's Legal Education and Action Fund (LEAF) warns that rights-oriented litigation is antithetical to feminism.[10] After an impressively broad analysis, Bogart concludes that the significant victories women and others have won in court run the risk of backlash, complacency, and fragmentation.[11] A middle school holds that litigation campaigns can serve to mobilize support, set public agendas, and produce important social and political changes.[12] Certainly a complete account of the recent impressive changes in legal status and public attitudes towards homosexual rights must include various litigation efforts since 1982.

One recent study sheds light on the question of comparative success rates in court.[13] It disaggregates the concept of "success" to look not only at who wins in particular court cases, but also how a particular case influences the policy status quo and whether it creates a favorable legal precedent for a group's work. Based on this more elaborate set of criteria, the study concludes that official language minority groups (OLMGs), feminists, and homosexual rights advocates have enjoyed strong success before the appellate courts in recent years. These three interests have enjoyed greater success in court than the Canadian Civil Liberties Association and organized labor, for example, and much more success than socially conservative groups like REAL Women.

Much work remains to be done on the operationalization of litigation success, but these three interests are undoubtedly successful appellate litigators today. Yet, we return to the puzzle. They are all self-described "disadvantaged" interests. How is it that they have become so successful? Understanding their success requires an understanding of three factors that influence how the Galanter sociolegal thesis is applied in Canada. We turn next to elaborating these three concepts, and then show how they contributed to the success of the three designated groups of "have nots" in their Charter litigation efforts since 1982.

Postindustrial Value Change

There is now a substantial body of evidence that the political cultures of advanced industrial states have changed, and changed in generally similar ways, over the last fifty years. This is first factor to consider in applying Galanter's thesis today. Students of postindustrial value change, or new politics, have focused attention on the emergence of new political agendas in many advanced industrial states. These new agendas give prominence to identity politics, environmental protection, animal rights, and quality-of-life issues. Lipset has described the new agendas as "a clean environment, a better culture, equal status for women and minorities, the quality of education, international relations, greater democratization, and a more permissive morality, particularly as affecting familial and sexual issues."[14] Inglehart describes this development as "postmaterialism."[15] There is little question that these changes have taken place in Canada.[16] Lipset, Inglehart, and others have observed that the most dynamic agent of this social change has not been the industrial proletariat. Instead, a new "oppositionist intelligentsia" drawn from and supported by the well-educated, wealthier strata of society has been driving social change.[17]

Value change brings more that just a new issue agenda to the politics of advanced industrial democracies. It also brings new modes of participating in politics. There has been an increase in unconventional, less hierarchical, and more elite-directing channels of political action. "Outside" tactics like protests, sit-ins, and boycotts have become more common.[18] Value change has spawned new kinds of interest groups promoting "an idea or cause" rather than the material interests of a particular occupation or segment of the business community.[19] While postindustrial groups are not organized on occupational lines, they do have a class character. Their concerns are most prevalent outside the working classes. Groups mobilizing around postindustrial concerns find their elites among the new "haves," the well-educated and well-informed knowledge workers of the economy.

Inglehart has long noted the link between value change and public interest litigation. In 1981, he wrote that postmaterialists form a minority in most nations, and are therefore "better equipped to attain their goals through bureaucratic institutions *or the courts* than through the electoral process."[20] He wrote that as the postmaterialist cohorts aged, postmaterialism "was no longer symbolized by the student with a protest placard, but by the public interest lawyer. . . ."[21] Politics by litigation plays to the strengths of the postmaterialist cohorts. It places a premium on the skills of highly educated professionals like lawyers. When litigation is married to civil rights and other social reform issues, it taps the political agenda of value change using a new mode of political participation.

The contending explanations of value change are controversial.[22] Our aim here is not to explain why political cultures have changed. There is, however, strong evidence that postindustrial value change is occurring, and occurring in Canada. This value change helps explain the reshuffling of the political deck that has taken place since Galanter's speculations. The emergence of new political agendas is connected to the emergence of new modes of political participation. Affluent and powerful social elites no longer stand four-square behind the social and political status quo. Over the past three decades, social reform and social justice have become a political agenda of the "haves." The political agenda of the "have nots" now resonates among social elites.

The Embedded State

As impressive as the scope of value change has been, value change alone cannot explain why self-styled disadvantaged groups have done so well in court. Postindustrial values are still held by a minority of citizens in Canada. To solve our puzzle, we must consider changes in the configurations and function of the state since Galanter's article appeared. Political scientists now have a rich understanding of the state's ability to shape its own political environment.[23] Institutionalists have shown how the state can act as an independent actor, pursuing policies independently of the preferences of citizens or social groups. Alan Cairns has noted the fragmentation in Canada of state and society, and the emergence of a fragmented state that is "embedded" in an equally fragmented society.[24] Various nodes of the state and their interested publics shape each other. Fragments of the state fragments can act as independent political actors. Battles between state actors and their associated fragments of society may shape policy outputs more than battles between social actors. Demands on the state thus often reflect prior state action, and allies within the state are a potent resource for any interest or movement. This fragmentation is not politically neutral. The embedded state helps some interests and hurts others.

In Canada, the embedded state concept is particularly salient. Since the 1960s, successive federal governments have pursued a series of high-profile campaigns for social reform.[25] The Pearson and Trudeau governments forged a new Canadian identity by undermining existing national symbols considered "too British" to hold the allegiance of French Canadians and non-British immigrants. These symbols were replaced with new, "modern," and "fully Canadian" ones. Policies such as bilingualism and multiculturalism redrew the contours of Canadian citizenship. In its early years, the Trudeau government pursued nationalist economic and cultural policies to reduce the American influence in Canadian society. The Pearson and Trudeau governments also quickly expanded the federal government's social programs. A richer welfare state would, it was hoped, buttress national unity by forging direct links between citizens and the federal government. Trudeau labeled his wide-ranging set of social reforms the "Just Society" program. More than just a catchall title for the Liberal Party's election platforms, the "Just Society" has become the defining mythology of the Trudeau years.[26] Under the rubric of the Just Society, the federal government forged a new postindustrial Canadian identity and Canadian political culture.

Part of the Just Society program involved the federal government helping to create and funding networks of interest groups. This started in the late-1960s, and the funding continues to this day.[27] Several objectives drove this "citizenship" dimension to the Just Society: promoting "citizen participation" in political and community affairs; ensuring that disadvantaged groups could take on a fuller measure of power in Canadian society; and promoting the redrawing of Canadian political culture in areas like bilingualism and multiculturalism. In response to the national unity challenge, the federal Secretary of State's Department began funding French-language minority groups. Later, when the Trudeau government announced its multiculturalism policy, it began funding a panoply of ethnic groups. Later still, when women's concerns moved up the national policy agenda, it began funding feminist groups. Eventually, community organizations of every description were drawn into the web of the Just Society. These programs were established and expanded as a result of deliberate cabinet decisions, but over time they carried on and evolved under pressure from the clientele that each one created for itself and from internal bureaucratic politics.[28]

The Just Society program also had a law-reform dimension.[29] As justice minister and then prime minister, Trudeau pursued a wide range of law reforms in areas like divorce, homosexuality, abortion, freedom of information and privacy, and legal aid. The Trudeau government also created two new federal agencies—the Law Reform Commission of Canada and the Canadian Human Rights Commission—that proved to be the intellectual seedbeds of the rights revolution that blossomed a decade later.

The 1982 constitutional reform effort was the jewel in the crown of Trudeau's social and legal reforms. Its centerpiece, the Charter of Rights, was not a response to grass-roots demands for new constitutional limits on the state. In part, it was intended to entrench and extend Trudeau's earlier reforms. Its language provisions entrenched bilingualism in constitutional law. Consequently, language politics was moved into a judicial system staffed by federally appointed judges who proved to be sympathetic to bilingualism. Criminal law reformers, many of whom had worked for the Law Reform Commission, successfully influenced the wording of the legal rights sections of the Charter and provided interpretive footholds for future judicial expansion. "Equality-seeking groups" strongly influenced the wording of the Charter's equality rights clause.

There were Tory Canadians who raised objections to the Just Society's attempt to re-create identity and culture. Trudeau's allies successfully painted them as reactionaries, Anglophiles, bigots, and un-Canadian.[30] However, many Canadians embraced the Pearson-Trudeau reforms. Bilingualism, multiculturalism, the Charter, and socialized Medicare are now widely considered part of the Canadian identity, so much so that the Progressive Conservative government of Brian Mulroney could not attack these pillars of the Pearson-Trudeau legacy. Indeed, the Mulroney government further entrenched multiculturalism and official bilingualism, and made no efforts to "de-fund" interest groups until its last year in power. The Just Society sank deep roots in Canadian politics.

Trudeau's efforts to spawn a new interest in law reform and rights issues were wildly successful. In the years since the birth of the Just Society, a "rights revolution" has swept Canadian politics. Charles Epp argues that in Canada and elsewhere interest groups can only create a rights revolution where there is a support structure for legal mobilization (SSLM)—advocacy organizations to organize rights litigation, dependable financing for rights litigation, and a community of sympathetic lawyers to undertake rights litigation. But where did Canada's SSLM come from? Epp traces each component of Canada's SSLM to the same place: government action. Many Canadian rights advocacy organizations depend on government support. Their liberal/egalitarian approach to law reform partly reflects the federal government's deliberate efforts to fund such groups. Canadian governments fund many kinds of rights litigation, especially through legal aid programs. Canada's public law schools control entry to the Canadian legal profession, and the growing interest in rights litigation among Canadian lawyers is due in part to the efforts of the law schools. Organizations like human rights commissions and law-reform commissions have been "institutional sites for liberal rights advocacy."[31] There has been "a fluid interchange" of personnel, resources, and ideas among these agencies, law schools, and rights advocacy organizations. In fact, Canadian governments have been deeply implicated in creating Canada's SSLM.

Canada's embedded state has been shaped by the Just Society and Trudeau's law-reform agenda. Nodes of the state are embedded in fragments of society and use state resources to promote law-reform ideas. Canada's support structure for legal mobilization has been developed in part through using state resources. This has upset the have–have not dichotomy and given some interests the resources to be repeat players in litigation.

Center-Periphery Dimension

One last factor explains the conceptual changes needed to understand recent Canadian developments through Galanter's thesis: the center-periphery dimension of Canadian politics. Center-periphery relations are a strong theme in Canadian political history.[32] The interests of the Montreal-Toronto-Ottawa metropolis have dominated the country's settlement and economic development since 1867. Consequently, the country has faced persistent problems of regional discontent from the Maritime provinces and more recently the West. Since the late 1960s Quebec secessionism has also challenged Canada's heartland elites.

The Fathers of Confederation anticipated these problems. The 1867 constitution gave federal authorities the disallowance, reservation, and declaratory powers,[33] powers that early federal governments used to rein in provincial administrations. Over time these powers have fallen into disuse. In their place, federal governments found they could use the courts to strengthen their position at the expense of the provinces. The 1867 constitution gave Canada a unitary court system, and empowered the federal cabinet to appoint all superior court judges. This arrangement not only gave federal authorities a useful patronage lever with the legal profession, but also ensured that Canada's judicial elite would be sympathetic to the concerns of the center. When Parliament created the Canadian Supreme Court in 1875, it allowed the federal cabinet to ask the new Court for advisory opinions on abstract legal questions. Federal cabinets have often used this power to enlist the Court as an ally in supervising provincial legislation and administration.[34]

Shapiro has documented how the judiciary can serve as an efficient mechanism for removing contentious disputes from local government and transferring them to national, or central, authorities.[35] The structure of appeals, he argues, is hard to explain except as a way of moving divisive issues out of local hands and into central hands. Judicial politics centralizes. As Shapiro notes, moving an issue into the courts plays to the advantage of central authorities. Central authorities benefit as courts take on more decision-making power. A corollary of Shapiro's thesis is that judicial politics helps those interests that are strong at the center and weak at the periphery. Such interests can use litigation to move issues out of local politics into national arenas. Thus, the structure of the judiciary is itself a political resource for both central authorities and some kinds of political interests.

Bzdera has persuasively applied Shapiro's analysis to Canada.[36] There has been an active debate about whether the Supreme Court of Canada is "biased' in its federalism cases,[37] but Bzdera's is the first systematic survey of the Court's overall impact on the center-periphery axis of Canadian politics. He concludes that in Canada, as in the United States, the European Union, and six other federal systems, the "main function" of the high court is "to favour and legitimate the gradual expansion of central legislative jurisdiction."[38] In Canada, he argues, the centralizing effect of the Supreme Court is aided by the federal control of Supreme Court appointments, its budget, and its establishment in the first place.

American interest groups have exploited the center-periphery implications of the American judiciary for many years. During the "laissez-faire" litigation campaigns of the 1890s and 1930s, business and financial interests used the federal courts to overcome periodic eruptions of antibusiness or anti-finance populism in the American hinterland. By litigating, they moved their political battles out of hostile local arenas and into the more sympathetic national arena. The NAACP played judicial politics to similar advantage from the 1930s to the 1960s. By litigating, they moved their political disputes out of local arenas where segregationist enjoyed the upper hand, and into the national arena. As black voters in northern cities became more important to the national Democratic Party, the NAACP enjoyed increasing success. Jack Peltason implicitly recognized the center-periphery aspect of the NAACP's success as early as 1955.

The Just Society's legal dimension exploited the centralizing potential of the Canadian judiciary. Trudeau saw his legal reforms, especially the Charter, as potentially powerful nationalizing and unifying forces. He anticipated the Charter would have a two-track effect. Rights-based judicial review would politicize nonregional issues like free speech, women's rights, and so forth. These issues would gradually push regionally divisive issues off the political agenda. Then, judicial review would transfer many political issues out of provincial politics and into the national judiciary.[39] In the end, the most contentious of rights issues would be settled in Ottawa at the Canadian Supreme Court. As Peter Russell has noted, the Charter's purpose was not so much to create new rights, but to shift decision-making power about rights into a nationalizing institution.[40] The Supreme Court has found room for provincial autonomy within its Charter jurisprudence.[41] Yet the centralizing bias of judicial politics remains.

While federalism creates a matrix of centralizing and decentralizing political opportunities that groups can exploit, judicial politics tends to centralization. This is important when applying the have–have not thesis in a federal state like Canada. Interests that are weak in the periphery can use litigation to transfer their disputes to the national level if that is a more advantageous forum for this. And this changes the way the have–have not dichotomy is applied.

To conclude, three developments help to explain why self-described "have not" groups have come out ahead in the Canadian courts since 1982. First, the emergence of postmaterialist politics changed the agenda of the "haves" in advanced industrial states like Canada. Galanter assumed that minority rights and social reform would always be the agenda of the "have nots," while majority rule and the social status quo would always be the agenda of the "haves." Today, the relatively wealthy, professionally trained, and highly educated postindustrialist cohort pursues a new political agenda of social reform. This new elite has an affinity for channels of political participation like litigation. Second, the emergence of the embedded state has changed Galanter's original equation. State agencies are autonomous political actors and can direct their own campaigns of social reform. Once fragments of the state emerge as autonomous actors, interests that have allies in the state, or who can count on the sympathies of state actors, have an important political resource. Third, using the courts to settle political disputes has a center-periphery effect. By transferring contentious disputes out of the local milieu and into the national arena, judicial politics gives an advantage to interests that are stronger at the center than at the periphery. Judicializing a political issue helps those interests that are politically vulnerable at the local level but valuable to governing national coalitions.

Official Language Minorities

The confederation of the British North American colonies in 1867 involved a complex set of trade-offs to protect the new colony's language and religious minorities. In Quebec, English Canadians were a minority, but they dominated the province's economy and the city of Montreal. Outside Quebec, most French Canadian communities were small and isolated. Federalism emerged from the Confederation debates as a way of protecting the autonomy of the new country's various communities. Yet federalism alone could not accommodate the concerns of the new colony's elites. They included explicit guarantees for the colony's various minorities in the Confederation constitution: bilingualism in Parliament, Quebec's legislature and courts, and denominational schools in Ontario and Quebec. As new provinces were admitted to the Confederation, Canada's heartland political elites imposed similar constitutional arrangements on Manitoba, Saskatchewan, and Alberta.

English Canadians in Quebec were strong enough to see that their language guarantees were respected for a century. Outside Quebec, French Canadian minorities quickly lost political influence. In the first twenty years of Manitoba's history, its governments tried several times to undo French language and Catholic schooling rights in the province.[42] In 1890, when the Manitoba legislature voted to abolish French language and Catholic schooling rights, it upset the compromises that kept the center's political elites together. The country was plunged into a deep national political crisis that realigned the Canadian political party system.

Manitoba's constitution seemed to provide a firm legal basis for these rights, and the province's French Canadians launched a court challenge to the new language legislation.[43] A lower-court judge declared the legislation invalid, but higher courts offered no support to the minority. Successive Manitoba governments went on to operate almost entirely in English for almost a century after 1890. In the decades that followed, French Canadian minorities in the other western provinces did not fare much better. They were isolated, poor, and politically weak. Over time, western French Canadians slowly assimilated into English-speaking society.[44] They illustrated the Galanter thesis well. They were "have nots" whose rights were not respected by provincial governments, and who were ignored by the courts.

Beginning in the 1960s, however, French Canadians outside Quebec became strategically important to the national government, and their legal status quickly improved. During the 1960s, a new Quebec nationalism emerged and made a number of political demands. These included a reformed federalism giving the Quebec government special powers over education, language, and economic development it could use to protect the French language. According to the new Quebec nationalism, Quebec was the primary home of French-speakers in North America. The decline of French Canadian communities outside Quebec demonstrated that French could only be secure where French speakers formed a majority.

These political developments directly threatened Quebec's English-speaking minority. As the new Quebec nationalism gave rise to secessionist movements, it began to threaten the interests of the entire heartland. First under Pearson and then under Trudeau, the federal government acted to thwart the new Quebec nationalism. Trudeau had been preoccupied with Quebec nationalism long before he entered national politics.[45] In his mind, the best response to nationalism was to make the country bilingual from coast to coast. Quebeckers, he thought, would abandon the nationalist cause if they could be convinced they could be at home anywhere in Canada. By focusing their political attention on national rather than provincial politics, they could use Canada as a great "sounding box" to amplify their influence in the world.

Trudeau's bilingualism program was electorally useful to the Liberal Party. According to Trudeau plan's, if the federal government made Canada bilingual and multinational, Quebec nationalism would disappear and Canada would become a world example of how diverse people could live together.[46] This idea proved popular in the Montreal-Toronto-Ottawa heartland. His government could, and did, introduce bilingualism in the federal government. New bilingual government services were established. French Canadians were recruited into national politics and into the senior ranks of the federal civil service. English-speakers in the federal civil service went back to school to learn French. Bilingual signs were erected on federal property from coast to coast, and bilingual government services were established in most major centers.

Bilingualism was not uniformly popular across the country, however. It was much less popular in the parts of the country that had no significant French-speaking population.[47] Trudeau realized that the fate of the tiny French-speaking communities in these parts of Canada would be the key test of bilingualism's ability to solve the national unity problem. To ensure the survival of these minorities, Ottawa established a policy to assist "official language minority groups" (OLMGs). In 1969, the Trudeau government created a Social Action Branch in the Secretary of State's Department to "animate" French Canadian minorities. Associations that represented French Canadian minorities began receiving federal funding. The Social Action Branch also dispatched professional organizers to mobilize these minorities to be more aggressive in demanding government services, especially French-language schooling. As OLMG policy developed, federal support created an extensive national network of associations representing French Canadian lawyers, journalists, youth, women, community groups, and cultural organizations.[48]

But federal bilingualism and the OLMG policy were inherently limited. Most of the government services that OLMGs needed to have in French to guarantee their survival were in provincial hands.[49] Trudeau could and did remake the federal government according to the imperatives of bilingualism, but social services, health, welfare, and, most importantly, education were all provincial responsibilities. Most provinces saw no reason to adopt bilingualism voluntarily. Western Canadian voters, in particular, saw no reason to think that the country's national unity problems were the result of their unwillingness to provide French language services to their tiny French Canadian communities. After the 1976 Quebec election, the Parti Québécois brought in Bill 101 to advance French-language unilingualism in the provincial government, the province's private sector, and Quebec's schools.

Trudeau had long realized that provincial governments would block national bilingualism. In 1965, before he entered national politics, he wrote that since few Canadians outside the heartland shared his analysis of the national unity problem, it "would not be very realistic to rely upon good will or purely political action" to secure bilingualism in provincial government services.[50] The provinces would only extend bilingual services if the obligation were "incorporated into constitutional law." If the federal government could convert questions of language policy into questions of constitutional language rights, it could transfer the issue into the courts and out of the hostile arena of provincial politics.

The strategy for judicializing language policy came in two parts. First, the federal government encouraged OLMGs to exploit the limited bilingualism guaranteed in some provincial constitutions like Manitoba's. It expanded the support structure for OLMG legal mobilization by creating the Court Challenges Program (CCP). Under the CCP, the federal government funded the legal costs of OLMGs that sued their provincial governments.[51] Second, Trudeau ensured that the 1982 Charter of Rights included several new language guarantees. He insisted that the Charter guarantee minority-language public schooling to the language minorities of all provinces. When eight provincial premiers demanded the power to exempt provincial statutes from judicial review under the Charter, Trudeau conceded, but on the condition that this new "legislative override" could not apply to language rights. Once the Charter was in place, Ottawa expanded the Court Challenges Program to ensure a steady stream of OLMG challenges to provincial school policies.[52] This maneuver neatly transferred the question of language and education out of provincial jurisdiction and into the courts. A stream of litigation ensued over the extent of minority language schooling required by the Charter's section 23.[53]

Trudeau's judicialization strategy was a remarkable success for the government and for the OLMGs. In Manitoba, French Canadians took renewed interest in the language rights guaranteed by their provincial constitution. Local plebiscites showed how unpopular bilingualism was in Manitoba, but the Supreme Court of Canada eventually overturned the province's 1890 law that made the provincial government unilingual. It then went on to strike down all the language-related legislation Manitoba had adopted since 1890. OLMGs used CCP money to take similar cases to the Supreme Court under Saskatchewan and Alberta's constitution, and in turn, the Court upheld the OLMGs' claims. The Supreme Court also declared most of the PQ government's language legislation unconstitutional, precipitating a series of political uproars in that province. Finally, the Court ordered the nine English-speaking provinces to create French-language public school boards under the control of French Canadian parents wherever there were enough students to warrant such boards.[54]

Over the past two decades, the Supreme Court has vigorously enforced minority language rights in Manitoba, Saskatchewan, and Alberta. Since the French Canadian communities in these provinces were isolated, poor, and powerless, does the Court's track record represent a triumph of the "have nots"? Perhaps it does. And yet, until the 1960s, the courts stood by while provincial governments repealed the rights of French Canadian minorities. Ottawa only took an interest in beleaguered western Francophone communities when the new Quebec nationalism threatened the heartland's political interests. The Liberals' national bilingualism policy served as the centerpiece of their campaign to forge a new, more modern Canadian identity, and it served to justify Ottawa's intervention in provincial jurisdiction. Judicial solicitude for OLMGs' "rights" followed these political initiatives. In effect, the federal government enlisted the Supreme Court in its campaign to centralize power over language by encouraging the Court to resurrect guarantees of language rights in provincial constitutions. When Trudeau brought in the Charter of Rights, he ensured that the Charter would limit provincial discretion and expand judicial discretion over language and education. The Court Challenges Program, a fragment of the state, ensured that legal costs would not be an obstacle to access to the courts. The recent litigation successes of the OLMGs must be understood in the context of Canada's embedded state and its center-periphery politics.

Feminists

No interest group has used Charter litigation more than the organized feminists have. Until 1982, Canadian feminists had a history of failed litigation campaigns. Feminist public interest litigation began in earnest in the 1970s. It drew its inspiration from American civil rights litigation and the success American feminists had had in court, especially in *Roe v. Wade*. On issue after issue, though, the Canadian courts dealt feminists a loss.[55] The courts refused to follow *Roe* and strike down Canada's criminal law on abortion. They refused to treat discrimination based on pregnancy as discrimination based on sex. They refused women equal access to Indian status and therefore to federal Indian benefits. However, since the mid-1980s Canadian feminists have had a complete reversal of fortunes in the courts.[56] In only a decade, they have won important litigation victories on issues like abortion, social services, pay equity, pornography, and discrimination based on pregnancy.[57] What accounts for the rapid change in litigation success?

Value change has contributed to a growing concern about the status of women in advanced industrial states. Postindustrial values favor more egalitarian relations between the sexes, and this has changed ideas about the family, marriage, work, and politics.[58] In the 1960s, new ideas about the place of women gave rise to a new feminist, or women's, movement in Canada and other countries. In 1967, in response to the emergence of the Canadian feminist movement, the Pearson government established the Royal Commission on the Status of Women. The commission's report was the catalyst for recruiting feminists to the Just Society program. It contained a list of prescriptions for changing the status of women in almost all sectors of Canadian society. It also recommended federal funding for feminist groups. Ottawa stepped in to support the National Advisory Committee on the Status of Women (NAC) in 1971, and in 1974 to support the new "Women's Bureau" in the Secretary of State's Department. The Secretary of State's Department created the Canadian Advisory Council on the Status of Women (CACSW) in 1973; the National Association of Women and the Law (NAWL) in 1974; the Canadian Congress for Learning Opportunities for Women in 1979; and the Canadian Day Care Advocacy Association in 1983.[59] Value change and state action reinforced each other.

When the Trudeau government announced its plans for the Charter in 1980, feminists saw an opportunity to undo the Supreme Court's decisions of the 1970s. They lobbied the Trudeau government to ensure women's rights were featured prominently in the Charter's text. During the hearings of the parliamentary committee on the proposed Charter, the federal government sought support for its efforts by bringing some interest groups, including feminists, into the drafting process. A series of battles between feminists and the

Trudeau government produced a "generously worded documents with significant interpretive flexibility" that favored feminist concerns.[60] Feminists were especially successful in redrafting the Charter's "equality rights" section.[61] This provision guaranteed equality "before and under the law" and "equal benefit and equal protection of the law" without discrimination based on, among other things, sex. Women in the federally funded network of feminist organizations created LEAF to take advantage of the new litigation opportunities the Charter provided. In 1984, the CACSW released a study that called for the formation of "a legal action fund to concentrate on issues of sex-based discrimination." With the adoption of the Charter two years earlier, the study declared, it was "an opportune moment to stress litigation as a vehicle for social change."[62] The feminist movement was already tied to the Secretary of State's Department, so LEAF's organizing committee was able to tap government grants to support its activities. The Court Challenges Program, which had previously funded OLMG litigation, was extended to include groups like LEAF, and LEAF soon became a top recipient of CCP funding.[63] LEAF deliberately followed the strategies of American rights-advocacy organization, with the objective of using "test cases" to pursue "systematic litigation" strategies.

Fragments of the Canadian state have contributed to a support structure for feminist legal mobilization in other ways. Various state offices—human rights commissions, legal departments, law-reform commissions, law schools, and judicial education programs—form a web of bureaucratic nodes for initiating, funding, legitimating, and implementing the claims of rights advocacy organizations. Canada's public universities recruit, train, and pay the salaries of many intellectuals whose ideas drive the feminist movement. Law school academics have been active on both sides of the debate about the efficacy of social reform by litigation. Yet law schools now produce a steady stream of "rights experts" to staff the bureaucracies, interest groups, and courts that pursue the politics of rights.

Advocacy scholarship was a calculated component of feminist strategy to maximize the political utility of Charter litigation. The same 1984 report that led to the creation of LEAF declared that "a critical component of this [systematic litigation] strategy [is] to build a theory of equality which is accepted by academics, lawyers and the judiciary. Legal writings in respected law journals, presentations of papers at legal seminars, and participation in judges' training sessions are all means of disseminating and legitimating such theories of equality."[64] Once LEAF was established, it adopted a self-styled campaign of "influencing the influencers" that included fostering supportive legal scholarship.[65] NAWL's sponsorship of the *Canadian Journal of Women and the Law* represents part of the implementation of this strategy.

The litigation track record of Canadian feminists, while not as successful as that of the OLMGs, has been impressive.[66] This success is not simply a matter of the triumph of the "have nots." As in other Western societies, feminism in Canada draws its strength from postindustrialist cohorts characterized by higher socioeconomic status. Other feminists have noted that the activists behind LEAF are largely white, wealthy, highly educated professional women, used to exercising considerable economic and social power.[67] LEAF, like the rest of the Canadian feminist movement, has been able to bring postmaterialist politics and state resources together to win in court.

Homosexual Rights

Canadian feminists set the standard for successfully judicializing the politics of gender, but homosexual rights activists and the interest group EGALE (Equality for Gays and Lesbians Everywhere) have learned the lessons of LEAF's litigation. The dramatic litigation advances of the Canadian homosexual rights movement in the past ten years illustrate the combined effect of postmaterialist politics and state autonomy. Canadian homosexuals were early beneficiaries of Trudeau's personal commitment to social and legal reform. Since then, Canada, like most advanced industrial states, has experienced the secular loosening of sexual mores associated with postmaterialism, and this has given gay rights issues good political currency.

Although Canadian homosexual rights activists demanded constitutional protection in the early 1970s,[68] they were not nearly as successful in influencing the drafting of the Charter as Canadian feminists were. Backbenchers tried to include sexual orientation as a prohibited ground of governmental discrimination under the Charter's equality rights section when the Charter was being drafted. The Trudeau government rebuffed these efforts, but Trudeau effectively gave judges the opportunity to extend the Charter's protection to new groups by making the list of prohibited grounds of discrimination open-ended.[69] Once the Charter was in place, homosexual rights activists planned litigation to persuade judges to extend equality rights protection to Canadian homosexuals. They expected protracted litigation on the issue, and this was not an unreasonable expectation. Trudeau had opposed putting sexual orientation in the Charter's text, and the Mulroney Progressive Conservatives soon replaced Trudeau's Liberals. Few provincial governments showed any enthusiasm for homosexual rights. To pave the way for their litigation, these activists started their own campaign of "influencing the influencers." Allies in the legal academy published law journal articles to establish the legitimacy of the various legal arguments for extending Charter protection to homosexuals. Yet when the first cases went to court, activists were surprised to find that getting equality rights protection for homosexuals "was a non-issue."[70] In 1986, the federal Justice Department issued a policy paper arguing that homosexuals should have equality rights protection under the Charter. Then, in 1990, when one of the first test cases on the issue went to appeal, it received funding from the Court Challenges Program and federal lawyers conceded that homosexuals should have equality rights protection. In 1995, the Supreme Court endorsed the proposition that homosexuals were a "protected" group under the equality rights provision of the Charter.

No Canadian episode illustrates the new importance of having allies in state institutions than the litigation campaign to have homosexual rights recognized in federal human rights legislation. In 1986, the Mulroney government announced its intention to expand the Canadian Human Rights Act (CHRA) to outlaw discrimination against homosexuals in areas of federal action. The issue deeply divided Mulroney's caucus, and the government was unable to produce legislation during its first mandate. Nonetheless, homosexual rights activists were buoyed by the willingness of the Justice Department to concede that homosexuals should have equality rights protection, and by the courts' willingness to accept this concession. They sued the federal government and asked the courts to extend the CHRA to cover discrimination based on sexual orientation. Their test case, financed by the Court Challenges Program, ended up at the Ontario Court of Appeals in 1992.[71] At the same time, the new Canadian minister of justice, Kim Campbell, made it clear that she intended to get the CHRA amended. Federal lawyers opted to pursue a weak defense of the CHRA on appeal, and in August 1992, the Ontario Court of Appeals extended the CHRA's protection to homosexuals. The Justice Department decided not to appeal to the Supreme Court of Canada. In November 1992, Justice Minister Campbell announced that the government no longer needed Parliament to amend the CHRA, because the courts had done so already. As in the case of bilingualism, federal government officials circumvented a hostile political environment for their policy objectives by enlisting the courts as allies. The government essentially allied itself with the courts to bypass the divided Conservative caucus and insert sexual orientation into the federal human rights code.

This homosexual rights litigation follows the pattern set by Canadian OLMG and feminist litigation. Homosexuals at first glance appear to be the kind of "have nots" that Galanter thought would do poorly in court, but as it turns out they have done quite well through litigation. A proper understanding of the new context of the Galanter theory shows why this is so: homosexual rights, like feminism, is a postmaterialist issue. The homosexual rights movement enjoys support among the wealthy, well-educated professionals of the postmaterialist classes. Homosexual rights activists also have strong allies in government, the legal academy, and the national media. Litigation allows them to transfer contentious policy issues into the courts and away from institutions where their cause is less likely to succeed.

Conclusion

Not all the public interest litigation in Canada is by self-described "disadvantaged" groups. Some conservative groups have been active in the Canadian courts. Socially conservative groups like the Evangelical Fellowship of Canada, REAL Women, and Focus on the Family Canada appeared at the Supreme Court during the 1990s to defend pro-life and traditional legal approaches to the family, but both of these efforts have largely failed. The National Citizens Coalition (NCC), a leading conservative political action group, has successfully used litigation to ensure free political speech during election campaigns.[72] Yet a closer look reveals how much the NCC has depended on adept forum-shopping to win. It launches cases in Alberta and tries to avoid appeals beyond the Alberta courts. When the Supreme Court heard the issue of campaign-time free speech, it sent a strong signal that it disapproves of the NCC precedents.[73]

Galanter's theory that the "haves come out ahead" in litigation is thus confirmed by Canada's experience under the Charter of Rights, but only when understood in light of certain changes to the wider political context. Value change has meant that a new agenda of social justice and quality-of-life issues now enjoys the sympathy of wealthier, more educated professional people. The greatest challenges to the sociopolitical status quo now come from the "have" classes. This has helped both the feminist and homosexual rights movements in Canada, whose activists and supporters are both characterized by higher socioeconomic profiles. The success of the OLMGs is in part attributable to the role bilingualism was intended to play in the new postindustrial Canadian nationalism.

The Canadian state's autonomy is the second political change that has contributed to the success of some interest group litigation under the Charter. All three of the interest groups studied have benefited from alliances with state actors. The Trudeau government supported the OLMGs as part of its national unity initiatives. The Secretary of State's Department provided core funding for both OLMGs and feminists, while the Court Challenges Program has been a funding source for the litigation efforts of all three groups. Access to decision-makers and support in the various rights bureaucracies—federal and provincial justice departments, human rights commissions, the law schools, and appeal court clerks—have been important resources for all three groups.

Finally, the center-periphery dynamic of Charter litigation has contributed to the success of OLMGs and gay rights activists. All three groups have been able to win policy concessions in the Supreme Court that they never would have achieved in provincial legislatures. The Canadian judiciary delivers the most controversial court cases to Ottawa, where they can be decided by judges appointed by the prime minister sitting in a Supreme Court that is funded by the federal government.

In other words, these self-described "disadvantaged" groups win because under the new conditions they are now among the "haves." And being among the "haves" has given them the resources required to become repeat players and succeed in judicial politics. Galanter recommended many of the legal reforms that Canada has adopted to help "have not" groups do better in the courts: universal legal aid, state support for litigation, and expanded law schools. With respect to Galanter, there is a certain paradox in his prescription for reform of the judiciary. If he really thought that the "haves" come out ahead in the courts, then why not keep as much policy as possible out of the courts? This was the prescription of the first generation of judicial progressives—the Holmes, Brandeis, and Frankfurter tradition. That Galanter did not choose this solution suggests that he was actually an early member of the second generation of judicial progressives, those who believed that an activist judiciary was not only consistent with but could even advance progressive politics and policy. As Silverstein has pointed out, the courts became more important to American progressives as the New Deal coalition splintered.[74] In 1974, Galanter was a self-proclaimed progressive writing at the beginning of the end of the Democratic Party's forty-year domination of American politics. In retrospect, Galanter's prescription may be understood as a program to empower the progressive elements of the faltering New Deal coalition.

In Canada, however, the progressive coalition was not faltering. On the contrary, under the banner of the Just Society program the Trudeau government was the driving force behind the adoption of many of the legal reforms prescribed by Galanter. In the end, Galanter's reform proposals could only be implemented by a governing national coalition that included the "have not" groups as either members or strategic allies.

Notes

An earlier version of this paper was presented at the conference commemorating the twenty-fifth anniversary of the publication of Marc Galanter's "Why the 'Haves' Come Out Ahead: Speculations on the Limits of Legal Change" [9 *Law & Society Review* 95–160 (1974)], held May 1998 at the University of Wisconsin. We thank Charles Epp for his comments and suggestions.

1. Ian Brodie, *Friends of the Court: The Privileging of Interest Group Litigants in Canada* (Albany: SUNY Press, 2002).

2. F. L. Morton and Avril Allen, "Feminists and the Courts: Measuring Success in Interest Group Litigation in Canada," *Canadian Journal of Political Science* 34 (2001): 55–84.

3. See, for example, the papers in the special issue of the *Law and Society Review* dedicated to the Galanter article (vol. 33, no. 4, 1999).

4. Joel B. Grossman, Herbert M. Kritzer, and Stewart Macaulay, "Do the 'Haves' Still Come Out Ahead?" *Law and Society Review* 33, no. 4 (1999): 303–810.

5. Charles R. Epp, "The Two Motifs of Why the 'Haves' Come Out Ahead and Its Heirs," *Law and Society Review* 33, no. 4 (1999): 1089–98. See also Epp's *The Rights Revolution: Lawyers, Activists, and the Supreme Court in Comparative Perspective* (Chicago and London: University of Chicago Press, 1998).

6. Peter McCormick, "Party Capability Theory and Appellate Success in the Supreme Court of Canada, 1949–1992," *Canadian Journal of Political Science* 26 (1993): 523–40.

7. Rainer Knopff and F. L. Morton, *The Charter Revolution and the Court Party* (Peterborough, Ont.: Broadview, 2000).

8. Rainer Knopff and F. L. Morton, *Charter Politics* (Toronto: Nelson Canada, 1992).

9. Michael Mandel, *The Charter of Rights and the Legalisation of Politics in Canada* (Toronto: Wall and Thompson, 1989), 50–51.

10. Sharene Razack, *Canadian Feminism and the Law: The Women's Legal Education and Action Fund Pursuit of Equality* (Toronto: Second Story Press, 1991), 25–26.

11. W. A. Bogart, *Courts and Country: The Limits of Litigation and the Social and Political Life of Canada* (Toronto: Oxford University Press, 1994).

12. Miriam Smith, *Lesbian and Gay Rights in Canada* (Toronto: University of Toronto Press, 1999); Didi Herman, "The Good, the Bad, and the Snugly: Sexual Orientation Perspectives on the Charter," in *Charting the Consequences: The Impact of Charter Rights on Law and Politics in Canada,* ed. David Schneiderman and Kate Sutherland (Toronto: University of Toronto Press, 1997).

13. Morton and Allen, "Feminists and the Courts."

14. S. M. Lipset, "The Industrial Proletariat and the Intelligentsia in a Comparative Perspective," in *Consensus and Conflict* (New Brunswick, N.J.: Transaction Books, 1987), 186.

15. Ronald Inglehart, *Culture Shift in Advanced Industrial Society* (Princeton: Princeton University Press, 1990).

16. Neil Nevitte, *The Decline of Deference: Canadian Value Change in Cross-National Perspective* (Peterborough, Ont.: Broadview, 1996); idem, "New Politics, the Charter, and Political Participation," in *Representation, Integration, and Political Parties in Canada,* ed. Herman Bakvis (Toronto: Dundurn Press, 1992); and Ian Brodie and Neil Nevitte, "Evaluating the Citizens' Constitution Theory," *Canadian Journal of Political Science* 26 (1993): 235–59.

17. Lipset, "The Industrial Proletariat and the Intelligentsia in a Comparative Perspective," 187.

18. Samuel H. Barnes et al., *Political Action: Mass Participation in Five Western Democracies* (Beverly Hills, Calif.: Sage, 1979).

19. Khayyam Z. Paltiel, "The Changing Environment and Role of Special Interest Groups," *Canadian Public Administration* 25 (1982): 198–210; Jack Walker, "The Origins and Maintenance of Interest Groups in America," *American Political Science Review* 77 (1983): 390–405.

20. Ronald Inglehart, "Post-materialism in an Environment of Insecurity," *American Political Science Review* 75 (1981): 893. Emphasis added.

21. Ibid., 894–95.

22. Harold Clarke and Nitish Dutt, "Measuring Value Change in Western Industrialized Societies: The Impact of Unemployment," *American Political Science Review* 85 (1991): 905–22; Ronald Inglehart and Paul Abramson, "Economic Security and Social Change," *American Political Science Review* 88 (1994): 336–55.

23. Eric A. Nordlinger, *On the Autonomy of the Democratic State* (Cambridge: Harvard University Press, 1981); Theda Skocpol, *Protecting Soldiers and Mothers: The Political Origins of Social Policy in the United States* (Cambridge: Harvard University Press, 1992).

24. Alan Cairns, "The Embedded State," in *Perspectives on the State,* ed. Keith Banting (Toronto: University of Toronto Press, 1985).

25. Peter Brimelow, *The Patriot Game: Canada and the Canadian Question Revisted* (Toronto: Key Porter, 1986).

26. Pierre Elliot Trudeau and Thomas Axworthy, eds., *Towards a Just Society: The Trudeau Years* (Markham, Ont.: Viking, 1990).

27. Leslie A. Pal, *Interests of State: The Politics of Language, Multiculturalism, and Feminism in Canada* (Montreal/Kingston: McGill-Queen's University Press, 1993); David J. Bercuson and Barry Cooper, *Derailed: The Betrayal of the National Dream* (Toronto: Key Porter, 1994).

28. Pal, *Interests of State.*

29. S. L. Sutherland, "The Justice Portfolio: Social Policy through Regulation," in *How Ottawa Spends: The Liberals, the Opposition and Federal Priorities, 1983,* ed. G. Bruce Doern (Toronto: Lorimer, 1983).

30. Brimelow, *Patriot Game.*

31. Epp, *Rights Revolution,* 186.

32. Donald V. Smiley, *The Federal Condition in Canada* (Toronto: McGraw-Hill Ryerson, 1987).

33. James R. Mallory, *Social Credit and the Federal Power in Canada* (Toronto: University of Toronto Press, 1954).

34. Jennifer Smith, "The Origins of Judicial Review in Canada," *Canadian Journal of Political Science* 16 (1983).

35. Martin Shapiro, *Courts: A Comparative Political Analysis* (Chicago: University of Chicago Press, 1981).

36. André Bzdera, "Comparative Analysis of Federal High Courts: A Political Theory," *Canadian Journal of Political Science* 26, no. 1 (1993): 1–29.

37. Peter Hogg, "Is the Supreme Court of Canada Biased in Constitutional Cases?" *Canadian Bar Review* 57, no. 3 (1979): 721–39; Peter Russell, *The Judiciary in Canada* (Scarborough, Ont.: McGraw-Hill-Ryerson, 1987); Frederick Vaughan, "Critics of the Judicial Committee of the Privy Council: The New Orthodoxy and an Alternative Explanation," *Canadian Journal of Political Science* 19, no. 3 (1986): 495–520; Alan Cairns, "The Judicial Committee and Its Critics," *Canadian Journal of Political Science* 4, no. 3 (1971): 301–345.

38. Bzdera, "Comparative Analysis of Federal High Courts," 19.

39. Rainer Knopff and F. L. Morton, "Nation-building and the Canadian Charter of Rights and Freedoms," in *Constitutionalism, Citizenship and Society in Canada,* ed. Alan Cairns and Cynthia Williams (Toronto: University of Toronto Press, 1985).

40. Peter Russell, "The Political Purposes of the Canadian Charter of Rights and Freedoms," *Canadian Bar Review* 61 (1983): 30–59.

41. James B. Kelley, "Reconciling Rights and Federalism during Review of the Charter of Rights and Freedoms: The Supreme Court of Canada and the Centralization Thesis," *Canadian Journal of Political Science* 34 (2001): 321–55.

42. Nelson Weisman, "The Questionable Relevance of the Constitution in Advancing Minority Cultural Rights in Manitoba," *Canadian Journal of Political Science* 25 (1992): 697–721.

43. Ibid.; also, Mandel, *Charter of Rights and the Legalisation of Politics in Canada,* 99.

44. Kenneth McRoberts, "Making Canada Bilingual: Illusions and Delusions of Federal Language Policy," in *Federalism and Political Community,* ed. David Shugarman and Reg Whitaker (Peterborough, Ont.: Broadview, 1989).

45. Pierre Elliot Trudeau, *Federalism and the French Canadians* (Toronto: Macmillan, 1968).

46. Brimelow, *Patriot Game.*

47. Bruce Pollard, "Minority Language Rights in Four Provinces," in *Canada, the State of the Federation, 1985,* ed. Peter Leslie (Kingston, Ont.: Institute for Governmental Relations, Queens University, 1985).

48. Pal, *Interests of State.*

49. Mandel, *Charter of Rights and the Legalisation of Politics in Canada.*

50. Pierre Elliot Trudeau, "Quebec and the Constitution Problem," an essay first published in 1965, reprinted in *Federalism and the French Canadians,* 49.

51. Ian Brodie, "Interest Group Litigation and the Embedded State: Canada's Court Challenges Program," *Canadian Journal of Political Science* 34 (2001): 357–76.

52. Brodie, *Friends of the Court.*

53. Christopher Manfredi, "Constitutional Rights and Interest Advocacy: Litigating Educational Reform in Canada and the United States," in *Equity and Community: The Charter, Interest Advocacy, and Representation,* ed. F. Leslie Seidle (Montreal: Institute for Research on Public Policy, 1993.

54. Ibid., 112–15.

55. Beth Atcheson, Mary Eberts, and Beth Symes, with Jennifer Stoddart, *Women and Legal Action: Precedents, Resources, and Strategies for the Future* (Ottawa: Canadian Advisory Council on the Status of Women, 1984).

56. Lynn Smith, "Have Equality of Rights Made Any Difference?" in *Protecting Rights and Freedoms: Essays on the Charter's Place in Canada's Political, Legal, and Intellectual Life,* ed. Philip Bryden, Steven Davis and Peter Russell (Toronto: University of Toronto Press, 1994).

57. F. L. Morton, *Morgentaler v. Borowski: Abortion, the Charter, and the Court* (Toronto: McClelland and Stewart, 1992).

58. Inglehart, *Cultural Shift in Advanced Industrial Society;* Nevitte, *Decline of Deference.*

59. Pal, *Interests of State.*

60. Manfredi, "Constitutional Rights and Interest Advocacy," 21.

61. Ibid.; Ian Brodie, "The Market for Political Status," *Comparative Politics* 28 (1996): 253–71; Penny Kome, *The Taking of Twenty-Eight: Women Challenge the Constitution* (Toronto: The Women's Press, 1983).

62. Atcheson, Eberts, and Symes, *Women and Legal Action,* 163.

63. Brodie, "Interest Group Litigation and the Embedded State."

64. Atcheson, Eberts, and Symes, *Women and Legal Action,* 172.

65. Razack, *Canadian Feminism and the Law,* 37.

66. Morton and Allen, "Feminists and the Courts."

67. Razack, *Canadian Feminism and the Law.*

68. Cynthia Williams, "The Changing Nature of Citizen Rights," in *Constitutionalism, State, and Society in Canada,* ed. Alan Cairns and Cynthia Williams (Toronto: University of Toronto Press, 1985).

69. Brodie, "The Market for Political Status."

70. Herman, "The Good, the Bad, and the Smugly," 203.

71. *Haig v. Canada* 5 O.R. (3d) 245 (1991).

72. Janet Hiebert, "Fair Elections and Freedom of Expression under the Charter," *Journal of Canadian Studies* 24 (1989–90): 72–86.

73. See *Libman v. Quebec (Attorney General),* 3 S.C.R. 569 (1997).

74. Mark Silverstein, *Judicious Choices: The New Politics of Supreme Court Confirmations* (New York: W.W. Norton, 1994).

CHAPTER 10

For the Love of Justice? Judicial Review in Canada and the United States

Raymond Bazowski

"The love of justice, the peaceful and legal introduction of the judge into the domain of politics," Tocqueville once noted in his customary epigrammatic fashion, "are perhaps the most outstanding characteristics of a free people."[1] So confident an observation about the providential political role open to the judiciary doubtless will strike many contemporary court-watchers as credulous. If anything, there is, at least in countries such as Canada and the United States that possess constitutional bills of rights, a strongly voiced concern that judges have demonstrated a reckless inclination to stray into areas that rightfully should be in the custody of elected officials. Apprehension over the misappropriation of the power of judicial review is typically funded by democratic considerations, though critics of the court also frequently allude to the modern republican doctrine of the separation of powers to sustain their case. This chapter will challenge both the general democratic and the more specifically republican argument used by opponents of an activist judiciary. I shall argue that, insofar as the problem of judicial review is posed as one of democratic arrogation, or of an illicit crossing of institutional boundaries, adversaries of the judiciary offer misleading reproaches and in consequence distract us from the more important questions that need to be asked about the court's role in democratic deliberations. These more important questions have to do with the inescapably political underpinning of judicial decision-making, and more specifically, with its historical provenance in an institutional setting that from time to time positively attracts legal norm-setting.

Of course it is hardly a novel observation to say that judicial rulings are motivated by political considerations. American legal realists in the 1920s, 1930s, and 1940s, for instance, famously challenged the then-prevailing formalism in legal thought, asserting both as a matter of description and as a matter of prescription that judges rely, and certainly should rely if suitably enlightened, on their personal and political convictions in reaching their decisions. More recently, scholars associated with the critical legal studies movement, feminist legal theory, and critical race theory have likewise drawn attention to the intrinsic politics of adjudication. While many of the insights contributed by these approaches to the study of the law are invaluable, they fail to account for the conspicuously irregular presence of courts in the affairs of a nation. If judicial review is unavoidably political, why do courts play a more or less capacious role at different times in American or Canadian history?

A theory of judicial review that aims to address this latter question must necessarily take into account the context of judicial decision-making. But context itself is a famously ambiguous word. What is the relevant context in explaining judicial decision-making? The practical answer, as in other lines of social and political inquiry, is that there is no single context that uniquely renders intelligible an institutional practice like judicial review. Rather, it is more fruitful to think of such a practice as the consequence of a multitude of factors that can be apprehended at different levels of analysis, and whose efficaciousness can never be established independently of each other. The law as an ever-evolving body of doctrine itself is one of those factors. Established legal doctrine does limit possible arguments available before the court, and it does figure as *reasons* for judgments. However, while the law has this structuring effect, it is not the single, or not necessarily even the most important, determining factor in judicial reasoning. Personal disposition, political and philosophical convictions, undiluted party politics, prejudices of the Burkean or more familiar sociological variety, horizons of meaning informed by class, gender, and ethnicity—all certainly come into play in the judicial process. As well, the politics of small groups is a significant element in explaining discrete judgments insofar as judges are compelled to build coalitions around their preferred rulings. Considerations of judicial independence and prestige also play a role, as do professional norms or collegial expectations.

Over and above these microlevel variables stand two pivotal macrolevel variables. One is the relationship between the court and other institutions of government, a relationship that is never simply captured by constitutional descriptions but rather is dynamically created and re-created in the process of politics itself. The second important macrovariable consists of those continuously shifting balances of power among the assorted cleavages that are the substructure of a nation's politics, disturbances amongst which periodically complicate established political patterns of economic and moral regulation. It is these two macrovariables that I take to be the crucial background of judicial review. They are background in several senses. First, saying that the institutional relationship is important in understanding judicial review stands as an invitation to explore the complex patterns of political interactions among different organs of government. For instance, if the power of courts relative to legislatures changes at different periods in a country's history, it is imperative to try to discern why that institutional relationship has varied, and how each branch of government managed its relationship with the other branches. As for the second relationship, that between those mutable balances of power among political cleavages and the process of judicial review, there are a number of analytic considerations that need to be acknowledged. To begin with, the prominent national questions that come before the court are themselves regularly related to, if not effectively produced by, these shifting balances of power established around politically salient divisions such as class, ethnicity, religion, gender, region, and so on. Moreover, judges generally are well aware of the political implications of the cases before them, in the sense of who stands to benefit from and who will be discomfited by particular rulings, and this knowledge inevitably figures in their own deliberations. Finally, although the shifting balances of power that comprise a nation's politics encompass a variety of actors, agendas, and undertakings, contemporary analysts of the court have tended to focus on the moral/political dimensions of constitutional adjudication, while understating if not entirely ignoring the way in which contests over economic organization play a central role in legislative as well as judicial politics.

All of this is to say that judges are never removed from politics. But it would be a mistake to conclude from this that judges are indistinguishable from elected officials. Rather, the relationship between the judiciary and elected branches of government itself constitutes a political process, the contours of which cannot be described a priori but can only be discerned empirically and, especially, historically. And this also means that the normative question of the role of courts in democratic deliberations can only sensibly be answered with reference to historical context. Accordingly, the first part of the chapter is devoted to a study of the operation of the power of judicial review in Canada and the United States over time. The comparison is instructive, because while these two countries share in the common law tradition, the differences in the way in which judicial review developed in each jurisdiction reveals much about the political construction of the court's power. The historical exploration will be followed by a brief survey of recent critiques of judicial review in both countries. Finally, the criticisms will themselves be subjected to critical analysis in light of the historical record, with special emphasis placed on how changing institutional relationships and assorted political and social transformations occasioned by developments in national capitalism have provided an important stimulus to the doctrinal directions adopted by courts. While no claim is made that these factors in any way exhaust the range of determinants of judicial decision-making, they do help throw into relief much of the broad doctrinal shifts that have occurred in both American and Canadian jurisprudence and, equally as significant, they help contextualize current debates on the democratic propriety of judicial review.

Evolution of Judicial Power

Neither in the United States nor in Canada did the original constitution-makers give much sustained thought to the role of the courts, particularly that of a final appellate tribunal, in their political artifices. In the United States provision for the establishment of a national supreme court was made in Article 3 of the Constitution, but there was from the beginning considerable uncertainty about its jurisdiction and authority. Even such shrewd statesmen as James Madison and Alexander Hamilton, who otherwise had so much to say about the appropriate organization of government for a large republic, were comparatively silent about the function of a supreme court. It was left to the workings of judicial politics itself to establish that function which retrospectively we have come to call the power of judicial review. The outlines of this story are well enough known. The politically canny judgment that Chief Justice Marshall devised in *Marbury v. Madison* in 1803 asserted the court's power to declare invalid federal legislation that violated the constitution while artfully finessing the contentious issue of what authorized the court to be the final interpreter of constitutional values. Marshall managed to accomplish this judicial sleight of hand all the while avoiding a direct confrontation with a hostile political executive by the brilliant expedient of refusing in the final instance to accept jurisdiction for the particular legal dispute that occasioned the case.

Thereafter, the court worked to consolidate its position as custodian of the constitution, a task that in this early period of American political history was shaped by the battle between Federalists who sought the creation of a strong national government and a legal regime favorable to mercantile and manufacturing interests, and Jeffersonian and later Jacksonian Democrats who spoke emphatically if inconsistently for agrarian interests and states' rights. In its first few decades the Court was concerned primarily with federalism issues, initially favoring federal over state powers and then, as its composition changed, endorsing state regulatory powers.[2] By the mid-nineteenth century, the judicial agenda was overtaken by the insuperable slavery issue, to which the Court contributed its own regrettable views in the *Dred Scott* case. In the aftermath of the Civil War the Court continued to sanction expanded state regulatory powers, in the process constricting the applicability of the newly passed Fourteenth Amendment. While the Court was thus willing to accommodate state regulation of the economy, it was generally uninterested in helping African Americans secure genuinely equal status in American society.[3]

At the turn of the century another noticeable shift occurred in the Court's conduct as it again became the champion of private property, eventually effecting a change in the way the Bill of Rights would be employed. Whereas jurisprudence in the preceding century held that the Bill of Rights was applicable only to the federal government,[4] by the early twentieth century the Court expanded its reach through such expedients as incorporating into the Fourteenth Amendment rights contained in the initial eight amendments.[5] This judicial strategy inaugurated a period of conservative rulings centering on "substantive due process" as a constitutional value and aimed at preventing both levels of government from unduly interfering in the rights of property. Unnerved finally by Roosevelt's indisputable electoral support and his court-packing scheme, the Court performed an about-face, abandoning its substantive due process interpretations and consenting to a vast increase in federal regulatory power under the auspices of the commerce clause. This particular doctrinal transformation was eventually fortified by a relatively coherent liberal approach to classic civil liberties and procedural rights,[6] and a belated attempt to reverse private and official discrimination against African Americans, signaled dramatically in *Brown v. Board of Education*.

In its most spirited liberal phase, the Court expanded procedural guarantees to criminal defendants and those subject to custodial investigation,[7] and adopted a progressive version of substantive due process, finding that the constitution protected privacy, thus limiting the capacity of government to engage in moral supervision.[8] Meanwhile, in its present manifestation the Court has been undoing some of what its immediate predecessor had accomplished—for instance, by being more indulgent of government as moral superintendent[9] while being less permissive of government attempts to remedy systemic inequalities.[10] Finally, after over half a century in which the Bill of Rights displaced classic federalism issues as the focus of constitutional law, there are indications that the Court presently is receptive to a revived federalism that harkens to a nineteenth-century view of states' rights, a view that not coincidentally corresponds to the efforts of Nixon and Reagan Republicans to disable many of the features of the modern regulatory welfare state.[11] At the very least, what all these doctrinal adjustments suggest is that the Court is ever ready to tack according to prevailing political winds, though full discussion of the significance of such adaptability must await an examination of comparable developments in Canadian jurisprudence.

The power of judicial review in the new nation of Canada was in a narrow legal respect conceptually unproblematic, even though controversy persists over the actual intentions of the constitution-makers. Those intentions notwithstanding, it was the British Judicial Committee of the Privy Council (JCPC) that initially acted as final appellate court in constitutional matters as well as civil and criminal law in Canada. Its constitutional charge derived from the fact that the British North America Act (1867) creating the Dominion of Canada was technically an imperial statute subject to the review of an imperial tribunal. When finally the Supreme Court of Canada displaced the JCPC, it simply assumed the latter's power of judicial review without seeking formal constitutional justification, relying instead on the implicit assumption that the logic of federalism requires a neutral umpire. The adoption of a new constitution in 1982 complete with a Charter of Rights and Freedoms helped resolve in part the legal status of the power of judicial review in Canada by explicitly recognizing the principle of constitutional supremacy.

Unconcerned with developing a rigorous justification of the power of judicial review, and almost exclusively concerned with federalism issues during the first century of Canadian political history, the JCPC and later the Supreme Court tended to style themselves as interpreters of the plain meaning of the constitution, ostensibly employing ordinary rules of statutory interpretation for this purpose. But such a self-attributed interpretative philosophy disguised differences in political perspectives, with the early Supreme Court an unambiguous supporter of federal power and the JCPC a progressively more vigorous defender of provincial rights. In this latter role the JCPC contributed in important ways to the attenuation of the federal trade and commerce, criminal, and residual powers, particularly in the first few decades of the twentieth century when the British tribunal frustrated several of the federal government's regulatory initiatives aimed at business.[12] In temper, if not in doctrinal detail, the JCPC appeared to share in the same judicial concern for the rights of capital that the American Supreme Court exhibited during this same period. When the Supreme Court succeeded the JCPC as the final appellate body, there was some restoration of federal powers consistent with the emergence of the postwar regulatory welfare state, but unlike in the United States the persistent strength of the provinces prevented a substantial centralization of power in the hands of the national government.

The recent addition of the Charter altered not simply the substance but also seemingly the style of judicial decision-making of the Supreme Court. For all intents and purposes the pre-Charter Supreme Court took an unassuming view of its powers vis-à-vis elected legislatures, from time to time striking down laws on jurisdictional grounds but otherwise ostensibly refraining from reviewing their substance. Of course, this portrayal of judicial restraint as deference to legislatures acting in their appropriate domain is less convincing once the wider political implications of judicial decision-making are brought into focus. For even if the Canadian court generally refused to involve itself in civil rights in its pre-Charter persona, its political influence was nonetheless felt in its federalism decisions, the latter frequently just as politically charged as civil rights cases, though usually engaging different political interests and audiences. On this view, what the Charter accomplished was not so much the mandating of a more activist court but the summoning of conditions favorable to a more *liberal* court.

That this more liberal court was influenced by American jurisprudence and judicial behavior is beyond contention. As Manfredi points out, the Canadian court has emulated its American counterpart in a variety of ways, including liberalizing its rules of standing, expanding the scope of admissible constitutional challenges to government action, developing creative remedies for rights violations, and generally making much more use of U.S. citations in their decisions.[13] As for its interpretation of Charter rights, the Canadian court has derived a great deal from American liberal jurisprudence in such areas as legal and equality rights. But at the same time it has been willing to tolerate limitations on these and other Charter rights under the aegis of sec.1, a clause that allows the government to defend an impugned law on grounds that it serves an important public purpose and to claim that whatever limitations the law might contain on Charter rights are both reasonable and justifiable in a democratic society.

Aside from this deliberately crafted constitutional clause meant to remind courts of the long-held principle of parliamentary supremacy, there have been other political factors at play giving rise to distinctive developments in Canadian jurisprudence. Perhaps the most notable of these are the calculated nation-building components of the Charter, such as the sections affirming official bilingualism and guaranteeing minority language education rights as well as mobility rights. Not only have these sections invited uniquely Canadian legal arguments, but they have from its inception made the explicit political purposes of this constitutional document a matter of national debate. In recent years that debate has centered on the power of judicial review, a debate that draws on, though in important ways is distinguishable from, similar controversies in the United States.

Critics of Judicial Review

Complaints about a peremptory or politically biased court have surfaced regularly in both the United States and Canada, generally from those disappointed with a particular line of judicial decisions. In the United States, for instance, Jeffersonian Democrats were often scathing in their assessments of the Marshall Court, while progressives in the early twentieth century routinely denounced the *Lochner* Court. More recently, the Warren-Brennan court has accumulated its share of condemnations from aggrieved segregationists and other political conservatives. In Canada the JCPC earned disapproval from partisans of a strong national government, while the Supreme Court has from time to time attracted the censure of provincial politicians and academic advocates of a more decentralized federal system. But just as in the United States, it has been the liberal bearing of the Charter-emboldened court that has prompted most sustained critical concern over the power of judicial review in Canada in recent years.

In the United States an important academic source for contemporary debates on the power of judicial review was Alexander Bickel, who in the early years of the Warren Court warned that judicial review is potentially a "countermajoritarian force" and for this reason is a "deviant institution in American democracy."[14] Defining the problem of judicial review as one of democracy, of a juridical minority potentially frustrating the will of a popularly elected legislative majority, Bickel hinted that the solution was to delineate a sphere in which judicial decision-making could be said to be consistent with the fundamental needs of democratic life. Succeeding debates between what in the United States came to be called interpretivists and noninterpretivists can be regarded as opposing attempts to define this appropriate sphere, each side accepting that the countermajoritarian dilemma describes a genuine normative problem. For the interpretivists the appropriate sphere is the Constitution itself, for which it is assumed that there is available to the Court an objective method of deciphering its meaning. Noninterpretivists, on the other hand, question the methodological and normative assumptions of such a literalist approach to jurisprudence, suggesting instead that judicial review be deliberately conducted as an exercise in value discovery where the court should feel free to draw on extralegal norms.

While these two broad approaches to constitutional interpretation hardly capture the full range of current American jurisprudential debate, they do mark off the politically most salient lines of division characteristic of that debate. These competing lines of interpretation do not, however, translate in the Canadian context quite the same way, even though their political subtext is certainly not unknown in Canada. The idea of original intent is difficult to apply in the Canadian context for a variety of reasons. The excessive centralization inscribed in the British North America Act, for instance, became disputed relatively early in Canadian history when an evolving provincial rights movement proposed an alternative constitutional narrative known as the compact theory of confederation, and subsequently as the JCPC effectively transformed the division of powers in its controverted rulings. The persistent discord among political elites over the form of the federation contributed to a situation in which Canadians as a citizen body failed to constitute themselves as a "sovereign people" through the performance of a defining covenantal act.[15] Symptomatic of that failure has been the abiding alienation of Quebec from the constitutional order. Thus, while possessed of a constitution organically evolved to fulfill basic framework requirements of government, Canadians have not been able to confidently lay claim to a foundational document around which there is a durable consensus. In these circumstances a jurisprudential argument that tries to invoke the authentic meaning of the constitution is likely to arouse acutely dissonant views about the text and its architects, a fact that does not exactly recommend originalism as an authoritative interpretative theory in Canadian constitutional law.

Besides the continuing political antagonism associated with the constitution, there are other reasons why arguments drawing on original intent just do not have the same purchase in Canada as they do in the United States. Significantly, the historical currency of the Charter likely undermines appeals to original intent. For while it might be relatively easy to determine the intent of the constitution-makers when they are historical contemporaries, this same fact can also diminish their authority in so important an enterprise as declaiming fundamental constitutional values, because it is hard to imagine present-day political leaders possessing the unimpeachable political wisdom that some might be disposed to attribute to more ancient constitution-makers. If proof be needed that the doctrine of original intent simply has not captured jurisprudential imagination in Canada to any significant degree, it merely has to be observed that almost as soon as members of the Supreme Court began to interpret the Charter, they announced their ambition to engage in a purposive analysis of its clauses that would not be limited to an examination of legislative intent. That this gesture earned no stern rebuke from the very legislatures that had just produced the Charter testifies to a legislative acceptance of a noninterpretivist judicial strategy in Canada. What finally confirms this political concession is the fact that federal and provincial governments have always had the opportunity to directly challenge judicial interpretations of the Charter by way of sec. 33, a clause authorizing legislative override of select Charter rights for five-year periods. The reluctance of legislatures other than in Quebec to use sec. 33 is a clear indication that they have resigned themselves to the court's interpretative prerogative.

With appeals to original intent generally unsuited to the circumstances of Canada, critics of judicial review in that country have tended to offer more straightforward democratic arguments. The best known of these critics, F. L Morton and Rainer Knopff, have for some time argued that the practice of judicial review under the Charter has led to a regrettable infusion of highly contestable values into the democratic political process.[16] The basis of their censure of Charter adjudication is that it is has all too frequently rewarded minority groups with gains incommensurate with the democratic legitimacy of their claims. Underlying this reproach is a relatively uncomplicated view of liberal democracy and constitutional rights. For Morton and Knopff, liberal democracy is all about pluralist politics, where conflicting partisan interests must acquire the skills of negotiation and compromise to participate in the shifting political coalitions that comprise legislative majorities. As for civil rights, they are proponents of that familiar version of liberal constitutionalism which depicts rights in the negative as legal limitations on the power of government, their egalitarian grammar restricted to pledges of formal equality. The problem with the Charter on this view is that as presently interpreted it subverts pluralist politics and liberal constitutionalism by encouraging numerically weak but politically militant groups, or what Morton and Knopff style as "court parties," to petition a sympathetic judiciary for policy privileges in the guise of constitutional rights. Aided by judges who increasingly are disposed to indulge in social engineering, court parties, in particular feminists and gays and lesbians, prefer constitutional litigation to conventional interest group political strategies, in the process inflating justice claims and discouraging the spirit of moderation and compromise at the center of democratic politics.

While Morton and Knopff are concerned primarily to delegitimize current Charter jurisprudence by exposing its partiality, another advocate of classic liberal constitutionalism, Christopher Manfredi, has a positive proposal to rein in a court supposedly infected with reformist hubris.[17] Liberal constitutionalism, Manfredi contends, means that the constitution is meant to restrain political power. Adapting a separation of powers argument derived from American political history, Manfredi suggests that when an unaccountable court itself threatens to usurp power by consistently thwarting elected governments, the appropriate solution would be to find an institutional mechanism that can check its political enthusiasms. To this end Manfredi proposes an amended sec. 33, limited in its operation to reversing a disputed judicial decision, and requiring the consent of a supermajority in Parliament or a provincial legislature. Moreover, Manfredi suggests that a legislative override undertaken under sec. 33 could be designed to cease with the dissolution of the enacting legislative body, making the subsequent election in part, at least, a referendum on that particular government measure. Manfredi's proposal is given in the spirit of the classic separation of powers doctrine, the underlying assumption being that the best chance of securing moderate government is to use ambition to counteract ambition—in this case, the ambition of an intemperate court.

The Judiciary and Democracy: A Reassessment

Of the several critics of the power of judicial review examined, certainly the most outspoken are unmistakably conservative, their criticisms as much directed at the content of contemporary jurisprudence as its ostensible encroachment on legislative authority. These criticisms accordingly have an empirical and normative dimension. Empirically, the claim is that from time to time courts engage sub rosa in legislative activity. Normatively, the claim is that such exercises of judicial power generally undermine democracy, and especially at present, because they support a radical political agenda at odds with majoritarian sentiments. The two claims, however, are not so easily distinguishable analytically. The reason is that while in theory courts and legislatures have distinct roles, in practice these roles are not quite so transparent and well defined, because judicial rulings always have consequences for the policy-making process. The more appropriate question, then, is not whether courts somehow have become unauthorized legislators but rather whether their own policy-related role has led in any serious and sustained way to the displacement of the democratic political process centered on elected legislatures.

Such a question is in the first instance historical and returns us to the evolving jurisprudence in the United States and Canada described previously. That brief sketch appeared to suggest that the courts have been politically consequential actors whose decisions shaped public policy, often in profound ways, at times directly contrary to the wishes of popularly elected legislatures. But is this image of an activist court periodically disdaining prevailing political convictions accurate? There are reasons to think that the scope of judicial activism has been exaggerated in conventional constitutional histories. For instance, in his well-known article on judicial decision-making, Robert Dahl insinuates that in the U.S. courts rarely have been ahead of popular opinion, and when sometimes they do stray from accepted constitutional norms the partisan appointment process inevitably repairs such departures.[18] Dahl takes it as a settled principle in democratic theory that courts shouldn't oblige majorities to political values not of their choosing, and that because of the operation of the party system in American political institutions they seldom do. Both contentions are, of course, problematic. Declaring that democracy requires courts to accommodate majority opinion has disturbing implications for the important intuition in liberal constitutionalism that vulnerable minorities often do need protection from majorities. And, in any event, partisan politics does not always ensure a correspondence between judicial philosophy and the political beliefs of the dominant political party, notwithstanding efforts to fill courts with politically compatible judges. These shortcomings in Dahl's account of the political nature of the judiciary point to the need for a more dynamic and sophisticated explanation of the relationship of courts to legislatures.

In their response to critics of Charter jurisprudence, Peter Hogg and Allison Bushell appear to provide precisely that type of explanation, centered on the concept of judicial dialogue.[19] According to Hogg and Bushell, where a judicial decision is capable of being reversed, modified, or avoided by the ordinary legislative process, it is worthwhile to suppose that there is a relationship between the Court and the legislature that can be characterized as a dialogue. The Canadian Charter facilitates this dialogue, because it features clauses such as sec. 33 and sec. 1, which offer legislatures room to contribute their own interpretation of contested constitutional values.[20] To substantiate their claim that a dialogue takes place in the Canadian constitutional setting, Hogg and Bushell surveyed the cases where laws were invalidated by the Court on Charter grounds and found that in two-thirds of these cases the relevant legislative body responded with amended laws, most of which incorporated minor refinements that did not compromise the objectives of the original legislation.[21] More realistic as an approach to understanding the political significance of constitutional jurisprudence, the work of Hogg and Bushell points to a dynamic relationship between the judiciary and legislatures not apprehended by a pure separation-of-powers doctrine. However, their account of dialogue remains doubtful both descriptively and prescriptively, on the one hand because their empirical evidence of legislative sequels in Charter cases is open to dispute, and, on the other, because their very conception of dialogue is rather implausibly based on a formal relationship in which the Court is represented as taking the interpretative lead while the legislatures are forever consigned to the role of respondent.[22] But perhaps the most serious problem in their version of judicial dialogue is that it is still not realistic enough, for in the end they continue to be absorbed by the same normative question as the critics of the Court. Concerned to show how certain textual provisions in the Charter encourage dialogue and hence assist rather than detract from democracy, Hogg and Bushell have no real way of explaining why judicial intercessions in the policy process have been so manifestly variable.

While suggestive, the dialogue thesis needs to be supplemented with broader institutional and sociological investigations into the complex articulation of political power and its multiple mediations. As it turns out, there have been a number of contributions from political scientists studying the constitutional process that can help explain the shifting political role of the courts and, in the process, supply a more reliable context against which the normative preoccupations of contemporary judicial critics can be assessed. For example, in American political science, self-described "new institutionalists" have been exploring ways in which judicial attitudes are constituted and regulated by the court's institutional structure, which not only has its own history but which also is mediated by relationships with other institutions in an environment that is inescapably political.[23] One such new institutionalist, Mark Graber, has proposed that the countermajoritarian dilemma that has so dominated contemporary discussion of the judiciary is largely an illusory problem in U.S. history, because constitutional dialogue continuously takes place between governing institutions on issues over which not only are there internal divisions within the ruling party, but which cut across prevailing political alignments altogether.[24] Except in such obvious instances as when there is a temporary lag between the ideological outlooks of courts and presidential administrations, Graber suggests that the judiciary tends to actively intrude into the policy-making field only when overtly or covertly invited by elected officials to conclude political conflicts they cannot or choose not to resolve themselves. "Judicial policymaking in these circumstances," Graber continues, "cannot be described as either majoritarian or countermajoritarian; it takes place when and because no legislative majority has formed."[25]

While Graber's thesis encourages us to look at judicial policy-making within a concrete political context where discord among political elites contributes to enhanced judicial power, the background conditions that give rise to such dissension themselves require attention. In contemporary judicial analysis an often overlooked background condition that provides much of the content of judicial decision-making, both directly and indirectly, is to be found in the historical developments within national capitalism.[26] Graber's premise about elite discord and judicial power, together with observations about the changing requirements of capitalist economies, can help explain many of the fluctuations in jurisprudence noted in the previous historical account of American and Canadian judicial review. For example, the exploits of the Marshall Court, so often portrayed as a contest between staunch Federalists promoting the interests of large financial and mercantile capitalists and equally staunch Jeffersonians championing the yeoman farmer and small business, ignores both the ideological transformations in American political parties in the first few decades of the nineteenth century and the growing acceptance of a commercial worldview and national political and territorial ambitions that united the principal political factions in both political parties. The result of this broad consensus over fundamental principles, Graber suggests, is that the most important rulings of the Marshall Court "are best understood as efforts to resolve the conflicts that divided members of the dominant national coalition, and not as efforts to revisit the conflicts that divided the governing majority from the political minority."[27]

Another turning point in American jurisprudence, the infamous *Dred Scott* decision, demonstrates more clearly still just how congressional elites, intent on keeping the explosive slavery issue out of the political realm, conspired to have the Court become the arbiter of this political quandary, which by the mid-nineteenth century was becoming an impediment to further development in the new territories.[28] Similarly, when the Supreme Court decided in *United States v. E. C. Knight* to exempt manufacturing from the Sherman Antitrust Act, this was not an instance of judicial usurpation of a congressional initiative; the Court was merely responding to an explicit invitation from lawmakers to give content to the law by interpreting which commercial activities were prohibited by the legislation. Significantly, when the executive branch finally did begin to pursue a consistent antitrust policy by century's end, the Supreme Court proved suitably compliant, steadfastly upholding federal prosecutions under the commerce clause.[29] The subsequent conversion of the *Lochner* Court to a substantive due process interpretation of property rights again was less radical than it might appear, for it did, after all, coincide with the unwavering pro-business attitude of the Harding and Coolidge administrations. And when it effected a "switch in time" and belatedly endorsed New Deal legislation in the face of its obvious public support, the Supreme Court did not merely act expediently but responded to fundamental shifts in the organization of capitalism with a jurisprudence more supportive of the emerging welfare state. As Gillman summarizes, these changes—in particular, the transformation from local production for local consumption to large-scale capitalist enterprise producing for national and international markets—confronted the Court with three interpretative complications: how to construe the federal division of powers when national and transnational companies began to dwarf local companies; how to modify nineteenth-century legal categories centered on ideas of health, safety, and the morality of the community to respond to the intensified class conflict produced by modern industrialism; and how to comprehend the emergence of the administrative state with its accompanying increase in executive power in light of an eighteenth-century doctrine of the separation of powers.[30] Once set in train, these several modifications in economic and political organization and accompanying social transformations could not but place strains on legal norms and doctrines developed in earlier times and for different socioeconomic circumstances.[31] This is not to say that changes in constitutional interpretations were inevitable, or altogether adequate to the forces that conjured them up,[32] but rather that the court's rulings affecting federalism or administrative law were drawn up in conditions where interpretative choices invariably would have broad nationwide impact, something of which the judges themselves were aware. In short, judges might make jurisprudential history, but not necessarily in circumstances or with materials of their own choosing.

If federalism jurisprudence is intimately related to shifts in the organization of capitalism, the same context helps explain the emergence of modern civil rights and civil liberties jurisprudence as well. Gillman notes that contemporary capitalism influenced civil rights rulings in at least two ways. First, the development of the modern regulatory and welfare state meant that government actively committed itself to intervening in market relations with legislation that at various times might favor particular groups such as labor or farmers. Once legislation targeted at certain structural economic inequalities became a political commonplace, the court was under some pressure to modify its established jurisprudence, which hitherto had given pride of place to the idea of formal equality.[33] By inventing the concept of "prejudices against discrete and insular minorities" in *Carolene Products,* Justice Stone signaled a new jurisprudential role for the Court that would be more hospitable to evolving substantive egalitarian sentiments on display in the political realm. Second, once the limited state gave way to the bureaucratic state, and once the Court surrendered its practice of appraising the public purpose of legislation, the traditional nineteenth-century protection of civil liberties conceived in terms of possessive individualism needed to find a new judicial footing. That new footing meant the renunciation of an ecumenical libertarian standpoint and a search for what have often been called "preferred freedoms."[34] Freedom of speech and freedom of assembly were obvious candidates for preferential attention from the court, because they stood as especially serviceable constitutional constraints on the growing power of the administrative state.

While the changing structure of capitalism is a crucial backdrop that helps illuminate broad developments in civil rights and civil liberties jurisprudence, the particular relationship between branches of government and substantive developments in civil society are the more immediate antecedents of judicial policy-making in this area. For example, the Court's role in ending segregation was helped along by both explicit and tacit support from successive administrations incapable of using ordinary legislative avenues because of a political stalemate in Congress. And as for the controversial role of the judiciary in deciding the constitutionality of state abortion laws, while not explicitly enticed to make abortion policy by legislators, the Court was drawn into this particular policy field, which had effectively been organized out of electoral politics because of its political volatility. The salience of abortion policy in American politics in recent years, and its partial resolution in the courtroom, is best understood against the background of a political process preoccupied in the post–World War II years with questions of economic production and distribution, as well as with national security. This particular focus encouraged the formation of nonparty movements representing people who were politicized by expanding postwar egalitarian attitudes but who, for one reason or another, were left out of the dominant political coalitions concerned with economic and security affairs. Typically, such movements, either shut out of or possessing only weak attachments to the established party system, have looked to alternative strategies, including litigation, in pursuit of their aims. The women's movement represents just such an instance where relative exclusion at the conventional political level had led to legal campaigns in support of goals such as reproductive rights. But at the same time, what success they have experienced at the judicial level in securing abortion rights has remained contingent on the continued aversion of legislators to seize decisively the issue.[35] The Court's policy role in this, as in other bids at social reform, has always been both informed and circumscribed by its relationship to other governing institutions and political dynamics occurring within civil society.

Just as in the United States, institutional politics and developments in civil society are the crucial context against which the policy-making role of the courts in Canada should be understood. Of course, the institutional nexus is more complicated in Canada, because for part of its history it was an imperial as well as a domestic relationship that framed constitutional politics. Without doubt, JCPC rulings exercised considerable influence in the development of Canadian federalism, modifying to a large degree the original constitutional arrangement of powers. But rather than view the imperial tribunal's decisions as examples of outright judicial arrogation of domestic political authority, it is more worthwhile, as Alan Cairns has suggested, to see the JCPC's controversial constitutional interpretations as being consistent with the underlying socioeconomic changes occurring in Canada in the early twentieth century, which had, in any event, inclined the nation to a more decentralized federal system.[36] Not only were JCPC judgments compatible with broad transformations in Canadian society, but they were also agreeable in the main to the discrete interests of dominant business classes, as J. R. Mallory long ago indicated.[37] Once the Canadian Court finally became supreme in fact as well as in name, it proved to be more receptive to arguments in support of national power; it remained cautious, however, about endorsing centralization. A degree of federal authority was restored through the Court's reading of the constitution's "peace, order and good government" clause, as well as the trade and commerce clause, which the JCPC had diluted; still, the Court moved warily, at once divided internally between supporters of classical federalism and advocates of federal power, and at the same time mindful of the need to gain for itself an air of legitimacy in its newly elevated role. In many ways, however, this role became increasingly superfluous, for just as the Supreme Court turned into the court of last resort, the federal and provincial governments began to experiment with cooperative programs, which belied the idea of a strict division of powers that had been so fundamental to previous constitutional jurisprudence.

During the era of cooperative federalism in Canada, overt federalism cases became less common as the postwar regulatory welfare state was constructed piecemeal, more often than not as a result of negotiations that led to the effective sharing of jurisdictions. Courts were mostly secondary players in postwar Canadian federalism, but unlike in the United States, constitutional disputes over the division of powers did not disappear entirely during this period. The political strains produced by sharing jurisdictions for purposes of welfare legislation and economic regulation contributed to an intensification of Quebec nationalism and to an increasingly combative form of executive federalism by the 1970s. Aggressive state-building strategies on the part of Quebec as well as other provinces, coupled with corporate ambitions to escape various regulatory and taxation regimes, led to renewed constitutional litigation on federalism grounds. In the late 1960s and 1970s, challenges over the ownership, taxation, and export of natural resources became troublesome constitutional issues.[38] In the 1980s and 1990s disagreements over environmental regulation found their way to the courts.[39] Other federalism issues of recent vintage include challenges to the ability of the federal government to regulate cigarette advertising or implement gun control under its criminal law power.[40] While the federal government was successful in all of these latter cases, this fact has hardly signified a dramatic shift of power to the national government wrought by a politically irresponsible Court. In large part, this is because a coordinate federalism had become so strongly entrenched in Canada in the twentieth century, as provincial governments grew in institutional competence and revenue-raising capacity, that it would be politically inconceivable for the Court to try to return the country to the quasi-federal union erected by nineteenth-century politicians.

The Trudeau government's promotion of a Charter of Rights in a revised constitution was partly a reaction to the centripetal forces at work in Canadian federalism that had accompanied contemporary province-building. A calculated effort to sidestep the increasingly intractable route of federal-provincial diplomacy, Trudeau's constitutional initiative was fashioned to be a populist appeal centered on the Charter of Rights. But there proved to be resistance from a majority of provincial premiers, the most common principled objection being that the Charter was an intolerable affront to parliamentary sovereignty. While failing to finally arrest the federal patriation strategy, the refractory premiers at least were able to secure a concession in the form of sec. 33, thereby complicating the political purposes of the Charter. On the one hand, the Charter was deliberately intended to realign political identities along national lines and shift political conflicts from the federal-provincial arena to the judicial one.[41] But conversely, the retention of the principle of parliamentary sovereignty in sec. 33 signaled that customary politics had not been eliminated. With so mixed a political message, it is not surprising that the Court's Charter-authorized political agenda would turn out not to be a straightforward matter. Initially active in upholding such national objectives as minority language education rights, the Supreme Court also failed spectacularly to resolve the language rights issue in Quebec, in the end aggravating rather than ameliorating political tensions in Canadian federalism. Overall, the Court's role as a homogenizing nation-builder has been decidedly modest, in contrast to the expectations held by both its supporters and detractors.[42]

If the Court has not discharged its nationalizing function in quite the way many had anticipated, its approach to civil rights and civil liberties has followed the same broad patterns observable in the United States, adjusted to certain political and institutional variations that distinguish Canadian judicial decision-making. Frequently tempted by governments to solve controversial problems for which they had hoped to avoid political responsibility,[43] the Canadian Court, just as its American counterpart, has been active most often in issues for which no clear political consensus exists. For example, in striking down the federal abortion law, the Canadian Court was in part following a cue supplied by federal officials including the prime minister, who had refused to include a clause in the Charter explaining that it did not derogate from Parliament's authority to legislate on abortion, despite being urged to do so by a number of parliamentarians. And, of course, when eventually confronted with a judicial annulment of its abortion law in 1988, which deliberately left open the possibility of legislative revision, Parliament at first temporized and then failed to secure agreement on any of its proposed amendments to the *Criminal Code.*

On the civil liberties front, the Canadian Court has varied the practice of the American judiciary of focusing on protecting preferred freedoms. In the Canadian case the presence of sec. 1 in the constitution permits the court to adopt a general libertarian stance while at the same time allowing it to defer to legislatures on the main objectives of state regulatory ventures. Empirical studies of judicial decision-making point to the practical consequences of this conflation of libertarian and deferential perspectives. After a preliminary spurt of activism in which the Court tried to stake out the interpretative doctrines it would employ in Charter litigation, the most noticeable tendencies have been for judicial nullifications based not on outright conflicts between laws and Charter rights, but rather on the basis of their overbreadth, or, more recently, on the basis of the impugnable conduct of public officials.[44] The significance of these recent trends is that the Court's incursions into policy fields have become relatively inconsiderable, and much more easily repairable.

Conclusion

What do these portraits of a comparatively unprepossessing Court, both in Canada and the United States, signify for the criticisms of judicial review summarized earlier? I would like to conclude by offering four propositions about normative critiques of judicial review in light of the discernible patterns in the actual decision-making of national courts. First, there is typically a divergence between empirically oriented and normative discourses on judicial review that raise some rather basic questions about the prescriptive foundation of the latter.[45] At the very least, there are strong reasons to think that the evidence to which critics of judicial review allude when constructing their arguments reflects a partiality that supports their particular normative preoccupations.

Second, these critics seldom subject to critical scrutiny the conception of democracy upon which their normative disapproval of judicial politics relies. Time and again the remonstrance is heard that courts are elite institutions that threaten democracy whenever they deviate from their narrow legal assignment. But once the majoritarian assumptions underlying modern representative democracy are scrutinized more closely, this particular line of criticism loses much of its purchase. Critics of judicial review characteristically see politics in terms of shifting combinations of interests that generate impermanent electoral and parliamentary majorities. However, as many observers have noted, this pluralist vision of democracy is neither descriptively accurate nor prescriptively consistent; it misrepresents the agenda-setting process in liberal democracies and is unwilling to acknowledge the class accents of the pluralist choir.

If the standard rendition of pluralism fails to capture adequately the political process at work in representative democracy, its more refined conceptual analogue, democratic elitism, might provide a better descriptive, if not normative, account of democratic politics. Democratic elitism regards government by the people as really government by elites periodically shuffled in elections. If the institutions of democratic government indeed are ultimately the domain of governing elites, competition among whom determines public policy, why deplore the judicial arena when its method of operation ostensibly is the same as that of legislatures? The customary reply is that legislatures, at least, are periodically renewable and therefore more accountable than courts. This may well serve as an answer in the abstract, but the theory of democratic elitism invites us to consider democracy concretely as a process of elite formation and alternation that responds indirectly to demands arising from the political arena. If the Court happens to be the site where some of these demands find a forum, there can be no a priori reason to decry this particular process of elite decision-making, because as a theory of governance, democratic elitism recommends only that there be some choices among elites. On this view, judicial policy-making is neither superior nor inferior to legislative policy-making, but rather is amenable to the same kind of analysis used to investigate all politics.

This observation leads to the third proposition about critics of judicial review. What the brief discussion of democratic elitism suggests is that judicial critics are moved not so much by the fact of judicial decision-making as by the implications it has for demand-setting in the overall political realm. This distinction is best illustrated by considering the separation of powers argument that is regularly used to reinforce the democratic critique of judicial review. Proponents of the device of separation of powers normally rely on its modern variant, so artfully described by Madison and Hamilton as an institutional arrangement where ambition is made to check ambition to produce moderate government. But is this argument for organizational principles formulated to limit the scope and activity of government appropriate in a political world where an executive-dominated administrative welfare state has now become commonplace? In the context of the modern bureaucratic state, allusions to the doctrine of separation of powers are used primarily to underwrite conservative critiques of economic regulation and state-sponsored redistribution, rather than to provide an occasion for discussing how judicial review can be made adequate to the current political environment. A theory of judicial review relevant to present-day politics might, for example, explore how due process or conceptions of natural justice should apply in administrative law or how social risk can be credibly assessed by courts, rather than how government should be confined in its reach.

Calling for a jurisprudential theory applicable to the reality of the modern state leads to a final proposition about the critics of judicial review. Opponents of the courts, it has been suggested, are more often than not motivated by fundamental objections to the nature of the political demands that make their way to the judiciary. The most familiar of these objections is that an impudent liberal Court has seized upon a series of abstract constitutional rights to privilege equality and identity claims that have no deep support in civil society. This admonition profoundly misconstrues the politics of rights on several different levels. To begin with, it depicts an aggressively independent Court challenging legislative majorities, a picture that is at odds with what empirical evidence actually demonstrates. But it also misapprehends the role of constitutional bills of rights in what many have termed the modern rights revolution. Constitutions and courts alone do not make for a rights revolution. As Charles Epp has shown in his careful comparative study of constitutional politics, rights litigation is a successful strategy only if there is an extensive and complex support structure, including availing organizations in civil society, that makes legal mobilization feasible.[46] But that structure itself presupposes a widespread public acceptance, if not positive endorsement, of the vocabulary of rights and the propriety of legal mobilization for political ends. That this acceptance has been reaching worldwide proportions is a fact attested to by a number of students of politics.[47] While the proximate causes of these developments vary from country to country, they nonetheless share in a philosophical patrimony with deep roots in modern liberalism. The libertarian and egalitarian sentiments that have combined to produce modern liberalism sustained a whole series of political transformations as they became the foundation for concrete citizenship rights. Once limited to formal conceptions of equality and a vigorous notion of individual liberty, citizenship rights were augmented and extended in the twentieth century with social rights, which in turn helped provoke both more varied egalitarian claims and increasingly insistent identity claims.[48] This is not to say that such claims are congruous and easily reconciled, but rather that they are part of a political process neither invented nor finally settled by courts. In fact, a less reified scrutiny of judicial review tells us that contemporary rights claimants are not nearly as successful as their adversaries would have it.[49] But at the same time, existing evidence also suggests that public approval of recent liberal jurisprudence is much greater than critics of the judiciary are willing to acknowledge.[50]

Where does that leave the question of judicial review and democracy? For all the shortcomings that attend this vehicle for resolving disputes over the division of powers and rights claims, it has become so integral a part of political decision-making in United States and Canada that recurring calls for court-curbing are not likely to meet with any success. Its place in political affairs an abiding reality, the judiciary's role in democratic deliberations is nonetheless contingent on the participatory culture and the mobilizing capacity of all citizens. Its democratic credentials are best established by the publicity it brings to contested political policies, and the Court might be a useful, albeit transient, forum for their promotion in circumstances where other political avenues are impeded. Over and above such strategic considerations, however, once it is acknowledged that the Court is irremediably political in a complex fashion, the democratic dilemma of judicial review might more accurately be conceptualized as a more general condition of democratic politics. That more general condition consists of the fact that democratic politics is a continuous process for which there can be no end point, and therefore no single set of political principles or policies can conclusively describe democratic purposes. Instead, such purposes are a matter of political contention, the Court being simply being one site for this contestation. Critics of judicial politics too often imagine a judiciary somehow limited to a world of legal principles safely distanced from contests over power that obtain in the democratic arena. If, however, power and principles are not so neatly separable, this vision of a sequestered court ironically represents a flight from politics rather than its democratic enhancement.

Notes

1. Alexis de Tocqueville, cited in A. V. Dicey, *Introduction to the Study of the Law of the Constitution* (London: Macmillan, 1960), 186.

2. The Marshall Court introduced interpretative doctrines regarding the implied power of Congress, the reach of the commerce power, and the applicability of the contract clause, which stood as weighty precedents strengthening the power of the national government and securing the rights of the propertied classes, in such rulings as *Sturgis v. Crowninshield* (1819), *Dartmouth College v. Woodward* (1819), *McCulloch v. Maryland* (1819), and *Gibbons v. Ogden* (1825). The subsequent Taney Court was more solicitous of states' rights, in the process elaborating a broad version of police power based on government's constitutional responsibility to promote the health, safety, morals, and welfare of its citizens. See, for example, *Charles River Bridge v. Warren Bridge* (1837) and *Mayor of New York v. Miln* (1837).

3. The relevant cases are: the *Slaughter-House Cases* (1873), *United States v. Cruikshank* (1876), *United States v. Reese* (1876), *Virginia v. Rives* (1880), *United States v. Harris* (1883), and, of course, *Plessy v. Ferguson* (1896).

4. The lead case establishing this interpretation was *Barron v. Baltimore* (1833), one of the last instances where Marshall had an opportunity to shape American federalism.

5. The seminal case was *Lochner v. New York* (1905).

6.Justice Stone furnished a hint of this liberal approach as early as *Carolene Products* (1938), where he suggested that courts should defer to legislative supervision of economic affairs but should subject to "more exacting judicial scrutiny" legislation that impedes the democratic political process, and that relies on "prejudices against discrete and insular minorities." See *United States v. Carolene Products Co.,* 304 U.S. 144 (1938), n. 4.

7.See *Gideon v. Wainright* (1963) and *Miranda v. Arizona* (1966).

8.See *Griswold v. Connecticut* (1965) and *Roe v. Wade* (1973).

9.See *Maher v. Roe* (1977), *Rust v. Sullivan* (1991), *Planned Parenthood of Southeastern Pennsylvania v. Casey* (1992), and *Bowers v. Hardwick* (1986).

10.See *Bakke v. Regents of the University of California* (1978), *City of Richmond, Virginia v. Croson* (1989), and *Adarand Constructors v. Pena* (1995).

11.See *U.S. v. Lopez* (1996), *Printz v. United States* (1997), and *Kimmel v. Florida Board of Regents* (2000). Of course, arguments favoring states' rights did fail spectacularly in *Bush v. Gore* 531 U.S. (2000), though the political motivation behind the Court's decision in this particular case is not hard to fathom.

12.The key cases in this judicial itinerary were *re Board of Commerce Act* and *Combines and Fair Prices Act* (1919, 1921), *Toronto Electric Commissioners v. Snider* (1925), *Employment and Social Insurance Act reference* (1937), *Natural Products Marketing Act reference* (1937), and *Labour Conventions Case* (1937).

13.Christopher Manfredi, "The Judicialization of Politics: Rights and Public Policy in Canada and the United States," in *Degrees of Freedom: Canada and the United States in a Changing World,* ed. Keith Banting, George Hoberg, and Richard Simeon (Montreal and Kingston: Queen's University Press, 1997).

14.Alexander M. Bickel, *The Least Dangerous Branch: The Supreme Court at the Bar of American Politics,* 2d ed. (New Haven and London: Yale University Press, 1986), 16, 18.

15.Peter H. Russell, *Constitutional Odyssey: Can Canadians Become a Sovereign People?* 2d ed. (Toronto: University of Toronto Press, 1993), 235.

16.See F. L. Morton and Rainer Knopff, *The Charter Revolution and the Court Party* (Peterborough, Ont.: Broadview Press, 2000); Rainer Knopff and F. L. Morton, *Charter Politics* (Scarborough, Ont.: Nelson, 1992); F. L. Morton and Rainer Knopff, "The Supreme Court as the Vanguard of the Intelligentsia: The Charter as Postmaterialist Politics," in *Canadian Constitutionalism, 1791–1991,* ed. Janet Ajzenstat (Ottawa: Canadian Study of Parliament Group, 1992).

17.See Christopher P. Manfredi, *Judicial Power and the Charter: Canada and the Paradox of Liberal Constitutionalism,* 2d ed. (Toronto: Oxford University Press, 2001).

18.Robert Dahl, "Decision-Making in a Democracy: The Supreme Court as National Policy-Maker," *Journal of Public Law* 6 (1958): 279–95.

19.Peter H. Hogg and Allison A. Bushell, "The Charter Dialogue between Courts and Legislatures," *Osgoode Hall Law Journal* 35, no. 1 (1997): 75–124.

20.American legal theorists who contemplate a dialogical relationship between courts and legislatures not infrequently refer to the Canadian Charter, and especially sec. 33, as an estimable illustration of how dialogue can be realized institutionally. See Guido Calabresi, "Foreword: Antidiscrimination and Constitutional Accountability (What the Bork-Brennan Debate Avoids)," *Harvard Law Review* 105 (1991): 124; Michael Perry, *The Constitution in the Courts* (New York: Oxford University Press, 1994), 196–201.

21.Hogg and Bushell, "The Charter Dialogue," 80–81.

22.See the empirical and normative criticisms of Hogg and Bushell offered by Christopher P. Manfredi and James B. Kelly, "Six Degrees of Dialogue: A Response to Hogg and Bushell," *Osgoode Hall Law Journal* 37, no. 3 (1999): 515–21.

23. For a sampling of new institutionalist writings on judicial politics, see Howard Gillman and Cornell Clayton, eds., *The Supreme Court in American Politics* (Lawrence: University Press of Kansas, 1999).

24.Mark Graber, "The Nonmajoritarian Difficulty: Legislative Deference to the Judiciary," *Studies in American Political Development* 7 (spring 1993): 35–73. See also idem, "Federalists or Friends of Adams: The Marshall Court and Party Politics," *Studies in American Political Development* 12 (fall 1998): 229–66; and idem, "The Problematic Establishment of Judicial Review," in Gillman and Clayton, eds., *The Supreme Court in American Politics,* 28–42.

25.Graber, "The Nonmajoritarian Difficulty," 38.

26.For a thoughtful summons to study the relationship between Supreme Court rulings and transitions in capitalism in the United States, see Howard Gillman, "Reconnecting the Modern Supreme Court to the Historical Evolution of American Capitalism," in Gillman and Clayton, *Supreme Court in American Politics,* 235–56.

27.Graber, "Federalist or Friends of Adams," 233.

28.Graber, "The Nonmajoritarian Difficulty," 46–50.

29. Ibid., 50–53.

30.Gillman, "Reconnecting the Modern Supreme Court," 241–46. See also Cass R. Sunstein, *After the Rights Revolution: Reconceiving the Regulatory State* (Cambridge: Harvard University Press, 1990).

31.F. D. Roosevelt certainly regarded as anachronistic the existing legal doctrines that were frustrating the implementation of New Deal legislation; he complained that they were better suited to the days of "horse and buggy." Roosevelt, cited in William E. Leuchtenburg, *The Supreme Court Reborn: The Constitutional Revolution in the Age of Roosevelt* (New York: Oxford University Press, 1995), 90.

32.For instance, Cass Sunstein contends that despite the Court's acquiescence to the realities of the modern regulatory state in the late 1930s, surviving common law attitudes to economic ordering continue to serve as encumbrances upon state regulatory activities. Sunstein, *After the Rights Revolution.*

33.According to Sunstein, prior to the 1930s judge-made doctrines in property, contract and tort law formed the interpretative baseline against which public law measures were assessed by courts, and that baseline was largely informed by the notion of formal equality. Ibid., 5–6.

34.Gillman points out that the term "preferred freedoms" was first employed in Justice Stone's dissent in *Jones v. Opelika* (1942) and attacked by Justice Frankfurter in *Kovacs v. Cooper* (1949). Gillman, "Reconnecting the Modern Supreme Court," 250. For discussions of how these freedoms came to be conceived in twentieth-century jurisprudence, see Howard Gillman, "Preferred Freedoms: The Progressive Expansion of State Power and the Rise of Modern Civil Liberties Jurisprudence," *Political Research Quarterly* 47 (1994): 623–53; G. Edward White, "The First Amendment Comes of Age: The Emergence of Free Speech in Twentieth Century America," *Michigan Law Review* 95 (1996): 299–392; Mark Graber, *Transforming Free Speech: The Ambiguous Legacy of Civil Libertarianism* (Berkeley: University of California Press, 1991).

35.See Eva R. Rubin, *Abortion, Politics, and the Courts: Roe v. Wade and its Aftermath,* rev. ed. (New York: Greenwood Press, 1987), chap. 6 and afterword.

36.Alan Cairns, "The Judicial Committee of the Privy Council and Its Critics," *Canadian Journal of Political Science* 4 (1971): 301–45.

37.J. R. Mallory, *Social Credit and the Federal Power in Canada* (Toronto: University of Toronto Press, 1976); and idem, "The Courts and the Sovereignty of the Canadian Parliament," *Canadian Journal of Economics* 10 (1944).

38.See *re Offshore Mineral Rights of British Columbia* (1967), *Canadian Industrial Gas & Oil Ltd. v. Government of Saskatchewan* (1978), *Central Canada Potash Co. Ltd.*, and *Attorney General of Canada v. Government of Saskatchewan* (1979).

39.See *The Queen v. Crown Zellerbach Canada, Ltd.* (1988), *Friends of Oldman River Society v. Canada* (1992), and *Regina v. Hydro-Quebec* (1997).

40.See *RJR-MacDonald v. Canada* (1995) and *re Firearms Act (Can)* (2000).

41.For a description of the nationwide constituencies the Charter was aimed at, and the transformations in politics it was meant to effect, see Alan C. Cairns, *Charter versus Federalism* (Montreal and Kingston: Queen's University Press, 1992), 33–61.

42.Yves De Montigny reports that the Charter "has not had the devastating impact on the legislative authority of Quebec (and of the other provinces) that some may have feared." De Montigny, "The Impact (Real or Apprehended) of the Canadian Charter of Rights and Freedoms on the Legislative Authority of Quebec," in *Charting the Consequences: The Impact of the Charter of Rights and Freedoms on Canadian Law and Politics,* ed. David Schneiderman and Kate Sutherland (Toronto: University of Toronto Press, 1997), 21. See also James B. Kelly, whose statistical analysis of Charter cases leads him to conclude that in recent years the Charter has had "a minimal impact on federal diversity. . . ." Kelly, "The Charter and Rebalancing of Liberal Constitutionalism, 1982–1997," *Osgoode Hall Law Journal* 37, no. 3 (1999): 685.

43.Former chief justice Lamar once complained that the reason why the Supreme Court has become so involved in policy issues in the era of the Charter is that "too often timid politicians have been afraid to confront them directly." Lamar, cited in Ian Greene, Carl Baar, Peter McCormick, George Szablowski, and Martin Thomas, *Final Appeal: Decision-Making in Canadian Courts of Appeal* (Toronto: James Lorimer & Co., 1998), 194.

44. See F. L. Morton, P. H. Russell, and T. Riddell, "The Canadian Charter of Rights and Freedoms: A Descriptive Analysis of the First Decade, 1982–1992," *National Journal of Constitutional Law* 5 (1994); Kelly, "The Charter of Rights and Freedoms and the Rebalancing of Liberal Constitutionalism"; and Hogg and Bushell, "The Charter Dialogue." This pattern has led some legal observers to characterize the Canadian Court as moderately activist. See, for example, P. H. Russell, "The Three Dimensions of Charter Politics," in *Canadian Politics,* ed. J. P. Bickerton and A.-G. Gagnon, 2d ed. (Peterborough, Ont.: Broadview Press, 1994), 352. Even in highly contested rulings such as *Vriend v. Alberta* (1998) and *M. v. H.* (1999), the court stopped short of a dramatic and wholesale reordering of legislative priorities.

45. On the issue of the divide between empirical and normative explorations of judicial review, see Rogers M. Smith, "Political Jurisprudence, the 'New Institutionalism,' and the Future of Public Law," *American Political Science Review* 82 (1988): 89–108; Miriam Smith, "Ghosts of the JCPC: Group Politics and Charter Litigation in Canadian Political Science," *Canadian Journal of Political Science* 35, no. 1 (March 2002).

46.Charles R. Epp, *The Rights Revolution: Lawyers, Activists, and Supreme Courts in Comparative Perspective* (Chicago: University of Chicago Press, 1998).See also idem, "Do Bills of Rights Matter? The Canadian Charter of Rights and Freedoms," *American Political Science Review* 90, no. 4 (December 1996): 765–79.

47.See, for instance, the contributions in C. Neal Tate and T. Vallinder, eds., *The Global Expansion of Judicial Power* (New York: New York University Press, 1995).

48.For a broad historical account of these developments, see Micahel Ignatieff, *The Rights Revolution* (Toronto: Anansi Press, 2000).

49.For disillusioned or positively scathing accounts of the social reform potential of judicial review, see Gerald N. Rosenberg, *The Hollow Hope* (Chicago: University of Chicago Press, 1991); Michael Mandel, *The Charter of Rights and the Legalization of Politics in Canada,* rev. ed. (Toronto: Thompson Educational Publishing, 1994); and Joel Bakan, *Constitutional Rights and Social Wrongs* (Toronto: University of Toronto Press, 1997).

50.See T. R. Marshall, *Public Opinion and the Supreme Court* (Boston: Unwin Hyman, 1989); Joseph Fletcher and Paul Howe, "Public Opinion and Canada's Courts," in *Judicial Power and Canadian Democracy,* ed. Paul Howe and Peter Russell (Montreal and Kingston: Queen's University Press, 2001), 255–96.

CHAPTER 11

Constitutional Amendment in Canada and the United States

Ian Greene

The revered British jurist A. V. Dicey thought that American democracy was in thrall to its courts. Unelected judges got to expound the meaning of the Constitution, and if the people's elected representatives disagreed, the enormous difficulty of amending the Constitution meant that there was little they could do about it.[1] Dicey argued that, in contrast, the United Kingdom remained a true democracy, because its unwritten constitution could be amended by Parliament through ordinary legislation. The British North America Act of 1867 that created the Dominion of Canada had some likeness to a written constitution in that it specified the division of powers between the federal parliament and the provincial legislatures, but it was subject to amendment as an ordinary statute of the British Parliament. After 1867, a constitutional convention developed that the B.N.A. Act could be amended in London at the request of a simple joint address from the Canadian Senate and House of Commons. It could therefore be argued from a Diceyan perspective that Canada, like the U.K., was governed in the final analysis by elected legislators rather than by appointed judges.[2]

In 1981, Prime Minister Pierre Trudeau proposed a domestic amending formula for the Canadian constitution along with a constitutional Charter of Rights. Much of the debate about this proposal centered around whether it was wise to abandon legislative supremacy in favor of judicial supremacy. After the constitutional reforms of 1982, it has become commonplace for academics to conclude that, like the United States, Canada has now succumbed to judicial supremacy, in part because the domestic amending formula has made the Canadian constitution as difficult to amend as the U.S. Constitution.

This chapter argues that despite a certain degree of constitutional rigidity, neither Canada nor the United States is trapped in a constitutional straightjacket preventing reasonable democratic change. Dicey's claims about the U.S. Constitution were exaggerated; he failed to notice how that Constitution can be altered in a de facto way through legislative action that either goes unchallenged or is legitimized through litigation. Although the attempts to amend the Canadian constitution through the Meech Lake Accord (1987–90) and the Charlottetown Accord (1992) were spectacular failures (because of breakdowns in the management processes at key points, or because they tried to accomplish too much), the Canadian constitution has nevertheless been amended nine times since 1982. This record, together with Canada's own reliance on informal constitutional alteration processes, indicates that the Canadian constitution, even more so than its U.S. counterpart, is more responsive to change than the conventional wisdom would have us believe. When there is a pressing need for constitutional change, this can often occur if leaders pursue a sensible strategy.

We will focus on the federal constitutions of Canada and the United States. Provincial and state constitutions, which are far easier to amend, lie beyond the scope of this inquiry. It should be noted, however, that in the United States there have been nearly six thousand successful amendments to state constitutions,[3] and there have been numerous amendments to the constitutions of the Canadian provinces.[4] If it is conceded that the state and provincial governments perform some of the more essential functions of government,[5] then "the constitutions" writ large in both the United States and Canada are less immune to change than a review of the relatively few amendments to the federal constitutions would indicate. For reasons of space we will also ignore the evolution of informal constitutional conventions, which provide some flexibility to the formal provisions of both the Canadian and American constitutions.[6]

The chapter will begin with a comparative overview of the formal amendment process in the United States and in Canada. It will then consider both the successes and failures of the formal and informal methods of constitutional revision in both countries, and the impact of the courts on constitutional revision. The chapter concludes with an analysis of lessons learned.

The Amendment Process

It is important to distinguish between the formal constitutional amendment process and informal methods of constitutional change that will be referred to as constitutional "alteration." Constitutional revision can result from either approach. Donald Lutz has argued that the rate of formal constitutional amendment is lower in jurisdictions in which constitutional amendment is difficult, and higher in jurisdictions with relatively lengthy constitutions.[7] As will be shown below, although the formal amendment process in both Canada and the United States is moderately difficult, it is somewhat less difficult in Canada. As well, the Canadian constitution is much lengthier than its U.S. counterpart. As predicted, the amendment rate in Canada is significantly higher than that in the United States.

The Canada Act of 1982, the last and final amendment of the Canadian constitution to be made by the British Parliament at the request of Canada, was by far the most significant constitutional amendment in Canada's history. It added the Charter of Rights and Freedoms to the constitution, enshrined some aboriginal rights, included a commitment to equalization payments in order to allow the poorer provinces to provide "reasonably comparable levels of public services," defined the written parts of the Canadian constitution that would have status superior to that of others, and provided no fewer than five domestic amending formulas (Part V of the Constitution Act, 1982). They are as follows:[8]

1. *The unanimity formula:* amendments affecting the office of the Queen or her Canadian representatives, the composition of the Supreme Court, the principle that no province may have fewer members of Parliament than senators, language rights that apply to the federal jurisdiction, and Part V itself, may only be made with the unanimous consent of Parliament and the ten provincial legislatures.
2. *The "some but not all" formula:* the parts of the constitution that affect one or more provinces and the federal government (such as constitutional provisions regarding the use of English or French within a particular province, denominational school rights, or a change in provincial borders) may be amended by the Parliament and the legislature for the province or provinces concerned acting together.
3. *Provincial governments may amend their own constitutions,* except for those parts of their constitutions that Part V states can only be amended by the unanimity formula, the "some but not all" formula, or the general amending formula. Provincial constitutions are not defined anywhere in the Canadian constitution, but the Supreme Court has defined them as any law that "bears on the operation of an organ of government of the province;"[9] this includes not only provincial legislation, but some parts of the C.A., 1867.
4. *Parliament may amend its own internal constitution* (such as matters dealing with parliamentary privilege, procedure, or the number of members of Parliament), except for those matters that Part V states can only be amended by one of the other amending formulas.
5. *The general amending formula:* All other parts of the constitution, including the Charter of Rights and the division of powers, may be amended with the agreement of Parliament and two-thirds of the provincial legislatures (i.e., seven out of ten), as long as these legislatures represent at least 50 percent of the Canadian population. (This procedure is often

> referred to as the "seven-fifty" formula.) A proclamation of amendment must be issued during the one-to-three-year period after the first resolution of amendment, which resolution could be initiated either by Parliament or by a provincial legislature. The following matters may be amended only through this formula: the principle of proportionate representation in the House of Commons, the powers of the Senate, the selection of senators and each province's allocation of senators, matters relating to the Supreme Court that are not covered by the unanimity formula, the establishment of new provinces, and the extension of the provinces into the territories.

Up to three provinces may opt out of an amendment made under the general procedure. This uniquely Canadian opting-out provision provides to each province a de facto internal veto over most constitutional amendments. It was devised in order to accommodate the demands of Quebec, British Columbia, and Alberta for amending formula vetoes during the 1981 constitutional negotiations. Moreover, if an amendment made under the seven-fifty formula were to result in a province losing power over education or culture, an opting-out province would be entitled to "reasonable compensation," meaning that the federal government would have to pay the opting-out province an amount equivalent to what it would have cost the federal government to operate the new program in the opting-out province. Compensation means that opting out becomes practically and not just theoretically possible with regard to education and culture. Trudeau agreed to compensate only for amendments affecting education and culture, because these are the matters that have traditionally been of greatest concern to Quebec. Quebec had originally demanded compensation for any amendment that it opted out of; however, Trudeau feared that providing the provinces with compensation for any amendment opted out of would lead to a highly uneven division of powers.

The procedures for amending the U.S. Constitution are much simpler. Article 5 of the Constitution is drafted so concisely that quoting it is the best way to describe its contents:

> The Congress, whenever two-thirds of both houses shall deem it necessary, shall propose amendments to this Constitution, or, on the application of the legislatures of two-thirds of the several States, shall call a convention for proposing amendments, which in either case shall be valid to all intents and purposes as part of this Constitution, when ratified by the legislatures of three-fourths of the several States, or by conventions in three-fourths thereof, as the one or the other mode of ratification may be proposed by the Congress, provided that[10] . . . no State, without its consent, shall be deprived of its equal suffrage in the Senate.

Only the first method for proposing amendments has ever been used successfully,[11] and in every instance but one (the Twenty-First Amendment, which repealed the Eighteenth) Congress prescribed ratification by state legislatures.[12] For any amendment proposed today, if ratification were to occur through the usual route, the assent of thirty-eight out of fifty state legislatures would be required. Because every state except Nebraska has a bicameral legislature, this means that the minimum number of legislatures needed to propose and ratify a constitutional amendment (including the two houses of Congress) is seventy-seven out of one hundred and one.[13] In Canada, eight out of eleven legislatures, including that of Ontario or Quebec, and the House of Commons[14] are needed to approve amendments to the central parts of the Canadian constitution—the Charter of Rights and the division of powers. It makes no difference in Canada whether an amendment is proposed by Parliament or by a provincial legislature.

Successes and Failures: The Canadian Record

Successes

Because the Canadian constitution reads more like a series of ordinary statutes than an American-style constitution and is much longer that its U.S. counterpart, it follows that it would be subject to amendment more frequently than the U.S. Constitution in order to keep the details up to date. In fact, between 1867 to 2001 the Canadian constitution was amended thirty-two times. Canada's record of thirty-two amendments over thirteen decades compares with the United States experience of seventeen amendments in twenty-one decades. (Although there are twenty-seven articles of amendment in the U.S. Constitution, the first ten amendments took effect in 1791 as a package, and so are counted here as one amendment, just as the omnibus amendments of 1982 in Canada are counted here as one amendment.) From a quantitative perspective, the rate of constitutional amendment (number of amendments divided by the number of years of constitutional history) in Canada is .24 (and .47 between 1982 and 2001), while in the United States, the rate is just .08, or one-third of the long-term Canadian rate.[15]

From 1867 until 1981, there were twenty-two amendments; three of these altered the division of powers between the federal and provincial governments. These three were the 1940 amendment that added unemployment insurance to the list of federal powers in section 91 of the Constitution Act, 1867; the 1951 amendment that placed old-age pensions in the list of concurrent federal and provincial powers; and the 1964 amendment that modified the definition of old-age pensions to include supplementary, survivors, and disability benefits.[16] In addition to the Statute of Westminster, other amendments added provinces or territories to the union, extended provincial boundaries to the north, or were relatively minor "housekeeping" amendments regarding central government institutions.[17]

There have been nine amendments between 1983 and 2001. The first amendment to proceed under the new amending procedures, which entrenched some aboriginal rights,[18] was proclaimed in 1983 and was effected according to the "seven-fifty" formula (although it actually received unanimous consent). Seven amendments employed the "some but not all" formula. Three of these (1987, 1997, and 1998) were in relation to religious education or denomination school rights in Newfoundland, and one in 1997 amended the position of denominational schools in Quebec.[19] An amendment in 1993 recognized the equality of the French and English linguistic communities in New Brunswick, and another in 1993 recognized the fixed link between Prince Edward Island and the mainland as fulfilling the federal obligation to provide a ferry service to the island. In 2001 an amendment changed the name of Newfoundland to "Newfoundland and Labrador." An amendment in 1985, which was brought about by the Parliament of Canada acting alone, updated the proportional representation of provincial populations in the House of Commons.[20]

Failures

Most Canadians are likely unaware of the number of successful constitutional amendments in their country. What is recalled are the failures, because of all the publicity surrounding them. The three failures that stand out are the inability of the first ministers to agree on a domestic amending formula between 1931 and 1982, the fumbling of the Meech Lake Accord, and the fumbling of the Charlottetown Accords in the early 1990s.

The Search for a Domestic Amending Formula. Between 1927 and 1980, the first ministers tried and failed six times to agree on a domestic amending formula for the Canadian constitution.[21] Pierre Trudeau claimed that the reason for the lack of progress was a fundamental disagreement about the locus of Canadian sovereignty.[22] At the 1927 constitutional conference, the premiers of Ontario and Quebec took the position that Canada is a "compact" of Francophones (represented primarily by Quebec) and the Anglophones (represented predominantly by Ontario). According to this theory, Quebec and Ontario, and perhaps other provinces, must necessarily have a veto over future change. No truly federal government could ever agree to the compact theory, and so the goal of developing a domestic amending formula seemed unreachable. The problem was exacerbated by the emerging demographic and economic prominence of Alberta and British Columbia during the 1970s; these provinces demanded equal treatment with Ontario and Quebec.

The deadlock was eventually broken after the dramatic attempt of the Trudeau government in 1981 to request Westminster to amend Canada's constitution one final time. Because the federal government took the position that provincial support for Parliament's request for the constitutional change was unnecessary, the request became known as a "unilateral" attempt to amend the constitution. The proposed amendment included a domestic amending procedure based on a formula developed in 1971 that, for a time, had the unanimous backing of all Canadian first ministers. The 1981 package also included a Charter of Rights and Freedoms that, among other things, also provided new guarantees for the French and English languages. Trudeau knew that most Canadians were not much interested in the amending formula issue and that language rights tended to be divisive. However, he gambled that Canadians could be mobilized to support a constitutional Charter of Rights, even if the Charter were attached to a domestic amending formula and new language rights.

Although the unilateral attempt to amend the constitution did have strong and broad public approval, it was vehemently opposed by eight provinces, three of which sent reference questions to their provincial courts of appeal to ask whether unilateral patriation was acceptable both in a legal and a conventional sense. The reference answers were appealed and arrived at the Supreme Court before Trudeau could persuade Westminster to approve the constitutional package. In September 1981, the Supreme Court ruled that unilaterial patriation was legally acceptable, but that it violated a constitutional convention of "substantial provincial consent" prior to requesting an amendment that affected provincial powers.[23] This decision set the stage for an agreement including nine provincial premiers and Trudeau on 5 November 1981. Both sides made significant compromises in order to achieve the agreement.

The separatist premier of Quebec, René Lévesque, did not participate in the informal late-night session that led to the 5 November agreement, but he had previously agreed to nearly everything included in it. When the agreement was announced, Lévesque attacked it for failing to recognize what he claimed was Quebec's historic veto over all constitutional changes. What he was referring to was Trudeau's insistence that provinces that opted out of a constitutional amendment made under the "seven-fifty" formula would be compensated *only* if the amendment affected education or culture. Thus, Quebec would not have a de facto veto over constitutional changes concerning matters other than education and culture. Although this point may seem relatively minor, the crux of the matter was that no Quebec government elected on a separatist platform could agree to a constitutional package that gave greater legitimacy to the Canadian regime. Lévesque contended that when the compromise agreement was reached, Quebec delegates were not present, and so Quebec had been "stabbed in the back."

The opposition Conservative Party took up the same refrain, and used the issue to help win the majority of seats both in Quebec and in Canada in the 1984 general election. (Trudeau had retired as prime minister in 1983.) The Conservatives promised to pursue another constitutional amendment that Quebec could agree to in its entirety. When the separatist Parti Québécois (PQ) government was defeated in the 1985 Quebec election by the federalist Liberals, the time seemed right to proceed with the amendment promised by the federal Conservatives.

Meech Lake. The Quebec Liberals spelled out five conditions for peace over the constitutional amendment issue; most important among them were a full Quebec veto for constitutional changes and the recognition of Quebec as a "distinct society." The other three conditions were a provincial role in making appointments to the Supreme Court of Canada, a shift to the provinces in power over immigration, and limits on the federal spending power. These conditions could actually be met without too much difficulty. Part V of the C.A., 1982 left each province with a de facto veto except with regard to financial compensation for amendments under the seven-fifty formula that affected matters other than education and culture; Part V could be amended to expand financial compensation for opting out by amending it with the unanimity formula. The other four conditions could be dealt with under the seven-fifty formula.

In fact, all the premiers and Prime Minister Mulroney agreed to a package for constitutional change—the "Meech Lake Accord"—that satisfied Quebec's five conditions in 1987. The only part of the accord requiring unanimous consent was the change to Part V regarding expanding compensation for opting out; the other changes came under the "seven-fifty" formula. Although the unanimous consent formula has no time limit, Quebec insisted on a three-year deadline. During the three years, provincial elections resulted in new governments in Manitoba, Newfoundland, and New Brunswick, and all three opposed the Meech Lake Accord. Their opposition reflected public sentiment outside of Quebec, which was critical of an important constitutional change made with very little public input and the failure of the accord to address constitutional issues like Senate reform and aboriginal self-government. A constitutional conference was held in 1990 that resulted in modifications that brought New Brunswick on board, but the three-year time limit passed before the accord could be ratified in the legislatures of Newfoundland and Manitoba. It should be remembered that had Quebec not imposed a strict three-year time limit on approval of the changes to Part V, which required unanimous consent, the Meech Lake Accord might have succeeded, as the other provisions had the requisite support under the seven-fifty formula.

Charlottetown. The failure of the Meech Lake Accord resulted in a dramatic rise of pro-sovereignist sentiments in Quebec. To combat the possibility of another Quebec referendum that might approve a sovereignty proposal, the first ministers tried to revive the Meech Lake agreement in a way that would overcome the public opposition that Meech Lake had encountered. This time, there was a great deal of public input, and there was an attempt to accommodate other significant demands for constitutional changes. The result was a lengthy and complex package agreed to by the first ministers in Charlottetown, Prince Edward Island, in 1992 that included an elected Senate, the right of aboriginal peoples to self-government, a nonjusticiable social and economic charter, a "Canada Clause" in addition to the "distinct society" clause for Quebec, a guarantee to Quebec of at least 25 percent of the seats in the House of Commons, as well as all of the elements of the Meech Lake Accord.

The first ministers decreed that the Charlottetown Accord would need to be approved in a national referendum, and that they would not proceed with the accord unless it was approved by a majority in each province. In the two months between the unveiling of the Charlottetown Accord and the referendum, public sentiment changed from strong support to skepticism. This waning of public support was partly a result of the accord's complexity, which made it nearly impossible either for experts or the public to evaluate it in two months. In the end, although most Canadians approved of much of the accord, many disagreed with at least one of the elements of it, and so voted against the entire package.[24] The accord was defeated by 54.4 percent to 44.6 percent nationally, and was also defeated in six provinces, including Quebec.

The legacy of the fifty-year search for a domestic amending formula, together with the failures of the Meech Lake and Charlottetown Accords, has left Canadians with the impression that constitutional amendment is a rare and heroic event. In fact, complex omnibus proposals, such as the 1982 constitutional accord and the Charlottetown Accord, are epic constitution-making events that can rarely succeed, but they do not reflect the reality of more simple and discrete constitutional amendments, which are by far more common.

Success and Failures: The American Record

Successes

There are twenty-seven articles of amendment appended to the U.S. Constitution. The first ten amendments, which form the core of the Bill of Rights, were proclaimed in 1791 as part of the constitution-making process of the late 1780s. Amendments 13 to 15, which abolished slavery, guaranteed equality, and extended the right to vote to male black Americans, were ratified in 1865, 1868, and 1870, respectively, as a response to the Civil War. Between 1791 and 1865, there were just two amendments ratified: Article 11 (1798) limited the extraterritorial jurisdiction of federal courts, and Article 12 (1804) established the procedure to be used in the electoral college for the election of the president and vice-president.

Amendments 16 and 17 were both ratified in 1913; the former gave Congress the power to collect income tax, and the latter modified section 3 of Article 1 by stipulating that senators would henceforth be elected instead of appointed by the state legislatures. Amendment 18 instituted prohibition in 1919, and Amendment 21 repealed it in 1933. Amendment 19 (1920) gave women the right to vote. The dates for the beginning and end of the presidential term of office were fixed by Amendment 20 in 1933, along with the date for the first day of Congress in each year, provisions regarding delays in approving presidential or vice-presidential qualifications, and provisions dealing with the death of presidential or vice-presidential candidates. Amendment 22 (1951) limited the presidential office to two terms, and Amendment 23 (1961) gave citizens living in the District of Columbia a vote in presidential elections. The Twenty-fourth Amendment of 1964 extended the right to vote in presidential and congressional elections to many hitherto disenfranchised blacks by declaring that failure to pay a poll tax could not interfere with the right to vote. The Kennedy assassination gave rise to Amendment 25 (1967), which ensured that there would not be a vacancy in the office of the president because of a president's death or a president's inability to discharge his or her duties. Amendment 26 of 1971 set the voting age at eighteen. The most recent amendment, the "Madison" amendment ratified in 1992, is unique in that it was first proposed 203 years earlier, in 1789.[25] It prohibits midterm increases in congressional pay.

The formal amendments to the U.S. Constitution, therefore, have dealt primarily with human rights issues and the institutions of government. Only one amendment has modified the division of powers—the Sixteenth Amendment, which gave Congress the power to collect income tax. And only two amendments have dealt with policy issues—the prohibition amendment and its repeal. Other changes have occurred through informal means.

Failures

About ten thousand amendments to the U.S. Constitution have been introduced into Congress, or formally proposed in one of the houses.[26] Many of these were introduced for humorous reasons or otherwise had no chance of success, but dozens came close to the proposal stage. Six amendments were formally proposed by Congress but then not ratified by the states.[27] The best-known failed amendment is the Equal Rights Amendment (ERA) proposal. The movement that won the right to vote for women through the Nineteenth Amendment in 1920 also advocated the equal treatment of women in all legislation. As a result, in 1923 a proposed amendment was introduced into Congress that would guarantee equal rights to men and women. The motion was defeated, but proponents had the amendment reintroduced in every subsequent session of Congress until it finally secured a majority in 1972. Congress stipulated a seven-year time limit for ratification by the states.

Twenty-two states ratified the amendment in 1972, and eight in 1973. Then opposition to the amendment began to build, and only five more states had ratified it by 1977, bringing the total number of ratifications to thirty-five out of the thirty-eight needed. Opposition to the ERA included conservative women's groups, employers that feared increased wage costs, and states' rights groups. In 1978, pressure from ERA supporters resulted in Congress extending the deadline for ratification to 1982, but the additional time could not save the amendment. From 1982 to 2001, the ERA has been reintroduced into every session of Congress, and proponents have continued to lobby for the amendment. The ratification of the Madison amendment in 1992 caused some to argue that if three additional states ratify the ERA (and none of the other thirty-five rescind their ratification), Congress has the power to extend the ratification period retroactively.[28]

There is nothing to prevent the federal and state governments from implementing the spirit of the ERA without a formal constitutional amendment, and many governments have done so. Part of the reason for the failure of the ERA may be that even among its supporters, there are those who see it more as a policy issue than a human rights issue. As the history of the prohibition amendment illustrates, policy issues do not fit well into an American-style constitution. They are dealt with more successfully by informal mechanisms of change.

The Impact of the Courts

Canada

Judicial decisions on the constitutionality of amending procedures. The Supreme Court's constitutional reference decision of 1981 is the judicial determination that has had the most dramatic impact on constitutional amendment in Canada.[29] In interviews that I conducted with three retired judges who participated in the decision, I asked whether the judges had calculated their opinion to try to force the opposing political camps to reach an agreement on constitutional change. Two reported that did they not consider how politicians might react to the decision. One judge, however, said that he and others were impressed with the arguments of the attorney general of Saskatchewan, and that the Saskatchewan approach (i.e., there is a convention of substantial provincial consent to amendments that impact provincial powers, but not unanimous provincial consent) presented an ingenious solution to an apparently intractable problem. It is clear that without the Supreme Court decision, which gave the federal government a legal victory but the provinces a moral one and which did not prescribe unanimous provincial consent,[30] the constitutional accord of 5 November 1981 could never have been achieved.

The second major decision on constitutional amendment procedure was the Quebec secession reference of 1996. The events leading up to this case date from the failure of the Charlottetown Accord. There followed a rise in nationalist sentiment in Quebec and the calculation of the PQ government of Jacques Parizeau that 1995 was an opportune time to hold a referendum on Quebec secession. The strategy of the federal government of Prime Minister Jean Chrétien had been to stay out of this debate, but that strategy backfired. The "yes" side came within 0.6 percent of winning on 30 October 1995.

Since 1996, Intergovernmental Affairs Minister Stephan Dion has been a forceful proponent of what has become known as the "Plan B" approach to fighting Quebec sovereignty. "Plan A"—the hands-off approach—had failed. Plan B refers to a more interventionist role for the federal government in attacking the sovereignist position. As part of the Plan B strategy, the federal government sent a reference question to the Supreme Court of Canada in 1997 asking (1) whether the Canadian constitution gives the Quebec government the right to implement the unilateral secession of Quebec, and (2) whether international law gives the Quebec government the right to unilateral secession.[31]

The government of Quebec refused to represent itself at the hearings, so the Supreme Court appointed André Joli-Cœur as amicus curiae to argue on behalf of the sovereignist side. Joli-Cœur argued that the Court ought not to answer the reference question, as secession was a political rather than a judicial matter. Although the Court could quite legitimately have refused to answer,[32] it may well be that the Court accepted the challenge because the judges thought they could make a contribution to the resolution of critical national issues, as they had in 1981. Moreover, as the judges themselves have pointed out in their recent public addresses, they have become used to a more activist role in public affairs since the advent of the Charter.[33]

The Court could have chosen to write a very short opinion; nearly all constitutional authorities agreed that the answer to the two questions was clearly "no."[34] However, the Supreme Court's judgment runs to some seventy-five pages. In answering the first question, the Court emphasized that the arguments in support of unilateral secession were based primarily on the principle of democracy. The Court wrote that democracy "means more than simple majority rule. . . . [C]onstitutional jurisprudence [shows that] democracy exists in the larger context of other constitutional values," such as "respect for the inherent dignity of the human person. . . ." The Court added that "a functioning democracy requires a continuous process of discussion . . . compromise, negotiation, and deliberation. . . . Inevitably, there will be dissenting voices. A democratic system of government is committed to considering those dissenting voices. . . ." The court concluded that "a clear majority vote in Quebec on a clear question in favour of secession" would mean that the federal government and the provinces would need to negotiate Quebec's secession in good faith. The terms, "a clear question" and "a clear majority" were intentionally not defined; these would have to be determined by the political process.[35]

In answering the second question regarding international law in the negative, the Court wrote that a right to secession only arises under international law when "a people" is governed as part of a colonial empire and "is subject to alien subjugation, domination or exploitation," and possibly also when "a people" is denied the "meaningful exercise of its right to self-determination" within the federation. These factors did not apply with regard to Quebec. Canada is "entitled to maintain its territorial integrity under international law and to have that territorial integrity recognized by other States. Quebec does not meet the threshold of a colonial people or an oppressed people."[36]

The Supreme Court's intervention on the Quebec secession issue outlines a way in which Quebec or any other province could attempt to secede from Canada in a constitutional way. What the Supreme Court formulated was a principled, bloodless approach to the settlement of internal unity issues. Even though the U.S. Civil War led to tens of thousands of casualties and immense destruction, Jay Winik has argued that the eventual settlement of the unity issue in fact represented one of the most civilized approaches to ending civil strife in the modern era.[37] Canada is more than a century behind the United States in coming to grips with the issue of whether the federation can be divided, and so can learn from history's lessons. The solution suggested by the Supreme Court may represent a step toward promoting greater respect for human dignity in breakup situations, although it places enormous faith in reason over passion.

Objections to judicial decisions that have given rise to amendments. Most scholars agree that the Judicial Committee of the Privy Council, from the 1890s until the 1930s, had been sympathetic to provincial rights arguments and tended to rule in their favor.[38] The result was a gradual transfer of power from the central government to the provinces, so that present-day Canada is arguably one of the most decentralized federations in the world. This judicial amendment of the constitution has arguably had as much impact on the day-to-day reality of the division of powers as all the formal amendments put together. The decentralizing impact of the JCPC began with the chairmanship of Lord Watson in the 1890s, and continued through to the end of the chairmanship of Viscount Haldane (1911 to 1928). Their decisions resulted in an erosion of the federal residual power, the federal Trade and Commerce power, and the federal criminal power. There is evidence that both of these law lords were convinced that because of the diverse nature of Canada, with its two linguistic communities, small population, and vast expanses, the 1867 constitution was too centralizing. In order to help ensure Canada's continued existence, Watson and Haldane often ruled in favor of provincial rights claims.[39]

Most of the JCPC decisions that shifted power to the provincial sphere were not appreciated by the federal government. However, there is only one instance where the results of a JCPC decision led to a constitutional amendment. This was the *Reference re Unemployment Insurance,* a decision of Haldane that declared that the power to legislate with regard to unemployment insurance was a provincial responsibility.[40] This decision resulted in section 91(2A), unemployment insurance, being added to the list of federal powers in a constitutional amendment of 1940.

Many expected that after the Canadian parliament legislated the end of appeals from Canada to the JCPC, the Supreme Court would exert a more centralizing influence on constitutional interpretation. However, the Supreme Court has taken the position that the JCPC decisions that resulted in decentralization ought generally to be followed. Several studies have indicated that the Supreme Court has tended to favor neither the provinces nor the central government on division of powers issues since 1949.[41]

In 1951, the Supreme Court was called on to decide the constitutionality of a scheme worked out by the federal government and Nova Scotia in which they delegated various powers to each other regarding old-age pensions. The reason for the elaborate plan was that the provincial governments had jurisdiction over pensions, but the federal government had the financial resources to implement them. The Supreme Court's decision declared the interdelegation procedure unconstitutional.[42] In reaction, section 94A, "old age pensions," was added to the list of concurrent federal and provincial powers by the Constitution Act, 1951. Similarly, when the old-age pension amendment needed to be updated to accommodate the Canada Pension Plan and the Quebec Pension Plan in 1964, an additional constitutional amendment was necessary. Thus, all three constitutional amendments that affected the division of powers from 1949 to 1982 were reactions to a judicial decision that had resulted in a straightjacket on governments bent on addressing social issues. One other amendment to the division of powers was also made in reaction to prior judicial interventions. Section 92A of the Constitution Act, 1867 gives the provinces additional powers over the regulation of non-renewable natural resources, forestry, and electrical energy, countering the impact of two Supreme Court of Canada decisions of the late 1970s that increased federal control over provincially owned natural resources.

Informal constitutional alteration. In federal countries, the division of powers is rarely crystal clear. Rather than going through a formal constitutional amendment process to clarify the situation, a government may simply declare that it has the constitutional power to accomplish a particular objective and enact the appropriate legislation. If no litigation results, or if litigation does result but the outcome is to uphold the legislation, then there has been a de facto alteration or clarification of the constitution that avoids the formal amendment process.

There are two general heads of power in the Canadian constitution that the federal government has used most often to justify enacting legislation when its constitutional competence to do so is uncertain: the "Peace, Order and Good Government" (POGG) clause (the preamble to sec. 91 of the C.A., 1867), and the "trade and commerce" clause (s. 91.2 of the C.A., 1867).[43] The provinces often defend uncertain legislation by referring to sec. 92.13, "property and civil rights," the subject matter that refers to private law.

The federal government has gained control over the following matters that have been justified by reference to the POGG clause:[44] radio and television broadcasting, offshore minerals, aeronautics, the National Capital Area, marine pollution, atomic energy, temporary wage and price controls during periods of high inflation, narcotics controls, the prosecution of offenses under federal statutes (except criminal offenses), wartime and crisis emergency powers, and postwar reconstruction. The "trade and commerce" clause has been used successfully to defend federal jurisdiction over the national marketing boards, the interprovincial marketing of petroleum, trademarks, and the regulation of competition. The provinces have justified jurisdiction over the following matters by referring to "property and civil rights": the regulation of business, the regulation of insurance, the professions and trades, labor relations, intraprovincial marketing regulations, the censorship of films, securities regulation, and debt adjustment.[45] The lists outlining the division of powers in sections 91 and 92 of the Constitution Act, 1867 would be far more complete and accurate if the subject matters listed in this paragraph were included in the federal and provincial lists of powers, respectively, given the Canadian approach of providing detailed lists in the constitution of both federal and provincial powers.

Another informal method of constitutional alteration is to enact legislation that, if respected, has the effect of changing the application of the written constitution. For example, after the narrow defeat in a referendum of the Quebec government's sovereignty proposal in 1995, Parliament enacted legislation to achieve two goals that had eluded it because of the failure of the Meech Lake and Charlottetown Accords: providing Quebec and other populous provinces with vetoes over constitutional change, and the recognition of Quebec as a "distinct society." Federal legislation[46] now prohibits any cabinet minister from proposing a motion to amend the constitution under the "seven-fifty" formula until resolutions of amendment have already been approved by Quebec, Ontario, British Columbia, two Atlantic provinces that represent 50 percent of the population of the Atlantic provinces, and two Prairie provinces similarly populated. This legislation was passed in tandem with a resolution recognizing Quebec as a "distinct society." Although the regional veto legislation and the distinct society resolution can be nullified by a simple act of Parliament, as long as they remain on the books they operate as key de facto pieces of the Canadian constitution.

A second use of ordinary legislation to bring about a de facto amendment of the constitution occurred in the spring of 2000, when Parliament enacted Bill C-20, "An Act to give effect to the requirement for clarity as set out in the opinion of the Supreme Court of Canada in the Quebec Secession Reference." This legislation was part of the federal government's "Plan B" national unity strategy, and was a followup to the Supreme Court's Quebec secession reference. The act requires the House of Commons to declare whether it considers a referendum question on a province's secession to be clear, and to do so within thirty days of a provincial legislature tabling a referendum question. If the House considers a referendum to be clear, and if there is eventually a majority vote in favor of the question, the act further requires the House to determine whether there has been a "clear" majority in favor of secession.

Because the Supreme Court of Canada has referred to legislative bills of rights and human rights acts that are supplemental to the Canadian Charter of Rights and Freedoms as "quasi-constitutional" documents,[47] and has sometimes given them priority when they conflict with other ordinary statutes, it would not be hard to imagine the Supreme Court assigning "quasi-constitutional" status to the federal constitutional amendment, distinct society, and clarity acts. Whether or not this occurs, if these acts withstand the test of time for a quarter century or so they will likely be regarded by at least some political observers as part of the Canadian constitution in the broad sense.

The United States

Judicial decisions on the constitutionality of amending procedures. Several judicial decisions in the United States have helped to clarify constitutional amendment procedures, although none has had an impact comparable to the Canadian decisions discussed above.[48] The Supreme Court has decided that although it is up to Congress to propose amendments, the president cannot be prevented from offering suggestions or guidance. The phrase, "two-thirds of both houses" in Article 5 means two-thirds of a quorum. "Legislatures" means legislative assemblies with or without the approval of the state governor; furthermore, the legislature cannot be forced to vote according to popular sentiments as expressed, for example, through a referendum. Tennessee's supreme court has ruled that the state legislature cannot limit the ratification process by legislating that the legislature is prohibited from ratifying an amendment that is proposed prior to an election for the legislature. State legislatures that have ratified a proposed amendment may not later rescind the ratification, although if a ratification vote fails at some point, that result may be overridden by a positive ratification vote in the future.[49]

Objections to judicial decisions that have given rise to amendments. Because constitutional amendment in the United States is so difficult, there is little opportunity to amend the Constitution to override judicial decisions about the meaning of the Constitution. The three Civil War amendments (13, 14, and 15) are an exception: they were necessitated by *Dred Scott v. Sanford,* the infamous decision in which all but two of the justices declared that the Constitution prevented the federal government from prohibiting slavery, even in a part of the Louisiana Purchase area.[50]

In 1918, the Supreme Court struck down a federal law prohibiting child labor as a violation of the limited federal jurisdiction over interstate commerce. As a result, Congress proposed a constitutional amendment in 1924 to prohibit child labor. By 1925, thirteen states still opposed ratification; only one more state's approval would have passed the amendment. However, after the Supreme Court's change of heart about the New Deal, the amendment became unnecessary. Congress enacted the Fair Labour Standards Act in 1938, which prohibited child labor, and the Supreme Court overturned its 1918 decision and upheld the federal legislation.[51]

The restrictive interpretation of due process by the Supreme Court during the *Lochner* era, and the resultant hamstringing of governments attempting to institute social programs designed to combat the Depression, compelled President Roosevelt to consider a constitutional amendment to counter the Supreme Court's rejection of the New Deal legislation. However, Roosevelt's advisors eventually persuaded him that because of the difficulty of change under Article 5, threatening to pack the court would be a strategy more likely to meet with success. Especially after Roosevelt had had a chance to appoint some judges to the Court, the Supreme Court deferred to Roosevelt's position that Congress and state legislatures already had the constitutional power to regulate social and economic matters.[52]

Informal constitutional alteration. Shortly after George Washington became president, details of government operation had to be worked out. This working out sometimes had the same impact as a formal constitutional amendment, but Article 5 was not invoked. For example, Washington behaved as if the cabinet's role was advisory, and he believed that he had the power to remove executive officers. These assumptions became constitutional conventions in the British sense, rather than formal constitutional amendments.[53]

When Thomas Jefferson had the opportunity as president to procure Louisiana from Napoleon, he at first believed that the purchase could only be brought about after a constitutional amendment. When he realized that the opportunity might be lost, he changed his mind and announced that the Constitution could be interpreted to permit the purchase.[54] Although there had been controversy about whether Jefferson had acted constitutionally in 1803, the Louisiana Purchase was not challenged in court, and later on the United States acquired new territories without controversy.

Other examples of constitutional change outside the formal amendment procedure are the creation of independent regulatory agencies, the institutionalization of judicial review as a result of Chief Justice Marshall's decision in *Marbury v. Madison,* and the development of political parties in spite of the belief of many of the fathers of the Constitution that the Constitution was designed to operate without political parties.[55]

During the late 1930s and early 1940s, Congress assumed vast new powers over the U.S. economy, and the president became much more involved in lawmaking than the classical theories of the constitutional separation of powers would have condoned.[56] These significant constitutional alterations were not effected through Article 5 but through an assumption of constitutional powers that was never successfully challenged.

Conclusion

Although Article 5 of the U.S. Constitution, and Part V of the Canada's Constitution Act, 1982 each make constitutional amendment cumbersome, the record shows that Canada's constitution is not as difficult to amend as the U.S. Constitution. From 1867 to 2001, the Canadian constitution has been amended thirty-two times (a rate of .24 times per year in the long term, or .47 between 1982 and 2001), compared with the U.S. record of seventeen amendments from 1789 to 2000 (a rate of only .08 times per year) . Canada's written constitution has always had a somewhat more flexible amending formula (both pre- and post-1982) than Article 5 of the U.S. Constitution. This greater flexibility was necessitated by the nature of the Canadian constitution. It is drafted more like a series of detailed ordinary statutes than as a concise constitution written with a patriotic flourish; as well, it is much longer than its U.S. counterpart. Because of these factors it will need formal amendment more frequently.

Regardless, the failures of the Meech Lake Accord and the Charlottetown Accord, together with the extraordinary amount of civic energy consumed by the 1982 constitutional amendment, have left Canadians with an image of their constitution as one that is nearly impossible to amend. The 1982 amendment was unique, however, in that what was at stake was the locus of sovereignty in Canada. Both the Meech Lake and Charlottetown Accords were attempted in the early days of the new amending procedure, when politicians were experimenting with the new amendment procedures. In addition, the Charlottetown Accord tried to attain general public support for far too many complex proposals for change at one time. In the United States, the failure of the ERA left many American supporters of the proposed amendment discouraged with the process of formal constitutional change. Too rarely do they remember that their goals might be achieved more effectively through informal means.

In both Canada and the United States constitutional change through informal mechanisms occurs fairly regularly, although without much publicity. The strategy is for a government to assume that the constitution gives it the power to enact a particular piece of legislation, and then to forge ahead. Sometimes constitutional litigation will result, and occasionally the government that is sailing into new constitutional waters will run aground. But the chances of the success of this strategy are often greater than the chances of success of formal constitutional amendment. Recently in Canada, an innovative strategy of the federal government has been to pursue de facto constitutional amendment through ordinary statutes that clarify or limit the federal role regarding some constitutional amendment procedures. Time will tell whether this gamble succeeds. It would be fair to conclude, then, that in both the United States and Canada the federal constitutions work as well as they do, both as blueprints for the structure and powers of government and as guarantors of democracy and rights, because constitutional alteration is possible outside the formal amendment process.

Dicey was wrong. A rigid constitutional amendment procedure does not necessarily mean that constitutional supremacy means judicial supremacy. There are plenty of opportunities for elected politicians to pursue democratic objectives either through formal constitutional amendment or by steering around formal constitutional amendment procedures. However, political leaders bent on constitutional change need to think carefully about which strategy to pursue. In hindsight, supporters of the ERA in the United States, and of the Charlottetown Accord in Canada, might have done better to consider advancing their objectives through informal means. Just the same, political leaders certainly do not have a free hand in interpreting the constitution as they see fit. The judiciary in both countries acts as a check against what the judges consider to be excessive or unreasonable constitutional alteration. Everything considered, it would be more accurate to describe the judicial role in constitutional amendment as an intermittent auditor of legislative initiative rather than as a "supreme" overseer.

Notes

1. A. V. Dicey, *Introduction to the Study of the Law of the Constitution,* 6th ed. (London: Macmillan, 1902), 145 ff.

2. The implications of the relation between the necessary rigidity of federal constitutions and democratic theory were not fully worked out by Dicey. See Douglas Verney, "The 'Reconciliation' of Parliamentary Supremacy and Federalism in Canada," *Journal of Commonwealth and Comparative Politics* 21 (1983): 22.

3. Donald Lutz, "Toward a Theory of Constitutional Amendment," *American Political Science Review* 88 (1994): 355.

4. Because provincial constitutions include all provincial laws that affect the organs of government in the province, it can be assumed that there have been numerous amendments to these laws.

5. Stephen M. Griffin, *American Constitutionalism: From Theory to Politics* (Princeton: Princeton University Press, 1996), 34–35.

6. Andrew Heard, *Canadian Constitutional Conventions: The Marriage of Law and Politics* (Toronto : Oxford University Press, 1991); and Alfred H. Kelly, Winfred A. Harbison, and Herman Belz, *The American Constitution: Its Origins and Development,* 6th ed. (New York: W. W. Norton, 1983).

7. Lutz, "Toward a Theory of Constitutional Amendment," 356, 157–58.

8. Part V of the C.A., 1982, secs. 38 to 49, describe the constitutional amendment machinery. The unanimity formula is contained in sec. 41; the "some but not all" formula in sec. 43; the provincial constitutions formula in sec. 45; the Parliament of Canada formula in sec. 44, and the general amending formula is covered in secs. 38, 39, 40, and 42. Where amendments must be approved by more than one legislature, any of the legislatures concerned may initiate the amendment (sec. 46).

9. *OPSEU v. Ont.* [1987] 2 S.C.R. 2, 33, at 40.

10. Omitted here is a spent clause.

11. Congress can set a time limit for ratification by the state legislatures for a particular amendment, or can decide not to impose a time limit. In recent times, the time limit has usually been seven years. An unresolved issue is whether a constitutional convention established by application of two-thirds of the state legislatures to Congress may propose only very specific amendments outlined in the petition to Congress, or whether such a convention could propose amendments without limit. See Morris D. Forkosch, "The Alternative Amending Clause in Article V: Reflections and Suggestions," *Minnesota Law Review* 51 (1967): 1053.

12. The one time state constitutional conventions were called for, Congress left it to the states to decide for themselves how they should be organized. Most states provided for a convention consisting of elected delegates pledged to vote for or against the amendment. See Everett S. Brown, "The Ratification of the Twenty-First Amendment," *American Political Science Review* 29 (1935): 1005.

13. See John Agresto, *The Supreme Court and Constitutional Democracy* (Ithaca and London: Cornell University Press, 1984), 109. According to Corwin, "A proposed amendment can be added to the Constitution by 38 States containing considerably less than half of the population of the country, or can be defeated by 13 containing less than one-twentieth of the population of the country." Edwin S. Corwin, *The Constitution and What It Means Today,* ed. Harold W. Chase and Craig R. Ducat, 14th ed. (Princeton: Princeton University Press, 1978), 271.

14. The Canadian Senate can hold up an amendment for six months but has no absolute veto.

15. The concept of "rate of constitutional amendment" was devised by Lutz ("Toward a Theory of Constitutional Amendment"), who calculated the U.S. rate at .13. However, the approach employed by Griffin in *American Constitutionalism,* whereby the first ten amendments are considered as one amending event, is arguably more accurate.

16. Sec. 91(2A) (unemployment insurance), and sec. 94A (pensions).

17. For example, the *Constitution Act, 1960,* 9 Eliz. II, c. 2 (U.K.) set the retirement age for federally appointed judges at seventy-five. See Guy Favreau, *The Amendment of the Constitution of Canada* (Ottawa: Queen's Printer, 1965).

18. Sec. 35.1 was added to the Constitution Act, 1982.

19. This amendment was effected despite the opposition of the Senate, because sec. 47 gives the Senate only a six-month suspensive veto over constitutional change.

20. For details of these amendments, see Peter Hogg, *Constitutional Law of Canada* (Toronto: Carswell, 2002), sec. 1.4.

21. The failed federal-provincial conferences were held in 1927, 1931, 1950, 1960, 1971, and 1980.

22. Pierre Trudeau, "Patriation and the Supreme Court," in *Against the Current: Selected Writings, 1939–1996,* ed. Gérard Pelletier (Toronto: McClelland & Stewart, 1996), 246, 249.

23. *A.-G. Man. et al. v. A.-G. Can. et al.* [1981] 2 S.C.R. 753.

24. Richard Johnston, André Blais, Elisabeth Gidengil, and Neil Nevitte, *The Challenge of Direct Democracy: The 1992 Canadian Referendum* (Montreal and Kingston: McGill-Queen's University Press, 1996).

25. Michigan became the thirty-eighth state to ratify this amendment. The proposal was passed by Congress in 1789 with no time limit. After the Michigan ratification in 1992, Congress passed a resolution declaring that the Madison amendment was now part of the Constitution in order to counter the arguments of skeptics who claimed that a resolution more than two hundred years old could not be revived. However, some argue that the Twenty-seventh Amendment is nevertheless invalid; see Sanford Levinson, "Authorizing Constitutional Text: On the Purported Twenty-Seventh Amendment," *Constitutional Commentary* 11 (1994): 101.

26. See Richard B. Bernstein with Jerome Agel, *Amending America* (New York: Times Books, 1993), 169, 181–98. Amendment proposals concerning the flag, the use of the English language, a balanced budget, and abortion have been common in recent years.

27. Ibid., 177.

28. See Allison Held, Sheryl Herndon, and Danielle Stager, "The Equal Rights Amendment: Why the ERA Remains Legally Viable and Properly Before the States," *William and Mary Journal of Women and the Law* (spring 1997); and David C. Huckabee, "Equal Rights Amendment: Ratification Issues," memorandum, 18 March 1996 (Congressional Research Service, Library of Congress, Washington, D.C.).

29. *A.-G. Man. et al. v. A.-G. Can. et al.*

30. Subsequently, the Supreme Court dismissed a challenge from Quebec, which argued that "substantial" consent must include Quebec. The Court explicitly rejected the compact theory of confederation. (*Re Objection by Quebec to Resolution to Amend the Constitution* [1982] 2 S.C.R. 793.)

31. *Reference re Secession of Quebec* [1998] 2 S.C.R. 217. The reference was framed after Guy Bertrand (a former sovereignist leader in Quebec turned federalist) began a litigation process in which he challenged the Quebec government's attempts to institute sovereignty on Charter of Rights grounds. When the Quebec government tried to block Bertrand's challenge, the federal government continued the litigation through the reference.

32. Lorne M. Sossin, *Boundaries of Judicial Review: The Law of Justiciability in Canada* (Toronto: Carswell-Thomson, 1999), 154–57, 197.

33. Ian Greene, Carl Baar, Peter McCormick, George Szablowski, and Martin Thomas, *Final Appeal: Decision-making in Canadian Courts of Appeal* (Toronto: Lorimer, 1998).

34. Hogg, *Constitutional Law,* chap. 5.7(a).

35. *Reference re Secession of Quebec,* pars. 149 and 64 (quoting opinion of Chief Justice Brian Dickson in *R. v. Oakes* [1986] 1 S.C.R. 103), and pars. 68, 150, and 151.

36. Ibid., pars. 133, 134, and 154.

37. Jay Winik, *April 1865: The Month That Saved America* (New York: Harper Collins, 2001), 365–88.

38. See Peter H. Russell, Rainer Knopff, and Ted Morton, *Federalism and the Charter: Leading Constitutional Decisions,* 5th ed. (Ottawa: Carleton University Press, 1989); and Hogg, *Constitutional Law,* chap. 4.8(b).

39. R. B. Haldane, Viscount, *Selected Addresses and Essays* (London: J. Murray, 1928); David R. Williams, *Duff: A Life in the Law* (Vancouver: University of British Columbia Press and Osgoode Society, 1984); and John T. Saywell, *The Lawmakers: Judicial Power and the Shaping of Canadian Federalism* (Toronto: University of Toronto Press, 2002).

40. *A.-G. Can. v. A.-G. Ont.* (Unemployment Insurance) [1937] A.C. 355.

41. Hogg, *Constitutional Law,* chap. 17.4 (a).

42. *A.-G. N.S. v. A.-G. Can.* [1951] S.C.R. 31 (Nova Scotia Interdelegation case).

43. The criminal law power (sec. 91.27 of the C.A., 1867), has also been used to justify some federal powers, for example, anticombines legislation, Sunday observance legislation, civil rights of action for breach of criminal statutes, and the regulation of abortion. See Hogg, *Constitutional Law,* chap. 19.

44. See Hogg, *Constitutional Law,* chap. 17.

45. See ibid., chaps. 20 and 21.

46. "An Act Respecting Constitutional Amendments," *Statutes of Canada* 1996, c. 1.

47. *Singh et al. v. Minister of Employment and Immigration* [1985] 1 S.C.R. 177.

48. See generally Corwin, *Constitution,* 268–69.

49. Some scholars, however, have argued that in spite of the Coleman decision, states can rescind a ratification prior to ratification by a thirty-eighth state. See William L. Dunker, "Constitutional Amendments—The Justiciability of Ratification and Retraction," *Tennessee Law Review* 41 (1972): 93.

50. 19 *Howard* 393 (1857).

51. See Bernstein, *Amending America,* 179–81.

52. Ibid., 39–40.

53. Griffin, *American Constitutionalism,* 31–33.

54. Ibid., 32.

55.Ibid., 33.

56.Ibid., 37.

Ran Hirschl is an Associate Professor of Political Science and Law at the University of Toronto. He studied law and political science at Tel Aviv University and at Yale University, where he received his Ph.D. in 1999. His research and teaching interests include comparative public law, constitutional and judicial politics. While at Yale and the University of Toronto, he received several prestigious fellowships and awards, including a Fulbright Scholar nomination, Visiting Fellowship at Princeton University's Program in Law and Public Affairs, a Connaught Research Fellowship in the Social Sciences, and a Canada Social Sciences and Humanities Research Council Research Grant. He has published extensively on comparative constitutional law and politics in journals such as *Comparative Politics, Law & Social Inquiry, Human Rights Quarterly, American Journal of Comparative Law, Israel Studies, Indiana Journal of Global Legal Studies, University of Richmond Law Review, Texas Law Review, Stanford Journal of International Law,* and the *Canadian Journal of Law and Jurisprudence,* as well as in several edited volumes, including *Marbury v. Madison: Documents and Commentary* (Congressional Quarterly, 2002), *The Democracy Sourcebook* (MIT, 2003), and *Constituting Women: The Gender of Constitutional Jurisprudence* (Cambridge, 2004). He is the author of *Towards Juristocracy: The Origins and Consequences of the New Constitutionalism* (Harvard University Press, 2004).

Contributors

Raymond Bazowski is Assistant Professor of Political Science and Director of the Undergraduate Program in Public Policy and Administration in the Department of Political Science of York University. He teaches courses on Canadian politics, public law, public policy, and political theory. His research interests include the philosophy of law, constitutional interpretation, and the intersection of law and public policy.

Ian Brodie is Assistant Professor of Political Science at the University of Western Ontario, where he teaches courses on Canadian politics, constitutional law, and law and public policy. He is the author of *Friends of the Court* and conducts research into the legal dimensions of politics, interest group litigation, and law and policy-making.

Sandra Clancy earned her doctorate in political science from the University of Toronto. Previously on the faculty of Stonehill College in Massachusetts, she is presently taking a hiatus from teaching in order to raise her young children. Her current research concerns the difficult choices women face regarding career and family.

Ian Greene is Associate Professor of Political Science and coordinator of the Graduate Diploma in Justice System Administration at York University, where he teaches courses in public law, ethical politics, and program evaluation. He is the author of *The Charter of Rights,* a pioneering study of Canada's new constitution. He is also a contributing author to *A Question of Ethics: Canadians Speak Out* and coauthor of *Final Appeal, Judges, and Judging* and *Honest Politics.* His academic articles appear in the *International Social Science Journal,* the *Canadian Journal of Political Science,* the *Osgoode Hall Law Journal, International Journal of Refugee Law,* and *Canadian Public Administration.* Prior to his academic career, he worked for three years as a middle manager for Alberta Social Services, and for one year as a minister's assistant.

Ran Hirschl is Assistant Professor of Political Science at the University of Toronto, where he teaches courses on comparative constitutionalism and judicial politics. He is presently completing a manuscript entitled *Constitutional Choices: A Comparative Inquiry into the Political Origins of the Constitutionalization of Rights* and has articles on the expansion of rights discourse internationally and the spread of judicial activism forthcoming in the *Stanford Journal of International Law, Comparative Politics,* and the *Harvard CRCL Law Review.* He completed the B.A. and M.A. in political science and the LL.B. at Tel-Aviv University prior to earning his Ph.D. from Yale in 1999. He is a member of the Executive Committee of the Canadian Bar Association in Ontario.

Samuel LaSelva is Associate Professor of Political Science at the University of British Columbia, where he teaches courses on political theory, the Canadian constitution, and jurisprudence. He has published numerous articles on problems in liberal political and legal theory. His book *The Moral Foundations of Canadian Federalism* won in 1998 the Smiley Prize, awarded by the Canadian Political Science Association to honor outstanding contributions to the study of Canadian politics. He is at work on a book about Canadian constitutional theory.

F. L. Morton is Professor of Political Science at the University of Calgary, where he teaches courses in comparative judicial process, constitutional law, and civil liberties in Canada, the United States, and France. His books include *The Charter Revolution and the Court Party* (with Rainer Knopff); *Morgentaler v. Borowoski: Abortion, The Charter, and the Courts; Charter Politics* (with Rainer Knopff); *Law, Politics, and the Judicial Process in Canada;* and *Federalism and the Charter: Leading Constitutional Decisions: A New Edition* (with Peter Russell and Rainer Knopff). Professor Morton is Convenor of the Research Committee on Comparative Judicial Studies Group (International Political Science Association) and Recipient of the 1995 Bora Laskin Fellowship in Human Rights Research.

Ronalda Murphy is Assistant Professor of Law at Dalhousie University Faculty of Law in Halifax, Nova Scotia. She teaches constitutional law, comparative constitutional law, evidence law, civil procedure, and the graduate seminar. She has an LL.B. from Dalhousie, an LL.M. from the University of Toronto, and an S.J.D. from Harvard University. Previously she worked in South Africa at the University of the Witswatersrand and in Toronto, Canada, as a civil litigation lawyer. She writes on legal topics relating to feminism, postmodernism, evidence in criminal trials, and constitutional change in South Africa and Canada.

Stephen L. Newman is Associate Professor of Political Science at York University, where he teaches political theory and American politics. He is the author of *Liberalism at Wits' End: The Libertarian Revolt against the Modern State.*

Sheldon Pollack is Associate Professor in the College of Business and Economics, with a joint appointment in the Department of Political Science, at the University of Delaware, where he teaches courses in law, political science, and legal studies. He is the author of *Revenue and Politics: The Failure of U.S. Tax Policy* and numerous articles on American law, politics, and taxation. Professor Pollack previously taught at the Wharton School of the University of Pennsylvania and has been a Guest Scholar at the Brookings Institution and the Urban Institute in Washington, D.C. He practiced law in Philadelphia for eight years.

Peter Russell is a University Professor at the University of Toronto, where he taught political science from 1958 to 1966. He has published extensively in the fields of comparative politics, judicial politics, and aboriginal politics. His book *Constitutional Odyssey: Can Canadians Become a Sovereign People?* is a leading treatise on Canada's constitutional struggles. Professor Russell is a Fellow and Foreign Secretary of the Royal Society of Canada and an Officer of the Order of Canada.

Robert Vipond is Professor and Chair of the Department of Political Science at the University of Toronto. He is the author of *Liberty and Community: Canadian Federalism and the Failure of the Constitution.*

Index